MOTOR RACING
The Records

MOTOR RACING
The Records

Ian Morrison

GUINNESS BOOKS

Ian Morrison, an established Guinness author and professional sports statistician, has been addicted to sports statistics and facts from an early age. His versatility is reflected in books on Motor Racing, Horse Racing, Rugby League, Rugby Union, Cycling, Snooker and Boxing. He has also provided biographical information on sports personalities, from sports as far apart as Archery and Weightlifting, for many publications, including several for the 1984 Los Angeles Olympics.

Special thanks to Neil Webster, Marlboro, and also to Philip Scott, National Motor Museum, for all their generous assistance. Also to Ray Davies for the loan of his excellent collection of books and magazines.

Editor: Beatrice Frei
Design and Layout: Alan Hamp

© Ian Morrison and Guinness Superlatives Ltd, 1987

Published in Great Britain by Guinness Superlatives Ltd,
33 London Road, Enfield, Middlesex

Typeset in Rockwell Light and Univers by
Wyvern Typesetting Ltd, Bristol
Printed and bound in Great Britain by R. J. Acford Ltd,
Chichester, Sussex

'Guinness' is a registered trade mark of Guinness Superlatives Ltd

British Library Cataloguing in Publication Data
Morrison, Ian, *1947 –*
 Guinness motor racing : the records.
 1. Automobile racing—History
 I. Title
 796.7'2'09   GV1029.15

 ISBN 0–85112–890–4

Cover illustration One of the successful Williams cars that has won the 1986 Constructors' Championship, driven by Nelson Piquet. (All Sport)

Page 1 The Alfa Romeo 159 in which Giuseppe Farina (ITA) won the first world title in 1950. (National Motor Museum)

Title page Action shortly after the start of the 1973 Le Mans. Eventual winner Henri Pescarlo (FRA) is lying fourth (No. 11). Pescarolo won the race four times, a total second only to Jacky Ickx of Belgium who has six wins. (National Motor Museum)

Contents

Abbreviations

ARG	Argentina	FRA	France	MC	Monaco
AUS	Australia	FRG	Federal Republic	NZ	New Zealand
AUT	Austria		of Germany	SAF	South Africa
BEL	Belgium	GER	Germany (pre-1945)	SIAM	Siam (now Thailand)
BRA	Brazil	GB	Great Britain	SPA	Spain
CAN	Canada	HOL	Holland	SWE	Sweden
CHI	Chile	IRE	Ireland	SWI	Switzerland
DEN	Denmark	ITA	Italy	USA	United States
FIN	Finland	MEX	Mexico	VEN	Venezuela

Introduction

Compiling a book about Motor Racing records is not difficult because it is a sport that has been well documented, statistically, over the years. The hard part was deciding what to put in and what to leave out.

Picking upon a starting point was easy and naturally 'Pole Position' went to the Formula One Grand Prix World Championship. But thereafter the task got increasingly harder. Apologies are made to those branches of the sport not covered, Formula Ford, Hill Climbing, Indycar racing and so on. Their role within the sport is, however, acknowledged as a vital one and must never be forgotten.

However, I have chosen to complement the Formula One statistics with comprehensive coverage of European Formula Two and British and European Formula Three Championships, which have all been excellent breeding grounds for many of today's top Formula One drivers.

Detailed coverage of Sports Car races are also included, as the Sports Car still has its special appeal and aura. The Can-Am and Tasman Cup series are, for the first time in a book of this nature, covered comprehensively and, while they no longer hold their place among the echelon of the Motor Racing world, there is no doubting their importance during the golden years in the 1960s.

Hopefully the blend of modern-day coverage, plus a sprinkling of nostalgia, and feature spreads will make interesting reading in one of the most comprehensively compiled statistical books on Motor Racing.

Ian Morrison.

Jody Scheckter (SAF), the 1979 world champion, in his championship-winning Ferrari 312T. (Michelin Tyre Co. Ltd.)

One of motor racing's first greats, Italy's Tazio
Nuvolari. (National Motor Museum)

History of Motor Racing

As man has always had the desire to compete, whether by running against one another, or throwing further than another man, it was obvious that with the advent of the motor car in the 19th-century, another form of rivalry would soon start.

The first ever race under mechanical power was believed to be the 31 km (19.3 miles) *La Velocipède* race around Paris in 1887. It was won by Count Jules Felix Philippe Albert de Dion at an average speed of 59 kph (37 mph). By the turn of the century road races were being held regularly, using Paris as a base, and the first real race was from Paris to Bordeaux, and back, in June 1895.

With competition becoming intense the first set of Motor Racing rules were drawn up for the Paris–Amsterdam–Paris race of 1898. Manufacturers were producing bigger and more powerful cars, and the rules, although crude, divided the cars into two categories – heavyweight and lightweight – those over 400 kg (882 lb) being classed as heavyweight.

The first great series of races, and forerunner to Grands Prix, was the Gordon Bennett series, introduced in 1900 and it was a real test of a manufacturer's skills, as the rules stipulated that all parts of each competing car had to be manufactured in its country of origin. Despite regulations regarding design, the sport was becoming dangerous as engines were built to be more powerful and, following the abandonment of the 1903 Paris–Madrid race due to many accidents, notably to pedestrians, road racing was banned. The sport moved to enclosed circuits such as Athy in Northern Ireland, and Taunus in Germany.

The Gordon Bennett races made way for the first Grand Prix in 1906 when Szisz of Romania won the inaugural French Grand Prix at Le Mans. The race was open to all-comers but the organizers felt a need for some control and imposed a weight limit of 1000 kg (2204 lb). Many manufacturers felt the production of cars was becoming costly and as a result the sport dwindled slightly in Europe but after the Americans introduced the famous Indianapolis 500 in 1911, interest picked up again on the continent.

Although the French Grand Prix was revived in 1912, it was not till after the war that it developed rapidly. Other countries followed France and staged Grands Prix, including Britain at the famous purpose-built Brooklands circuit.

One of the world's great races was born in 1923, when the first Le Mans 24-hour race was held. Four years later the most famous of all road races, the Mille Miglia, was created. The inter-war era saw the birth of some great cars, none of which could match the elegance and speed of the Type 35 Bugatti which first appeared in 1924, and was to be credited with more than 2000 wins during its life-time.

Great cars helped to develop great drivers and wealthy Britons Lord Howe and Sir Henry Birkin were two of the many aristocrats that tried their hand at the sport. But it was on the continent that the cream of the drivers could be found. Louis Chiron (Fra), Hermann Lang (Ger) and Rudolf Caracciola (Ger) were three of the leading drivers of the era but the greatest of all drivers before the second war was Italy's Tazio Nuvolari. The legendary Enzo Ferrari rates him the best driver ever, and coming from the man with Ferrari's wealth of experience and knowledge, he must be right.

The great strides forward by the manufacturers led to stringent controls over sizes of engine, car etc, which changed regularly. A 3-litre capacity was imposed in 1921, this was reduced to 2 litres in 1922. The carrying of the riding mechanic, which was vital at one time, was dropped in 1925 because of its dangers. The engine capacity was reduced even further, to 1½ litres in 1926 but then a Formula Libre, with no engine size legislation, came into force in 1928.

Restrictions were re-introduced in 1938 which limited supercharged engines to 3-litres, and unsupercharged engines to 4½ litres. After the war the supercharged capacity was reduced to 1½ litres.

Formula Two was introduced in 1947 to cater for the new breed of younger driver who wanted to break into the sport but could not afford to get into Grand Prix racing. Formula Two soon became a great grooming ground and was, for many years, a nursery for the leading Formula One drivers of the future. The original Formula Two restrictions were for 2000cc cars unsupercharged, or 500cc supercharged.

Formula Three was born in 1950 but more

The last of the great 'Paris' races at the turn of the century, the Paris–Madrid race, 1903, was prematurely halted due to the high number of accidents involving pedestrians. (National Motor Museum)

significantly, that year saw the birth of the Formula One drivers' championship. Seven races made up the first championship and the first was run at Silverstone on Saturday, 13 May 1950. The race, and the first year's championship, was won by Dr Giuseppe Farina (Ita) in his Alfa Romeo. Alfa drivers also occupied second and third places in the championship through Juan Manuel Fangio (Arg) and Luigi Fagioli (Ita).

It was the Argentinian Fangio who was to dominate the early years of the championship, winning the title on a record five occasions between 1951–57. Continental manufacturers like Ferrari, Mercedes-Benz and Maserati were invincible in the early years of the championship but, when the first championship for manufacturers was introduced in 1958, it was the British-made Vanwall that took the title.

Further changes in Grand Prix rules had been made, and in 1952 and 1953 the World Championship was run to Formula Two rules. When it reverted to Formula One rules in 1954, new limits of 750cc for supercharged engines, and 2500cc for unsupercharged engines were imposed.

The unpopular 1½-litre formula was introduced in 1961 but this was increased in 1966 to 1½ litres supercharged, 3 litres unsupercharged.

Manufacturers were looking at different techniques in an effort to beat off their rivals. Colin Chapman introduced his gas powered turbine Lotus 56B in 1971 and Ken Tyrrell his famous 6-wheeled Project 34 in 1976. But the appearance of the turbocharged Renault at the 1977 British Grand Prix was the most significant introduction into the sport within the last ten years.

Initially viewed with doubt, it was not long, however, before most manufacturers were following the French team's lead and developing turbocharged engines. The power produced by turbochargers greatly increased the engine's output. Consequently, greater speeds enhanced danger. The governing body therefore announced further changes in legislation in 1986 which will mean the phasing out of turbocharging completely by 1989.

With or without turbochargers, Motor Racing has produced some great drivers. In the two years prior to instituting of the 1½-litre formula in 1961, the Cooper–Climax, driven by Jack Brabham, swept all before them as the Australian installed himself as one of the all-time greats, first as a driver, and later as a constructor.

Mike Hawthorn had become Britain's first World Champion in 1958 but the great British monopoly of the World Championship started in 1962 when

Graham Hill won the first of his two titles, but then perhaps the greatest driver of the modern era, Jim Clark, won the first of his two titles in 1963.

John Surtees kept the British flag flying in 1964, before Clark won his second title a year later. In 1968, however, that rare talent of Clark's was taken from the sport when he lost his life in an inexplicable accident during a Formula Two race at West Germany's Hockenheim circuit.

Britain's Jackie Stewart carried on where Clark left off and, had it not been for a decision to retire early, could have dominated the sport longer than he did, and could well have added to his collection of three world titles.

Austria's Niki Lauda joined the list of Motor Racing legends in 1977 when he won a second world title just a year after cheating death in an horrific accident at the Nurburgring. Lauda won the title a

This picture clearly shows how motor racing is used as an advertising platform. (West Zakspeed)

third time in 1984 after coming out of retirement to beat Marlboro-McLaren team mate Alain Prost by a mere half a point. But since that defeat, Frenchman Prost has written his own name into Motor Racing history as only the fourth man to defend successfully his world crown, which he did in 1986.

Motor Racing champions exist beyond the world of Formula One: Britain's Derek Bell and Belgium's Jacky Ickx have established themselves as the best Sports Car drivers, and A. J. Foyt is the hero of all Americans, after his record-breaking four Indianapolis 500 wins. But Motor Racing goes even deeper than that and today's Hill Climb champion, or Formula Ford champion, could well be tomorrow's World Champion.

Formula One World Championship

The first Formula One World Championship race took place at Silverstone on 13 May 1950 and was won by Italian Giuseppe Farina, who became the first World Champion four months later.

Seven races made up the first championship and that number has fluctuated over the years. Sixteen races made up the 1986 championship.

Between 1950 and 1960 the Indianapolis 500 was included in the championship but it was rare for a European Grand Prix driver to compete in the race, and vice versa. Because of its limited appeal among Grand Prix drivers, it has been ignored for some record purposes in the statistical section to be found at the end of this chapter.

The World Championships of 1952 and 1953 were run on Formula Two rules, but race results etc have been included for record purposes.

Note: Average speed is given for first driver only.

Results

1950

British GP

13 May: Silverstone
325 km / 202 miles
1 G. Farina   Alfa Romeo
   146.34 kph / 90.95 mph
2 L. Fagioli   Alfa Romeo
3 R. Parnell   Alfa Romeo
4 Y. Giraud-
   Cabantous   Lago-Talbot
5 L. Rosier   Lago-Talbot
6 F. R. Gerard   ERA
Fastest lap: G. Farina
   151.28 kph / 94.02 mph
Pole position: G. Farina

Monaco GP

21 May: Monte Carlo
318 km / 198 miles
1 J. M. Fangio   Alfa Romeo
   98.68 kph / 61.33 mph
2 A. Ascari   Ferrari
3 L. Chiron   Maserati
4 R. Sommer   Ferrari
5 'B. Bira'   Maserati
6 F. R. Gerard   ERA
Fastest lap: J. M. Fangio
   103.12 kph / 64.09 mph
Pole position: J. M. Fangio

1950 Alfa Romeo 158

Indianapolis 500

30 May: Indianapolis
805 km / 500 miles
1 J. Parsons   Wynn's Friction
     Proof
   199.52 kph / 124.00 mph
2 W. Holland   Blue Crown
3 M. Rose   Howard Keck
4 C. Green   John Zink
5 J. Chitwood/T.
   Bettenhausen   Wolfe
6 L. Wallard   Blue Crown
Fastest lap: W. Holland
   207.56 kph / 129.00 mph
Pole position: W. Faulkner (Grant
   Piston Ring)
(Due to adverse weather conditions
race stopped after 555 km / 345 miles)

Swiss GP

4 June: Bremgarten
306 km / 190 miles
1 G. Farina   Alfa Romeo
   149.25 kph / 92.76 mph
2 L. Fagioli   Alfa Romeo
3 L. Rosier   Lago-Talbot
4 'B. Bira'   Maserati
5 F. Bonetto   Maserati
6 E. De Graffen-
   ried   Maserati
Fastest lap: G. Farina
   162.15 kph / 100.78 mph
Pole position: J. M. Fangio (Alfa
   Romeo)

Belgian GP

18 June: Spa
494 km / 307 miles
1 J. M. Fangio   Alfa Romeo
   177.07 kph / 110.05 mph
2 L. Fagioli   Alfa Romeo
3 L. Rosier   Lago-Talbot
4 G. Farina   Alfa Romeo
5 A. Ascari   Ferrari
6 L. Villoresi   Ferrari
Fastest lap: G. Farina
   185.68 kph / 115.40 mph
Pole position: G. Farina

French GP

2 July: Rheims
500 km / 311 miles
1 J. M. Fangio   Alfa Romeo
   168.69 kph / 104.84 mph
2 L. Fagioli   Alfa Romeo
3 P. Whitehead   Ferrari
4 R. Manzon   Simca-Gordini
5 P. Etancelin/
   E. Chaboud   Lago-Talbot
6 C. Pozzi/
   L. Rosier   Lago-Talbot
Fastest lap: J. M. Fangio
   180.79 kph / 112.36 mph
Pole position: J. M. Fangio

Italian GP

3 September: Monza
504 km / 313 miles
1 G. Farina   Alfa Romeo
   176.39 kph / 109.63 mph
2 D. Serafini/
   A. Ascari   Ferrari
3 L. Fagioli   Alfa Romeo
4 L. Rosier   Lago-Talbot
5 P. Etancelin   Lago-Talbot
6 E. De Graffen-
   ried   Maserati
Fastest lap: J. M. Fangio (Alfa Romeo)
   188.96 kph / 117.44 mph
Pole position: J. M. Fangio

World Drivers' Championship

Pts	Driver	Wins	
30	Giuseppe Farina (ITA)	3	British GP, Swiss GP, Italian GP
27	Juan Manuel Fangio (ARG)	3	Monaco GP, Belgian GP, French GP
24	Luigi Fagioli (ITA)	–	
13	Louis Rosier (FRA)	–	
11	Alberto Ascari (ITA)	–	
8	Johnny Parsons (USA)	1	Indianapolis 500
6	Bill Holland (USA)	–	
5	'B. Bira' (SIAM)	–	
4	Louis Chiron (MON)	–	
4	Reg Parnell (GB)	–	
4	Maurie Rose (USA)	–	
4	Peter Whitehead (GB)	–	

Pts	Driver	Wins
3	Yves Giraud-Cabantous (FRA)	–
3	Phillipe Etancelin (FRA)	–
3	Cecil Green (USA)	–
3	Robert Manzon (FRA)	–
3	Dorino Serafini (ITA)	–
3	Raymond Sommer (FRA)	–
2	Felice Bonetto (ITA)	–
1	Tony Bettenhausen (USA)	–
1	Eugene Chaboud (FRA)	–
1	Joeie Chitwood (USA)	–

Points scoring: First five to count with points as follows: 8–6–4–3–2 plus one point for the fastest lap. Best four results to count.

1951 Ferrari 375

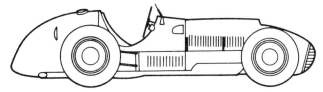

1951

Swiss GP

27 May: Bremgarten
306 km / 190 miles
1 J. M. Fangio Alfa Romeo
 143.28 kph / 89.05 mph
2 P. Taruffi Ferrari
3 G. Farina Alfa Romeo
4 C. Sanesi Alfa Romeo
5 E. De Graffen-
 ried Alfa Romeo
6 A. Ascari Ferrari
Fastest lap: J. M. Fangio
 153.18 kph / 95.18 mph
Pole position: J. M. Fangio

Indianapolis 500

30 May: Indianapolis
805 km / 500 miles
1 L. Wallard Belanger
 203.12 kph / 126.24 mph
2 M. Nazaruk Robbins
3 J. McGrath/
 M. Ayulo Hinkle
4 A. Linden Leitenberger
5 B. Ball Blakely
6 H. Banks . Blue Crown
Fastest lap: L. Wallard
 215.30 kph / 133.81 mph
Pole position: D. Nalon (Novi Purelube)

Belgian GP

17 June: Spa
508 km / 316 miles
1 G. Farina Alfa Romeo
 183.94 kph / 114.3 mph
2 A. Ascari Ferrari
3 L. Villoresi Ferrari
4 L. Rosier Lago-Talbot
5 Y. Giraud-
 Canbantous Lago-Talbot
6 A. Pilette Lago-Talbot
Fastest lap: J. M. Fangio (Alfa Romeo)
 193.90 kph / 120.51 mph
Pole position: J. M. Fangio

French GP

1 July: Rheims
602 km / 374 miles
1 J. M. Fangio/
 L. Fagioli Alfa Romeo
 178.55 kph / 110.97 mph
2 A. Ascari/
 F. Gonzalez Ferrari
3 L. Villoresi Ferrari
4 R. Parnell Ferrari
5 G. Farina Alfa Romeo
6 L. Chiron Lago-Talbot
Fastest lap: J. M. Fangio
 190.33 kph / 118.29 mph
Pole position: J. M. Fangio

British GP

14 July: Silverstone
418 km / 260 miles
1 F. Gonzalez Ferrari
 154.64 kph / 96.11 mph
2 J. M. Fangio Alfa Romeo
3 L. Villoresi Ferrari
4 F. Bonetto Alfa Romeo
5 R. Parnell BRM
6 C. Sanesi Alfa Romeo
Fastest lap: G. Farina (Alfa Romeo)
 160.88 kph / 99.99 mph
Pole position: F. Gonzalez

German GP

29 July: Nurburgring
456 km / 283 miles
1 A. Ascari Ferrari
 134.77 kph / 83.76 mph
2 J. M. Fangio Alfa Romeo
3 F. Gonzalez Ferrari
4 L. Villoresi Ferrari
5 P. Taruffi Ferrari
6 R. Fischer Ferrari
Fastest lap: J. M. Fangio
 137.79 kph / 85.64 mph
Pole position: A. Ascari

Italian GP

16 September: Monza
504 km / 313 miles
1 A. Ascari Ferrari
 185.89 kph / 115.53 mph
2 F. Gonzalez Ferrari
3 G. Farina/
 F. Bonetto Alfa Romeo
4 L. Villoresi Ferrari
5 P. Taruffi Ferrari
6 A. Simon Simca-Gordini
Fastest lap: G. Farina
 195.52 kph / 121.49 mph
Pole position: J. M. Fangio (Alfa Romeo)

Spanish GP

28 October: Pedralbes
442 km / 275 miles
1 J. M. Fangio Alfa Romeo
 158.90 kph / 98.76 mph
2 F. Gonzalez Ferrari
3 G. Farina Alfa Romeo
4 A. Ascari Ferrari
5 F. Bonetto Alfa Romeo
6 E. de Graffen-
 ried Alfa Romeo
Fastest lap: J. M. Fangio
 169.27 kph / 105.20 mph
Pole position: A. Ascari

World Drivers' Championship

Pts	Driver	Wins	
31	Juan Manuel Fangio (ARG)	3	Swiss GP, French GP*, Spanish GP
25	Alberto Ascari (ITA)	2	German GP, Italian GP
24	Jose Froilan Gonzalez (ARG)	1	British GP
19	Giuseppe Farina (ITA)	1	Belgian GP
15	Luigi Villoresi (ITA)	–	

World Drivers' Championship—*Cont.*

Pts	Driver	Wins
10	Piero Taruffi (ITA)	–
9	Lee Wallard (USA)	1 Indianapolis
7	Felice Bonetto (ITA)	–
6	Mike Nazaruk (USA)	–
5	Reg Parnell (GB)	–
4	Luigi Fagioli (ITA)	1 French GP*
3	Andy Linden (USA)	–
3	Louis Rosier (FRA)	–
3	Consalvo Sanesi (ITA)	–
2	Manuel Ayulo (USA)	–

Pts	Driver	Wins
2	Bobby Ball (USA)	–
2	Yves Giraud-Cabantous (FRA)	–
2	Emmanuel de Graffenried (SWI)	–
2	Jack McGrath (USA)	–

* Indicates shared drive

Points scoring: First five to count with points as follows: 8–6–4–3–2 plus one point for the fastest lap. Best four results to count.

1952 Ferrari 500F2

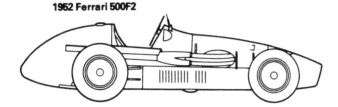

1952

German GP

3 August: Nurburgring
411 km / 255 miles
1 A. Ascari   Ferrari
   132.26 kph / 82.20 mph
2 G. Farina   Ferrari
3 R. Fischer   Ferrari
4 P. Taruffi   Ferrari
5 J. Behra   Gordini
6 R. Laurent   Ferrari
Fastest lap: A. Ascari
   135.71 kph / 84.33 mph
Pole position: A. Ascari

Swiss GP

18 May: Bremgarten
451 km / 280 miles
1 P. Taruffi   Ferrari
   149.38 kph / 92.78 mph
2 R. Fischer   Ferrari
3 J. Behra   Gordini
4 K. Wharton   Frazer-Nash
5 A. Brown   Cooper-Bristol
6 E. de Graffen-
   ried   Maserati-Plate
Fastest lap: P. Taruffi
   154.84 kph / 96.25 mph
Pole position: G. Farina (Ferrari)

Indianapolis 500

30 May: Indianapolis
805 km / 500 miles
1 T. Ruttman   Agajanian
   207.43 kph / 128.92 mph
2 J. Rathmann   Grancor-Wynn
3 S. Hanks   Bardahl
4 D. Carter   Belanger
5 A. Cross   Bowes Seal Fast
6 J. Bryan   Peter Schmidt
Fastest lap: W. Vukovich (Fuel
   Injection)
   217.44 kph / 135.14 mph
Pole position: F. Agabashian
   (Cummins Diesel)

Belgian GP

22 June: Spa
508 km / 316 miles
1 A. Ascari   Ferrari
   165.94 kph / 103.13 mph
2 G. Farina   Ferrari
3 R. Manzon   Gordini
4 M. Hawthorn   Cooper-Bristol
5 P. Frere   HWM
6 A. Brown   Cooper-Bristol
Fastest lap: A. Ascari
   172.87 kph / 107.44 mph
Pole position: A. Ascari

French GP

6 July: Rouen-Les Essarts
387 km / 240 miles
1 A. Ascari   Ferrari
   128.94 kph / 80.14 mph
2 G. Farina   Ferrari
3 P. Taruffi   Ferrari
4 R. Manzon   Gordini
5 M. Trintignant   Gordini
6 P. Collins   HWM
Fastest lap: G. Farina
   136.03 kph / 84.57 mph
Pole position: A. Ascari

British GP

19 July: Silverstone
400 km / 249 miles
1 A. Ascari   Ferrari
   146.29 kph / 90.92 mph
2 P. Taruffi   Ferrari
3 M. Hawthorn   Cooper-Bristol
4 D. Poore   Connaught
5 E. Thompson   Connaught
6 G. Farina   Ferrari
Fastest lap: A. Ascari
   151.37 kph / 94.08 mph
Pole position: G. Farina

Dutch GP

17 August: Zandvoort
377 km / 234 miles
1 A. Ascari   Ferrari
   130.57 kph / 81.15 mph
2 G. Farina   Ferrari
3 L. Villoresi   Ferrari
4 M. Hawthorn   Cooper-Bristol
5 R. Manzon   Gordini
6 M. Trintignant   Gordini
Fastest lap: A. Ascari
   137.48 kph / 85.43 mph
Pole position: A. Ascari

Italian GP

7 September: Monza
504 km / 313 miles
1 A. Ascari   Ferrari
   176.67 kph / 109.80 mph
2 F. Gonzalez   Maserati
3 L. Villoresi   Ferrari
4 G. Farina   Ferrari
5 F. Bonetto   Maserati
6 A. Simon   Ferrari
Fastest lap: A. Ascari and F. Gonzalez
   179.86 kph / 111.76 mph
Pole position: A. Ascari

World Drivers' Championship

Pts	Driver	Wins
36	Alberto Ascari (ITA)	6 Belgian GP, French GP British GP, German GP, Dutch GP, Italian GP
24	Giuseppe Farina (ITA)	–
22	Piero Taruffi (ITA)	1 Swiss GP
10	Rudi Fischer (SWI)	–
10	Mike Hawthorn (GB)	–
9	Robert Manzon (FRA)	–
8	Troy Ruttman (USA)	1 Indianapolis
8	Luigi Villoresi (ITA)	–
6½	Jose Froilan Gonzalez (ARG)	–
6	Jean Behra (FRA)	–
6	Jim Rathmann (USA)	–
4	Sam Hanks (USA)	–
3	Duane Carter (USA)	–
3	Dennis Poore (GB)	–

World Drivers' Championship—*Cont.*

Pts	Driver	Wins
3	Ken Wharton (GB)	–
2	Felice Bonetto (ITA)	–
2	Alan Brown (GB)	–
2	Art Cross (USA)	–
2	Paul Frere (BEL)	–
2	Eric Thompson (GB)	–
2	Maurice Trintignant (FRA)	–
1	Bill Vukovich (USA)	–

Points scoring: First five to count with points as follows:
8–6–4–3–2 plus one point for the fastest lap. Best four
results to count.

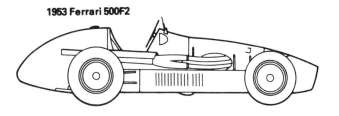

1953 Ferrari 500F2

1953

Argentine GP

18 January: Buenos Aires
379 km / 236 miles
1 A. Ascari   Ferrari
   125.73 kph / 78.14 mph
2 L. Villoresi   Ferrari
3 F. Gonzalez   Maserati
4 M. Hawthorn   Ferrari
5 O. Galvez   Maserati
6 J. Behra   Gordini
Fastest lap: A. Ascari
   129.93 kph / 80.74 mph
Pole position: A. Ascari

Indianapolis 500

30 May: Indianapolis
805 km / 500 miles
1 W. Vukovich   Fuel Injection
   207.14 kph / 128.92 mph
2 A. Cross   Springfield
                      Welding
3 S. Hanks/
   D. Carter   Bardahl
4 F. Agabashian/
   P. Russo   Grancor-Elgin
5 J. McGrath   Hinkle
6 J. Daywalt   Sumar
Fastest lap: W. Vukovich
   218.61 kph / 135.87 mph
Pole position: W. Vukovich

Dutch GP

7 Jun: Zandvoort
376 km / 234 miles
1 A. Ascari   Ferrari
   130.39 kph / 81.04 mph
2 G. Farina   Ferrari
3 F. Bonetto/
   F. Gonzalez   Maserati
4 M. Hawthorn   Ferrari
5 E. de Graffen-
   ried   Maserati
6 M. Trintignant   Gordini
Fastest lap: L. Villoresi (Ferrari)
   133.79 kph / 83.15 mph
Pole position: A. Ascari

Belgian GP

21 June: Spa
508 km / 316 miles
1 A. Ascari   Ferrari
   180.96 kph / 112.47 mph
2 L. Villoresi   Ferrari
3 O. Marimon   Maserati
4 E. de Graffen-
   ried   Maserati
5 M. Trintignant   Gordini
6 M. Hawthorn   Ferrari
Fastest lap: F. Gonzalez (Maserati)
   185.47 kph / 115.27 mph
Pole position: J. M. Fangio (Maserati)

French GP

5 July: Rheims
500 km / 311 miles
1 M. Hawthorn   Ferrari
   182.86 kph / 113.65 mph
2 J. M. Fangio   Maserati
3 F. Gonzalez   Maserati
4 A. Ascari   Ferrari
5 G. Farina   Ferrari
6 L. Villoresi   Ferrari
Fastest lap: J. M. Fangio
   186.50 kph / 115.91 mph
Pole position: A. Ascari

British GP

18 July: Silverstone
424 km / 263 miles
1 A. Ascari   Ferrari
   149.59 kph / 92.97 mph
2 J. M. Fangio   Maserati
3 G. Farina   Ferrari
4 F. Gonzalez   Maserati
5 M. Hawthorn   Ferrari
6 F. Bonetto   Maserati
Fastest lap: F. Gonzalez/A. Ascari
   154.13 kph / 95.79 mph
Pole position: A. Ascari

German GP

2 August: Nurburgring
411 km / 255 miles
1 G. Farina   Ferrari
   134.98 kph / 83.89 mph
2 J. M. Fangio   Maserati
3 M. Hawthorn   Ferrari
4 F. Bonetto   Maserati
5 E. de Graffen-
   ried   Maserati
6 S. Moss   Cooper-Alta
Fastest lap: A. Ascari (Ferrari)
   137.76 kph / 85.62 mph
Pole position: A. Ascari

Swiss GP

23 August: Bremgarten
473 km / 294 miles
1 A. Ascari   Ferrari
   156.35 kph / 97.17 mph
2 G. Farina   Ferrari
3 M. Hawthorn   Ferrari
4 F. Bonetto/
   J. M. Fangio   Maserati
5 H. Lang   Maserati
6 L. Villoresi   Ferrari
Fastest lap: A. Ascari
   162.44 kph / 100.96 mph
Pole position: J. M. Fangio

Italian GP

13 September: Monza
504 km / 313 miles
1 J. M. Fangio   Maserati
   178.10 kph / 110.69 mph
2 G. Farina   Ferrari
3 L. Villoresi   Ferrari
4 M. Hawthorn   Ferrari
5 M. Trintignant   Gordini
6 R. Mieres   Gordini
Fastest lap: J. M. Fangio
   182.14 kph / 113.20 mph
Pole position: A. Ascari (Ferrari)

World Drivers' Championship

Pts	Driver	Wins
34½	Alberto Ascari (ITA)	5 Argentine GP, Dutch GP, Belgian GP, British GP, Swiss GP
28	Juan Manuel Fangio (ARG)	1 Italian GP
26	Giuseppe Farina (ITA)	1 German GP
19	Mike Hawthorn (GB)	1 French GP

Pts	Driver	Wins
17	Luigi Villoresi (ITA)	–
13½	Jose Froilan Gonzalez (ARG)	–
9	Bill Vukovich (USA)	1 Indianapolis 500
7	Emmanuel de Graffenried (SWI)	–
6½	Felice Bonetto (ITA)	–

World Drivers' Championship—*Cont.*

Pts	Driver	Wins
6	Art Cross (USA)	–
4	Onofre Marimon (ARG)	–
4	Maurice Trintignant (FRA)	–
2	Duane Carter (USA)	–
2	Oscar Galvez (ARG)	–
2	Sam Hanks (USA)	–
2	Hermann Lang (FRG)	–
2	Jack McGrath (USA)	–
1½	Fred Agabashian (USA)	–
1½	Paul Russo (USA)	–

Points scoring: First five to count with points as follows:
8–6–4–3–2 plus one point for the fastest lap. Best four
results to count.

1954

Argentine GP

17 January: Buenos Aires
340 km / 211 miles
1 J. M. Fangio   Maserati
   112.84 kph / 70.13 mph
2 G. Farina   Ferrari
3 F. Gonzalez   Ferrari
4 M. Trintignant   Ferrari
5 E. Bayol   Gordini
6 H. Schell   Maserati
Fastest lap: F. Gonzalez
   129.95 kph / 80.76 mph
Pole position: G. Farina

Indianapolis 500

31 May: Indianapolis
805 km / 500 miles
1 W. Vukovich   Fuel Injection
   210.52 kph / 130.84 mph
2 J. Bryan   Dean Van Lines
3 J. McGrath   Hinkle
4 T. Ruttman/
   D. Carter   Auto Shippers
5 M. Nazaruk   McNamara
6 F. Agabashian   Merz
Fastest lap: J. McGrath
   226.12 kph / 140.54 mph
Pole position: J. McGrath

Belgian GP

20 June: Spa
508 km / 315 miles
1 J. M. Fangio   Maserati
   185.16 kph / 115.08 mph
2 M. Trintignant   Ferrari
3 S. Moss   Maserati
4 F. Gonzalez/
   M. Hawthorn   Ferrari
5 A. Pilette   Gordini
6 'B. Bira'   Maserati
Fastest lap: J. M. Fangio
   191.42 kph / 118.97 mph
Pole position: J. M. Fangio

1954 Mercedes-Benz W196 Streamliner

French GP

4 July: Rheims
506 km / 315 miles
1 J. M. Fangio   Mercedes-Benz
   186.64 kph / 115.97 mph
2 K. Kling   Mercedes-Benz
3 R. Manzon   Ferrari
4 'B. Bira'   Maserati
5 L. Villoresi   Maserati
6 J. Behra   Gordini
Fastest lap: H. Herrmann
   (Mercedes-Benz)
   195.43 kph / 121.46 mph
Pole position: J. M. Fangio

British GP

17 July: Silverstone
424 km / 263 miles
1 F. Gonzalez   Ferrari
   144.31 kph / 89.69 mph
2 M. Hawthorn   Ferrari
3 O. Marimon   Maserati
4 J. M. Fangio   Mercedes-Benz
5 M. Trintignant   Ferrari
6 R. Mieres   Maserati
Fastest lap: F. Gonzalez/M. Hawthorn/
O. Marimon/J. M. Fangio/S. Moss
(Maserati)/A. Ascari (Maserati)/
J. Behra (Gordini)
   154.13 kph / 95.79 mph
Pole position: J. M. Fangio

German GP

1 August: Nurburgring
502 km / 312 miles
1 J. M. Fangio   Mercedes-Benz
   133.37 kph / 82.87 mph
2 F. Gonzalez/
   M. Hawthorn   Ferrari
3 M. Trintignant   Ferrari
4 K. Kling   Mercedes-Benz
5 S. Mantovani   Maserati
6 P. Taruffi   Ferrari
Fastest lap: K. Kling
   137.97 kph / 85.75 mph
Pole position: J. M. Fangio

Swiss GP

22 August: Bremgarten
480 km / 299 miles
1 J. M. Fangio   Mercedes-Benz
   159.56 kph / 99.17 mph
2 F. Gonzalez   Ferrari
3 H. Herrmann   Mercedes-Benz
4 R. Mieres   Maserati
5 S. Mantovani   Maserati
6 K. Wharton   Maserati
Fastest lap: J. M. Fangio
   164.90 kph / 101.97 mph
Pole position: F. Gonzalez

Italian GP

5 September: Monza
504 km / 313 miles
1 J. M. Fangio   Mercedes-Benz
   180.17 kph / 111.98 mph
2 J. M. Hawthorn   Ferrari
3 F. Gonzalez/
   U. Maglioli   Ferrari
4 H. Herrmann   Mercedes-Benz
5 M. Trintignant   Ferrari
6 F. Wacker   Gordini
Fastest lap: F. Gonzalez
   187.73 kph / 116.66 mph
Pole position: J. M. Fangio

Spanish GP

24 October: Pedralbes
505 km / 314 miles
1 M. Hawthorn   Ferrari
   156.38 kph / 97.16 mph
2 L. Musso   Maserati
3 J. M. Fangio   Mercedes-Benz
4 R. Mieres   Maserati
5 K. Kling   Mercedes-Benz
6 F. Godia   Maserati
Fastest lap: A. Ascari (Lancia)
   161.97 kph / 100.64 mph
Pole position: A. Ascari

World Drivers' Championship

Pts	Driver	Wins
42	Juan Manuel Fangio (ARG)	6 Argentine GP, Belgian GP, French GP, German GP, Swiss GP, Italian GP
25½	Jose Froilan Gonzalez (ARG)	1 British GP
24⁹⁄₁₄	Mike Hawthorn (GB)	1 Spanish GP
17	Maurice Trintignant (FRA)	–
12	Karl Kling (FRG)	–
8	Hans Herrmann (FRG)	–
8	Bill Vukovich (USA)	1 Indianapolis 500
6	Jimmy Bryan (USA)	–
6	Giuseppe Farina (ITA)	–
6	Roberto Mieres (ARG)	–
6	Luigi Musso (ITA)	–
5	Jack McGrath (USA)	–

World Drivers' Championship—*Cont.*

Pts	Driver	Wins
4½	Onofre Marimon (ARG)	–
4½	Stirling Moss (GB)	–
4	Sergio Mantovani (ITA)	
4	Robert Manzon (FRA)	–
3	'B. Bira' (SIAM)	–
2	Elie Bayol (FRA)	–
2	Umberto Maglioli (ITA)	–
2	Mike Nazaruk (USA)	–
2	Andre Pilette (BEL)	–
2	Luigi Villoresi (ITA)	–
1½	Duane Carter (USA)	–
1½	Troy Ruttman (USA)	–
1½	Alberto Ascari (ITA)	–
½	Jean Behra (FRA)	–

1955

Argentine GP

16 January: Buenos Aires
376 km / 233 miles
1 J. M. Fangio   Mercedes-Benz
  124.74 kph / 77.51 mph
2 F. Gonzalez/
  G. Farina/M.
  Trintignant   Ferrari
3 G. Farina/
  U. Maglioli/M.
  Trintignant   Ferrari
4 H. Herrmann/
  K. Kling/
  S. Moss   Mercedes-Benz
5 R. Mieres   Maserati
6 H. Schell/
  J. Behra   Maserati
Fastest lap: J. M. Fangio
  130.05 kph / 80.81 mph
Pole position: F. Gonzalez

Monaco GP

22 May: Monte Carlo
315 km / 195 miles
1 M. Trintignant   Ferrari
  105.91 kph / 65.81 mph
2 E. Castellotti   Lancia
3 J. Behra/
  C. Perdisa   Maserati
4 G. Farina   Ferrari
5 L. Villoresi   Lancia
6 L. Chiron   Lancia
Fastest lap: J. M. Fangio
  (Mercedes-Benz)
  110.57 kph / 68.70 mph
Pole position: J. M. Fangio

Indianapolis 500

30 May: Indianapolis
805 km / 500 miles
1 B. Sweikert   John Zink
  206.29 kph / 128.21 mph
2 T. Betten-
  hausen/
  P. Russo   Chapman
3 J. Davies   Bardahl
4 J. Thomson   Schmidt
5 W. Faulkner/
  B. Homeier   Merz
6 A. Linden   Massaglia
Fastest lap: W. Vukovich (Hopkins)
  227.44 kph / 141.35 mph
Pole position: J. Hoyt (Jim Robins)

Belgian GP

5 June: Spa
508 km / 316 miles
1 J. M. Fangio   Mercedes-Benz
  191.24 kph / 118.83 mph
2 S. Moss   Mercedes-Benz
3 G. Farina   Ferrari
4 P. Frere   Ferrari
5 R. Mieres/
  J. Behra   Maserati
6 M. Trintignant   Ferrari
Fastest lap: J. M. Fangio
  195.05 kph / 121.21 mph
Pole position: E. Castellotti (Lancia)

Dutch GP

19 June: Zandvoort
419 km / 261 miles
1 J. M. Fangio   Mercedes-Benz
  144.17 kph / 89.60 mph
2 S. Moss   Mercedes-Benz
3 L. Musso   Maserati
4 R. Mieres   Maserati
5 E. Castellotti   Ferrari
6 J. Behra   Maserati
Fastest lap: R. Mieres
  149.60 kph / 92.96 mph
Pole position: J. M. Fangio

British GP

16 July: Aintree
434 km / 270 miles
1 S. Moss   Mercedes-Benz
  139.16 kph / 86.47 mph
2 J. M. Fangio   Mercedes-Benz
3 K. Kling   Mercedes-Benz
4 P. Taruffi   Mercedes-Benz
5 L. Musso   Maserati
6 M. Hawthorn/
  E. Castellotti   Ferrari
Fastest lap: S. Moss
  144.36 kph / 89.70 mph
Pole position: S. Moss

Italian GP

11 September: Monza
500 km / 311 miles
1 J. M. Fangio   Mercedes-Benz
  206.79 kph / 128.49 mph
2 P. Taruffi   Mercedes-Benz
3 E. Castellotti   Ferrari
4 J. Behra   Maserati
5 C. Menditeguy   Maserati
6 U. Maglioli   Ferrari
Fastest lap: S. Moss (Mercedes-Benz)
  215.70 kph / 134.03 mph
Pole position: J. M. Fangio

**1955 Mercedes-Benz W196
Open wheeler**

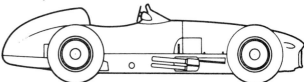

World Drivers' Championship

Pts	Driver	Wins	
40	Juan Manuel Fangio (ARG)	4	Argentine GP, Belgian GP, Dutch GP, Italian GP
23	Stirling Moss (GB)	1	British GP
11⅓	Eugenio Castellotti (ITA)	–	
10⅓	Maurice Trintignant (FRA)	1	Monaco GP
9	Giuseppe Farina (ITA)	–	
9	Piero Taruffi (ITA)	–	
8	Bob Sweikert (USA)	1	Indianapolis 500
7	Roberto Mieres (ARG)	–	
6	Jean Behra (FRA)	–	
6	Luigi Musso (ITA)	–	
5	Karl Kling (FRG)	–	
4	Jimmy Davies (USA)	–	
3	Tony Bettenhausen (USA)	–	
3	Paul Frere (BEL)	–	
3	Paul Russo (USA)	–	
3	Johnny Thomson (USA)	–	

World Drivers' Championship—*Cont.*

Pts	Driver	Wins
2	Jose Froilan Gonzalez (ARG)	–
2	Carlos Menditeguy (ARG)	–
2	Cesare Perdisa (ITA)	–
2	Luigi Villoresi (ITA)	–
1⅓	Umberto MagliOli (ITA)	–
1	Walt Faulkner (USA)	–
1	Hans Herrmann (FRG)	–
1	Bill Homeier (USA)	–
1	Bill Vukovich (USA)	–

Points scoring: First five drivers in each race to score.
Points as follows: 8–6–4–3–2. Plus 1 point for the fastest lap in each race. Best five results only to count.

1956

Argentine GP

22 January: Buenos Aires
383 km / 238 miles
1 L. Musso/
   J. M. Fangio   Lancia-Ferrari
   127.76 kph / 79.39 mph
2 J. Behra   Maserati
3 M. Hawthorn   Maserati
4 C. Landi/
   G. Gerini   Maserati
5 O. Gendebien   Lancia-Ferrari
6 A. Uria/
   O. Gonzalez   Maserati
Fastest lap: J. M. Fangio
   133.74 kph / 83.11 mph
Pole position: J. M. Fangio

Monaco GP

13 May: Monte Carlo
315 km / 195 miles
1 S. Moss   Maserati
   104.51 kph / 64.94 mph
2 P. Collins/
   J. M. Fangio   Lancia-Ferrari
3 J. Behra   Maserati
4 J. M. Fangio/
   E. Castellotti   Lancia-Ferrari
5 H. da Silva
   Ramos   Gordini
6 E. Bayol/
   A. Pilette   Gordini
Fastest lap: J. M. Fangio
   108.45 kph / 67.39 mph
Pole position: J. M. Fangio

Indianapolis 500

30 May: Indianapolis
805 km / 500 miles
1 P. Flaherty   John Zink
   206.74 kph / 128.49 mph
2 S. Hanks   Jones & Maley
3 D. Freeland   Bob Estes
4 J. Parsons   Agajanian
5 D. Rathmann   McNamara
6 B. Sweikert   D-A. Lubricant
Fastest lap: P. Russo (Novi Vespa)
   232.37 kph / 144.42 mph
Pole position: P. Flaherty

1956 Lancia-Ferrari

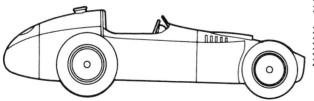

Belgian GP

3 June: Spa
508 km / 316 miles
1 P. Collins   Lancia-Ferrari
   190.61 kph / 118.44 mph
2 P. Frere   Lancia-Ferrari
3 C. Perdisa/
   S. Moss   Maserati
4 H. Schell   Vanwall
5 L. Villoresi   Maserati
6 A. Pilette   Lancia-Ferrari
Fastest lap: S. Moss
   199.58 kph / 124.01 mph
Pole position: J. M. Fangio
   (Lancia-Ferrari)

French GP

1 July: Rheims
506 km / 315 miles
1 P. Collins   Lancia-Ferrari
   196.80 kph / 122.29 mph
2 E. Castellotti   Lancia-Ferrari
3 J. Behra   Maserati
4 J. M. Fangio   Lancia-Ferrari
5 C. Perdisa/
   S. Moss   Maserati
6 L. Rosier   Maserati
Fastest lap: J. M. Fangio
   204.98 kph / 127.37 mph
Pole position: J. M. Fangio

British GP

14 July: Silverstone
476 km / 296 miles
1 J. M. Fangio   Lancia-Ferrari
   158.76 kph / 98.65 mph
2 A. de Portago/
   P. Collins   Lancia-Ferrari
3 J. Behra   Maserati
4 J. Fairman   Connaught
5 H. Gould   Maserati
6 L. Villoresi   Maserati
Fastest lap: S. Moss (Maserati)
   164.32 kph / 102.10 mph
Pole position: S. Moss

German GP

5 August: Nurburgring
502 km / 312 miles
1 J. M. Fangio   Lancia-Ferrari
   137.66 kph / 85.54 mph
2 S. Moss   Maserati
3 J. Behra   Maserati
4 F. Godia   Maserati
5 L. Rosier   Maserati
Only five finished
Fastest lap: J. M. Fangio
   141.19 kph / 87.73 mph
Pole position: J. M. Fangio

Italian GP

2 September: Monza
500 km / 311 miles
1 S. Moss   Maserati
   208.79 kph / 129.73 mph
2 P. Collins/
   J. M. Fangio   Lancia-Ferrari
3 R. Flockhart   Connaught
4 F. Godia   Maserati
5 J. Fairman   Connaught
6 L. Piotti   Maserati
Fastest lap: S. Moss
   217.92 kph / 135.41 mph
Pole position: J. M. Fangio

World Drivers' Championship

Pts	Driver	Wins
30	Juan Manuel Fangio (ARG)	3 Argentine GP*, British GP, German GP
27	Stirling Moss (GB)	2 Monaco GP, Italian GP
25	Peter Collins (GB)	2 Belgian GP, French GP
22	Jean Behra (FRA)	–
8	Pat Flaherty (USA)	1 Indianapolis 500
7½	Eugenio Castellotti (ITA)	–
6	Paul Frere (BEL)	–
6	Sam Hanks (USA)	–
6	Francesca Godia (SPA)	–
5	Jack Fairman (GB)	–
4	Mike Hawthorn (GB)	–
4	Ron Flockhart (GB)	–
4	Don Freeland (USA)	–
4	Luigi Musso (ITA)	1 Argentine GP*
3	Alfonso de Portago (SPA)	–
3	Johnny Parsons (USA)	–
3	Cesare Perdisa (ITA)	–
3	Harry Schell (USA)	–
2	Luigi Villoresi (ITA)	

World Drivers' Championship—*Cont.*

Pts	Driver	Wins
2	Olivier Gendebien (BEL)	–
2	Horace Gould (GB)	–
2	Dick Rathmann (USA)	–
2	Louis Rosier (FRA)	–
2	Nano da Silva Ramos (BRA)	–
1½	Gerino Gerini (ITA)	–
1½	Chico Landi (BRA)	–
1	Paul Russo (USA)	–

* Indicates shared drive
Points scoring: First five drivers in each race to score.
Points as follows: 8–6–4–3–2. Plus 1 point for the fastest lap in each race. Best five results only to count.

1957

Argentine GP

13 January: Buenos Aires
391 km / 243 miles
1 J. M. Fangio   Maserati
   129.73 kph / 80.61 mph
2 J. Behra   Maserati
3 C. Menditeguy   Maserati
4 H. Schell   Maserati
5 F. Gonzalez/
   A. de Portago   Lancia-Ferrari
6 C. Perdisa/
   W. von Trips/
   P. Collins   Lancia-Ferrari
Fastest lap: S. Moss (Maserati)
   134.51 kph / 83.58 mph
Pole position: S. Moss

Monaco GP

19 May: Monte Carlo
330 km / 205 miles
1 J. M. Fangio   Maserati
   104.16 kph / 64.72 mph
2 C. A. S. Brooks   Vanwall
3 M. Gregory   Maserati
4 S. Lewis-Evans   Connaught
5 M. Trintignant   Lancia-Ferrari
6 J. Brabham   Cooper-Climax
Fastest lap: J. M. Fangio
   107.22 kph / 66.62 mph
Pole position: J. M. Fangio

Indianapolis 500

30 May: Indianapolis
805 km / 500 miles
1 S. Hanks   Belond Exhaust
   218.18 kph / 135.60 mph
2 J. Rathmann   Chiropractic
3 J. Bryan   Dean Van Lines
4 P. Russo   Novi Auto Air
5 A. Linden   McNamara
6 J. Boyd   Bowes Seal Fast
Fastest lap: J. Rathmann
   230.77 kph / 143.43 mph
Pole position: P. O'Connor (Sumar)

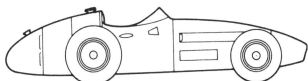

1957 Maserati 250F

French GP

7 July: Rouen
504 km / 313 miles
1 J. M. Fangio   Maserati
   160.96 kph / 100.02 mph
2 L. Musso   Lancia-Ferrari
3 P. Collins   Lancia-Ferrari
4 M. Hawthorn   Lancia-Ferrari
5 J. Behra   Maserati
6 H. Schell   Maserati
Fastest lap: L. Musso
   165.55 kph / 102.87 mph
Pole position: J. M. Fangio

British GP

20 July: Aintree
435 km / 270 miles
1 C. A. S. Brooks/
   S. Moss   Vanwall
   139.68 kph / 86.79 mph
2 L. Musso   Lancia-Ferrari
3 M. Hawthorn   Lancia-Ferrari
4 M. Trintignant/
   P. Collins   Lancia-Ferrari
5 R. Salvadori   Cooper-Climax
6 F. R. Gerard   Cooper-Bristol
Fastest lap: S. Moss
   145.81 kph / 90.60 mph
Pole position: S. Moss

German GP

4 August: Nurburgring
502 km / 312 miles
1 J. M. Fangio   Maserati
   142.95 kph / 88.82 mph
2 M. Hawthorn   Lancia-Ferrari
3 P. Collins   Lancia-Ferrari
4 L. Musso   Lancia-Ferrari
5 S. Moss   Vanwall
6 J. Behra   Maserati
Fastest lap: J. M. Fangio
   147.32 kph / 91.54 mph
Pole position: J. M. Fangio

Pescara GP

18 August: Pescara
460 km / 286 miles
1 S. Moss   Vanwall
   154.00 kph / 95.70 mph
2 J. M. Fangio   Maserati
3 H. Schell   Maserati
4 M. Gregory   Maserati
5 S. Lewis-Evans   Vanwall
6 G. Scarlatti   Maserati
Fastest lap: S. Moss
   157.50 kph / 97.88 mph
Pole position: J. M. Fangio

Italian GP

8 September: Monza
500 km / 311 miles
1 S. Moss   Vanwall
   193.56 kph / 120.27 mph
2 J. M. Fangio   Maserati
3 W. von Trips   Lancia-Ferrari
4 M. Gregory   Maserati
5 G. Scarlatti/
   H. Schell   Maserati
6 M. Hawthorn   Lancia-Ferrari
Fastest lap: C. A. S. Brooks (Vanwall)
   199.61 kph / 124.03 mph
Pole position: S. Lewis-Evans (Vanwall)

World Drivers' Championship

Pts	Driver	Wins	
40	Juan Manuel Fangio (ARG)	4	Argentine GP, Monaco GP, French GP, German GP
25	Stirling Moss (GB)	3	British GP*, Pescara GP, Italian GP
16	Luigi Musso (ITA)	–	
13	Mike Hawthorn (GB)	–	
11	Tony Brooks (GB)	1	British GP*
10	Masten Gregory (USA)	–	
9½	Peter Collins (GB)	–	
8	Harry Schell (USA)	–	
8	Sam Hanks (USA)	1	Indianapolis 500
8	Jean Behra (FRA)	–	
7	Jim Rathmann (USA)	–	
5	Stuart Lewis-Evans (GB)	–	
4	Wolfgang von Trips (FRG)	–	
4	Carlos Menditeguy (ARG)	–	
4	Jimmy Bryan (USA)	–	
3½	Maurice Trintignant (FRA)	–	
3	Paul Russo (USA)	–	

World Drivers' Championship—*Cont.*

Pts	Driver	Wins
2	Roy Salvadori (GB)	–
2	Andy Linden (USA)	–
1	Giorgio Scarlatti (ITA)	–
1	Alfonso de Portago (SPA)	–
1	Jose Froilan Gonzalez (ARG)	–

* Indicates shared drive
Points scoring: First five drivers in each race to score.
Points as follows: 8–6–4–3–2. Plus 1 point for the fastest lap
in each race. Best five results only to count.

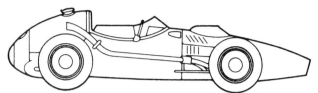

1958 Ferrari 246

1958

Argentine GP

19 January: Buenos Aires
313 km / 194 miles
1 S. Moss   Cooper-Climax
    134.56 kph / 83.61 mph
2 L. Musso   Ferrari
3 M. Hawthorn   Ferrari
4 J. M. Fangio   Maserati
5 J. Behra   Maserati
6 H. Schell   Maserati
Fastest lap: J. M. Fangio
    138.34 kph / 85.96 mph
Pole position: J. M. Fangio

Monaco GP

18 May: Monte Carlo
315 km / 195 miles
1 M. Trintignant   Cooper-Climax
    109.41 kph / 67.99 mph
2 L. Musso   Ferrari
3 P. Collins   Ferrari
4 J. Brabham   Cooper-Climax
5 H. Schell   BRM
6 C. Allison   Lotus-Climax
Fastest lap: M. Hawthorn (Ferrari)
    112.55 kph / 69.93 mph
Pole position: C. A. S. Brooks
    (Vanwall)

Dutch GP

25 May: Zandvoort
315 km / 195 miles
1 S. Moss   Vanwall
    151.16 kph / 93.95 mph
2 H. Schell   BRM
3 J. Behra   BRM
4 R. Salvadori   Cooper-Climax
5 M. Hawthorn   Ferrari
6 C. Allison   Lotus-Climax
Fastest lap: S. Moss
    154.66 kph / 96.10 mph
Pole position: S. Lewis-Evans
    (Vanwall)

Indianapolis 500

30 May: Indianapolis
805 km / 500 miles
1 J. Bryan   Belond Exhaust
    215.27 kph / 133.79 mph
2 G. Amick   Demler
3 J. Boyd   Bowes Seal Fast
4 T. Betten-
    hausen   Jones & Maley
5 J. Rathmann   Leader Card
6 J. Reece   John Zink
Fastest lap: T. Bettenhausen
    232.18 kph / 144.30 mph
Pole position: D. Rathmann
    (McNamara)

Belgian GP

15 June: Spa
338 km / 210 miles
1 C. A. S. Brooks   Vanwall
    209.09 kph / 129.92 mph
2 M. Hawthorn   Ferrari
3 S. Lewis-Evans   Vanwall
4 C. Allison   Lotus-Climax
5 H. Schell   BRM
6 O. Gendebien   Ferrari
Fastest lap: M. Hawthorn
    213.01 kph / 132.36 mph
Pole position: M. Hawthorn

French GP

6 July: Rheims
415 km / 258 miles
1 M. Hawthorn   Ferrari
    201.90 kph / 125.45 mph
2 S. Moss   Vanwall
3 W. von Trips   Ferrari
4 J. M. Fangio   Maserati
5 P. Collins   Ferrari
6 J. Brabham   Cooper-Climax
Fastest lap: M. Hawthorn
    206.25 kph / 128.16 mph
Pole position: M. Hawthorn

British GP

19 July: Silverstone
353 km / 220 miles
1 P. Collins   Ferrari
  164.23 kph / 102.05 mph
2 M. Hawthorn   Ferrari
3 R. Salvadori   Cooper-Climax
4 S. Lewis-Evans   Vanwall
5 H. Schell   BRM
6 J. Brabham   Cooper-Climax
Fastest lap: M. Hawthorn
  168.23 kph / 104.53 mph
Pole position: S. Moss (Vanwall)

German GP

3 August: Nurburgring
342 km / 213 miles
1 C. A. S. Brooks   Vanwall
  145.34 kph / 90.31 mph
2 R. Salvadori   Cooper-Climax
3 M. Trintignant   Cooper-Climax
4 W. von Trips   Ferrari
5 B. McLaren   Cooper-Climax*
6 E. Barth   Porsche*
* Did not receive championship points
as they were in the Formula Two race
that ran concurrent with the Formula
One Grand Prix.
Fastest lap: S. Moss (Vanwall)
  149.50 kph / 92.91 mph
Pole position: M. Hawthorn (Ferrari)

Portuguese GP

24 August: Oporto
370 km / 230 miles
1 S. Moss   Vanwall
  169.03 kph / 105.03 mph
2 M. Hawthorn   Ferrari
3 S. Lewis-Evans   Vanwall
4 J. Behra   BRM
5 W. von Trips   Ferrari
6 H. Schell   BRM
Fastest lap: M. Hawthorn
  178.20 kph / 110.75 mph
Pole position: S. Moss

Italian GP

7 September: Monza
403 km / 250 miles
1 C. A. S. Brooks   Vanwall
  195.05 kph / 121.22 mph
2 M. Hawthorn   Ferrari
3 P. Hill   Ferrari
4 M. Gregory/
    C. Shelby   Maserati
5 R. Salvadori   Cooper-Climax
6 G. Hill   Lotus-Climax
Fastest lap: P. Hill
  201.17 kph / 125.00 mph
Pole position: S. Moss (Vanwall)

Moroccan GP

19 October: Ain-Diab, Casablanca
403 km / 251 miles
1 S. Moss   Vanwall
  187.43 kph / 116.46 mph
2 M. Hawthorn   Ferrari
3 P. Hill   Ferrari
4 J. Bonnier   BRM
5 H. Schell   BRM
6 M. Gregory   Maserati
Fastest lap: S. Moss
  192.46 kph / 119.59 mph
Pole position: M. Hawthorn

Above Britain's Tony Brooks won at Spa, the Nurburgring and Monza in 1958 to finish third in the Drivers' Championship, but there was no joy for him at Silverstone where he could only finish seventh. (National Motor Museum)

Left Between 1950–60 the Indianapolis 500 was part of the Formula One World Championship. Jimmy Bryan won the 1958 race in his Belond Special and he collected eight championship points. (National Motor Museum)

World Drivers' Championship

Pts	Driver	Wins	
42	Mike Hawthorn (GB)	1	French GP
41	Stirling Moss (GB)	4	Argentine GP, Dutch GP, Portuguese GP, Moroccan GP
24	Tony Brooks (GB)	3	Belgian GP, German GP, Italian GP
15	Roy Salvadori (GB)	–	
14	Peter Collins (GB)	1	British GP
14	Harry Schell (USA)	–	
12	Maurice Trintignant (FRA)	1	Monaco GP
12	Luigi Musso (ITA)	–	
11	Stuart Lewis-Evans (GB)	–	
9	Phil Hill (USA)	–	
9	Wolfgang von Trips (FRG)	–	
9	Jean Behra (FRA)	–	
8	Jimmy Bryan (USA)	1	Indianapolis 500
7	Juan Manuel Fangio (ARG)	–	
6	George Amick (USA)	–	
4	Tony Bettenhausen (USA)	–	
4	Johnny Boyd (USA)	–	
3	Jack Brabham (AUS)	–	
3	Cliff Allison (GB)	–	
3	Jo Bonnier (SWE)	–	
2	Jim Rathmann (USA)	–	

Points scoring: First five drivers in each race to score. Points as follows: 8–6–4–3–2. Plus 1 point for the fastest lap in each race. Best six results only to count. No points awarded for a shared win.

Constructors' Cup

Pts	Manufacturer	Wins	
48	Vanwall	6	Dutch GP, Belgian GP, German GP, Portuguese GP, Italian GP, Moroccan GP
40	Ferrari	2	French GP, British GP
31	Cooper-Climax	2	Argentine GP, Monaco GP
18	BRM	–	
9	Maserati	–	
3	Lotus-Climax	–	

Points scoring: Best six results from ten rounds (Indianapolis excluded). Points 8–6–4–3–2.

Stirling Moss

If one name was synonymous with motor racing in Britain in the 1950s, it was that of Stirling Moss. He was to motor racing what Denis Compton was to cricket and Stanley Matthews was to football. But, despite his popularity and wealth of talent, Moss never won the coveted World Drivers' Championship and is, undoubtedly, the greatest driver never to have won the title.

Born at West Kensington in London in 1929, Moss started his racing career in Hill Climbs at the age of 17, before developing into one of the great Endurance and Formula One drivers of the 1950s. He was just as at home behind the wheel of a Sports Car as he was in a Grand Prix car, and his passion for all branches of the sport possibly hindered his quest for the world title.

His first Grand Prix was the 1951 Swiss when he was in a British HWM but he had to wait four years for his first success. Moss's loyalty to British manufacturers like Cooper, Jaguar, Frazer-Nash and ERA certainly hindered his early progress as they could not provide cars good enough to compete with the European manufacturers. He came close to joining the Italian giant Ferrari but did eventually join an overseas manufacturer in 1954, when he joined Ferrari's rivals, Maserati.

Above, left Stirling Moss in his role of interviewer, talking to Dan Gurney (USA). (National Motor Museum)

Above The familiar sight of Stirling Moss in his No. 7 car. On this occasion it is a Vanwall at Goodwood in 1957. (National Motor Museum)

Left Moss driving a Lotus-Climax during the 1961 Belgian Grand Prix at Spa. He went into the race as joint leader in the championship with Wolfgang von Trips (FRG) but Moss finished out of the points in eighth place. (National Motor Museum)

The great Fangio (Arg) was also in the Maserati team but they only had one race together as team-mates before Fangio moved on to Mercedes. The pair of them teamed up again the following season when Moss also joined the German manufacturer.

Both men had cars capable of winning the world title but that honour went to the Argentinian, while Moss had to be content with the runner-up position although he did record his first Grand Prix victory at Aintree in 1955. That year was also memorable for Moss because, with co-driver Denis Jenkinson, he became the first, and only, Briton to win the Mille Miglia classic.

When Mercedes pulled out of racing in 1956 Moss went back to Maserati and Fangio to Lancia. The Argentinian beat the Englishman by a mere three points in that year's championship.

Fangio and Moss teamed up again at Maserati in 1957, but their renewed partnership was only brief as Moss soon moved to Vanwall. The pair of them, however, dominated the championship once more but the final championship positions read: 1st Fangio, 2nd Moss, for a third successive year.

With Fangio retiring after the 1958 French Grand Prix the way was surely open for Moss to win his first world title. Although Moss won four rounds, he lost out to fellow Briton Mike Hawthorn by one point, despite Hawthorn only winning one championship race.

Moss was never to get that close to the title again and his career ended on Easter Monday 1962, after a high-speed crash at Goodwood. Moss escaped with his life but the famous 'Lucky No. 7' car of his was not seen in a Formula One Grand Prix again although he did later return to saloon car racing. He still maintains contact with motor racing in Britain and the name of Stirling Moss still remains synonymous with the sport.

1959

Monaco GP

10 May: Monte Carlo
315 km / 195 miles
1 J. Brabham   Cooper-Climax
    107.36 kph / 66.71 mph
2 C. A. S. Brooks   Ferrari
3 M. Trintignant   Cooper-Climax
4 P. Hill   Ferrari
5 B. McLaren   Cooper-Climax
6 R. Salvadori   Cooper-Maserati
Fastest lap: J. Brabham
    112.77 kph / 70.07 mph
Pole position: S. Moss
    (Cooper-Climax)

Indianapolis 500

30 May: Indianapolis
805 km / 500 miles
1 R. Ward   Leader Card
    218.60 kph / 135.86 mph
2 J. Rathmann   Simoniz
3 J. Thomson   Racing Associates
4 T. Betten-
    hausen   Hoover M.E.
5 P. Goldsmith   Demler
6 J. Boyd   Bowes Seal Fast
Fastest lap: J. Thomson
    233.98 kph / 145.42 mph
Pole position: J. Thomson

Dutch GP

31 May: Zandvoort
314 km / 195 miles
1 J. Bonnier   BRM
    150.41 kph / 93.46 mph
2 J. Brabham   Cooper-Climax
3 M. Gregory   Cooper-Climax
4 I. Ireland   Lotus-Climax
5 J. Behra   Ferrari
6 P. Hill   Ferrari
Fastest lap: S. Moss (Cooper-Climax)
    156.09 kph / 96.99 mph
Pole position: J. Bonnier

French GP

5 July: Rheims
415 km / 258 miles
1 C. A. S. Brooks   Ferrari
    205.05 kph / 127.43 mph
2 P. Hill   Ferrari
3 J. Brabham   Cooper-Climax
4 O. Gendebien   Ferrari
5 B. McLaren   Cooper-Climax
6 R. Flockhart   BRM
Fastest lap: S. Moss (BRM)
    209.29 kph / 130.05 mph
Pole position: C. A. S. Brooks

British GP

18 July: Aintree
362 km / 225 miles
1 J. Brabham   Cooper-Climax
    144.65 kph / 89.88 mph
2 S. Moss   BRM
3 B. McLaren   Cooper-Climax
4 H. Schell   BRM
5 M. Trintignant   Cooper-Climax
6 R. Salvadori   Aston Martin
Fastest lap: S. Moss/B. McLaren
    148.56 kph / 92.31 mph
Pole position: J. Brabham

German GP

2 August: Avus
498 km / 309 miles
1 C. A. S. Brooks   Ferrari
    236.04 kph / 146.67 mph
2 D. Gurney   Ferrari
3 P. Hill   Ferrari
4 M. Trintignant   Cooper-Climax
5 J. Bonnier   BRM
6 I. Burgess   Cooper-Maserati
Fastest lap: C. A. S. Brooks
    239.97 kph / 149.14 mph
Pole position:
    (Heat 1) J. Brabham
        (Cooper-Climax)
    (Heat 2) C. A. S. Brooks
Race held over two heats each of 30
laps. Aggregate times taken

Portuguese GP

23 August: Monsanto
337 km / 210 miles
1 S. Moss   Cooper-Climax
    153.40 kph / 95.32 mph
2 M. Gregory   Cooper-Climax
3 D. Gurney   Ferrari
4 M. Trintignant   Cooper-Climax
5 H. Schell   BRM
6 R. Salvadori   Aston Martin
Fastest lap: S. Moss
    156.58 kph / 97.30 mph
Pole position: S. Moss

Italian GP

13 September: Monza
414 km / 257 miles
1 S. Moss   Cooper-Climax
    200.18 kph / 124.38 mph
2 P. Hill   Ferrari
3 J. Brabham   Cooper-Climax
4 D. Gurney   Ferrari
5 C. Allison   Ferrari
6 O. Gendebien   Ferrari
Fastest lap: P. Hill
    206.14 kph / 128.11 mph
Pole position: S. Moss

United States GP

12 December: Sebring
352 km / 218 miles
1 B. McLaren   Cooper-Climax
    159.06 kph / 98.83 mph
2 M. Trintignant   Cooper-Climax
3 C. A. S. Brooks   Ferrari
4 J. Brabham   Cooper-Climax
5 I. Ireland   Lotus-Climax
6 W. von Trips   Ferrari
Fastest lap: M. Trintignant
    162.85 kph / 101.19 mph
Pole position: S. Moss
    (Cooper-Climax)

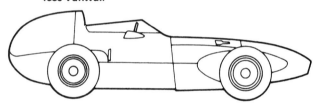

1959 Vanwall

World Drivers' Championship

Pts	Driver	Wins	
31	Jack Brabham (AUS)	2	Monaco GP, British GP
27	Tony Brooks (GB)	2	French GP, German GP
25½	Stirling Moss (GB)	2	Portuguese GP, Italian GP
20	Phil Hill (USA)	–	
19	Maurice Trintignant (FRA)	–	
16½	Bruce McLaren (NZ)	1	United States GP
13	Dan Gurney (USA)	–	
10	Jo Bonnier (SWE)	1	Dutch GP
10	Masten Gregory (USA)	–	
8	Rodger Ward (USA)	1	Indianapolis 500
6	Jim Rathmann (USA)	–	
5	Harry Schell (USA)	–	
5	Innes Ireland (GB)	–	
5	Johnny Thomson (USA)	–	
3	Olivier Gendebien (BEL)	–	
3	Tony Bettenhausen (USA)	–	
2	Cliff Allison (GB)	–	
2	Jean Behra (FRA)	–	
2	Paul Goldsmith (USA)	–	

Points scoring: First five drivers in each race to score.
Points as follows: 8–6–4–3–2. Plus 1 point for the fastest
lap in each race. Best five results only to count.

Constructors' Cup

Pts	Manufacturer	Wins	
40	Cooper-Climax	5	Monaco GP, British GP, Portuguese GP, Italian GP, United States GP
32	Ferrari	2	French GP, German GP
18	BRM	1	Dutch GP
5	Lotus-Climax	–	

Points scoring: Best five results from eight rounds (Indianapolis excluded). Best placed car of each manufacturer only to score. Points 8–6–4–3–2.

1960

Argentine GP

7 February: Buenos Aires
313 km / 194 miles
1 B. McLaren   Cooper-Climax
   133.18 kph / 82.77 mph
2 C. Allison   Ferrari
3 M. Trintignant/
   S. Moss   Cooper-Climax
4 C. Menditeguy   Cooper-Maserati
5 W. von Trips   Ferrari
6 I. Ireland   Lotus-Climax
Fastest lap: S. Moss
   142.36 kph / 88.48 mph
Pole position: S. Moss

Monaco GP

29 May: Monte Carlo
315 km / 195 miles
1 S. Moss   Lotus-Climax
   108.60 kph / 67.48 mph
2 B. McLaren   Cooper-Climax
3 P. Hill   Ferrari
4 C. A. S. Brooks Cooper-Climax
5 J. Bonnier   BRM
6 R. Ginther   Ferrari
Fastest lap: B. McLaren
   117.69 kph / 73.13 mph
Pole position: S. Moss

Indianapolis 500

30 May: Indianapolis
805 km / 500 miles
1 J. Rathmann   Ken Paul
   223.28 kph / 138.77 mph
2 R. Ward   Leader Card
3 P. Goldsmith   Demler
4 D. Branson   Bob Estes
5 J. Thomson   Adams Quarter-
                   Horse
6 E. Johnson   Jim Robbins
Fastest lap: J. Rathmann
   235.12 kph / 146.13 mph
Pole position: E. Sachs (Dean Van
Lines)

Dutch GP

6 June: Zandvoort
314 km / 195 miles
1 J. Brabham   Cooper-Climax
   154.90 kph / 96.27 mph
2 I. Ireland   Lotus-Climax
3 G. Hill   BRM
4 S. Moss   Lotus-Climax
5 W. von Trips   Ferrari
6 R. Ginther   Ferrari
Fastest lap: S. Moss
   160.90 kph / 99.99 mph
Pole position: S. Moss

Belgian GP

19 June: Spa
508 km / 315 miles
1 J. Brabham   Cooper-Climax
   215.02 kph / 133.63 mph
2 B. McLaren   Cooper-Climax
3 O. Gendebien   Cooper-Climax
4 P. Hill   Ferrari
5 J. Clark   Lotus-Climax
6 L. Bianchi   Cooper-Climax
Fastest lap: J. Brabham/P. Hill/
   I. Ireland (Lotus-Climax)
   218.89 kph / 136.01 mph
Pole position: J. Brabham

French GP

3 July: Rheims
415 km / 258 miles
1 J. Brabham   Cooper-Climax
   212.69 kph / 131.19 mph
2 O. Gendebien   Cooper-Climax
3 B. McLaren   Cooper-Climax
4 H. Taylor   Cooper-Climax
5 J. Clark   Lotus-Climax
6 R. Flockhart   Lotus-Climax
Fastest lap: J. Brabham
   217.32 kph / 135.06 mph
Pole position: J. Brabham

British GP

16 July: Silverstone
363 km / 225 miles
1 J. Brabham   Cooper-Climax
   174.90 kph / 108.69 mph
2 J. Surtees   Lotus-Climax
3 I. Ireland   Lotus-Climax
4 B. McLaren   Cooper-Climax
5 C. A. S. Brooks Cooper-Climax
6 W. von Trips   Ferrari
Fastest lap: G. Hill (BRM)
   179.60 kph / 111.62 mph
Pole position: J. Brabham

Portuguese GP

14 August: Oporto
407 km / 253 miles
1 J. Brabham   Cooper-Climax
   175.82 kph / 109.27 mph
2 B. McLaren   Cooper-Climax
3 J. Clark   Lotus-Climax
4 W. von Trips   Ferrari
5 C. A. S. Brooks Cooper-Climax
6 I. Ireland   Lotus-Climax
Fastest lap: J. Surtees (Lotus-Climax)
   180.70 kph / 112.31 mph
Pole position: J. Surtees

Italian GP

4 September: Monza
500 km / 311 miles
1 P. Hill   Ferrari
   212.51 kph / 132.06 mph
2 R. Ginther   Ferrari
3 W. Mairesse   Ferrari
4 G. Cabianca   Cooper-Ferrari
5 W. von Trips   Ferrari*
6 H. Herrmann   Porsche*
* Due to boycott of race by British
teams Formula Two cars were allowed
to compete to make up the numbers
Fastest lap: P. Hill
   220.00 kph / 136.73 mph
Pole position: P. Hill

United States GP

20 November: Riverside
395 km / 246 miles
1 S. Moss   Lotus-Climax
   159.31 kph / 99.00 mph
2 I. Ireland   Lotus-Climax
3 B. McLaren   Cooper-Climax
4 J. Brabham   Cooper-Climax
5 J. Bonnier   BRM
6 P. Hill   Cooper-Climax
Fastest lap: J. Brabham
   163.15 kph / 101.38 mph
Pole position: S. Moss

World Drivers' Championship

Pts	Driver	Wins	
43	Jack Brabham (AUS)	5	Dutch GP, Belgian GP, French GP, British GP, Portuguese GP
34	Bruce McLaren (NZ)	1	Argentine GP
19	Stirling Moss (GB)	2	Monaco GP, United States GP
18	Innes Ireland (GB)	–	
16	Phil Hill (USA)	1	Italian GP
10	Olivier Gendebien (BEL)	–	
10	Wolfgang von Trips (FRG)	–	
8	Jim Rathmann (USA)	1	Indianapolis 500
8	Richie Ginther (USA)	–	
8	Jim Clark (GB)	–	
7	Tony Brooks (GB)	–	

World Drivers' Championship—*Cont.*

Pts	Driver	Wins
6	Cliff Allison (GB)	–
6	John Surtees (GB)	–
6	Rodger Ward (USA)	–
4	Graham Hill (GB)	–
4	Willy Mairesse (BEL)	–
4	Paul Goldsmith (USA)	–
4	Jo Bonnier (SWE)	–
3	Carlos Menditeguy (ARG)	–
3	Henry Taylor (GB)	–
3	Giulio Cabianca (ITA)	–
3	Don Branson (USA)	–
2	Johnny Thomson (USA)	–
1	Lucien Bianchi (BEL)	–
1	Ron Flockhart (GB)	–
1	Hans Herrmann (FRG)	–
1	Eddie Johnson (USA)	–

Points scoring: First six drivers in each race to score.
Points as follows: 8–6–4–3–2–1. Best six results only to count.

Constructors' Cup

Pts	Manufacturer	Wins	
48	Cooper-Climax	6	Argentine GP, Dutch GP, Belgian GP, French GP, British GP, Portuguese GP
34	Lotus-Climax	2	Monaco GP, United States GP
26	Ferrari	1	Italian GP
8	BRM	–	
3	Cooper-Maserati	–	
3	Cooper-Ferrari	–	

Points scoring: Best six results from nine rounds (Indianapolis excluded). Best placed car of each manufacturer only to score. Points: 8–6–4–3–2–1.

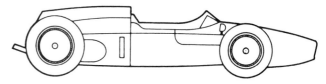

1960 Cooper-Climax

1961

Monaco GP

14 May: Monte Carlo
315 km / 195 miles
1 S. Moss   Lotus-Climax
    113.76 kph / 70.70 mph
2 R. Ginther   Ferrari
3 P. Hill   Ferrari
4 W. von Trips   Ferrari
5 D. Gurney   Porsche
6 B. McLaren   Cooper-Climax
Fastest lap: R. Ginther/S. Moss
    115.93 kph / 72.05 mph
Pole position: S. Moss

Dutch GP

22 May: Zandvoort
314 km / 195 miles
1 W. von Trips   Ferrari
    154.80 kph / 96.21 mph
2 P. Hill   Ferrari
3 J. Clark   Lotus-Climax
4 S. Moss   Lotus-Climax
5 R. Ginther   Ferrari
6 J. Brabham   Cooper-Climax
Fastest lap: J. Clark
    158.03 kph / 98.21 mph
Pole position: P. Hill

● When he appeared at the San Sebastian Grand Prix in Spain in September 1924, Sir Henry Segrave became the first driver to wear a crash helmet in a motor race.

Belgian GP

18 June: Spa
423 km / 263 miles
1 P. Hill   Ferrari
    206.20 kph / 128.15 mph
2 W. von Trips   Ferrari
3 R. Ginther   Ferrari
4 O. Gendebien   Ferrari
5 J. Surtees   Cooper-Climax
6 D. Gurney   Porsche
Fastest lap: R. Ginther
    211.60 kph / 131.53 mph
Pole position: P. Hill

French GP

2 July: Rheims
432 km / 268 miles
1 G. Baghetti   Ferrari
    192.82 kph / 119.85 mph
2 D. Gurney   Porsche
3 J. Clark   Lotus-Climax
4 I. Ireland   Lotus-Climax
5 B. McLaren   Cooper-Climax
6 G. Hill   BRM-Climax
Fastest lap: P. Hill
    203.18 kph / 126.25 mph
Pole position: P. Hill

British GP

15 July: Aintree
362 km / 225 miles
1 W. von Trips   Ferrari
    135.02 kph / 83.91 mph
2 P. Hill   Ferrari
3 R. Ginther   Ferrari
4 J. Brabham   Cooper-Climax
5 J. Bonnier   Porsche
6 R. Salvadori   Cooper-Climax
Fastest lap: C. A. S. Brooks
    (BRM-Climax)
    147.54 kph / 91.68 mph
Pole position: P. Hill

German GP

6 August: Nurburgring
341 km / 212 miles
1 S. Moss   Lotus-Climax
    148.54 kph / 92.30 mph
2 W. von Trips   Ferrari
3 P. Hill   Ferrari
4 J. Clark   Lotus-Climax
5 J. Surtees   Cooper-Climax
6 B. McLaren   Cooper-Climax
Fastest lap: P. Hill
    152.69 kph / 94.88 mph
Pole position: P. Hill

Italian GP

10 September: Monza
430 km / 267 miles
1 P. Hill   Ferrari
    209.36 kph / 130.11 mph
2 D. Gurney   Porsche
3 B. McLaren   Cooper-Climax
4 J. Lewis   Cooper-Climax
5 C. A. S. Brooks BRM-Climax
6 R. Salvadori   Cooper-Climax
Fastest lap: G. Baghetti (Ferrari)
    213.74 kph / 132.83 mph
Pole position: W. von Trips (Ferrari)

United States GP

8 October: Watkins Glen
370 km / 230 miles
1 I. Ireland   Lotus-Climax
    166.03 kph / 103.17 mph
2 D. Gurney   Porsche
3 C. A. S. Brooks BRM-Climax
4 B. McLaren   Cooper-Climax
5 G. Hill   BRM-Climax
6 J. Bonnier   Porsche
Fastest lap: S. Moss (Lotus-Climax)
    170.23 kph / 105.80 mph
Pole position: J. Brabham
    (Cooper-Climax)

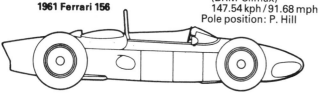

1961 Ferrari 156

World Drivers' Championship

Pts	Driver	Wins	
34	Phil Hill (USA)	2	Belgian GP, Italian GP
33	Wolfgang von Trips (FRG)	2	Dutch GP, British GP
21	Stirling Moss (GB)	2	Monaco GP, German GP
21	Dan Gurney (USA)	–	
16	Richie Ginther (USA)	–	
12	Innes Ireland (GB)	1	United States GP
11	Jim Clark (GB)	–	
11	Bruce McLaren (NZ)	–	
9	Giancarlo Baghetti (ITA)	1	French GP
6	Tony Brooks (GB)	–	
4	Jack Brabham (AUS)	–	
4	John Surtees (GB)	–	
3	Olivier Gendebien (BEL)	–	
3	Jack Lewis (GB)	–	
3	Jo Bonnier (SWE)	–	

Pts	Driver	Wins
3	Graham Hill (GB)	–
2	Roy Salvadori (GB)	–

Points scoring: First six drivers in each race to score. Points as follows: 9–6–4–3–2–1. Best five results only to count.

Constructors' Cup

Pts	Manufacturer	Wins	
45	Ferrari	5	Dutch GP, Belgian GP, French GP, British GP, Italian GP
35	Lotus-Climax	3	Monaco GP, German GP, United States GP
22	Porsche	–	
14	Cooper-Climax	–	
7	BRM-Climax	–	

Points scoring: Best five results from eight rounds. Best placed car of each manufacturer only to score. Points: 9–6–4–3–2–1.

1962

Dutch GP

20 May: Zandvoort
335 km / 208 miles
1 G. Hill   BRM
    153.57 kph / 95.44 mph
2 T. Taylor   Lotus-Climax
3 P. Hill   Ferrari
4 G. Baghetti   Ferrari
5 A. Maggs   Cooper-Climax
6 C. G. de
    Beaufort   Porsche
Fastest lap: B. McLaren
    (Cooper-Climax)
    159.88 kph / 99.36 mph
Pole position: J. Surtees
    (Lola-Climax)

Monaco GP

3 June: Monte Carlo
315 km / 195 miles
1 B. McLaren   Cooper-Climax
    113.37 kph / 70.46 mph
2 P. Hill   Ferrari
3 L. Bandini   Ferrari
4 J. Surtees   Lola-Climax
5 J. Bonnier   Porsche
6 G. Hill   BRM
Fastest lap: J. Clark (Lotus-Climax)
    118.54 kph / 73.67 mph
Pole position: J. Clark

Belgian GP

17 June: Spa
451 km / 280 miles
1 J. Clark   Lotus-Climax
    212.24 kph / 131.90 mph
2 G. Hill   BRM
3 P. Hill   Ferrari
4 R. Rodriguez   Ferrari
5 J. Surtees   Lola-Climax
6 J. Brabham   Lotus-Climax
Fastest lap: J. Clark
    215.57 kph / 133.98 mph
Pole position: G. Hill

• Janet Guthrie (USA), became the first woman, in 1977, to qualify for the Indianapolis 500. She finished 29th.

French GP

8 July: Rouen
353 km / 220 miles
1 D. Gurney   Porsche
    163.94 kph / 101.89 mph
2 A. Maggs   Cooper-Climax
3 R. Ginther   BRM
4 B. McLaren   Cooper-Climax
5 J. Surtees   Lola-Climax
6 C. G. de
    Beaufort   Porsche
Fastest lap: G. Hill (BRM)
    172.01 kph / 106.90 mph
Pole position: J. Clark (Lotus-Climax)

British GP

21 July: Aintree
362 km / 225 miles
1 J. Clark   Lotus-Climax
    148.44 kph / 92.25 mph
2 J. Surtees   Lola-Climax
3 B. McLaren   Cooper-Climax
4 G. Hill   BRM
5 J. Brabham   Lotus-Climax
6 A. Maggs   Cooper-Climax
Fastest lap: J. Clark
    151.10 kph / 93.91 mph
Pole position: J. Clark

German GP

5 August: Nurburgring
342 km / 212 miles
1 G. Hill   BRM
    129.30 kph / 80.35 mph
2 J. Surtees   Lola-Climax
3 D. Gurney   Porsche
4 J. Clark   Lotus-Climax
5 B. McLaren   Cooper-Climax
6 R. Rodriguez   Ferrari
Fastest lap: G. Hill
    134.03 kph / 83.30 mph
Pole position: D. Gurney

Italian GP

16 September: Monza
495 km / 307 miles
1 G. Hill   BRM
    198.91 kph / 123.62 mph
2 R. Ginther   BRM
3 B. McLaren   Cooper-Climax
4 W. Mairesse   Ferrari
5 G. Baghetti   Ferrari
6 J. Bonnier   Porsche
Fastest lap: G. Hill
    202.32 kph / 125.73 mph
Pole position: J. Clark (Lotus-Climax)

United States GP

7 October: Watkins Glen
370 km / 230 miles
1 J. Clark   Lotus-Climax
    174.58 kph / 108.48 mph
2 G. Hill   BRM
3 B. McLaren   Cooper-Climax
4 J. Brabham   Brabham-Climax
5 D. Gurney   Porsche
6 M. Gregory   Lotus-BRM
Fastest lap: J. Clark
    177.64 kph / 110.40 mph
Pole position: J. Clark

South African GP

29 December: East London
321 km / 200 miles
1 G. Hill   BRM
    150.55 kph / 93.57 mph
2 B. McLaren   Cooper-Climax
3 A. Maggs   Cooper-Climax
4 J. Brabham   Brabham-Climax
5 I. Ireland   Lotus-Climax
6 N. Lederle   Lotus-Climax
Fastest lap: J. Clark (Lotus-Climax)
    155.03 kph / 96.35 mph
Pole position: J. Clark

1962 BRM

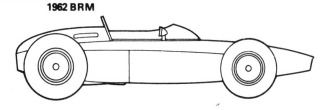

World Drivers' Championship

Pts	Driver	Wins	
42	Graham Hill (GB)	4	Dutch GP, German GP, Italian GP, South African GP
30	Jim Clark (GB)	3	Belgian GP, British GP, United States GP
27	Bruce McLaren (NZ)	1	Monaco GP
19	John Surtees (GB)	–	
15	Dan Gurney (USA)	1	French GP
14	Phil Hill (USA)	–	
13	Tony Maggs (SAF)	–	
10	Richie Ginther (USA)	–	
9	Jack Brabham (AUS)	–	
6	Trevor Taylor (GB)	–	
5	Giancarlo Baghetti (ITA)	–	
4	Lorenzo Bandini (ITA)	–	
4	Ricardo Rodriguez (MEX)	–	
3	Willy Mairesse (BEL)	–	
3	Jo Bonnier (SWE)	–	
2	Innes Ireland (GB)	–	
2	Carel Godin de Beaufort (HOL)	–	
1	Masten Gregory (USA)	–	
1	Neville Lederle (SAF)	–	

Points scoring: First six drivers in each race to score. Points as follows: 9–6–4–3–2–1. Best five results only to count.

Constructors' Cup

Pts	Manufacturer	Wins	
42	BRM	4	Dutch GP, German GP, Italian GP, South African GP
36	Lotus-Climax	3	Belgian GP, British GP, United States GP
29	Cooper-Climax	1	Monaco GP
19	Lola-Climax	–	
18	Porsche	1	French GP
18	Ferrari	–	
6	Brabham-Climax	–	
1	Lotus-BRM	–	

Points scoring: Best five results from nine rounds. Best placed car of each manufacturer only to score. Points: 9–6–4–3–2–1.

1963

Monaco GP

26 May: Monte Carlo
315 km / 195 miles
1 G. Hill BRM
 116.56 kph / 72.42 mph
2 R. Ginther BRM
3 B. McLaren Cooper-Climax
4 J. Surtees Ferrari
5 A. Maggs Cooper-Climax
6 T. Taylor Lotus-Climax
Fastest lap: J. Surtees
 119.81 kph / 74.45 mph
Pole position: J. Clark (Lotus-Climax)

Belgian GP

9 June: Spa
451 km / 280 miles
1 J. Clark Lotus-Climax
 183.63 kph / 114.10 mph
2 B. McLaren Cooper-Climax
3 D. Gurney Brabham-Climax
4 R. Ginther BRM
5 J. Bonnier Cooper-Climax
6 C. G. de
 Beaufort Porsche
Fastest lap: J. Clark
 213.19 kph / 132.47 mph
Pole position: G. Hill (BRM)

Dutch GP

23 June: Zandvoort
335 km / 208 miles
1 J. Clark Lotus-Climax
 156.96 kph / 97.53 mph
2 D. Gurney Brabham-Climax
3 J. Surtees Ferrari
4 I. Ireland BRP-BRM
5 R. Ginther BRM
6 L. Scarfiotti Ferrari
Fastest lap: J. Clark
 161.10 kph / 100.10 mph
Pole position: J. Clark

French GP

30 June: Rheims
440 km / 273 miles
1 J. Clark Lotus-Climax
 210.67 kph / 125.31 mph
2 A. Maggs Cooper-Climax
3 G. Hill BRM
4 J. Brabham Brabham-Climax
5 D. Gurney Brabham-Climax
6 J. Siffert Lotus-BRM
Fastest lap: J. Clark
 211.06 kph / 131.15 mph
Pole position: J. Clark

British GP

20 July: Silverstone
386 km / 240 miles
1 J. Clark Lotus-Climax
 172.75 kph / 107.35 mph
2 J. Surtees Ferrari
3 G. Hill BRM
4 R. Ginther BRM
5 L. Bandini BRM
6 J. Hall Lotus-BRM
Fastest lap: J. Surtees
 176.65 kph / 109.76 mph
Pole position: J. Clark

German GP

4 August: Nurburgring
342 km / 213 miles
1 J. Surtees Ferrari
 154.22 kph / 95.83 mph
2 J. Clark Lotus-Climax
3 R. Ginther BRM
4 G. Mitter Porsche
5 J. Hall Lotus-BRM
6 J. Bonnier Cooper-Climax
Fastest lap: J. Surtees
 155.82 kph / 96.82 mph
Pole position: J. Clark

Italian GP

8 September: Monza
495 km / 307 miles
1 J. Clark Lotus-Climax
 205.58 kph / 127.74 mph
2 R. Ginther BRM
3 B. McLaren Cooper-Climax
4 I. Ireland BRP-BRM
5 J. Brabham Brabham-Climax
6 A. Maggs Cooper-Climax
Fastest lap: J. Clark
 209.28 kph / 130.05 mph
Pole position: J. Surtees (Ferrari)

United States GP

6 October: Watkins Glen
407 km / 253 miles
1 G. Hill BRM
 175.29 kph / 108.92 mph
2 R. Ginther BRM
3 J. Clark Lotus-Climax
4 J. Brabham Brabham-Climax
5 L. Bandini Ferrari
6 C. G. de
 Beaufort Porsche
Fastest lap: J. Clark
 178.83 kph / 111.14 mph
Pole position: G. Hill

Mexican GP

27 October: Mexico City
325 km / 202 miles
1 J. Clark Lotus-Climax
 150.15 kph / 93.30 mph
2 J. Brabham Brabham-Climax
3 R. Ginther BRM
4 G. Hill BRM
5 J. Bonnier Cooper-Climax
6 D. Gurney Brabham-Climax
Fastest lap: J. Clark
 152.42 kph / 94.71 mph
Pole position: J. Clark

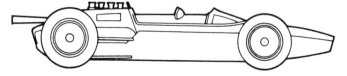

1963 Lotus-Climax 25

South African GP

28 December: East London
333 km / 207 miles
1 J. Clark   Lotus-Climax
   153.05 kph / 95.10 mph
2 D. Gurney   Brabham-Climax
3 G. Hill   BRM
4 B. McLaren   Cooper-Climax
5 L. Bandini   Ferrari
6 J. Bonnier   Cooper-Climax
Fastest lap: D. Gurney
   158.34 kph / 98.41 mph
Pole position: J. Clark

Constructors' Cup

Pts	Manufacturer	Wins	
54	Lotus-Climax	7	Belgian GP, Dutch GP, French GP, British GP, Italian GP, Mexican GP, South African GP
36	BRM	2	Monaco GP, United States GP
28	Brabham-Climax	–	
26	Ferrari	1	German GP
25	Cooper-Climax	–	
6	BRP-BRM	–	
5	Porsche	–	
4	Lotus-BRM	–	

Points scoring: Best six results from ten rounds.
Best placed car of each manufacturer only to score.
Points: 9–6–4–3–2–1.

World Drivers' Championship

Pts	Driver	Wins	
54	Jim Clark (GB)	7	Belgian GP, Dutch GP, French GP, British GP, Italian GP, Mexican GP, South African GP
29	Graham Hill (GB)	2	Monaco GP, United States GP
29	Richie Ginther (USA)		
22	John Surtees (GB)	1	German GP
19	Dan Gurney (USA)	–	
17	Bruce McLaren (NZ)	–	
14	Jack Brabham (AUS)	–	
9	Tony Maggs (SAF)	–	
6	Innes Ireland (GB)	–	
6	Lorenzo Bandini (ITA)	–	
6	Jo Bonnier (SWE)	–	
3	Gerhard Mitter (FRG)	–	
3	Jim Hall (USA)	–	
2	Carel Godin de Beaufort (HOL)	–	
1	Trevor Taylor (GB)	–	
1	Ludovico Scarfiotti (ITA)	–	
1	Jo Siffert (SWI)	–	

Points scoring: First six drivers in each race to score.
Points as follows: 9–6–4–3–2–1. Best six results only to count.

1964

Monaco GP

10 May: Monte Carlo
315 km / 195 miles
1 G. Hill   BRM
   116.88 kph / 72.64 mph
2 R. Ginther   BRM
3 P. Arundell   Lotus-Climax
4 J. Clark   Lotus-Climax
5 J. Bonnier   Cooper-Climax
6 M. Hailwood   Lotus-BRM
Fastest lap: G. Hill
   120.55 kph / 74.92 mph
Pole position: J. Clark

Dutch GP

24 May: Zandvoort
335 km / 208 miles
1 J. Clark   Lotus-Climax
   157.71 kph / 98.02 mph
2 J. Surtees   Ferrari
3 P. Arundell   Lotus-Climax
4 G. Hill   BRM
5 C. Amon   Lotus-BRM
6 R. Anderson   Brabham-Climax
Fastest lap: J. Clark
   162.62 kph / 101.07 mph
Pole position: D. Gurney
   (Brabham-Climax)

Belgian GP

14 June: Spa
451 km / 280 miles
1 J. Clark   Lotus-Climax
   213.68 kph / 132.79 mph
2 B. McLaren   Cooper-Climax
3 J. Brabham   Brabham-Climax
4 R. Ginther   BRM
5 G. Hill   BRM
6 D. Gurney   Brabham-Climax
Fastest lap: D. Gurney
   221.42 kph / 137.61 mph
Pole position: D. Gurney

French GP

28 June: Rouen
373 km / 232 miles
1 D. Gurney   Brabham-Climax
   175.01 kph / 108.77 mph
2 G. Hill   BRM
3 J. Brabham   Brabham-Climax
4 P. Arundell   Lotus-Climax
5 R. Ginther   BRM
6 B. McLaren   Cooper-Climax
Fastest lap: J. Brabham
   179.20 kph / 111.37 mph
Pole position: J. Clark (Lotus-Climax)

British GP

11 July: Brands Hatch
341 km / 212 miles
1 J. Clark   Lotus-Climax
   151.47 kph / 94.14 mph
2 G. Hill   BRM
3 J. Surtees   Ferrari
4 J. Brabham   Brabham-Climax
5 L. Bandini   Ferrari
6 P. Hill   Cooper-Climax
Fastest lap: J. Clark
   155.36 kph / 96.56 mph
Pole position: J. Clark

German GP

2 August: Nurburgring
342 km / 213 miles
1 J. Surtees   Ferrari
   155.40 kph / 96.58 mph
2 G. Hill   BRM
3 L. Bandini   Ferrari
4 J. Siffert   Brabham-BRM
5 M. Trintignant   BRM
6 A. Maggs   BRM
Fastest lap: J. Surtees
   158.20 kph / 98.31 mph
Pole position: J. Surtees

Austrian GP

23 August: Zeltweg
336 km / 209 miles
1 L. Bandini   Ferrari
   159.62 kph / 99.20 mph
2 R. Ginther   BRM
3 R. Anderson   Brabham-Climax
4 A. Maggs   BRM
5 I. Ireland   BRP-BRM
6 J. Bonnier   Brabham-Climax
Fastest lap: D. Gurney
   (Brabham-Climax)
   163.46 kph / 101.57 mph
Pole position: G. Hill (BRM)

Italian GP

6 September: Monza
449 km / 279 miles
1 J. Surtees   Ferrari
   205.60 kph / 127.78 mph
2 B. McLaren   Cooper-Climax
3 L. Bandini   Ferrari
4 R. Ginther   BRM
5 I. Ireland   BRP-BRM
6 M. Spence   Lotus-Climax
Fastest lap: J. Surtees
   209.51 kph / 130.19 mph
Pole position: J. Surtees

United States GP

4 October: Watkins Glen
407 km / 253 miles
1 G. Hill   BRM
   178.77 kph / 111.10 mph
2 J. Surtees   Ferrari
3 J. Siffert   Brabham-BRM
4 R. Ginther   BRM
5 W. Hansgen   Lotus-Climax
6 T. Taylor   BRP-BRM
Fastest lap: J. Clark (Lotus-Climax)
   183.25 kph / 113.89 mph
Pole position: J. Clark

1964 Ferrari 158

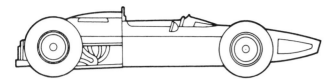

Mexican GP

25 October: Mexico City
325 km / 202 miles
1	D. Gurney	Brabham-Climax
	150.16 kph / 93.32 mph	
2	J. Surtees	Ferrari
3	L. Bandini	Ferrari
4	M. Spence	Lotus-Climax
5	J. Clark	Lotus-Climax
6	P. Rodriguez	Ferrari

Fastest lap: J. Clark
 152.07 kph / 94.49 mph
Pole position: J. Clark

John Surtees (left) was the 1964 world champion. The man next to him, Stirling Moss, never won the world title despite his long and illustrious Formula One career. (National Motor Museum)

World Drivers' Championship

Pts	Driver	Wins	
40	John Surtees (GB)	2	German GP, Italian GP
39	Graham Hill (GB)	2	Monaco GP, United States GP
32	Jim Clark (GB)	3	Dutch GP, Belgian GP, British GP
23	Lorenzo Bandini (ITA)	1	Austrian GP
23	Richie Ginther (USA)	–	
19	Dan Gurney (USA)	2	French GP, Mexican GP
13	Bruce McLaren (NZ)	–	
11	Jack Brabham (AUS)	–	
11	Peter Arundell (GB)	–	
7	Jo Siffert (SWI)	–	
5	Bob Anderson (GB)	–	
4	Tony Maggs (SAF)	–	
4	Mike Spence (GB)	–	
4	Innes Ireland (GB)	–	
3	Jo Bonnier (SWE)	–	
2	Chris Amon (NZ)	–	
2	Walter Hansgen (USA)	–	
2	Maurice Trintignant (FRA)	–	
1	Trevor Taylor (GB)	–	
1	Mike Hailwood (GB)	–	
1	Phil Hill (USA)	–	
1	Pedro Rodriguez (MEX)	–	

Points scoring: First six drivers in each race to score. Points as follows: 9–6–4–3–2–1. Best six results only to count.

Constructors' Cup

Pts	Manufacturer	Wins	
45	Ferrari	3	German GP, Austrian GP, Italian GP
42	BRM	2	Monaco GP, United States GP
37	Lotus-Climax	3	Dutch GP, Belgian GP, British GP
30	Brabham-Climax	2	French GP, Mexican GP
16	Cooper-Climax	–	
7	Brabham-BRM	–	
5	BRP-BRM	–	
3	Lotus-BRM	–	

Points scoring: Best six results from ten rounds. Best placed car of each manufacturer only to score. Points: 9–6–4–3–2–1.

1965

South African GP

1 January: East London
333 km / 207 miles
1	J. Clark	Lotus-Climax
	157.63 kph / 97.97 mph	
2	J. Surtees	Ferrari
3	G. Hill	BRM
4	M. Spence	Lotus-Climax
5	B. McLaren	Cooper-Climax
6	J. Stewart	BRM

Fastest lap: J. Clark
 161.06 kph / 100.10 mph
Pole position: J. Clark

Monaco GP

30 May: Monte Carlo
315 km / 195 miles
1	G. Hill	BRM
	119.60 kph / 74.34 mph	
2	L. Bandini	Ferrari
3	J. Stewart	BRM
4	J. Surtees	Ferrari
5	B. McLaren	Cooper-Climax
6	J. Siffert	Brabham-BRM

Fastest lap: G. Hill
 123.44 kph / 76.72 mph
Pole position: G. Hill

Belgian GP

13 June: Spa
451 km / 280 miles
1	J. Clark	Lotus-Climax
	188.51 kph / 117.16 mph	
2	J. Stewart	BRM
3	B. McLaren	Cooper-Climax
4	J. Brabham	Brabham-Climax
5	G. Hill	BRM
6	R. Ginther	Honda

Fastest lap: J. Clark
 200.67 kph / 124.72 mph
Pole position: G. Hill

French GP

27 June: Clermont-Ferrand
322 km / 200 miles
1	J. Clark	Lotus-Climax
	143.56 kph / 89.22 mph	
2	J. Stewart	BRM
3	J. Surtees	Ferrari
4	D. Hulme	Brabham-Climax
5	G. Hill	BRM
6	J. Siffert	Brabham-BRM

Fastest lap: J. Clark
 145.79 kph / 90.59 mph
Pole position: J. Clark

British GP

10 July: Silverstone
377 km / 234 miles
1	J. Clark	Lotus-Climax
	180.25 kph / 112.02 mph	
2	G. Hill	BRM
3	J. Surtees	Ferrari
4	M. Spence	Lotus-Climax
5	J. Stewart	BRM
6	D. Gurney	Brabham-Climax

Fastest lap: G. Hill
 183.90 kph / 114.29 mph
Pole position: J. Clark

Dutch GP

18 July: Zandvoort
335 km / 208 miles
1	J. Clark	Lotus-Climax
	162.30 kph / 100.87 mph	
2	J. Stewart	BRM
3	D. Gurney	Brabham-Climax
4	G. Hill	BRM
5	D. Hulme	Brabham-Climax
6	R. Ginther	Honda

Fastest lap: J. Clark
 166.58 kph / 103.53 mph
Pole position: G. Hill

German GP

1 August: Nurburgring
342 km / 213 miles
1 J. Clark   Lotus-Climax
   160.54 kph / 99.76 mph
2 G. Hill   BRM
3 D. Gurney   Brabham-Climax
4 J. Rindt   Cooper-Climax
5 J. Brabham   Brabham-Climax
6 L. Bandini   Ferrari
Fastest lap: J. Clark
   162.87 kph / 101.22 mph
Pole position: J. Clark

Italian GP

12 September: Monza
437 km / 272 miles
1 J. Stewart   BRM
   209.92 kph / 130.46 mph
2 G. Hill   BRM
3 D. Gurney   Brabham-Climax
4 L. Bandini   Ferrari
5 B. McLaren   Cooper-Climax
6 R. Attwood   Lotus-BRM
Fastest lap: J. Clark (Lotus-Climax)
   214.70 kph / 133.43 mph
Pole position: J. Clark

Constructors' Cup

Pts	Manufacturer	Wins	
54	Lotus-Climax	6	South African GP, Belgian GP, French GP, British GP, Dutch GP, German GP
45	BRM	3	Monaco GP, Italian GP, United States GP
27	Brabham-Climax	–	
26	Ferrari	–	
14	Cooper-Climax	–	
11	Honda	1	Mexican GP
5	Brabham-BRM	–	
2	Lotus-BRM	–	

Points scoring: Best six results from ten rounds.
Best placed car of each manufacturer only to score.
Points: 9–6–4–3–2–1.

United States GP

3 October: Watkins Glen
407 km / 253 miles
1 G. Hill   BRM
   173.74 kph / 107.98 mph
2 D. Gurney   Brabham-Climax
3 J. Brabham   Brabham-Climax
4 L. Bandini   Ferrari
5 P. Rodriguez   Ferrari
6 J. Rindt   Cooper-Climax
Fastest lap: G. Hill
   185.30 kph / 115.16 mph
Pole position: G. Hill

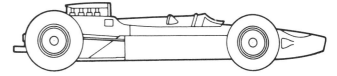

1965 Lotus-Climax 33

World Drivers' Championship

Pts	Driver	Wins	
54	Jim Clark (GB)	6	South African GP, Belgian GP, French GP, British GP, Dutch GP, German GP
40	Graham Hill (GB)	2	Monaco GP, United States GP
33	Jackie Stewart (GB)	1	Italian GP
25	Dan Gurney (USA)	–	
17	John Surtees (GB)	–	
13	Lorenzo Bandini (ITA)	–	
11	Richie Ginther (USA)	1	Mexican GP
10	Mike Spence (GB)	–	
10	Bruce McLaren (NZ)	–	
9	Jack Brabham (AUS)	–	
5	Denny Hulme (NZ)	–	
5	Jo Siffert (SWI)	–	
4	Jochen Rindt (AUT)	–	
2	Pedro Rodriguez (MEX)	–	
2	Ron Bucknum (USA)	–	
2	Dick Attwood (GB)	–	

Points scoring: First six drivers in each race to score. Points as follows: 9–6–4–3–2–1. Best six results only to count.

Mexican GP

24 October: Mexico City
325 km / 202 miles
1 R. Ginther   Honda
   151.66 kph / 94.26 mph
2 D. Gurney   Brabham-Climax
3 M. Spence   Lotus-Climax
4 J. Siffert   Brabham-BRM
5 R. Bucknum   Honda
6 R. Attwood   Lotus-BRM
Fastest lap: D. Gurney
   155.39 kph / 96.55 mph
Pole position: J. Clark (Lotus-Climax)

1966

Monaco GP

22 May: Monte Carlo
315 km / 195 miles
1 J. Stewart   BRM
   123.14 kph / 76.52 mph
2 L. Bandini   Ferrari
3 G. Hill   BRM
4 B. Bondurant   BRM
(Only four classified)
Fastest lap: L. Bandini
   126.08 kph / 78.34 mph
Pole position: J. Clark (Lotus-Climax)

Belgian GP

12 June: Spa
395 km / 245 miles
1 J. Surtees   Ferrari
   183.36 kph / 113.93 mph
2 J. Rindt   Cooper-Maserati
3 L. Bandini   Ferrari
4 J. Brabham   Brabham-Repco
5 R. Ginther   Cooper-Maserati
(Only five classified)
Fastest lap: J. Surtees
   196.21 kph / 121.92 mph
Pole position: J. Surtees

French GP

3 July: Rheims
398 km / 248 miles
1 J. Brabham   Brabham-Repco
   220.32 kph / 136.90 mph
2 M. Parkes   Ferrari
3 D. Hulme   Brabham-Repco
4 J. Rindt   Cooper-Maserati
5 D. Gurney   Eagle-Climax
6 J. Taylor   Brabham-BRM
Fastest lap: L. Bandini (Ferrari)
   227.62 kph / 141.44 mph
Pole position: L. Bandini

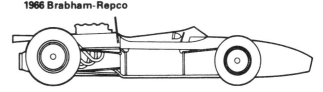

1966 Brabham-Repco

British GP

16 July: Brands Hatch
341 km / 212 miles
1 J. Brabham   Brabham-Repco
   153.66 kph / 95.48 mph
2 D. Hulme   Brabham-Repco
3 G. Hill   BRM
4 J. Clark   Lotus-Climax
5 J. Rindt   Cooper-Maserati
6 B. McLaren   McLaren-
                     Serenissima
Fastest lap: J. Brabham
   158.28 kph / 98.35 mph
Pole position: J. Brabham

Dutch GP

24 July: Zandvoort
377 km / 234 miles
1 J. Brabham   Brabham-Repco
   161.11 kph / 100.11 mph
2 G. Hill   BRM
3 J. Clark   Lotus-Climax
4 J. Stewart   BRM
5 M. Spence   Lotus-BRM
6 L. Bandini   Ferrari
Fastest lap: D. Hulme
   (Brabham-Repco)
   166.61 kph / 103.53 mph
Pole position: J. Brabham

German GP

7 August: Nurburgring
342 km / 213 miles
1 J. Brabham   Brabham-Repco
   139.61 kph / 86.75 mph
2 J. Surtees   Cooper-Maserati
3 J. Rindt   Cooper-Maserati
4 G. Hill   BRM
5 J. Stewart   BRM
6 L. Bandini   Ferrari
Fastest lap: J. Surtees
   155.23 kph / 96.45 mph
Pole position: J. Clark (Lotus-Climax)

Italian GP

4 September: Monza
391 km / 243 miles
1 L. Scarfiotti   Ferrari
   218.75 kph / 135.92 mph
2 M. Parkes   Ferrari
3 D. Hulme   Brabham-Repco
4 J. Rindt   Cooper-Maserati
5 M. Spence   Lotus-BRM
6 R. Anderson   Brabham-Climax
Fastest lap: L. Scarfiotti
   224.03 kph / 139.20 mph
Pole position: M. Parkes

United States GP

2 October: Watkins Glen
400 km / 248 miles
1 J. Clark   Lotus-BRM
   184.98 kph / 114.94 mph
2 J. Rindt   Cooper-Maserati
3 J. Surtees   Cooper-Maserati
4 J. Siffert   Cooper-Maserati
5 B. McLaren   McLaren-Ford
6 P. Arundell   Lotus-Climax
Fastest lap: J. Surtees
   191.26 kph / 118.85 mph
Pole position: J. Brabham
   (Brabham-Repco)

Mexican GP

23 October: Mexico City
325 km / 202 miles
1 J. Surtees   Cooper-Maserati
   154.04 kph / 95.72 mph
2 J. Brabham   Brabham-Repco
3 D. Hulme   Brabham-Repco
4 R. Ginther   Honda
5 D. Gurney   Eagle-Climax
6 J. Bonnier   Cooper-Maserati
Fastest lap: R. Ginther
   158.24 kph / 98.33 mph
Pole position: J. Surtees

Jack Brabham enjoyed wearing the victor's laurel wreath 14 times beween 1959–70. This win was victory number ten in the 1966 Dutch Grand Prix. (National Motor Museum)

World Drivers' Championship

Pts	Driver	Wins	
42	Jack Brabham (AUS)	4	French GP, British GP, Dutch GP, German GP
28	John Surtees (GB)	2	Belgian GP, Mexican GP
22	Jochen Rindt (AUT)	–	
18	Denny Hulme (NZ)	–	
17	Graham Hill (GB)	–	
16	Jim Clark (GB)	1	United States GP
14	Jackie Stewart (GB)	1	Monaco GP
12	Mike Parkes (GB)	–	
12	Lorenzo Bandini (ITA)	–	
9	Ludovico Scarfiotti (ITA)	1	Italian GP
5	Richie Ginther (USA)	–	
4	Mike Spence (GB)	–	
4	Dan Gurney (USA)	–	
3	Bob Bondurant (USA)	–	
3	Jo Siffert (SWI)	–	
3	Bruce McLaren (NZ)	–	
1	John Taylor (GB)	–	
1	Bob Anderson (GB)	–	
1	Peter Arundell (GB)	–	
1	Jo Bonnier (SWE)	–	

Points scoring: First six drivers in each race to score.
Points as follows: 9–6–4–3–2–1. Best five results only to count.

Constructors' Cup

Pts	Manufacturer	Wins	
42	Brabham-Repco	4	French GP, British GP, Dutch GP, German GP
31	Ferrari	2	Belgian GP, Italian GP
30	Cooper-Maserati	1	Mexican GP
22	BRM	1	Monaco GP
13	Lotus-BRM	1	United States GP
8	Lotus-Climax	–	
4	Eagle-Climax	–	
3	Honda	–	
2	McLaren-Ford	–	
1	Brabham-BRM	–	
1	McLaren-Serenissima	–	
1	Brabham-Climax	–	

Points scoring: Best five results from nine rounds.
Best placed car of each manufacturer only to score.
Points: 9–6–4–3–2–1.

1967

South African GP

2 January: Kyalami
328 km / 204 miles
1 P. Rodriguez   Cooper-Maserati
   156.26 kph / 97.09 mph
2 J. Love   Cooper-Climax
3 J. Surtees   Honda
4 D. Hulme   Brabham-Repco
5 R. Anderson   Brabham-Climax
6 J. Brabham   Brabham-Repco
Fastest lap: D. Hulme
   163.95 kph / 101.87 mph
Pole position: J. Brabham

Monaco GP

7 May: Monte Carlo
315 km / 195 miles
1 D. Hulme   Brabham-Repco
   122.14 kph / 75.90 mph
2 G. Hill   Lotus-BRM
3 C. Amon   Ferrari
4 B. McLaren   McLaren-BRM
5 P. Rodriguez   Cooper-Maserati
6 M. Spence   BRM
Fastest lap: J. Clark (Lotus-Climax)
   126.50 kph / 78.61 mph
Pole position: J. Brabham
   (Brabham-Repco)

Dutch GP

4 June: Zandvoort
377 km / 234 miles
1 J. Clark   Lotus-Ford
   168.09 kph / 104.44 mph
2 J. Brabham   Brabham-Repco
3 D. Hulme   Brabham-Repco
4 C. Amon   Ferrari
5 M. Parkes   Ferrari
6 L. Scarfiotti   Ferrari
Fastest lap: J. Clark
   171.38 kph / 106.49 mph
Pole position: G. Hill (Lotus-Ford)

Belgian GP

18 June: Spa
395 km / 245 miles
1 D. Gurney   Eagle-Weslake
   234.95 kph / 145.99 mph
2 J. Stewart   BRM
3 C. Amon   Ferrari
4 J. Rindt   Cooper-Maserati
5 M. Spence   BRM
6 J. Clark   Lotus-Ford
Fastest lap: D. Gurney
   239.55 kph / 148.85 mph
Pole position: J. Clark

French GP

2 July: Le Mans
354 km / 220 miles
1 J. Brabham   Brabham-Repco
   159.17 kph / 98.90 mph
2 D. Hulme   Brabham-Repco
3 J. Stewart   BRM
4 J. Siffert   Cooper-Maserati
5 C. Irwin   BRM
6 P. Rodriguez   Cooper-Maserati
Fastest lap: G. Hill (Lotus-Ford)
   164.64 kph / 102.29 mph
Pole position: G. Hill

British GP

15 July: Silverstone
377 km / 234 miles
1 J. Clark   Lotus-Ford
   189.33 kph / 117.64 mph
2 D. Hulme   Brabham-Repco
3 C. Amon   Ferrari
4 J. Brabham   Brabham-Repco
5 P. Rodriguez   Cooper-Maserati
6 J. Surtees   Honda
Fastest lap: D. Hulme
   194.92 kph / 121.12 mph
Pole position: J. Clark

German GP

6 August: Nurburgring
343 km / 213 miles
1 D. Hulme   Brabham-Repco
   163.20 kph / 101.41 mph
2 J. Brabham   Brabham-Repco
3 C. Amon   Ferrari
4 J. Surtees   Honda
5 J. Bonnier   Cooper-Maserati
6 G. Ligier   Brabham-Repco
Fastest lap: D. Gurney (Eagle-
   Weslake)
   166.04 kph / 103.17 mph
Pole position: J. Clark (Lotus-Ford)

Canadian GP

27 August: Mosport
356 km / 221 miles
1 J. Brabham   Brabham-Repco
   133.01 kph / 82.65 mph
2 D. Hulme   Brabham-Repco
3 D. Gurney   Eagle-Weslake
4 G. Hill   Lotus-Ford
5 M. Spence   BRM
6 C. Amon   Ferrari
Fastest lap: J. Clark (Lotus-Ford)
   171.47 kph / 106.54 mph
Pole position: J. Clark

Italian GP

10 September: Monza
391 km / 243 miles
1 J. Surtees   Honda
   226.12 kph / 140.50 mph
2 J. Brabham   Brabham-Repco
3 J. Clark   Lotus-Ford
4 J. Rindt   Cooper-Maserati
5 M. Spence   BRM
6 J. Ickx   Cooper-Maserati
Fastest lap: J. Clark
   233.90 kph / 145.34 mph
Pole position: J. Clark

United States GP

1 October: Watkins Glen
400 km / 248 miles
1 J. Clark   Lotus-Ford
   194.66 kph / 120.95 mph
2 G. Hill   Lotus-Ford
3 D. Hulme   Brabham-Repco
4 J. Siffert   Cooper-Maserati
5 J. Brabham   Brabham-Repco
6 J. Bonnier   Cooper-Maserati
Fastest lap: G. Hill
   201.90 kph / 125.46 mph
Pole position: G. Hill

Mexican GP

22 October: Mexico City
325 km / 202 miles
1 J. Clark   Lotus-Ford
   163.22 kph / 101.42 mph
2 J. Brabham   Brabham-Repco
3 D. Hulme   Brabham-Repco
4 J. Surtees   Honda
5 M. Spence   BRM
6 P. Rodriguez   Cooper-Maserati
Fastest lap: J. Clark
   166.47 kph / 103.44 mph
Pole position: J. Clark

World Drivers' Championship

Pts	Driver	Wins	
51	Denny Hulme (NZ)	2	Monaco GP, German GP
46	Jack Brabham (AUS)	2	French GP, Canadian GP
41	Jim Clark (GB)	4	Dutch GP, British GP, United States GP, Mexican GP
20	John Surtees (GB)	1	Italian GP
20	Chris Amon (NZ)	–	
15	Pedro Rodriguez (MEX)	1	South African GP
15	Graham Hill (GB)	–	
13	Dan Gurney (USA)	1	Belgian GP
10	Jackie Stewart (GB)	–	
9	Mike Spence (GB)	–	
6	John Love (SAF)	–	
6	Jochen Rindt (AUT)	–	
6	Jo Siffert (SWI)	–	
3	Bruce McLaren (NZ)	–	
3	Jo Bonnier (SWE)	–	
2	Chris Irwin (GB)	–	
2	Mike Parkes (GB)	–	
2	Bob Anderson (GB)	–	
1	Ludovico Scarfiotti (ITA)	–	
1	Guy Ligier (FRA)	–	
1	Jacky Ickx (BEL)	–	

Points scoring: First six drivers in each race to score. Points as follows: 9–6–4–3–2–1. Best five results from first six races plus best four results from next five races only to count.

Constructors' Cup

Pts	Manufacturer	Wins	
63	Brabham-Repco	4	Monaco GP, French GP, Canadian GP, German GP
44	Lotus-Ford	4	Dutch GP, British GP, United States GP, Mexican GP
28	Cooper-Maserati	1	South African GP
20	Honda	1	Italian GP
20	Ferrari	–	
17	BRM		
13	Eagle-Weslake	1	Belgian GP
6	Cooper-Climax	–	
6	Lotus-BRM	–	
3	McLaren-BRM	–	
2	Brabham-Climax	–	

Points scoring: Best five results from first six races plus best four results from remaining five races to count. Best placed car of each manufacturer only to score. Points: 9–6–4–3–2–1.

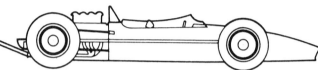

1967 Lotus-Ford 49

The Brabham team provided the winner and runner-up in the 1967 world championship. Brabham himself was second to New Zealander Denny Hulme. (National Motor Museum)

1968

South African GP

1 January: Kyalami
328 km / 204 miles
1 J. Clark   Lotus-Ford
   172.89 kph / 107.42 mph
2 G. Hill   Lotus-Ford
3 J. Rindt   Brabham-Repco
4 C. Amon   Ferrari
5 D. Hulme   McLaren-BRM
6 J. P. Beltoise Matra-Ford
Fastest lap: J. Clark
   176.51 kph / 109.68 mph
Pole position: J. Clark

Spanish GP

12 May: Jarama
306 km / 190 miles
1 G. Hill   Lotus-Ford
   135.84 kph / 84.40 mph
2 D. Hulme   McLaren-Ford
3 B. Redman   Cooper-BRM
4 L. Scarfiotti   Cooper-BRM
5 J. P. Beltoise Matra-Ford
(only five classified)
Fastest lap: J. P. Beltoise
   138.80 kph / 86.24 mph
Pole position: C. Amon (Ferrari)

Monaco GP

26 May: Monte Carlo
252 km / 156 miles
1 G. Hill   Lotus-Ford
   125.24 kph / 77.82 mph
2 R. Attwood   BRM
3 L. Bianchi   Cooper-BRM
4 L. Scarfiotti   Cooper-BRM
5 D. Hulme   McLaren-Ford
(only five classified)
Fastest lap: R. Attwood
   128.51 kph / 79.85 mph
Pole position: G. Hill

Belgian GP

9 June: Spa
395 km / 245 miles
1 B. McLaren   McLaren-Ford
   236.80 kph / 147.14 mph
2 P. Rodriguez   BRM
3 J. Ickx   Ferrari
4 J. Stewart   Matra-Ford
5 J. Oliver   Lotus-Ford
6 L. Bianchi   Cooper-BRM
Fastest lap: J. Surtees (Honda)
   241.14 kph / 149.84 mph
Pole position: C. Amon (Ferrari)

Dutch GP

23 June: Zandvoort
377 km / 234 miles
1 J. Stewart   Matra-Ford
   136.25 kph / 84.66 mph
2 J. P. Beltoise Matra
3 P. Rodriguez   BRM
4 J. Ickx   Ferrari
5 S. Moser   Brabham-Repco
6 C. Amon   Ferrari
Fastest lap: J. P. Beltoise
   142.52 kph / 88.56 mph
Pole position: C. Amon

French GP

7 July: Rouen
393 km / 244 miles
1 J. Ickx   Ferrari
   161.66 kph / 100.45 mph
2 J. Surtees   Honda
3 J. Stewart   Matra-Ford
4 V. Elford   Cooper-BRM
5 D. Hulme   McLaren-Ford
6 P. Courage   BRM
Fastest lap: P. Rodriguez (BRM)
   179.10 kph / 111.29 mph
Pole position: J. Rindt
   (Brabham-Repco)

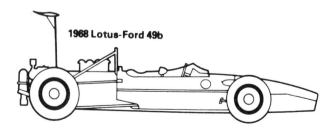

1968 Lotus-Ford 49b

British GP

20 July: Brands Hatch
341 km / 212 miles
1 J. Siffert   Lotus-Ford
     168.70 kph / 104.83 mph
2 C. Amon   Ferrari
3 J. Ickx   Ferrari
4 D. Hulme   McLaren-Ford
5 J. Surtees   Honda
6 J. Stewart   Matra-Ford
Fastest lap: J. Siffert
     171.16 kph / 106.35 mph
Pole position: G. Hill (Lotus-Ford)

German GP

4 August: Nurburgring
320 km / 199 miles
1 J. Stewart   Matra-Ford
     137.94 kph / 85.71 mph
2 G. Hill   Lotus-Ford
3 J. Rindt   Brabham-Repco
4 J. Ickx   Ferrari
5 J. Brabham   Brabham-Repco
6 P. Rodriguez   BRM
Fastest lap: J. Stewart
     142.72 kph / 88.68 mph
Pole position: J. Ickx

Italian GP

8 September: Monza
390 km / 243 miles
1 D. Hulme   McLaren-Ford
     234.02 kph / 145.41 mph
2 J. Servoz-Gavin   Matra-Ford
3 J. Ickx   Ferrari
4 P. Courage   BRM
5 J. P. Beltoise   Matra
6 J. Bonnier   McLaren-BRM
Fastest lap: J. Oliver (Lotus-Ford)
     239.31 kph / 148.70 mph
Pole position: J. Surtees (Honda)

Canadian GP

22 September: St. Jovite
384 km / 239 miles
1 D. Hulme   McLaren-Ford
     156.47 kph / 97.22 mph
2 B. McLaren   McLaren-Ford
3 P. Rodriguez   BRM
4 G. Hill   Lotus-Ford
5 V. Elford   Cooper-BRM
6 J. Stewart   Matra-Ford
Fastest lap: J. Siffert (Lotus-Ford)
     161.44 kph / 100.31 mph
Pole position: J. Rindt
     (Brabham-Repco)

United States GP

6 October: Watkins Glen
400 km / 248 miles
1 J. Stewart   Matra-Ford
     200.99 kph / 124.90 mph
2 G. Hill   Lotus-Ford
3 J. Surtees   Honda
4 D. Gurney   McLaren-Ford
5 J. Siffert   Lotus-Ford
6 B. McLaren   McLaren-Ford
Fastest lap: J. Stewart
     204.31 kph / 126.96 mph
Pole position: M. Andretti
     (Lotus-Ford)

Mexican GP

3 November: Mexico City
325 km / 202 miles
1 G. Hill   Lotus-Ford
     167.05 kph / 103.80 mph
2 B. McLaren   McLaren-Ford
3 J. Oliver   Lotus-Ford
4 P. Rodriguez   BRM
5 J. Bonnier   Honda
6 J. Siffert   Lotus-Ford
Fastest lap: J. Siffert
     172.70 kph / 107.31 mph
Pole position: J. Siffert

Two youngsters, Graham Hill (left) and Jackie Stewart. The pair of them occupied the first two places in the 1968 championship. (National Motor Museum)

World Drivers' Championship

Pts	Driver	Wins	
48	Graham Hill (GB)	3	Spanish GP, Monaco GP, Mexican GP
36	Jackie Stewart (GB)	3	Dutch GP, German GP, United States GP
33	Denny Hulme (NZ)	2	Italian GP, Canadian GP
27	Jacky Ickx (BEL)	1	French GP
22	Bruce McLaren (NZ)	1	Belgian GP
18	Pedro Rodriguez (MEX)	–	
12	Jo Siffert (SWI)	1	British GP
12	John Surtees (GB)	–	
11	Jean-Pierre Beltoise (FRA)	–	
10	Chris Amon (NZ)	–	
9	Jim Clark (GB)	1	South African GP
8	Jochen Rindt (AUT)	–	
6	Dick Attwood (GB)	–	
6	Johnny Servoz-Gavin (FRA)	–	
6	Jackie Oliver (GB)	–	
6	Ludovico Scarfiotti (ITA)	–	
5	Lucien Bianchi (BEL)	–	
5	Vic Elford (GB)	–	
4	Brian Redman (GB)	–	
4	Piers Courage (GB)	–	
3	Dan Gurney (USA)	–	
3	Jo Bonnier (SWE)	–	
2	Silvio Moser (SWI)	–	
2	Jack Brabham (AUS)	–	

Points scoring: First six drivers in each race to score. Points as follows: 9–6–4–3–2–1. Best five results from first half of the season plus the best five results from the second half of the season to count.

Constructors' Cup

Pts	Manufacturer	Wins	
62	Lotus-Ford	5	South African GP, Spanish GP, Monaco GP, British GP, Mexican GP
49	McLaren-Ford	3	Belgian GP, Italian GP, Canadian GP
45	Matra-Ford	3	Dutch GP, German GP, United States GP
32	Ferrari	1	French GP
28	BRM	–	
14	Honda	–	
14	Cooper-BRM	–	
10	Brabham-Repco	–	
8	Matra	–	
3	McLaren-BRM	–	

Points scoring: Best five results from first six races plus best five results from remaining six races. Best placed car of each manufacturer only to score. Points: 9–6–4–3–2–1.

A Sad Day At Hockenheim

Jim Clark's two sponsors, Lotus and Ford, both wanted him to drive on Sunday 7 April, 1968. Lotus boss Colin Chapman wanted Clark to compete in the Deutschland Trophae Formula Two race at the Hockenheim circuit, set among the pine forests of Heidelberg, while Ford wanted him to drive their new 3-litre prototype in the BOAC 500-mile international sports car race at Brands Hatch. The arguments over who he should drive for went on until the last minute when it was decided that Clark should make the fateful trip to Germany.

The race around the fast but treacherous circuit was scheduled for 20 laps and was the first of eight races to count towards the European Formula Two Championship. Clark was visibly unhappy in his Lotus-Cosworth and, despite being the race favourite, was struggling in eighth place on the sixth lap when, coming out of a gentle right-hand curve, he lost control of the car. It careered down the track for 500 yards before somersaulting three or four times and crashing broadside into a clump of trees before disintegrating 'into 100 pieces', as a trackside official described it. The wreckage was strewn over an area of 150-yard radius, confirming the official's description.

Clark was rushed to the clinic at Heidelberg University but was dead on arrival as a result of a broken neck, skull fracture and multiple internal injuries.

Ironically, it was Clark's first competitive drive at Hockenheim, and it was the circuit's first fatality. Hockenheim was a fast circuit but was regarded as one of the safest. Colin Chapman, however, had his doubts and was convinced that if it had barriers around it, similar to those at Monaco, Clark would never have died.

What caused the accident remains a mystery, although a cut in one of the rear tyres was discovered over a week later, but according to Lotus it was impossible to be categoric as to the real cause. The nearest driver to Clark capable of giving an eye witness account was Robin Widdows (GB) in a McLaren-Ford, but he saw little, except the blur in the distance of Clark's vehicle leaving the track.

The accident happened out of sight of the public enclosures and the 80 000 spectators rose to their feet in a stunned numbness when the tannoy announced that Clark was dead. Clark's Lotus team-mate Graham Hill (GB) pulled out of the race which was eventually won by Frenchman Jean-Pierre Beltoise.

Jim Clark, the greatest driver produced by Britain, had survived many high-speed crashes in the past—at Aintree, Brands Hatch and Monaco, but he could not survive the 275-kph (170-mph) crash on that sad day at Hockenheim in 1968.

Colin Chapman (left) and Jim Clark shared many successful moments together. Clark is seen holding the Ferodo Trophy awarded to Chapman in 1965 for the achievements of his Lotus team. Clark himself was the recipient of the trophy in 1963. (National Motor Museum)

1969

South African GP

1 March: Kyalami
328 km / 204 miles
1 J. Stewart   Matra-Ford
    178.03 kph / 110.62 mph
2 G. Hill   Lotus-Ford
3 D. Hulme   McLaren-Ford
4 J. Siffert   Lotus-Ford
5 B. McLaren   McLaren-Ford
6 J. P. Beltoise   Matra-Ford
Fastest lap: J. Stewart
    181.05 kph / 112.50 mph
Pole position: J. Brabham
    (Brabham-Ford)

Spanish GP

4 May: Montjuich
341 km / 212 miles
1 J. Stewart   Matra-Ford
    149.52 kph / 92.91 mph
2 B. McLaren   McLaren-Ford
3 J. P. Beltoise   Matra-Ford
4 D. Hulme   McLaren-Ford
5 J. Surtees   BRM
6 J. Ickx   Brabham-Ford
Fastest lap: J. Rindt (Lotus-Ford)
    154.54 kph / 96.02 mph
Pole position: J. Rindt

Monaco GP

18 May: Monte Carlo
252 km / 156 miles
1 G. Hill   Lotus-Ford
    129.04 kph / 80.18 mph
2 P. Courage   Brabham-Ford
3 J. Siffert   Lotus-Ford
4 R. Attwood   Lotus-Ford
5 B. McLaren   McLaren-Ford
6 D. Hulme   McLaren-Ford
Fastest lap: J. Stewart (Matra-Ford)
    133.04 kph / 82.67 mph
Pole position: J. Stewart

Dutch GP

21 June: Zandvoort
377 km / 234 miles
1 J. Stewart   Matra-Ford
    178.71 kph / 111.04 mph
2 J. Siffert   Lotus-Ford
3 C. Amon   Ferrari
4 D. Hulme   McLaren-Ford
5 J. Ickx   Brabham-Ford
6 J. Brabham   Brabham-Ford
Fastest lap: J. Stewart
    182.00 kph / 113.09 mph
Pole position: J. Rindt (Lotus-Ford)

French GP

6 July: Clermont-Ferrand
306 km / 190 miles
1 J. Stewart   Matra-Ford
    157.25 kph / 97.71 mph
2 J. P. Beltoise   Matra-Ford
3 J. Ickx   Brabham-Ford
4 B. McLaren   McLaren-Ford
5 V. Elford   McLaren-Ford
6 G. Hill   Lotus-Ford
Fastest lap: J. Stewart
    158.72 kph / 98.62 mph
Pole position: J. Stewart

British GP

19 July: Silverstone
396 km / 246 miles
1 J. Stewart   Matra-Ford
    204.79 kph / 127.25 mph
2 J. Ickx   Brabham-Ford
3 B. McLaren   McLaren-Ford
4 J. Rindt   Lotus-Ford
5 P. Courage   Brabham-Ford
6 V. Elford   McLaren-Ford
Fastest lap: J. Stewart
    208.58 kph / 129.61 mph
Pole position: J. Rindt

German GP

3 August: Nurburgring
320 km / 199 miles
1 J. Ickx   Brabham-Ford
    174.50 kph / 108.43 mph
2 J. Stewart   Matra-Ford
3 B. McLaren   McLaren-Ford
4 G. Hill   Lotus-Ford
5 J. Siffert   Lotus-Ford
6 J. P. Beltoise   Matra-Ford
Fastest lap: J. Ickx
    177.24 kph / 110.13 mph
Pole position: J. Ickx

Italian GP

7 September: Monza
391 km / 243 miles
1 J. Stewart   Matra-Ford
    236.52 kph / 146.97 mph
2 J. Rindt   Lotus-Ford
3 J. P. Beltoise   Matra-Ford
4 B. McLaren   McLaren-Ford
5 P. Courage   Brabham-Ford
6 P. Rodriguez   Ferrari
Fastest lap: J. P. Beltoise
    242.96 kph / 150.97 mph
Pole position: J. Rindt

Canadian GP

20 September: Mosport
356 km / 221 miles
1 J. Ickx   Brabham-Ford
    178.93 kph / 111.18 mph
2 J. Brabham   Brabham-Ford
3 J. Rindt   Lotus-Ford
4 J. P. Beltoise   Matra-Ford
5 B. McLaren   McLaren-Ford
6 J. Servoz-Gavin   Matra-Ford
Fastest lap: J. Ickx
    184.67 kph / 114.78 mph
Pole position: J. Ickx

United States GP

5 October: Watkins Glen
400 km / 248 miles
1 J. Rindt   Lotus-Ford
    203.36 kph / 126.36 mph
2 P. Courage   Brabham-Ford
3 J. Surtees   BRM
4 J. Brabham   Brabham-Ford
5 P. Rodriguez   Ferrari
6 S. Moser   Brabham-Ford
Fastest lap: J. Rindt
    207.11 kph / 128.69 mph
Pole position: J. Rindt

Mexican GP

19 October: Mexico City
325 km / 202 miles
1 D. Hulme   McLaren-Ford
    170.83 kph / 106.15 mph
2 J. Ickx   Brabham-Ford
3 J. Brabham   Brabham-Ford
4 J. Stewart   Matra-Ford
5 J. P. Beltoise   Matra-Ford
6 J. Oliver   BRM
Fastest lap: J. Ickx
    174.67 kph / 108.54 mph
Pole position: J. Brabham

World Drivers' Championship

Pts	Driver	Wins	
63	Jackie Stewart (GB)	6	South African GP, Spanish GP, Dutch GP, French GP, British GP, Italian GP
37	Jacky Ickx (BEL)	2	German GP, Canadian GP
26	Bruce McLaren (NZ)	–	
22	Jochen Rindt (AUT)	1	United States GP
21	Jean-Pierre Beltoise (FRA)	–	
20	Denny Hulme (NZ)	1	Mexico GP
19	Graham Hill (GB)	1	Monaco GP
16	Piers Courage (GB)	–	
15	Jo Siffert (SWI)	–	
14	Jack Brabham (AUS)	–	
6	John Surtees (GB)	–	
4	Chris Amon (NZ)	–	
3	Dick Attwood (GB)	–	
3	Pedro Rodriguez (MEX)	–	
3	Vic Elford (GB)	–	
1	Johnny Servoz-Gavin (FRA)	–	
1	Silvio Moser (SWI)	–	
1	Jackie Oliver (GB)	–	

Points scoring: First six drivers in each race to score. Points as follows: 9–6–4–3–2–1. Best five results from first six races plus the best four results from the next five races to count.

Brooklands

Brooklands has a legendary place in motor racing history, not only in Britain, but world-wide. As the first purpose-built motor racing circuit in the world it was the forerunner of many of today's great circuits and must, therefore, never be forgotten.

Opened in 1907, it was the idea of motoring enthusiast Hugh Fortesque Locke-King and he invested £150 000 of his own money in the circuit. It was built to a design by Colonel H.C.L. Holden on part of Lord North-cliffe's estate near Weybridge in Surrey.

For more than 30 years Brook-lands was the home of hundreds of races, the scene of many record attempts, and the testing ground for manufacturers who were res-tricted to the 20 mph speed limit on Britain's roads at the time.

Three different circuits were used: The Outer Circuit (the full course) measured 4.45 km (2.77 miles); the Short Course took in everything except the Home Banking, and was 4.21 km (2.62 miles) long; and the Moun-tain Course used only the Home Banking and Finishing Straight and measured 1.88 km (1.17 miles). A simulated road course, the Campbell Course, was added in 1937 and ran in an anti-clockwise direction.

Because it was the first pur-pose-built circuit, the designer had little knowledge of such mat-ters and based his design on that of a horse race track. Consequent-ly it was virtually oval-shaped. It bordered the railway line, 20 miles from London. Part of the track which went over the river Wey was supported by a ferro-concrete bridge—revolutionary in its day.

The actual surface consisted of a flimsy 6-in (15-cm) layer of concrete, a far cry from the resi-lient surfaces that take today's high-speed cars. Because of the hammering the great Bugattis and the like gave Brooklands during the summer months, extensive repairs had to be carried out each winter.

The most striking feature at Brooklands, the two steep banked bends, were known as the Byfleet Banking and the Members Bank-ing, which reached a maximum height of nearly 9 m (29 ft). Such severe bends would never be allowed in the safety conscious world of Grand Prix racing today.

The first race at Brooklands was in July 1907 and the first British Grand Prix (then known as the RAC Grand Prix) was held at Brooklands in 1926 and won by Robert Senechal and Louis Wag-ner in a Delage at an average speed of 115.22 kph (71.61 mph). Motor cycling was also popular at Brooklands and the great John Cobb was synonymous with the circuit and his lap record of 230.80 kph (143.44 mph) in a 24-litre Napier-Railton stood at the time of the circuit's closure.

Apart from a brief period during the First World War, when the Royal Flying Corps had use of the area inside the circuit, Brooklands was used continuously from 1907 to the outbreak of the Second World War. On that occasion the site was taken over by the Vickers-Armstrong aircraft factory but it was never suitably repaired and racing never returned to Brooklands. The site was sold to Vickers for £300 000 in 1946 and thus was brought about the end of a motor racing legend.

As the drivers 'jockey' for vantage positions, the width and severity of the banking at Brooklands can clearly be seen as the drivers head towards the railway straight. (National Motor Museum)

1969 Matra MS 80

Constructors' Cup

Pts	Manufacturer	Wins	
66	Matra-Ford	6	South African GP, Spanish GP, Dutch GP, French GP, British GP, Italian GP
49	Brabham-Ford	2	German GP, Canadian GP
47	Lotus-Ford	2	Monaco GP, United States GP
38	McLaren-Ford	1	Mexican GP
7	BRM	–	
7	Ferrari	–	

Points scoring: Best five results from first six races plus best results from remaining five races. Best placed car of each manufacturer only to score. Points: 9–6–4–3–2–1.

1970

South African GP

7 March: Kyalami
328 km / 204 miles
1 J. Brabham   Brabham-Ford
   179.76 kph / 111.70 mph
2 D. Hulme   McLaren-Ford
3 J. Stewart   March-Ford
4 J. P. Beltoise   Matra-Simca
5 J. Miles   Lotus-Ford
6 G. Hill   Lotus-Ford
Fastest lap: J. Surtees
   (McLaren-Ford)/J. Brabham
   182.84 kph / 113.61 mph
Pole position: J. Stewart

Spanish GP

19 April: Jarama
306 km / 190 miles
1 J. Stewart   March-Ford
   140.36 kph / 87.22 mph
2 B. McLaren   McLaren-Ford
3 M. Andretti   March-Ford
4 G. Hill   Lotus-Ford
5 J. Servoz-Gavin   March-Ford
(only five classified)
Fastest lap: J. Brabham
   (Brabham-Ford)
   145.38 kph / 90.33 mph
Pole position: J. Brabham

Monaco GP

10 May: Monte Carlo
252 km / 156 miles
1 J. Rindt   Lotus-Ford
   131.72 kph / 81.85 mph
2 J. Brabham   Brabham-Ford
3 H. Pescarolo   Matra-Simca
4 D. Hulme   McLaren-Ford
5 G. Hill   Lotus-Ford
6 P. Rodriguez   BRM
Fastest lap: J. Rindt
   136.08 kph / 84.56 mph
Pole position: J. Stewart
   (March-Ford)

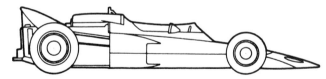

1970 Lotus 72

Belgian GP

7 June: Spa
395 km / 245 miles
1 P. Rodriguez   BRM
   241.31 kph / 149.94 mph
2 C. Amon   March-Ford
3 J. P. Beltoise   Matra-Simca
4 I. Giunti   Ferrari
5 R. Stommelen   Brabham-Ford
6 H. Pescarolo   Matra-Simca
Fastest lap: C. Amon
   244.74 kph / 152.08 mph
Pole position: J. Stewart
   (March-Ford)

Dutch GP

21 June: Zandvoort
335 km / 208 miles
1 J. Rindt   Lotus-Ford
   181.78 kph / 112.95 mph
2 J. Stewart   March-Ford
3 J. Ickx   Ferrari
4 C. Regazzoni   Ferrari
5 J. P. Beltoise   Matra-Simca
6 J. Surtees   McLaren-Ford
Fastest lap: J. Ickx
   190.52 kph / 118.38 mph
Pole position: J. Rindt

French GP

5 July: Clermont-Ferrand
306 km / 190 miles
1 J. Rindt   Lotus-Ford
   158.39 kph / 98.42 mph
2 C. Amon   March-Ford
3 J. Brabham   Brabham-Ford
4 D. Hulme   McLaren-Ford
5 H. Pescarolo   Matra-Simca
6 D. Gurney   McLaren-Ford
Fastest lap: J. Brabham
   160.43 kph / 99.69 mph
Pole position: J. Ickx (Ferrari)

British GP

18 July: Brands Hatch
341 km / 212 miles
1 J. Rindt   Lotus-Ford
   174.91 kph / 108.69 mph
2 J. Brabham   Brabham-Ford
3 D. Hulme   McLaren-Ford
4 C. Regazzoni   Ferrari
5 C. Amon   March-Ford
6 G. Hill   Lotus-Ford
Fastest lap: J. Brabham
   178.73 kph / 111.06 mph
Pole position: J. Rindt

German GP

2 August: Hockenheim
339 km / 211 miles
1 J. Rindt   Lotus-Ford
   199.67 kph / 124.07 mph
2 J. Ickx   Ferrari
3 D. Hulme   McLaren-Ford
4 E. Fittipaldi   Lotus-Ford
5 R. Stommelen   Brabham-Ford
6 H. Pescarolo   Matra-Simca
Fastest lap: J. Ickx
   202.83 kph / 126.03 mph
Pole position: J. Ickx

Austrian GP

16 August: Osterreichring
355 km / 220 miles
1 J. Ickx   Ferrari
   208.04 kph / 129.27 mph
2 C. Regazzoni   Ferrari
3 R. Stommelen   Brabham-Ford
4 P. Rodriguez   BRM
5 J. Oliver   BRM
6 J. P. Beltoise   Matra-Simca
Fastest lap: J. Ickx/C. Regazzoni
   211.95 kph / 131.70 mph
Pole position: J. Rindt (Lotus-Ford)

Italian GP

6 September: Monza
390 km / 243 miles
1 C. Regazzoni   Ferrari
   236.70 kph / 147.08 mph
2 J. Stewart   March-Ford
3 J. P. Beltoise   Matra-Simca
4 D. Hulme   McLaren-Ford
5 R. Stommelen   Brabham-Ford
6 F. Cevert   March-Ford
Fastest lap: C. Regazzoni
   242.96 kph / 150.97 mph
Pole position: J. Ickx (Ferrari)

Canadian GP

20 September: St Jovite
384 km / 239 miles
1 J. Ickx   Ferrari
   162.97 kph / 101.27 mph
2 C. Regazzoni   Ferrari
3 C. Amon   March-Ford
4 P. Rodriguez   BRM
5 J. Surtees   Surtees-Ford
6 P. Gethin   McLaren-Ford
Fastest lap: C. Regazzoni
   166.51 kph / 103.47 mph
Pole position: J. Stewart
   (Tyrrell-Ford)

United States GP

4 October: Watkins Glen
400 km / 248 miles
1 E. Fittipaldi   Lotus-Ford
   204.05 kph / 126.79 mph
2 P. Rodriguez   BRM
3 R. Wisell   Lotus-Ford
4 J. Ickx   Ferrari
5 C. Amon   March-Ford
6 D. Bell   Surtees-Ford
Pole position: J. Ickx
   212.39 kph / 131.97 mph
Pole position: J. Ickx

Mexican GP

18 October: Mexico City
325 km / 202 miles
1 J. Ickx   Ferrari
   171.85 kph / 106.78 mph
2 C. Regazzoni   Ferrari
3 D. Hulme   McLaren-Ford
4 C. Amon   March-Ford
5 J. P. Beltoise   Matra-Simca
6 P. Rodriguez   BRM
Fastest lap: J. Ickx
   174.57 kph / 108.47 mph
Pole position: C. Regazzoni

Constructors' Cup

Pts	Manufacturer	Wins	
59	Lotus-Ford	6	Monaco GP, Dutch GP, French GP, British GP, German GP, United States GP
52	Ferrari	4	Austrian GP, Italian GP, Canadian GP, Mexican GP
48	March-Ford	1	Spanish GP
35	Brabham-Ford	1	South African GP
35	McLaren-Ford	–	
23	Matra-Simca	–	
23	BRM	1	Belgian GP
3	Surtees-Ford	–	

Points scoring: Best six results from first seven races plus best five results from remaining six races. Best placed car of each manufacturer only to score. Points: 9–6–4–3–2–1.

World Drivers' Championship

Pts	Driver	Wins	
45	Jochen Rindt (AUT)	5	Monaco GP, Dutch GP, French GP, British GP, German GP
40	Jacky Ickx (BEL)	3	Austrian GP, Canadian GP, Mexican GP
33	Clay Regazzoni (SWI)	1	Italian GP
27	Denny Hulme (NZ)	–	
25	Jack Brabham (AUS)	1	South African GP
25	Jackie Stewart (GB)	1	Spanish GP
23	Pedro Rodriguez (MEX)	1	Belgian GP
23	Chris Amon (NZ)	–	
16	Jean-Pierre Beltoise (FRA)	–	
12	Emerson Fittipaldi (BRA)	1	United States GP
10	Rolf Stommelen (FRG)	–	
8	Henri Pescarolo (FRA)	–	
7	Graham Hill (GB)	–	
6	Bruce McLaren (NZ)	–	
4	Mario Andretti (USA)	–	
4	Reine Wisell (SWE)	–	
3	Ignazio Giunti (ITA)	–	
3	John Surtees (GB)	–	
2	John Miles (GB)	–	
2	Johnny Servoz-Gavin (FRA)	–	
2	Jackie Oliver (GB)	–	
1	Dan Gurney (USA)	–	
1	Francois Cevert (FRA)	–	
1	Peter Gethin (GB)	–	
1	Derek Bell (GB)	–	

Points scoring: First six drivers in each race to score. Points as follows: 9–6–4–3–2–1. Best six results from first seven races plus the best five results from the remaining six races to count.

● Johnny Dumfries, winner of the British Formula Three Championship, and runner-up in the European Championship in 1984, was not in motor racing for the money. The 26-year-old Earl of Dumfries was heir to a £100 million fortune.

Jochen Rindt (AUT) having difficulty lifting the splendid trophy after winning the 1970 British Grand Prix. Less than two months later Rindt lost his life at Monza but went on to become the first, and only, posthumous world champion. (National Motor Museum)

1971

South African GP

6 March: Kyalami
324 km / 201 miles
1 M. Andretti   Ferrari
   180.80 kph / 112.35 mph
2 J. Stewart   Tyrrell-Ford
3 C. Regazzoni   Ferrari
4 R. Wisell   Lotus-Ford
5 C. Amon   Matra-Simca
6 D. Hulme   McLaren-Ford
Fastest lap: M. Andretti
   183.99 kph / 114.33 mph
Pole position: J. Stewart

Spanish GP

18 April: Montjuich
284 km / 177 miles
1 J. Stewart   Tyrrell-Ford
   156.41 kph / 97.19 mph
2 J. Ickx   Ferrari
3 C. Amon   Matra-Simca
4 P. Rodriguez   BRM
5 D. Hulme   McLaren-Ford
6 J. P. Beltoise   Matra-Simca
Fastest lap: J. Ickx
   160.36 kph / 99.64 mph
Pole position: J. Ickx

Monaco GP

23 May: Monte Carlo
252 km / 156 miles
1 J. Stewart   Tyrrell-Ford
   134.36 kph / 83.49 mph
2 R. Peterson   March-Ford
3 J. Ickx   Ferrari
4 D. Hulme   McLaren-Ford
5 E. Fittipaldi   Lotus-Ford
6 R. Stommelen   Surtees-Ford
Fastest lap: J. Stewart
   137.74 kph / 85.59 mph
Pole position: J. Stewart

Dutch GP

20 June: Zandvoort
294 km / 182 miles
1 J. Ickx   Ferrari
   151.38 kph / 94.06 mph
2 P. Rodriguez   BRM
3 C. Regazzoni   Ferrari
4 R. Peterson   March-Ford
5 J. Surtees   Surtees-Ford
6 J. Siffert   BRM
Fastest lap: J. Ickx
   158.98 kph / 98.78 mph
Pole position: J. Ickx

French GP

4 July: Paul Ricard
320 km / 199 miles
1 J. Stewart   Tyrrell-Ford
   179.70 kph / 111.66 mph
2 F. Cevert   Tyrrell-Ford
3 E. Fittipaldi   Lotus-Ford
4 J. Siffert   BRM
5 C. Amon   Matra-Simca
6 R. Wisell   Lotus-Ford
Fastest lap: J. Stewart
   183.33 kph / 113.92 mph
Pole position: J. Stewart

British GP

17 July: Silverstone
320 km / 199 miles
1 J. Stewart   Tyrrell-Ford
   209.99 kph / 130.48 mph
2 R. Peterson   March-Ford
3 E. Fittipaldi   Lotus-Ford
4 H. Pescarolo   March-Ford
5 R. Stommelen   Surtees-Ford
6 J. Surtees   Surtees-Ford
Fastest lap: J. Stewart
   212.24 kph / 131.88 mph
Pole position: C. Regazzoni (Ferrari)

German GP

1 August: Nurburgring
274 km / 170 miles
1 J. Stewart   Tyrrell-Ford
   184.19 kph / 114.45 mph
2 F. Cevert   Tyrrell-Ford
3 C. Regazzoni   Ferrari
4 M. Andretti   Ferrari
5 R. Peterson   March-Ford
6 T. Schenken   Brabham-Ford
Fastest lap: F. Cevert
   186.79 kph / 116.07 mph
Pole position: J. Stewart

Austrian GP

15 August: Osterreichring
319 km / 198 miles
1 J. Siffert   BRM
   211.86 kph / 131.64 mph
2 E. Fittipaldi   Lotus-Ford
3 T. Schenken   Brabham-Ford
4 R. Wisell   Lotus-Ford
5 G. Hill   Brabham-Ford
6 H. Pescarolo   March-Ford
Fastest lap: J. Siffert
   216.10 kph / 134.28 mph
Pole position: J. Siffert

Italian GP

5 September: Monza
317 km / 197 miles
1 P. Gethin   BRM
   242.62 kph / 150.75 mph
2 R. Peterson   March-Ford
3 F. Cevert   Tyrrell-Ford
4 M. Hailwood   Surtees-Ford
5 H. Ganley   BRM
6 C. Amon   Matra-Simca
Fastest lap: H. Pescarolo
   (March-Ford)
   247.02 kph / 153.49 mph
Pole position: C. Amon

Canadian GP

19 September: Mosport
253 km / 157 miles
1 J. Stewart   Tyrrell-Ford
   131.88 kph / 81.95 mph
2 R. Peterson   March-Ford
3 M. Donohue   McLaren-Ford
4 D. Hulme   McLaren-Ford
5 R. Wisell   Lotus-Ford
6 F. Cevert   Tyrrell-Ford
Fastest lap: D. Hulme
   137.64 kph / 85.52 mph
Pole position: J. Stewart

United States GP

3 October: Watkins Glen
321 km / 199 miles
1 F. Cevert   Tyrrell-Ford
   185.24 kph / 115.10 mph
2 J. Siffert   BRM
3 R. Peterson   March-Ford
4 H. Ganley   BRM
5 J. Stewart   Tyrrell-Ford
6 C. Regazzoni   Ferrari
Fastest lap: J. Ickx (Ferrari)
   189.09 kph / 117.50 mph
Pole position: J. Stewart

World Drivers' Championship

Pts	Driver	Wins	
62	Jackie Stewart (GB)	6	Spanish GP, Monaco GP, French GP, British GP, German GP, Canadian GP
33	Ronnie Peterson (SWE)	–	
26	Francois Cevert (FRA)	1	United States GP
19	Jacky Ickx (BEL)	1	Dutch GP
19	Jo Siffert (SWI)	1	Austrian GP
16	Emerson Fittipaldi (BRA)	–	
13	Clay Regazzoni (SWI)	–	
12	Mario Andretti (USA)	1	South African GP
9	Peter Gethin (GB)	1	Italian GP
9	Pedro Rodriguez (MEX)	–	
9	Chris Amon (NZ)	–	
9	Reine Wisell (SWE)	–	
9	Denny Hulme (NZ)	–	
5	Tim Schenken (AUS)	–	
5	Howden Ganley (NZ)	–	
4	Mark Donohue (USA)	–	
4	Henri Pescarolo (FRA)	–	
3	Mike Hailwood (GB)	–	
3	Rolf Stommelen (FRG)	–	
3	John Surtees (GB)	–	
2	Graham Hill (GB)	–	
1	Jean-Pierre Beltoise (FRA)	–	

Points scoring: First six drivers in each race to score. Points as follows: 9–6–4–3–2–1. Best five results from first six races plus the best four results from the remaining five races to count.

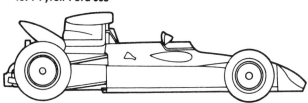

1971 Tyrell-Ford 003

Constructors' Cup

Pts	Manufacturer	Wins	
73	Tyrrell-Ford	7	Spanish GP, Monaco GP, French GP, British GP, German GP, Canadian GP, United States GP
36	BRM	2	Austrian GP, Italian GP
33	Ferrari	2	South African GP, Dutch GP
33	March-Ford	–	
21	Lotus-Ford	–	
10	McLaren-Ford	–	
9	Matra-Simca	–	
8	Surtees-Ford	–	
5	Brabham-Ford	–	

Points scoring: Best five results from first six races plus best four results from remaining five races. Best placed car of each manufacturer only to score. Points: 9–6–4–3–2–1.

1972

Argentine GP

23 January: Buenos Aires
318 km / 197 miles
1 J. Stewart   Tyrrell-Ford
   161.61 kph / 100.42 mph
2 D. Hulme   McLaren-Ford
3 J. Ickx   Ferrari
4 C. Regazzoni   Ferrari
5 T. Schenken   Surtees-Ford
6 R. Peterson   March-Ford
Fastest lap: J. Stewart
   163.48 kph / 101.58 mph
Pole position: C. Reutemann
  (Brabham-Ford)

South African GP

4 March: Kyalami
324 km / 201 miles
1 D. Hulme   McLaren-Ford
   183.83 kph / 114.23 mph
2 E. Fittipaldi   Lotus-Ford
3 P. Revson   McLaren-Ford
4 M. Andretti   Ferrari
5 R. Peterson   March-Ford
6 G. Hill   Brabham-Ford
Fastest lap: M. Hailwood
  (Surtees-Ford)
   187.25 kph / 116.35 mph
Pole position: J. Stewart
  (Tyrrell-Ford)

Spanish GP

1 May: Jarama
306 km / 190 miles
1 E. Fittipaldi   Lotus-Ford
   148.63 kph / 92.35 mph
2 J. Ickx   Ferrari
3 C. Regazzoni   Ferrari
4 A. de Adamich   Surtees-Ford
5 P. Revson   McLaren-Ford
6 C. Pace   March-Ford
Fastest lap: J. Ickx
   151.28 kph / 94.00 mph
Pole position: J. Ickx

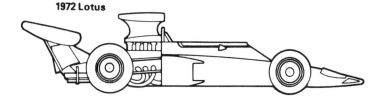

1972 Lotus

Monaco GP

14 May: Monte Carlo
252 km / 156 miles
1 J. P. Beltoise   BRM
   102.76 kph / 63.85 mph
2 J. Ickx   Ferrari
3 E. Fittipaldi   Lotus-Ford
4 J. Stewart   Tyrrell-Ford
5 B. Redman   McLaren-Ford
6 C. Amon   Matra-Simca
Fastest lap: J. P. Beltoise
   113.22 kph / 70.35 mph
Pole position: E. Fittipaldi

Belgian GP

4 June: Nivelles
317 km / 197 miles
1 E. Fittipaldi   Lotus-Ford
   182.42 kph / 113.35 mph
2 F. Cevert   Tyrrell-Ford
3 D. Hulme   McLaren-Ford
4 M. Hailwood   Surtees-Ford
5 C. Pace   March-Ford
6 C. Amon   Matra-Simca
Fastest lap: C. Amon
   185.89 kph / 115.51 mph
Pole position: E. Fittipaldi

French GP

2 July: Clermont–Ferrand
306 km / 190 miles
1 J. Stewart   Tyrrell-Ford
   163.45 kph / 101.57 mph
2 E. Fittipaldi   Lotus-Ford
3 C. Amon   Matra-Simca
4 F. Cevert   Tyrrell-Ford
5 R. Peterson   March-Ford
6 M. Hailwood   Surtees-Ford
Fastest lap: C. Amon
   166.75 kph / 103.61 mph
Pole position: D. Hulme
  (McLaren-Ford)

British GP

15 July: Brands Hatch
324 km / 201 miles
1 E. Fittipaldi   Lotus-Ford
   180.34 kph / 112.06 mph
2 J. Stewart   Tyrrell-Ford
3 P. Revson   McLaren-Ford
4 C. Amon   Matra-Simca
5 D. Hulme   McLaren-Ford
6 A. Merzario   Ferrari
Fastest lap: J. Stewart
   182.78 kph / 113.57 mph
Pole position: J. Ickx (Ferrari)

German GP

30 July: Nurburgring
320 km / 199 miles
1 J. Ickx   Ferrari
   187.68 kph / 116.62 mph
2 C. Regazzoni   Ferrari
3 R. Peterson   March-Ford
4 H. Ganley   BRM
5 B. Redman   McLaren-Ford
6 G. Hill   Brabham-Ford
Fastest lap: J. Ickx
   189.59 kph / 117.81 mph
Pole position: J. Ickx

Austrian GP

13 August: Osterreichring
319 km / 198 miles
1 E. Fittipaldi   Lotus-Ford
   214.52 kph / 133.30 mph
2 D. Hulme   McLaren-Ford
3 P. Revson   McLaren-Ford
4 M. Hailwood   Surtees-Ford
5 C. Amon   Matra-Simca
6 H. Ganley   BRM
Fastest lap: D. Hulme
   216.43 kph / 134.48 mph
Pole position: E. Fittipaldi

Italian GP

10 September: Monza
317 km / 197 miles
1 E. Fittipaldi   Lotus-Ford
   211.81 kph / 131.61 mph
2 M. Hailwood   Surtees-Ford
3 D. Hulme   McLaren-Ford
4 P. Revson   McLaren-Ford
5 G. Hill   Brabham-Ford
6 P. Gethin   BRM
Fastest lap: J. Ickx (Ferrari)
   215.89 kph / 134.15 mph
Pole position: J. Ickx

Canadian GP

24 September: Mosport
317 km / 197 miles
1 J. Stewart   Tyrrell-Ford
  183.90 kph / 114.27 mph
2 P. Revson   McLaren-Ford
3 D. Hulme   McLaren-Ford
4 C. Reutemann   Brabham-Ford
5 C. Regazzoni   Ferrari
6 C. Amon   Matra-Simca
Fastest lap: J. Stewart
  189.17 kph / 117.57 mph
Pole position: P. Revson

United States GP

8 October: Watkins Glen
321 kph / 199 mph
1 J. Stewart   Tyrrell-Ford
  189.09 kph / 117.49 mph
2 F. Cevert   Tyrrell-Ford
3 D. Hulme   McLaren-Ford
4 R. Peterson   March-Ford
5 J. Ickx   Ferrari
6 M. Andretti   Ferrari
Fastest lap: J. Stewart
  192.50 kph / 119.61 mph
Pole position: D. Hulme

World Drivers' Championship

Pts	Driver	Wins	
61	Emerson Fittipaldi (BRA)	5	Spanish GP, Belgian GP, British GP, Austrian GP, Italian GP
45	Jackie Stewart (GB)	4	Argentine GP, French GP, Canadian GP, United States GP
39	Denny Hulme (NZ)	1	South African GP
27	Jacky Ickx (BEL)	1	German GP
23	Peter Revson (USA)	–	
15	Francois Cevert (FRA)	–	
15	Clay Regazzoni (SWI)	–	
13	Mike Hailwood (GB)	–	

Pts	Driver	Wins	
12	Ronnie Peterson (SWE)	–	
12	Chris Amon (NZ)	–	
9	Jean-Pierre Beltoise (FRA)	1	Monaco GP
4	Mario Andretti (USA)	–	
4	Howden Ganley (NZ)	–	
4	Brian Redman (GB)	–	
4	Graham Hill (GB)	–	
3	Andrea de Adamich (ITA)	–	
3	Carlos Reutemann (ARG)	–	
3	Carlos Pace (BRA)	–	
2	Tim Schenken (AUS)	–	
1	Arturo Merzario (ITA)	–	
1	Peter Gethin (GB)	–	

Points scoring: First six drivers in each race to score. Points as follows: 9–6–4–3–2–1. Best five results from first six races plus the best five results from the remaining six races to count.

Constructors' Cup

Pts	Manufacturer	Wins	
61	Lotus-Ford	5	Spanish GP, Belgian GP, British GP, Austrian GP, Italian GP
51	Tyrrell-Ford	4	Argentine GP, French GP, Canadian GP, United States GP
47	McLaren-Ford	1	South African GP
33	Ferrari	1	German GP
18	Surtees-Ford	–	
15	March-Ford	–	
14	BRM	1	Monaco GP
12	Matra-Simca	–	
7	Brabham-Ford	–	

Points scoring: Best five results from first six races plus best five results from remaining six races. Best placed car of each manufacturer only to score. Points: 9–6–4–3–2–1.

1973

Argentine GP

28 January: Buenos Aires
321 km / 200 miles
1 E. Fittipaldi   Lotus-Ford
  165.69 kph / 102.95 mph
2 F. Cevert   Tyrrell-Ford
3 J. Stewart   Tyrrell-Ford
4 J. Ickx   Ferrari
5 D. Hulme   McLaren-Ford
6 W. Fittipaldi   Brabham-Ford
Fastest lap: E. Fittipaldi
  169.11 kph / 105.08 mph
Pole position: C. Regazzoni (BRM)

Brazilian GP

11 February: Interlagos
318 km / 198 miles
1 E. Fittipaldi   Lotus-Ford
  183.82 kph / 114.22 mph
2 J. Stewart   Tyrrell-Ford
3 D. Hulme   McLaren-Ford
4 A. Merzario   Ferrari
5 J. Ickx   Ferrari
6 C. Regazzoni   BRM
Fastest lap: E. Fittipaldi/D. Hulme
  184.88 kph / 114.88 mph
Pole position: R. Peterson
  (Lotus-Ford)

South Africa GP

3 March: Kyalami
324 km / 201 miles
1 J. Stewart   Tyrrell-Ford
  188.53 kph / 117.14 mph
2 P. Revson   McLaren-Ford
3 E. Fittipaldi   Lotus-Ford
4 A. Merzario   Ferrari
5 D. Hulme   McLaren-Ford
6 G. Follmer   Shadow-Ford
Fastest lap: E. Fittipaldi
  191.63 kph / 119.07 mph
Pole position: D. Hulme

Spanish GP

29 April: Montjuich
284 km / 177 miles
1 E. Fittipaldi   Lotus-Ford
  157.49 kph / 97.86 mph
2 F. Cevert   Tyrrell-Ford
3 G. Follmer   Shadow-Ford
4 P. Revson   McLaren-Ford
5 J. P. Beltoise   BRM
6 D. Hulme   McLaren-Ford
Fastest lap: R. Peterson (Lotus-Ford)
  162.84 kph / 101.19 mph
Pole position: R. Peterson.

Belgian GP

20 May: Zolder
295 km / 184 miles
1 J. Stewart   Tyrrell-Ford
  173.38 kph / 107.74 mph
2 F. Cevert   Tyrrell-Ford
3 E. Fittipaldi   Lotus-Ford
4 A. de Adamich   Brabham-Ford
5 N. Lauda   BRM
6 C. Amon   Tecno
Fastest lap: F. Cevert
  177.85 kph / 110.51 mph
Pole position: R. Peterson
  (Lotus-Ford)

Monaco GP

3 June: Monte Carlo
256 km / 159 miles
1 J. Stewart   Tyrrell-Ford
  130.30 kph / 80.96 mph
2 E. Fittipaldi   Lotus-Ford
3 R. Peterson   Lotus-Ford
4 F. Cevert   Tyrrell-Ford
5 P. Revson   McLaren-Ford
6 D. Hulme   McLaren-Ford
Fastest lap: E. Fittipaldi
  133.95 kph / 83.23 mph
Pole position: J. Stewart

Swedish GP

17 June: Anderstorp
321 km / 200 miles
1 D. Hulme   McLaren-Ford
   165.17 kph / 102.63 mph
2 R. Peterson   Lotus-Ford
3 F. Cevert   Tyrrell-Ford
4 C. Reutemann   Brabham-Ford
5 J. Stewart   Tyrrell-Ford
6 J. Ickx   Ferrari
Fastest lap: D. Hulme
   167.91 kph / 104.33 mph
Pole position: R. Peterson

French GP

1 July: Paul Ricard
314 km / 195 miles
1 R. Peterson   Lotus-Ford
   185.26 kph / 115.12 mph
2 F. Cevert   Tyrrell-Ford
3 C. Reutemann   Brabham-Ford
4 J. Stewart   Tyrrell-Ford
5 J. Ickx   Ferrari
6 J. Hunt   March-Ford
Fastest lap: D. Hulme (McLaren-Ford)
   188.45 kph / 117.10 mph
Pole position: J. Stewart

British GP

14 July: Silverstone
316 km / 196 miles
1 P. Revson   McLaren-Ford
   212.03 kph / 131.75 mph
2 R. Peterson   Lotus-Ford
3 D. Hulme   McLaren-Ford
4 J. Hunt   March-Ford
5 F. Cevert   Tyrrell-Ford
6 C. Reutemann   Brabham-Ford
Fastest lap: J. Hunt
   215.75 kph / 134.06 mph
Pole position: R. Peterson

Dutch GP

29 July: Zandvoort
304 km / 189 miles
1 J. Stewart   Tyrrell-Ford
   184.03 kph / 114.35 mph
2 F. Cevert   Tyrrell-Ford
3 J. Hunt   March-Ford
4 P. Revson   McLaren-Ford
5 J. P. Beltoise BRM
6 G. van Lennep   Williams-Ford
Fastest lap: R. Peterson (Lotus-Ford)
   189.44 kph / 117.71 mph
Pole position: R. Peterson

German GP

5 August: Nurburgring
320 km / 199 miles
1 J. Stewart   Tyrrell-Ford
   187.96 kph / 116.79 mph
2 F. Cevert   Tyrrell-Ford
3 J. Ickx   McLaren-Ford
4 C. Pace   Surtees-Ford
5 W. Fittipaldi   Brabham-Ford
6 E. Fittipaldi   Lotus-Ford
Fastest lap: C. Pace
   190.56 kph / 118.41 mph
Pole position: J. Stewart

Austrian GP

19 August: Osterreichring
319 km / 198 miles
1 R. Peterson   Lotus-Ford
   215.64 kph / 133.99 mph
2 J. Stewart   Tyrrell-Ford
3 C. Pace   Surtees-Ford
4 C. Reutemann   Brabham-Ford
5 J. P. Beltoise BRM
6 C. Regazzoni   BRM
Fastest lap: C. Pace
   218.72 kph / 135.91 mph
Pole position: E. Fittipaldi
   (Lotus-Ford)

Italian GP

9 September: Monza
317 km / 197 miles
1 R. Peterson   Lotus-Ford
   213.45 kph / 132.63 mph
2 E. Fittipaldi   Lotus-Ford
3 P. Revson   McLaren-Ford
4 J. Stewart   Tyrrell-Ford
5 F. Cevert   Tyrrell-Ford
6 C. Reutemann   Brabham-Ford
Fastest lap: J. Stewart
   218.15 kph / 135.55 mph
Pole position: R. Peterson

Canadian GP

23 September: Mosport
317 km / 197 miles
1 P. Revson   McLaren-Ford
   159.53 kph / 99.13 mph
2 E. Fittipaldi   Lotus-Ford
3 J. Oliver   Shadow-Ford
4 J. P. Beltoise BRM
5 J. Stewart   Tyrrell-Ford
6 H. Ganley   Williams-Ford
Fastest lap: E. Fittipaldi
   188.71 kph / 117.26 mph
Pole position: R. Peterson
   (Lotus-Ford)

United States GP

7 October: Watkins Glen
321 km / 199 miles
1 R. Peterson   Lotus-Ford
   189.99 kph / 118.06 mph
2 J. Hunt   March-Ford
3 C. Reutemann   Brabham-Ford
4 D. Hulme   McLaren-Ford
5 P. Revson   McLaren-Ford
6 E. Fittipaldi   Lotus-Ford
Fastest lap: J. Hunt
   192.47 kph / 119.60 mph
Pole position: R. Peterson

World Drivers' Championship

Pts	Driver	Wins	
71	Jackie Stewart (GB)	5	South African GP, Belgian GP, Monaco GP, Dutch GP, German GP
55	Emerson Fittipaldi (BRA)	3	Argentine GP, Brazilian GP, Spanish GP
52	Ronnie Peterson (SWE)	4	French GP, Austrian GP, Italian GP, United States GP
47	Francois Cevert (FRA)	–	
38	Peter Revson (USA)	2	British GP, Canadian GP
26	Denny Hulme (NZ)	1	Swedish GP
16	Carlos Reutemann (ARG)	–	
14	James Hunt (GB)	–	
12	Jacky Ickx (BEL)	–	
9	Jean-Pierre Beltoise (FRA)	–	
7	Carlos Pace (BRA)	–	
6	Arturo Merzario (ITA)	–	
5	George Follmer (USA)	–	
4	Jackie Oliver (GB)	–	
3	Andrea de Adamich (ITA)	–	
3	Wilson Fittipaldi (BRA)	–	
2	Niki Lauda (AUT)	–	
2	Clay Regazzoni (SWI)	–	
1	Chris Amon (NZ)	–	
1	Gijs van Lennep (HOL)	–	
1	Howden Ganley (NZ)	–	

Points scoring: First six drivers in each race to score. Points as follows: 9–6–4–3–2–1. Best seven results from first eight races plus the best six results from the remaining seven races to count.

Constructors' Cup

Pts	Manufacturer	Wins	
92	Lotus-Ford	7	Argentine GP, Brazilian GP, Spanish GP, French GP, Austrian GP, Italian GP, United States GP
82	Tyrrell-Ford	5	South African GP, Belgian GP, Monaco GP, Dutch GP, German GP
58	McLaren-Ford	3	Swedish GP, British GP, Canadian GP
22	Brabham-Ford	–	
14	March-Ford	–	
12	Ferrari	–	
12	BRM	–	
9	Shadow-Ford	–	
7	Surtees-Ford	–	
2	Williams-Ford	–	
1	Tecno	–	

Points scoring: Best seven results from first eight races plus best six results from remaining seven races. Best placed car of each manufacturer only to score. Points: 9–6–4–3–2–1.

1973 Tyrell-Ford 006

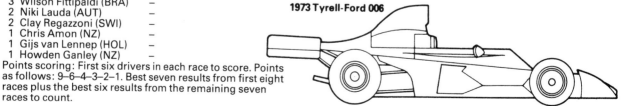

1974

Argentine GP

13 January: Buenos Aires
316 km / 197 miles
1 D. Hulme   McLaren-Ford
   187.85 kph / 116.72 mph
2 N. Lauda   Ferrari
3 C. Regazzoni   Ferrari
4 M. Hailwood   McLaren-Ford
5 J. P. Beltoise   BRM
6 P. Depailler   Tyrrell-Ford
Fastest lap: C. Regazzoni
   191.66 kph / 119.09 mph
Pole position: R. Peterson
   (Lotus-Ford)

Brazilian GP

27 January: Interlagos
255 km / 158 miles
1 E. Fittipaldi   McLaren-Ford
   180.62 kph / 112.23 mph
2 C. Regazzoni   Ferrari
3 J. Ickx   Lotus-Ford
4 C. Pace   Surtees-Ford
5 M. Hailwood   McLaren-Ford
6 R. Peterson   Lotus-Ford
Fastest lap: C. Regazzoni
183.63 kph / 114.10 mph
Pole position: E. Fittipaldi

South African GP

30 March: Kyalami
320 km / 199 miles
1 C. Reutemann   Brabham-Ford
   187.05 kph / 116.23 mph
2 J. P. Beltoise   BRM
3 M. Hailwood   McLaren-Ford
4 P. Depailler   Tyrrell-Ford
5 H. Stuck   March-Ford
6 A. Merzario   Williams-Ford
Fastest lap: C. Reutemann
   189.03 kph / 117.46 mph
Pole position: N. Lauda (Ferrari)

Spanish GP

28 April: Jarama
286 km / 178 miles
1 N. Lauda   Ferrari
   142.40 kph / 88.48 mph
2 C. Regazzoni   Ferrari
3 E. Fittipaldi   McLaren-Ford
4 H. Stuck   March-Ford
5 J. Scheckter   Tyrrell-Ford
6 D. Hulme   McLaren-Ford
Fastest lap: N. Lauda
151.62 kph / 94.21 mph
Pole position: N. Lauda

Belgian GP

12 May: Nivelles
317 km / 197 miles
1 E. Fittipaldi   McLaren-Ford
   182.02 kph / 113.10 mph
2 N. Lauda   Ferrari
3 J. Scheckter   Tyrrell-Ford
4 C. Regazzoni   Ferrari
5 J. P. Beltoise   BRM
6 D. Hulme   McLaren-Ford
Fastest lap: D. Hulme
   188.00 kph / 116.82 mph
Pole position: C. Regazzoni

Monaco GP

26 May: Monte Carlo
256 km / 159 miles
1 R. Peterson   Lotus-Ford
   129.94 kph / 80.74 mph
2 J. Scheckter   Tyrrell-Ford
3 J. P. Jarier   Shadow-Ford
4 C. Regazzoni   Ferrari
5 E. Fittipaldi   McLaren-Ford
6 J. Watson   Brabham-Ford
Fastest lap: R. Peterson
   134.25 kph / 83.42 mph
Pole position: N. Lauda (Ferrari)

Swedish GP

9 June: Anderstorp
321 km / 200 miles
1 J. Scheckter   Tyrrell-Ford
   162.72 kph / 101.11 mph
2 P. Depailler   Tyrrell-Ford
3 J. Hunt   Hesketh-Ford
4 E. Fittipaldi   McLaren-Ford
5 J. P. Jarier   Shadow-Ford
6 G. Hill   Lola-Ford
Fastest lap: P. Depailler
   165.76 kph / 103.00 mph
Pole position: P. Depailler

Dutch GP

23 June: Zandvoort
317 km / 197 miles
1 N. Lauda   Ferrari
   184.63 kph / 114.72 mph
2 C. Regazzoni   Ferrari
3 E. Fittipaldi   McLaren-Ford
4 M. Hailwood   McLaren-Ford
5 J. Scheckter   Tyrrell-Ford
6 P. Depailler   Tyrrell-Ford
Fastest lap: R. Peterson (Lotus-Ford)
   186.81 kph / 116.08 mph
Pole position: N. Lauda

French GP

7 July: Dijon-Prenois
263 km / 163 miles
1 R. Peterson   Lotus-Ford
   192.72 kph / 119.75 mph
2 N. Lauda   Ferrari
3 C. Regazzoni   Ferrari
4 J. Scheckter   Tyrrell-Ford
5 J. Ickx   Lotus-Ford
6 D. Hulme   McLaren-Ford
Fastest lap: J. Scheckter
   197.34 kph / 122.62 mph
Pole position: N. Lauda

British GP

20 July: Brands Hatch
320 km / 199 miles
1 J. Scheckter   Tyrrell-Ford
   186.26 kph / 115.74 mph
2 E. Fittipaldi   McLaren-Ford
3 J. Ickx   Lotus-Ford
4 C. Regazzoni   Ferrari
5 N. Lauda   Ferrari
6 C. Reutemann   Brabham-Ford
Fastest lap: N. Lauda
   189.31 kph / 117.63 mph
Pole position: N. Lauda

German GP

4 August: Nurburgring
320 km / 199 miles
1 C. Regazzoni   Ferrari
   188.83 kph / 117.33 mph
2 J. Scheckter   Tyrrell-Ford
3 C. Reutemann   Brabham-Ford
4 R. Peterson   Lotus-Ford
5 J. Ickx   Lotus-Ford
6 T. Pryce   Shadow-Ford
Fastest lap: J. Scheckter
   190.69 kph / 118.49 mph
Pole position: N. Lauda (Ferrari)

Austrian GP

18 August: Osterreichring
319 km / 198 miles
1 C. Reutemann   Brabham-Ford
   215.80 kph / 134.09 mph
2 D. Hulme   McLaren-Ford
3 J. Hunt   Hesketh-Ford
4 J. Watson   Brabham-Ford
5 C. Regazzoni   Ferrari
6 V. Brambilla   March-Ford
Fastest lap: C. Regazzoni
   218.88 kph / 136.01 mph
Pole position: N. Lauda (Ferrari)

Italian GP

8 September: Monza
301 km / 187 miles
1 R. Peterson   Lotus-Ford
   217.42 kph / 135.10 mph
2 E. Fittipaldi   McLaren-Ford
3 J. Scheckter   Tyrrell-Ford
4 A. Merzario   Williams-Ford
5 C. Pace   Brabham-Ford
6 D. Hulme   McLaren-Ford
Fastest lap: C. Pace
220.89 kph / 137.26 mph
Pole position: N. Lauda (Ferrari)

Canadian GP

22 September: Mosport
317 km / 197 miles
1 E. Fittipaldi   McLaren-Ford
   189.13 kph / 117.52 mph
2 C. Regazzoni   Ferrari
3 R. Peterson   Lotus-Ford
4 J. Hunt   Hesketh-Ford
5 P. Depailler   Tyrrell-Ford
6 D. Hulme   McLaren-Ford
Fastest lap: N. Lauda (Ferrari)
   193.41 kph / 120.18 mph
Pole position: E. Fittipaldi

United States GP

6 October: Watkins Glen
321 km / 199 miles
1 C. Reutemann   Brabham-Ford
   191.71 kph / 119.12 mph
2 C. Pace   Brabham-Ford
3 J. Hunt   Hesketh-Ford
4 E. Fittipaldi   McLaren-Ford
5 J. Watson   Brabham-Ford
6 P. Depailler   Tyrrell-Ford
Fastest lap: C. Pace
   194.47 kph / 120.84 mph
Pole position: C. Reutemann

World Drivers' Championship

Pts	Driver	Wins	
55	Emerson Fittipaldi (BRA)	3	Brazilian GP, Belgian GP, Canadian GP
52	Clay Regazzoni (SWI)	1	German GP
45	Jody Scheckter (SAF)	2	Swedish GP, British GP
38	Niki Lauda (AUT)	2	Spanish GP, Dutch GP
35	Ronnie Peterson (SWE)	3	Monaco GP, French GP, Italian GP
32	Carlos Reutemann (ARG)	3	South African, GP, Austrian GP, United States GP
20	Denny Hulme (NZ)	1	Argentine GP
15	James Hunt (GB)	–	
14	Patrick Depailler (FRA)	–	
12	Jacky Ickx (BEL)	–	
12	Mike Hailwood (GB)	–	
11	Carlos Pace (BRA)	–	
10	Jean-Pierre Beltoise (FRA)	–	
6	John Watson (GB)	–	
6	Jean-Pierre Jarier (FRA)	–	
5	Hans-Joachim Stuck (FRG)	–	
4	Arturo Merzario (ITA)	–	
1	Vittorio Brambilla (ITA)	–	
1	Graham Hill (GB)	–	
1	Tom Pryce (GB)	–	

Points scoring: First six drivers in each race to score. Points as follows: 9–6–4–3–2–1. Best seven results from first eight races plus the best six results from the remaining seven races.

Constructors' Cup

Pts	Manufacturer	Wins	
73	McLaren-Ford	4	Argentine GP, Brazilian GP, Belgian GP, Canadian GP
65	Ferrari	3	Spanish GP, Dutch GP, German GP
52	Tyrrell-Ford	2	Swedish GP, British GP
42	Lotus-Ford	3	Monaco GP, French GP, Italian GP
35	Brabham-Ford	3	South African GP, Austrian GP, United States GP
15	Hesketh-Ford	–	
10	BRM	–	
7	Shadow-Ford	–	
6	March-Ford	–	
4	Williams-Ford	–	
3	Surtees-Ford	–	
1	Lola-Ford	–	

Points scoring: Best seven results from the first eight races plus the best six results from the remaining seven races. Best placed car of each manufacturer only to score. Points: 9–6–4–3–2–1.

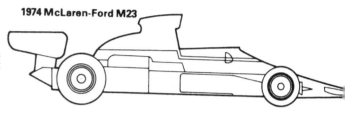

1974 McLaren-Ford M23

1975

Argentine GP

12 January: Buenos Aires
316 km / 197 miles
1 E. Fittipaldi   McLaren-Ford
     190.86 kph / 118.60 mph
2 J. Hunt   Hesketh-Ford
3 C. Reutemann   Brabham-Ford
4 C. Regazzoni   Ferrari
5 P. Depailler   Tyrrell-Ford
6 N. Lauda   Ferrari
Fastest lap: J. Hunt
     193.72 kph / 120.37 mph
Pole position: J. P. Jarier
     (Shadow-Ford) Did not start race

Brazilian GP

26 January: Interlagos
318 km / 198 miles
1 C. Pace   Brabham-Ford
     182.49 kph / 113.39 mph
2 E. Fittipaldi   McLaren-Ford
3 J. Mass   McLaren-Ford
4 C. Regazzoni   Ferrari
5 N. Lauda   Ferrari
6 J. Hunt   Hesketh-Ford
Fastest lap: J. P. Jarier (Shadow-Ford)
     185.88 kph / 115.50 mph
Pole position: J. P. Jarier

South African GP

1 March: Kyalami
320 km / 199 miles
1 J. Scheckter   Tyrrell-Ford
     185.96 kph / 115.55 mph
2 C. Reutemann   Brabham-Ford
3 P. Depailler   Tyrrell-Ford
4 C. Pace   Brabham-Ford
5 N. Lauda   Ferrari
6 J. Mass   McLaren-Ford
Fastest lap: C. Pace
     191.38 kph / 118.92 mph
Pole position: C. Pace

Spanish GP

27 April: Montjuich
110 km / 68 miles
1 J. Mass   McLaren-Ford
     153.76 kph / 95.54 mph
2 J. Ickx   Lotus-Ford
3 C. Reutemann   Brabham-Ford
4 J. P. Jarier   Shadow-Ford
5 V. Brambilla   March-Ford
6 Sig. L. Lombardi   March-Ford
Fastest lap: M. Andretti
     (Parnelli-Ford)
     160.36 kph / 99.64 mph
Pole position: N. Lauda (Ferrari)

Monaco GP

11 May: Monte Carlo
246 km / 153 miles
1 N. Lauda   Ferrari
     121.55 kph / 75.53 mph
2 E. Fittipaldi   McLaren-Ford
3 C. Pace   Brabham-Ford
4 R. Peterson   Lotus-Ford
5 P. Depailler   Tyrrell-Ford
6 J. Mass   McLaren-Ford
Fastest lap: P. Depailler
     133.09 kph / 82.70 mph
Pole position: N. Lauda

Belgian GP

25 May: Zolder
298 km / 185 miles
1 N. Lauda   Ferrari
     172.29 kph / 107.05 mph
2 J. Scheckter   Tyrrell-Ford
3 C. Reutemann   Brabham-Ford
4 P. Depailler   Tyrrell-Ford
5 C. Regazzoni   Ferrari
6 T. Pryce   Shadow-Ford
Fastest lap: C. Regazzoni
     176.85 kph / 109.89 mph
Pole position: N. Lauda

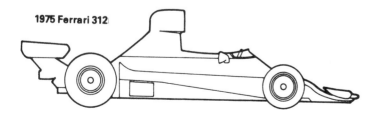

1975 Ferrari 312

● Bruno Giacomelli (Ita) and Elisio Salazar (Chi) were well down the starting grid for the 1982 Belgian Grand Prix. They had a shunt before either of them reached the starting line, and never took part in the race.

Swedish GP

8 June: Anderstorp
321 km / 200 miles
1 N. Lauda   Ferrari
   161.66 kph / 100.45 mph
2 C. Reutemann   Brabham-Ford
3 C. Regazzoni   Ferrari
4 M. Andretti   Parnelli-Ford
5 M. Donohue   Penske-Ford
6 A. Brise   Hill-Ford
Fastest lap: N. Lauda
   163.88 kph / 101.83 mph
Pole position: V. Brambilla
   (March-Ford)

Dutch GP

22 June: Zandvoort
317 km / 197 miles
1 J. Hunt   Hesketh-Ford
   177.80 kph / 110.48 mph
2 N. Lauda   Ferrari
3 C. Regazzoni   Ferrari
4 C. Reutemann   Brabham-Ford
5 C. Pace   Brabham-Ford
6 T. Pryce   Shadow-Ford
Fastest lap: N. Lauda
   186.58 kph / 115.93 mph
Pole position: N. Lauda

French GP

6 July: Paul Ricard
314 km / 195 miles
1 N. Lauda   Ferrari
   187.65 kph / 116.60 mph
2 J. Hunt   Hesketh-Ford
3 J. Mass   McLaren-Ford
4 E. Fittipaldi   McLaren-Ford
5 M. Andretti   Parnelli-Ford
6 P. Depailler   Tyrrell-Ford
Fastest lap: J. Mass
   189.11 kph / 117.51 mph
Pole position: N. Lauda

British GP

19 July: Silverstone
264 km / 164 miles
1 E. Fittipaldi   McLaren-Ford
   193.15 kph / 120.02 mph
2 C. Pace   Brabham-Ford
3 J. Scheckter   Tyrrell-Ford
4 J. Hunt   Hesketh-Ford
5 M. Donohue   March-Ford
6 V. Brambilla   March-Ford
Fastest lap: C. Regazzoni (Ferrari)
   209.97 kph / 130.47 mph
Pole position: T. Pryce (Shadow-Ford)

German GP

3 August: Nurburgring
320 km / 199 miles
1 C. Reutemann   Brabham-Ford
   189.47 kph / 117.73 mph
2 J. Laffite   Williams-Ford
3 N. Lauda   Ferrari
4 T. Pryce   Shadow-Ford
5 A. Jones   Hill-Ford
6 G. van Lennep   Ensign-Ford
Fastest lap: C. Regazzoni (Ferrari)
   192.79 kph / 119.79 mph
Pole position: N. Lauda

Austrian GP

17 August: Osterreichring
171 km / 107 miles
1 V. Brambilla   March-Ford
   177.50 kph / 110.29 mph
2 J. Hunt   Hesketh-Ford
3 T. Pryce   Shadow-Ford
4 J. Mass   McLaren-Ford
5 R. Peterson   Lotus-Ford
6 N. Lauda   Ferrari
Fastest lap: V. Brambilla
   186.83 kph / 116.09 mph
Pole position: N. Lauda

Italian GP

7 September: Monza
301 km / 187 miles
1 C. Regazzoni   Ferrari
   218.03 kph / 135.48 mph
2 E. Fittipaldi   McLaren-Ford
3 N. Lauda   Ferrari
4 C. Reutemann   Brabham-Ford
5 J. Hunt   Hesketh-Ford
6 T. Pryce   Shadow-Ford
Fastest lap: C. Regazzoni
   223.50 kph / 138.88 mph
Pole position: N. Lauda

United States GP

5 October: Watkins Glen
321 km / 199 miles
1 N. Lauda   Ferrari
   186.84 kph / 116.10 mph
2 E. Fittipaldi   McLaren-Ford
3 J. Mass   McLaren-Ford
4 J. Hunt   Hesketh-Ford
5 R. Peterson   Lotus-Ford
6 J. Scheckter   Tyrrell-Ford
Fastest lap: E. Fittipaldi
   189.27 kph / 117.60 mph
Pole position: N. Lauda

World Drivers' Championship

Pts	Driver	Wins	
64½	Niki Lauda (AUT)	5	Monaco GP, Belgian GP, Swedish GP, French GP, United States GP
45	Emerson Fittipaldi (BRA)	2	Argentine GP, British GP
37	Carlos Reutemann (ARG)	1	German GP
33	James Hunt (GB)	1	Dutch GP
25	Clay Regazzoni (SWI)	1	Italian GP
24	Carlos Pace (BRA)	1	Brazilian GP
20	Jody Scheckter (SAF)	1	South African GP
20	Jochen Mass (FRG)	1	Spanish GP*
12	Patrick Depailler (FRA)	–	
8	Tom Pryce (GB)	–	
6½	Vittorio Brambilla (ITA)	1	Austrian GP*
6	Jacques Laffite (FRA)	–	
6	Ronnie Peterson (SWE)	–	
5	Mario Andretti (USA)	–	
4	Mark Donohue (USA)	–	
3	Jacky Ickx (BEL)	–	
2	Alan Jones (AUS)	–	
1½	Jean-Pierre Jarier (FRA)	–	
1	Tony Brise (GB)	–	
1	Gijs van Lennep (HOL)	–	
½	Lella Lombardi (ITA)	–	

* Only half points awarded
Points scoring: First six drivers in each race to score. Points as follows: 9–6–4–3–2–1. Best seven results from first eight races plus the best five results from the remaining six races.

Constructors' Cup

Pts	Manufacturer	Wins	
72½	Ferrari	6	Monaco GP, Belgian GP, Swedish GP, French GP, Italian GP, United States GP
54	Brabham-Ford	2	Brazilian GP, German GP
53	McLaren-Ford	3	Argentine GP, Spanish GP*, British GP
33	Hesketh-Ford	1	Dutch GP
25	Tyrrell-Ford	1	South African GP
9½	Shadow-Ford	–	
9	Lotus-Ford	–	
7½	March-Ford	1	Austrian GP*
6	Williams-Ford	–	
5	Parnelli-Ford	–	
3	Hill-Ford	–	
2	Penske-Ford	–	
1	Ensign-Ford	–	

* Half points only at stake
Points scoring: Best seven results from the first eight races plus the best five results from the remaining six races. Best placed car of each manufacturer only to score. Points: 9–6–4–3–2–1.

● Carlos Reutemann (Arg) became the first man, in 1978, to win both the US Grand Prix and US Grand Prix (West) in the same season.

James Hunt's Year

The 1976 World Championship was divided into two halves: that of Niki Lauda and James Hunt. As the Austrian dominated the first eight races of the 16-race championship in defence of his world title, Hunt dominated the second half after Lauda's horrific accident at the Nurburgring in August.

Hunt was in his first season with McLaren when his talent influenced them to sign him as leader, after his former team, Hesketh, folded at the end of 1975. The 29-year-old former public schoolboy and ex-junior Wimbledon tennis starlet was entrusted with the McLaren M23 and, after snatching pole position from the Ferrari of Niki Lauda in the first race of the season, the Brazilian Grand Prix at Interlagos, it looked like a promising start for the new team.

Lauda, however, went on to win the first race of the season as Hunt crashed out on lap 33. The South African Grand Prix at Kyalami was also won by Lauda but Hunt came close to catching him at the end, losing by just over a second. Hunt was put out of the new US Grand Prix (West) at Long Beach, following a shunt with Patrick Depailler (Fra) as Lauda finished second to stretch his lead to 18 points. Hunt overtook Lauda to win the Spanish Grand Prix at Jarama, the fourth of the championship, but then the season-long wrangling and arguing started when it was ruled that Hunt's car was 1.8 cm (0.7 in) too wide and he was stripped of his

points, Lauda being promoted to first place. Naturally an appeal was made by the McLaren team but the dispute was not resolved for many weeks. Consequently Lauda's lead stretched to 27 points.

Ferrari, headed by Lauda, were first and second in Belgium while Hunt retired on lap 36. Lauda added nine more points after leading from start to finish at Monaco while Hunt was again out of the scoring, and seemingly out of the championship. The Austrian pulled away further with a third to Hunt's fifth in Sweden to stretch his lead to a mammoth 47 points.

The turning point for Hunt came in the last race of the first half of the season when Lauda retired from the French Grand Prix with a rare mechanical fault and Hunt took full advantage by winning. The day after the race, the appeals committee reinstated the Englishman as winner of the Spanish Grand Prix. Suddenly Lauda's lead was cut to 26 points.

More trouble was to follow Hunt at the British Grand Prix at

Brands when he was involved in a shunt at the first bend after Lauda and Clay Regazzoni (Swi) collided. The race was restarted and Hunt took part after illegally receiving repairs to his car. While Hunt went on to win the race from Lauda, he was disqualified two months later, with the maximum points going to the defending champion.

The German Grand Prix was next and Hunt scored another victory to pull himself to within 14 points of Lauda but the race was marred by the horrific accident to the Austrian who was badly burned in his wrecked car.

With Lauda sidelined, the way was open for Hunt to close the gap even further. He could only manage fourth at the Osterreichring but gained maximum points at Zandvoort two weeks later. Only two points separated the two men going into the Italian Grand Prix at Monza when, six weeks after his accident, Lauda was back behind the wheel and, amazingly, increased his lead in the championship with a fourth place after Hunt failed to finish.

James Hunt (left) and Niki Lauda (AUT) were engaged in one of the most dramatic finishes to a Grand Prix season in 1976. Hunt ended as champion by just one point

A rare picture of Britain's dual 1976 world champions on two and four wheels, Barry Sheene (left) and James Hunt

Before the next race, the Canadian Grand Prix, it was announced that Hunt had been stripped of his points from the British Grand Prix. Hunt, and the McLaren team, were incensed by the decision and went out and won the Canadian and US Grands Prix (East) in successive weeks.

Lauda only picked up four points from the two races. And so, with one race in the championship remaining, Lauda led by two points.

Mount Fuji, Japan, was the scene of the final act as Japan played host to its first World Championship Grand Prix. Appalling weather conditions forced Lauda to withdraw after just two laps—a decision few, except Enzo Ferrari, criticized. Hunt had to

finish in the first three to win the title. He led for most of the first 60 laps but was forced to make a tyre change. He slipped to fifth with just four laps to go but, miraculously, he hauled himself to third place and hung on to win the championship by just one point.

Hunt became the first Briton since Jackie Stewart in 1973 to win the title, but the real hero of the most dramatic of World Championships was Niki Lauda.

1976

Brazilian GP

25 January: Interlagos
318 km / 198 miles
1 N. Lauda   Ferrari
   181.47 kph / 112.76 mph
2 P. Depailler   Tyrrell-Ford
3 T. Pryce   Shadow-Ford
4 H. Stuck   March-Ford
5 J. Scheckter   Tyrrell-Ford
6 J. Mass   McLaren-Ford
Fastest lap: J. P. Jarier (Shadow-Ford)
   184.80 kph / 114.83 mph
Pole position: J. Hunt (McLaren-Ford)

South African GP

6 March: Kyalami
320 km / 199 miles
1 N. Lauda   Ferrari
   187.74 kph / 116.65 mph
2 J. Hunt   McLaren-Ford
3 J. Mass   McLaren-Ford
4 J. Scheckter   Tyrrell-Ford
5 J. Watson   Penske-Ford
6 M. Andretti   Parnelli-Ford
Fastest lap: N. Lauda
   189.49 kph / 117.74 mph
Pole position: J. Hunt

United States GP (West)

28 March: Long Beach
260 km / 162 miles
1 C. Regazzoni   Ferrari
   137.72 kph / 85.57 mph
2 N. Lauda   Ferrari
3 P. Depailler   Tyrrell-Ford
4 J. Laffite   Ligier-Matra
5 J. Mass   McLaren-Ford
6 E. Fittipaldi   Fittipaldi-Ford
Fastest lap: C. Regazzoni
   140.87 kph / 87.53 mph
Pole position: C. Regazzoni

Spanish GP

2 May: Jarama
255 km / 159 miles
1 J. Hunt   McLaren-Ford
   149.69 kph / 93.01 mph
2 N. Lauda   Ferrari
3 G. Nilsson   Lotus-Ford
4 C. Reutemann   Brabham-
                     Alfa Romeo
5 C. Amon   Ensign-Ford
6 C. Pace   Brabham-
                     Alfa Romeo
Fastest lap: J.Mass (McLaren-Ford)
   151.43 kph / 94.10 mph
Pole position: J. Hunt

Belgian GP

16 May: Zolder
298 km / 185 miles
1 N. Lauda   Ferrari
   173.98 kph / 108.10 mph
2 C. Regazzoni   Ferrari
3 J. Laffite   Ligier-Matra
4 J. Scheckter   Tyrrell-Ford
5 A. Jones   Surtees-Ford
6 J. Mass   McLaren-Ford
Fastest lap: N. Lauda
   178.45 kph / 110.88 mph
Pole position: N. Lauda

Monaco GP

30 May: Monte Carlo
258 km / 160 miles
1 N. Lauda   Ferrari
   129.32 kph / 80.35 mph
2 J. Scheckter   Tyrrell-Ford
3 P. Depailler   Tyrrell-Ford
4 H. Stuck   March-Ford
5 J. Mass   McLaren-Ford
6 E. Fittipaldi   Fittipaldi-Ford
Fastest lap: C. Regazzoni (Ferrari)
   132.07 kph / 82.06 mph
Pole position: N. Lauda

Swedish GP

13 June: Anderstorp
289 km / 180 miles
1 J. Scheckter   Tyrrell-Ford
   162.38 kph / 100.90 mph
2 P. Depailler   Tyrrell-Ford
3 N. Lauda   Ferrari
4 J. Laffite   Ligier-Matra
5 J. Hunt   McLaren-Ford
6 C. Regazzoni   Ferrari
Fastest lap: M. Andretti (Lotus-Ford)
   164.37 kph / 102.13 mph
Pole position: J. Scheckter

French GP

4 July: Paul Ricard
314 km / 195 miles
1 J. Hunt   McLaren-Ford
   186.42 kph / 115.84 mph
2 P. Depailler   Tyrrell-Ford
3 J. Watson   Penske-Ford
4 C. Pace   Brabham-
                     Alfa Romeo
5 M. Andretti   Lotus-Ford
6 J. Scheckter   Tyrrell-Ford
Fastest lap: N. Lauda (Ferrari)
   188.43 kph / 117.09 mph
Pole position: N. Lauda

British GP

18 July: Brands Hatch
320 km / 199 miles
1 N. Lauda   Ferrari
   183.84 kph / 114.23 mph
2 J. Scheckter   Tyrrell-Ford
3 J. Watson   Penske-Ford
4 T. Pryce   Shadow-Ford
5 A. Jones   Surtees-Ford
6 E. Fittipaldi   Fittipaldi-Ford
Fastest lap: N. Lauda
   189.49 kph / 117.74 mph
Pole position: N. Lauda

German GP

1 August: Nurburgring
320 km / 199 miles
1 J. Hunt   McLaren-Ford
   188.59 kph / 117.18 mph
2 J. Scheckter   Tyrrell-Ford
3 J. Mass   McLaren-Ford
4 C. Pace   Brabham-
                     Alfa Romeo
5 G. Nilsson   Lotus-Ford
6 R. Stommelen   Brabham-
                     Alfa Romeo
Fastest lap: J. Scheckter
   190.82 kph / 118.57 mph
Pole position: J. Hunt

Austrian GP

15 August: Osterreichring
319 km / 198 miles
1 J. Watson   Penske-Ford
   212.43 kph / 132.00 mph
2 J. Laffite   Ligier-Matra
3 G. Nilsson   Lotus-Ford
4 J. Hunt   McLaren-Ford
5 M. Andretti   Lotus-Ford
6 R. Peterson   March-Ford
Fastest lap: J. Hunt
   221.81 kph / 137.83 mph
Pole position: J. Hunt

Dutch GP

29 August: Zandvoort
317 km / 197 miles
1 J. Hunt   McLaren-Ford
   181.34 kph / 112.68 mph
2 C. Regazzoni   Ferrari
3 M. Andretti   Lotus-Ford
4 T. Pryce   Shadow-Ford
5 J. Scheckter   Tyrrell-Ford
6 V. Brambilla   March-Ford
Fastest lap: C. Regazzoni
   184.21 kph / 114.46 mph
Pole position: R. Peterson
   (March-Ford)

Italian GP

12 September: Monza
302 km / 187 miles
1 R. Peterson   March-Ford
   199.75 kph / 124.12 mph
2 C. Regazzoni   Ferrari
3 J. Laffite   Ligier-Matra
4 N. Lauda   Ferrari
5 J. Scheckter   Tyrrell-Ford
6 P. Depailler   Tyrrell-Ford
Fastest lap: R. Peterson
   206.12 kph / 128.08 mph
Pole position: J. Laffite

Canadian GP

3 October: Mosport
317 km / 197 miles
1 J. Hunt   McLaren-Ford
   189.65 kph / 117.84 mph
2 P. Depailler   Tyrrell-Ford
3 M. Andretti   Lotus-Ford
4 J. Scheckter   Tyrrell-Ford
5 J. Mass   McLaren-Ford
6 C. Regazzoni   Ferrari
Fastest lap: P. Depailler
   193.00 kph / 119.92 mph
Pole position: J. Hunt

United States GP

10 October: Watkins Glen
321 km / 199 miles
1 J. Hunt   McLaren-Ford
   187.37 kph / 116.43 mph
2 J. Scheckter   Tyrrell-Ford
3 N. Lauda   Ferrari
4 J. Mass   McLaren-Ford
5 H. Stuck   March-Ford
6 J. Watson   Penske-Ford
Fastest lap: J. Hunt
   190.22 kph / 118.20 mph
Pole position: J. Hunt

Japanese GP

24 October: Fuji
318 km / 198 miles
1 M. Andretti   Lotus-Ford
   183.62 kph / 114.09 mph
2 P. Depailler   Tyrrell-Ford
3 J. Hunt   McLaren-Ford
4 A. Jones   Surtees-Ford
5 C. Regazzoni   Ferrari
6 G. Nilsson   Lotus-Ford
Fastest lap: M. Hasemi (Kojima-Ford)
   200.59 kph / 124.64 mph
Pole position: M. Andretti

Constructors' Cup

Pts	Manufacturer	Wins	
83	Ferrari	6	Brazilian GP, South African GP, United States GP (West), Belgian GP, Monaco GP, British GP
74	McLaren-Ford	6	Spanish GP, French GP, German GP, Dutch GP, Canadian GP, United States GP
71	Tyrrell-Ford	1	Swedish GP
29	Lotus-Ford	1	Japanese GP
20	Ligier-Matra	–	
20	Penske-Ford	1	Austrian GP
19	March-Ford	1	Italian GP
10	Shadow-Ford	–	
9	Brabham-Alfa Romeo	–	
7	Surtees-Ford	–	
3	Fittipaldi-Ford	–	
2	Ensign-Ford	–	
1	Parnelli-Ford	–	

Points scoring: Best seven results from the first eight races plus the best seven results from the remaining eight races. Best placed car of each manufacturer only to score. Points: 9–6–4–3–2–1.

World Drivers' Championship

Pts	Driver	Wins	
69	James Hunt (GB)	6	Spanish GP, French GP, German GP, Dutch GP, Canadian GP, United States GP
68	Niki Lauda (AUT)	5	Brazilian GP, South African GP, Belgian GP, Monaco GP, British GP
49	Jody Scheckter (SAF)	1	Swedish GP
39	Patrick Depailler (FRA)	–	
31	Clay Regazzoni (SWI)	1	United States GP (West)
22	Mario Andretti (USA)	1	Japanese GP
20	John Watson (GB)	1	Austrian GP
20	Jacques Laffite (FRA)	–	
19	Jochen Mass (FRG)		
11	Gunnar Nilsson (SWE)		
10	Ronnie Peterson (SWE)	1	Italian GP
10	Tom Pryce (GB)		
8	Hans-Joachim Stuck (FRG)	–	
7	Carlos Pace (BRA)	–	
7	Alan Jones (AUS)	–	
3	Carlos Reutemann (ARG)	–	
3	Emerson Fittipaldi (BRA)	–	
2	Chris Amon (NZ)	–	
1	Rolf Stommelen (FRG)	–	
1	Vittorio Brambilla (ITA)	–	

Points scoring: First six drivers in each race to score. Points as follows: 9–6–4–3–2–1. Best seven results from first eight races plus the best seven results from the remaining eight races.

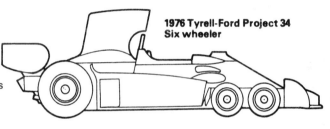

1976 Tyrell-Ford Project 34 Six wheeler

1977

Argentine GP

9 January: Buenos Aires
316 km / 197 miles
1 J. Scheckter   Wolf-Ford
   189.44 kph / 117.71 mph
2 C. Pace   Brabham-Alfa Romeo
3 C. Reutemann   Ferrari
4 E. Fittipaldi   Fittipaldi-Ford
5 M. Andretti   Lotus-Ford
6 C. Regazzoni   Ensign-Ford
Fastest lap: J. Hunt (McLaren-Ford)
   193.46 kph / 120.21 mph
Pole position: J. Hunt

Brazilian GP

23 January: Interlagos
318 km / 198 miles
1 C. Reutemann   Ferrari
   181.73 kph / 112.92 mph
2 J. Hunt   McLaren-Ford
3 N. Lauda   Ferrari
4 E. Fittipaldi   Fittipaldi-Ford
5 G. Nilsson   Lotus-Ford
6 R. Zorzi   Shadow-Ford
Fastest lap: J. Hunt
   185.43 kph / 115.22 mph
Pole position: J. Hunt

South African GP

5 March: Kyalami
320 km / 199 miles
1 N. Lauda   Ferrari
   187.64 kph / 116.59 mph
2 J. Scheckter   Wolf-Ford
3 P. Depailler   Tyrrell-Ford
4 J. Hunt   McLaren-Ford
5 J. Mass   McLaren-Ford
6 J. Watson   Brabham-Alfa Romeo
Fastest lap: J. Watson
   190.32 kph / 118.26 mph
Pole position: J. Hunt

United States GP (West)

3 April: Long Beach
259 km / 162 miles
1 M. Andretti   Lotus-Ford
   139.84 kph / 86.89 mph
2 N. Lauda   Ferrari
3 J. Scheckter   Wolf-Ford
4 P. Depailler   Tyrrell-Ford
5 E. Fittipaldi   Fittipaldi-Ford
6 J. P. Jarier   Penske-Ford
Fastest lap: N. Lauda
   141.42 kph / 87.88 mph
Pole position: N. Lauda

Spanish GP

8 May: Jarama
255 km / 159 miles
1 M. Andretti   Lotus-Ford
   148.92 kph / 92.53 mph
2 C. Reutemann   Ferrari
3 J. Scheckter   Wolf-Ford
4 J. Mass   McLaren-Ford
5 G. Nilsson   Lotus-Ford
6 H. Stuck   Brabham-Alfa Romeo
Fastest lap: J. Laffite (Ligier-Matra)
   151.66 kph / 94.24 mph
Pole position: M. Andretti

Monaco GP

22 May: Monte Carlo
252 km / 156 miles
1 J. Scheckter   Wolf-Ford
   128.12 kph / 79.61 mph
2 N. Lauda   Ferrari
3 C. Reutemann   Ferrari
4 J. Mass   McLaren-Ford
5 M. Andretti   Lotus-Ford
6 A. Jones   Shadow-Ford
Fastest lap: J. Scheckter
   130.92 kph / 81.35 mph
Pole position: J. Watson
(Brabham-Alfa Romeo)

Belgian GP

5 June: Zolder
298 km / 185 miles
1   G. Nilsson   Lotus-Ford
    155.53 kph / 96.64 mph
2   N. Lauda   Ferrari
3   R. Peterson   Tyrrell-Ford
4   V. Brambilla   Surtees-Ford
5   A. Jones   Shadow-Ford
6   H. Stuck   Brabham-
                    Alfa Romeo
Fastest lap: G. Nilsson
    175.63 kph / 109.13 mph
Pole position: M. Andretti
    (Lotus-Ford)

Swedish GP

19 June: Anderstorp
289 km / 180 miles
1   J. Laffite   Ligier-Matra
    162.34 kph / 100.87 mph
2   J. Mass   McLaren-Ford
3   C. Reutemann   Ferrari
4   P. Depailler   Tyrrell-Ford
5   J. Watson   Brabham-
                    Alfa Romeo
6   M. Andretti   Lotus-Ford
Fastest lap: M. Andretti
    165.11 kph / 102.59 mph
Pole position: M. Andretti

Jacques Laffite (FRA) won his first Grand Prix at Anderstoorp in 1977, driving a Ligier. (The Goodyear Tyre & Rubber Co. Ltd.)

1977 Wolf

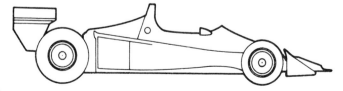

French GP

3 July: Dijon–Prenois
304 km / 189 miles
1   M. Andretti   Lotus-Ford
    183.01 kph / 113.71 mph
2   J. Watson   Brabham-
                    Alfa Romeo
3   J. Hunt   McLaren-Ford
4   G. Nilsson   Lotus-Ford
5   N. Lauda   Ferrari
6   C. Reutemann   Ferrari
Fastest lap: M. Andretti
    185.49 kph / 115.26 mph
Pole position: M. Andretti

British GP

16 July: Silverstone
321 km / 199 miles
1   J. Hunt   McLaren-Ford
    209.79 kph / 130.35 mph
2   N. Lauda   Ferrari
3   G. Nilsson   Lotus-Ford
4   J. Mass   McLaren-Ford
5   H. Stuck   Brabham-
                    Alfa Romeo
6   J. Laffite   Ligier-Matra
Fastest lap: J. Hunt
    213.40 kph / 132.60 mph
Pole position: J. Hunt

German GP

31 July: Hockenheim
319 km / 198 miles
1   N. Lauda   Ferrari
    208.53 kph / 129.57 mph
2   J. Scheckter   Wolf-Ford
3   H. Stuck   Brabham-
                    Alfa Romeo
4   C. Reutemann   Ferrari
5   V. Brambilla   Surtees-Ford
6   P. Tambay   Ensign-Ford
Fastest lap: N. Lauda
    210.71 kph / 130.93 mph
Pole position: J. Scheckter

Austrian GP

14 August: Osterreichring
321 km / 199 miles
1   A. Jones   Shadow-Ford
    197.93 kph / 122.99 mph
2   N. Lauda   Ferrari
3   H. Stuck   Brabham-
                    Alfa Romeo
4   C. Reutemann   Ferrari
5   R. Peterson   Tyrrell-Ford
6   J. Mass   McLaren-Ford
Fastest lap: J. Watson (Brabham-
    Alfa Romeo) 211.89 kph / 131.66 mph
Pole position: N. Lauda

Dutch GP

28 August: Zandvoort
317 km / 197 miles
1   N. Lauda   Ferrari
    186.87 kph / 116.12 mph
2   J. Laffite   Ligier-Matra
3   J. Scheckter   Wolf-Ford
4   E. Fittipaldi   Fittipaldi-Ford
5   P. Tambay   Ensign-Ford
6   C. Reutemann   Ferrari
Fastest lap: N. Lauda
    190.19 kph / 118.18 mph
Pole position: M. Andretti
    (Lotus-Ford)

Italian GP

11 September: Monza
302 km / 187 miles
1   M. Andretti   Lotus-Ford
    206.02 kph / 128.01 mph
2   N. Lauda   Ferrari
3   A. Jones   Shadow-Ford
4   J. Mass   McLaren-Ford
5   C. Regazzoni   Ensign-Ford
6   R. Peterson   Tyrrell-Ford
Fastest lap: M. Andretti
    210.70 kph / 130.92 mph
Pole position: J. Hunt (McLaren-Ford)

United States GP

2 October: Watkins Glen
321 km / 199 miles
1   J. Hunt   McLaren-Ford
    162.51 kph / 100.98 mph
2   M. Andretti   Lotus-Ford
3   J. Scheckter   Wolf-Ford
4   N. Lauda   Ferrari
5   C. Regazzoni   Ensign-Ford
6   C. Reutemann   Ferrari
Fastest lap: R. Peterson (Tyrrell-Ford)
    174.92 kph / 108.69 mph
Pole position: J. Hunt

Canadian GP

9 October: Mosport
317 km / 197 miles
1   J. Scheckter   Wolf-Ford
    189.95 kph / 118.03 mph
2   P. Depailler   Tyrrell-Ford
3   J. Mass   McLaren-Ford
4   A. Jones   Shadow-Ford
5   P. Tambay   Ensign-Ford
6   V. Brambilla   Surtees-Ford
Fastest lap: M. Andretti (Lotus-Ford)
    194.36 kph / 120.77 mph
Pole position: M. Andretti

Japanese GP

23 October: Fuji
318 km / 198 miles
1   J. Hunt   McLaren-Ford
    207.84 kph / 129.15 mph
2   C. Reutemann   Ferrari
3   P. Depailler   Tyrrell-Ford
4   A. Jones   Shadow-Ford
5   J. Laffite   Ligier-Matra
6   R. Patrese   Shadow-Ford
Fastest lap: J. Scheckter (Wolf-Ford)
    211.20 kph / 131.24 mph
Pole position: M. Andretti
    (Lotus-Ford)

World Drivers' Championship

Pts	Driver	Wins	
72	Niki Lauda (AUT)	3	South African GP, German GP, Dutch GP
55	Jody Scheckter (SAF)	3	Argentine GP, Monaco GP, Canadian GP
47	Mario Andretti (USA)	4	United States GP (West), Spanish GP, French GP, Italian GP
42	Carlos Reutemann (ARG)	1	Brazilian GP
40	James Hunt (GB)	3	British GP, United States GP, Japanese GP
25	Jochen Mass (FRG)	–	
22	Alan Jones (AUS)	1	Austrian GP
20	Gunnar Nilsson (SWE)	1	Belgian GP
20	Patrick Depailler (FRA)	–	
18	Jacques Laffite (FRA)	1	Swedish GP
12	Hans-Joachim Stuck (FRG)	–	
11	Emerson Fittipaldi (BRA)	–	
9	John Watson (GB)	–	
7	Ronnie Peterson (SWE)	–	
6	Carlos Pace (BRA)	–	
6	Vittorio Brambilla (ITA)	–	
5	Clay Regazzoni (SWI)	–	
5	Patrick Tambay (FRA)	–	
1	Jean-Pierre Jarier (FRA)	–	
1	Riccardo Patrese (ITA)	–	
1	Renzo Zorzi (ITA)	–	

Points scoring: first six drivers in each race to score. Points as follows: 9–6–4–3–2–1. Best eight results from first nine races plus the best seven results from the remaining eight races.

Constructors' Cup

Pts	Manufacturer	Wins	
95	Ferrari	4	Brazilian GP, South African GP, German GP, Dutch GP
62	Lotus-Ford	5	United States GP (West), Spanish GP, Belgian GP, French GP, Italian GP
60	McLaren-Ford	3	British GP, United States GP, Japanese GP
55	Wolf-Ford	3	Argentine GP, Monaco GP, Canadian GP
27	Brabham-Alfa Romeo	–	
27	Tyrrell-Ford	–	
23	Shadow-Ford	1	Austrian GP
18	Ligier-Matra	1	Swedish GP
11	Fittipaldi-Ford	–	
10	Ensign-Ford	–	
6	Surtees-Ford	–	
1	Penske-Ford	–	

Points scoring: Best eight results from the first nine races plus the best seven results from the remaining eight races. Best placed car of each manufacturer only to score. Points: 9–6–4–3–2–1.

1978

Argentine GP

15 January: Buenos Aires
316 km / 197 miles
1 M. Andretti   Lotus-Ford
    191.82 kph / 119.19 mph
2 N. Lauda   Brabham-Alfa Romeo
3 P. Depailler   Tyrrell-Ford
4 J. Hunt   McLaren-Ford
5 R. Peterson   Lotus-Ford
6 P. Tambay   McLaren-Ford
Fastest lap: G. Villeneuve (Ferrari)
    195.75 kph / 121.63 mph
Pole position: M. Andretti

Brazilian GP

29 January: Rio de Janeiro
317 km / 197 miles
1 C. Reutemann   Ferrari
    172.89 kph / 107.43 mph
2 E. Fittipaldi   Fittipaldi-Ford
3 N. Lauda   Brabham-Alfa Romeo
4 M. Andretti   Lotus-Ford
5 C. Regazzoni   Shadow-Ford
6 D. Pironi   Tyrrell-Ford
Fastest lap: C. Reutemann
    175.72 kph / 109.19 mph
Pole position: R. Peterson
    (Lotus-Ford)

South African GP

4 March: Kyalami
320 km / 199 miles
1 R. Peterson   Lotus-Ford
    187.81 kph / 116.70 mph
2 P. Depailler   Tyrrell-Ford
3 J. Watson   Brabham-Alfa Romeo
4 A. Jones   Williams-Ford
5 J. Laffite   Ligier-Matra
6 D. Pironi   Tyrrell-Ford
Fastest lap: M. Andretti (Lotus-Ford)
    191.64 kph / 119.08 mph
Pole position: N. Lauda
    (Brabham-Alfa Romeo)

United States GP (West)

2 April: Long Beach
262 km / 163 mph
1 C. Reutemann   Ferrari
    140.17 kph / 87.10 mph
2 M. Andretti   Lotus-Ford
3 P. Depailler   Tyrrell-Ford
4 R. Peterson   Lotus-Ford
5 J. Laffite   Ligier-Matra
6 R. Patrese   Arrows-Ford
Fastest lap: A. Jones (Williams-Ford)
    142.35 kph / 88.45 mph
Pole position: C. Reutemann

Monaco GP

7 May: Monte Carlo
248 km / 154 miles
1 P. Depailler   Tyrrell-Ford
    129.33 kph / 80.36 mph
2 N. Lauda   Brabham-Alfa Romeo
3 J. Scheckter   Wolf-Ford
4 J. Watson   Brabham-Alfa Romeo
5 D. Pironi   Tyrrell-Ford
6 R. Patrese   Arrows-Ford
Fastest lap: N. Lauda
    134.50 kph / 83.57 mph
Pole position: C. Reutemann (Ferrari)

Belgian GP

21 May: Zolder
298 km / 185 miles
1 M. Andretti   Lotus-Ford
    179.24 kph / 111.38 mph
2 R. Peterson   Lotus-Ford
3 C. Reutemann   Ferrari
4 G. Villeneuve   Ferrari
5 J. Laffite   Ligier-Matra
6 D. Pironi   Tyrrell-Ford
Fastest lap: R. Peterson
    184.57 kph / 114.69 mph
Pole position: M. Andretti

1978 Lotus 78

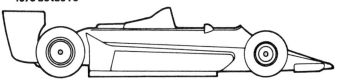

Spanish GP

4 June: Jarama
255 km / 159 miles
1　M. Andretti　　Lotus-Ford
　　150.51 kph / 93.52 mph
2　R. Peterson　　Lotus-Ford
3　J. Laffite　　Ligier-Matra
4　J. Scheckter　　Wolf-Ford
5　J. Watson　　Brabham-
　　　　　　　　　Alfa Romeo
6　J. Hunt　　McLaren-Ford
Fastest lap: M. Andretti
　　153.08 kph / 95.12 mph
Pole position: M. Andretti

Swedish GP

17 June: Anderstorp
282 km / 175 miles
1　N. Lauda　　Brabham-
　　　　　　　　　Alfa Romeo
　　167.61 kph / 104.15 mph
2　R. Patrese　　Arrows-Ford
3　R. Peterson　　Lotus-Ford
4　P. Tambay　　McLaren-Ford
5　C. Regazzoni　　Shadow-Ford
6　E. Fittipaldi　　Fittipaldi-Ford
Fastest lap: N. Lauda
　　171.06 kph / 106.29 mph
Pole position: M. Andretti
　　(Lotus-Ford)

French GP

2 July: Paul Ricard
314 km / 195 miles
1　M. Andretti　　Lotus-Ford
　　190.41 kph / 118.31 mph
2　R. Peterson　　Lotus-Ford
3　J. Hunt　　McLaren-Ford
4　J. Watson　　Brabham-
　　　　　　　　　Alfa Romeo
5　A. Jones　　Williams-Ford
6　J. Scheckter　　Wolf-Ford
Fastest lap: C. Reutemann (Ferrari)
　　192.67 kph / 119.72 mph
Pole position: J. Watson

British GP

16 July: Brands Hatch
320 km / 199 miles
1　C. Reutemann　　Ferrari
　　187.66 kph / 116.61 mph
2　N. Lauda　　Brabham-
　　　　　　　　　Alfa Romeo
3　J. Watson　　Brabham-
　　　　　　　　　Alfa Romeo
4　P. Depailler　　Tyrrell-Ford
5　H. Stuck　　Shadow-Ford
6　P. Tambay　　McLaren-Ford
Fastest lap: N. Lauda
　　192.65 kph / 119.71 mph
Pole position: R. Peterson
　　(Lotus-Ford)

German GP

30 July: Hockenheim
306 km / 190 miles
1　M. Andretti　　Lotus-Ford
　　208.26 kph / 129.41 mph
2　J. Scheckter　　Wolf-Ford
3　J. Laffite　　Ligier-Matra
4　E. Fittipaldi　　Fittipaldi-Ford
5　D. Pironi　　Tyrrell-Ford
6　H. Rebaque　　Lotus-Ford
Fastest lap: R. Peterson (Lotus-Ford)
　　211.39 kph / 131.35 mph
Pole position: M. Andretti

Austrian GP

13 August: Osterreichring
321 km / 199 miles
1　R. Peterson　　Lotus-Ford
　　189.95 kph / 118.03 mph
2　P. Depailler　　Tyrrell-Ford
3　G. Villeneuve　　Ferrari
4　E. Fittipaldi　　Fittipaldi-Ford
5　J. Laffite　　Ligier-Matra
6　V. Brambilla　　Surtees-Ford
Fastest lap: R. Peterson
　　207.45 kph / 128.91 mph
Pole position: R. Peterson

Dutch GP

27 August: Zandvoort
317 km / 197 miles
1　M. Andretti　　Lotus-Ford
　　188.16 kph / 116.91 mph
2　R. Peterson　　Lotus-Ford
3　N. Lauda　　Brabham-
　　　　　　　　　Alfa Romeo
4　J. Watson　　Brabham-
　　　　　　　　　Alfa Romeo
5　E. Fittipaldi　　Fittipaldi-Ford
6　G. Villeneuve　　Ferrari
Fastest lap: N. Lauda
　　191.20 kph / 118.81 mph
Pole position: M. Andretti

Italian GP

10 September: Monza
232 km / 144 miles
1　N. Lauda　　Brabham-
　　　　　　　　　Alfa Romeo
　　207.52 kph / 128.95 mph
2　J. Watson　　Brabham-
　　　　　　　　　Alfa Romeo

3　C. Reutemann　　Ferrari
4　J. Laffite　　Ligier-Matra
5　P. Tambay　　McLaren-Ford
6　M. Andretti　　Lotus-Ford
Fastest lap: M. Andretti
　　212.56 kph / 132.08 mph
Pole position: M. Andretti

United States GP

1 October: Watkins Glen
321 km / 199 miles
1　C. Reutemann　　Ferrari
　　190.85 kph / 118.59 mph
2　A. Jones　　Williams-Ford
3　J. Scheckter　　Wolf-Ford
4　J. P. Jabouille　　Renault
5　E. Fittipaldi　　Fittipaldi-Ford
6　P. Tambay　　McLaren-Ford
Fastest lap: J. P. Jarier (Lotus-Ford)
　　196.53 kph / 122.12 mph
Pole position: M. Andretti
　　(Lotus-Ford)

Canadian GP

8 October: Montreal
315 km / 196 miles
1　G. Villeneuve　　Ferrari
　　160.40 kph / 99.67 mph
2　J. Scheckter　　Wolf-Ford
3　C. Reutemann　　Ferrari
4　R. Patrese　　Arrows-Ford
5　P. Depailler　　Tyrrell-Ford
6　D. Daly　　Ensign-Ford
Fastest lap: A. Jones (Williams-Ford)
　　165.18 kph / 102.64 mph
Pole position: J. P. Jarier (Lotus-Ford)

World Drivers' Championship

Pts	Driver	Wins	
64	Mario Andretti (USA)	6	Argentine GP, Belgian GP, Spanish GP, French GP, German GP, Dutch GP
51	Ronnie Peterson (SWE)	2	South African GP, Austrian GP
48	Carlos Reutemann (ARG)	4	Brazilian GP, United States GP (West), British GP, United States GP
44	Niki Lauda (AUT)	2	Swedish GP, Italian GP
34	Patrick Depailler (FRA)	1	Monaco GP
25	John Watson (GB)	–	
24	Jody Scheckter (SAF)	–	
19	Jacques Laffite (FRA)	–	
17	Gilles Villeneuve (CAN)	1	Canadian GP
17	Emerson Fittipaldi (BRA)	–	
11	Alan Jones (AUS)	–	
11	Riccardo Patrese (ITA)	–	
8	James Hunt (GB)	–	
8	Patrick Tambay (FRA)	–	
7	Didier Pironi (FRA)	–	
4	Clay Regazzoni (SWI)	–	
3	Jean-Pierre Jabouille (FRA)	–	
2	Hans-Joachim Stuck (FRG)	–	
1	Hector Rebaque (MEX)	–	
1	Vittorio Brambilla (ITA)	–	
1	Derek Daly (IRE)	–	

Points scoring: First six drivers in each race to score. Points as follows: 9–6–4–3–2–1. Best seven results from first eight races plus the best seven results from the remaining eight races.

Constructors' Cup

Pts	Manufacturer	Wins	
86	Lotus-Ford	8	Argentine GP, South African GP, Belgian GP, Spanish GP, French GP, German GP, Austrian GP, Dutch GP
58	Ferrari	5	Brazilian GP, United States GP (West), British GP, United States GP, Canadian GP
53	Brabham-Alfa Romeo	2	Swedish GP, Italian GP
38	Tyrrell-Ford	1	Monaco GP
24	Wolf-Ford	–	

Pts	Manufacturer	Wins
19	Ligier-Matra	–
17	Fittipaldi-Ford	–
15	McLaren-Ford	–
11	Williams-Ford	–
11	Arrows-Ford	–
6	Shadow-Ford	–
3	Renault	–
1	Surtees-Ford	–
1	Ensign-Ford	–

Points scoring: Best seven results from the first eight races plus the best seven results from the remaining eight races. Best placed car of each manufacturer only to score. Points: 9–6–4–3–2–1.

1979

Argentine GP

21 January: Buenos Aires
316 km / 197 miles
1 J. Laffite   Ligier-Ford
    197.59 kph / 122.78 mph
2 C. Reutemann   Lotus-Ford
3 J. Watson   McLaren-Ford
4 P. Depailler   Ligier-Ford
5 M. Andretti   Lotus-Ford
6 E. Fittipaldi   Fittipaldi-Ford
Fastest lap: J. Laffite
    200.97 kph / 124.88 mph
Pole position: J. Laffite

Brazilian GP

4 February: Interlagos
315 km / 196 miles
1 J. Laffite   Ligier-Ford
    188.67 kph / 117.23 mph
2 P. Depailler   Ligier-Ford
3 C. Reutemann   Lotus-Ford
4 D. Pironi   Tyrrell-Ford
5 G. Villeneuve   Ferrari
6 J. Scheckter   Ferrari
Fastest lap: J. Laffite
    190.55 kph / 118.40 mph
Pole position: J. Laffite

South African GP

3 March: Kyalami
320 km / 199 miles
1 G. Villeneuve   Ferrari
    188.60 kph / 117.19 mph
2 J. Scheckter   Ferrari
3 J. P. Jarier   Tyrrell-Ford
4 M. Andretti   Lotus-Ford
5 C. Reutemann   Lotus-Ford
6 N. Lauda   Brabham-
                        Alfa Romeo
Fastest lap: G. Villeneuve
    198.54 kph / 123.38 mph
Pole position: J. P. Jabouille (Renault)

United States GP (West)

8 April: Long Beach
262 km / 163 miles
1 G. Villeneuve   Ferrari
    141.31 kph / 87.81 mph
2 J. Scheckter   Ferrari
3 A. Jones   Williams-Ford
4 M. Andretti   Lotus-Ford
5 P. Depailler   Ligier-Ford
6 J. P. Jarier   Tyrrell-Ford
Fastest lap: G. Villeneuve
    144.28 kph / 89.65 mph
Pole position: G. Villeneuve

Spanish GP

29 April: Jarama
255 km / 159 miles
1 P. Depailler   Ligier-Ford
    154.45 kph / 95.97 mph
2 C. Reutemann   Lotus-Ford
3 M. Andretti   Lotus-Ford
4 J. Scheckter   Ferrari
5 J. P. Jarier   Tyrrell-Ford
6 D. Pironi   Tyrrell-Ford
Fastest lap: G. Villeneuve (Ferrari)
    160.45 kph / 99.70 mph
Pole position: J. Laffite (Ligier-Ford)

Belgian GP

13 May: Zolder
298 km / 185 miles
1 J. Scheckter   Ferrari
    179.02 kph / 111.24 mph
2 J. Laffite   Ligier-Ford
3 D. Pironi   Tyrrell-Ford
4 C. Reutemann   Lotus-Ford
5 R. Patrese   Arrows-Ford
6 J. Watson   McLaren-Ford
Fastest lap: J. Scheckter
    186.23 kph / 115.72 mph
Pole position: J. Laffite

Monaco GP

27 May: Monte Carlo
252 km / 156 miles
1 J. Scheckter   Ferrari
    130.90 kph / 81.34 mph
2 C. Regazzoni   Williams-Ford
3 C. Reutemann   Lotus-Ford
4 J. Watson   McLaren-Ford
5 P. Depailler   Ligier-Ford
6 J. Mass   Arrows-Ford
Fastest lap: P. Depailler
    134.24 kph / 83.41 mph
Pole position: J. Scheckter

French GP

1 July: Dijon-Prenois
304 km / 189 miles
1 J. P. Jabouille   Renault
    191.32 kph / 118.88 mph
2 G. Villeneuve   Ferrari
3 R. Arnoux   Renault
4 A. Jones   Williams-Ford
5 J. P. Jarier   Tyrrell-Ford
6 C. Regazzoni   Williams-Ford
Fastest lap: R. Arnoux
    197.80 kph / 122.91 mph
Pole position: J. P. Jabouille

British GP

14 July: Silverstone
321 km / 199 miles
1 C. Regazzoni   Williams-Ford
    223.37 kph / 138.80 mph
2 R. Arnoux   Renault
3 J. P. Jarier   Tyrrell-Ford
4 J. Watson   McLaren-Ford
5 J. Scheckter   Ferrari
6 J. Ickx   Ligier-Ford
Fastest lap: C. Regazzoni
    228.31 kph / 141.87 mph
Pole position: A. Jones
    (Williams-Ford)

German GP

29 July: Hockenheim
306 km / 190 miles
1 A. Jones   Williams-Ford
    216.09 kph / 134.27 mph
2 C. Regazzoni   Williams-Ford
3 J. Laffite   Ligier-Ford
4 J. Scheckter   Ferrari
5 J. Watson   McLaren-Ford
6 J. Mass   Arrows-Ford
Fastest lap: G. Villeneuve (Ferrari)
    218.40 kph / 135.71 mph
Pole position: J. P. Jabouille (Renault)

Austrian GP

12 August: Osterreichring
321 km / 199 miles
1 A. Jones   Williams-Ford
    219.71 kph / 136.52 mph
2 G. Villeneuve   Ferrari
3 J. Laffite   Ligier-Ford
4 J. Scheckter   Ferrari
5 C. Regazzoni   Williams-Ford
6 R. Arnoux   Renault
Fastest lap: R. Arnoux
    223.82 kph / 139.08 mph
Pole position: R. Arnoux

Dutch GP

26 August: Zandvoort
317 km / 197 miles
1 A. Jones   Williams-Ford
    187.67 kph / 116.62 mph
2 J. Scheckter   Ferrari
3 J. Laffite   Ligier-Ford
4 N. Piquet   Brabham-
                        Alfa Romeo
5 J. Ickx   Ligier-Ford
6 J. Mass   Arrows-Ford
Fastest lap: G. Villeneuve (Ferrari)
    191.52 kph / 119.00 mph
Pole position: R. Arnoux (Renault)

Italian GP

9 September: Monza
290 km / 180 miles
1 J. Scheckter   Ferrari
    212.19 kph / 131.85 mph
2 G. Villeneuve   Ferrari
3 C. Regazzoni   Williams-Ford
4 N. Lauda   Brabham-
                     Alfa Romeo
5 M. Andretti   Lotus-Ford
6 J. P. Jarier   Tyrrell-Ford
Fastest lap: C. Regazzoni
    218.41 kph / 135.71 mph
Pole position: J. P. Jabouille
    (Renault)

Canadian GP

30 September: Montreal
318 km / 197 miles
1 A. Jones   Williams-Ford
    169.93 kph / 105.59 mph
2 G. Villeneuve   Ferrari
3 C. Regazzoni   Williams-Ford
4 J. Scheckter   Ferrari
5 D. Pironi   Tyrrell-Ford
6 J. Watson   McLaren-Ford
Fastest lap: A. Jones
    173.94 kph / 108.08 mph
Pole position: A. Jones

United States GP

7 October: Watkins Glen
321 km / 199 miles
1 G. Villeneuve   Ferrari
    171.33 kph / 106.46 mph
2 R. Arnoux   Renault
3 D. Pironi   Tyrrell-Ford
4 E. de Angelis   Shadow-Ford
5 H. Stuck   ATS-Ford
6 J. Watson   McLaren-Ford
Fastest lap: N. Piquet (Brabham-Ford)
    195.55 kph / 121.51 mph
Pole position: A. Jones
    (Williams-Ford)

World Drivers' Championship

Pts	Driver	Wins	
51	Jody Scheckter (SAF)	3	Belgian GP, Monaco GP, Italian GP
47	Gilles Villeneuve (CAN)	3	South African GP, United States GP (West), United States GP
40	Alan Jones (AUS)	4	German GP, Austrian GP, Dutch GP, Canadian GP
36	Jacques Laffite (FRA)	2	Argentine GP, Brazilian GP
29	Clay Regazzoni (SWI)	1	British GP
20	Patrick Depailler (FRA)	1	Spanish GP
20	Carlos Reutemann (ARG)	–	
17	Rene Arnoux (FRA)	–	
15	John Watson (GB)	–	
14	Didier Pironi (FRA)	–	
14	Jean-Pierre Jarier (FRA)	–	
14	Mario Andretti (USA)	–	
9	Jean-Pierre Jabouille (FRA)	1	French GP
4	Niki Lauda (AUT)	–	
3	Nelson Piquet (BRA)	–	
3	Elio de Angelis (ITA)	–	
3	Jacky Ickx (BEL)	–	
3	Jochen Mass (FRG)	–	
2	Riccardo Patrese (ITA)	–	
2	Hans-Joachim Stuck (FRG)	–	
1	Emerson Fittipaldi (BRA)	–	

Points scoring: First six drivers in each race to score. Points as follows: 9–6–4–3–2–1. Best four results from first seven races plus the best four results from the remaining eight races.

Constructors' Cup

Pts	Manufacturer	Wins	
113	Ferrari	6	South African GP, United States GP (West), Belgian GP, Monaco GP, Italian GP, United States GP
75	Williams-Ford	5	British GP, German GP, Austrian GP, Dutch GP, Canadian GP
61	Ligier-Ford	3	Argentine GP, Brazilian GP, Spanish GP
39	Lotus-Ford	–	
28	Tyrrell-Ford	–	
26	Renault	1	French GP
15	McLaren-Ford	–	
7	Brabham-Alfa Romeo	–	
5	Arrows-Ford	–	
3	Shadow-Ford	–	
2	ATS-Ford	–	
1	Fittipaldi-Ford	–	

Points scoring: First six cars in each race to score, results from all 15 rounds counted. Points: 9–6–4–3–2–1.

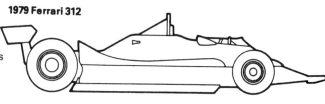

1979 Ferrari 312

1980

Argentine GP

13 January: Buenos Aires
316 km / 197 miles
1 A. Jones   Williams-Ford
    183.44 kph / 113.99 mph
2 N. Piquet   Brabham-Ford
3 K. Rosberg   Fittipaldi-Ford
4 D. Daly   Tyrrell-Ford
5 B. Giacomelli   Alfa Romeo
6 A. Prost   McLaren-Ford
Fastest lap: A. Jones
    194.53 kph / 120.87 mph
Pole position: A. Jones

Brazilian GP

27 January: Interlagos
315 km / 196 miles
1 R. Arnoux   Renault
    188.93 kph / 117.40 mph
2 E. de Angelis   Lotus-Ford
3 A. Jones   Williams-Ford
4 D. Pironi   Ligier-Ford
5 A. Prost   McLaren-Ford
6 R. Patrese   Arrows-Ford
Fastest lap: R. Arnoux
    192.42 kph / 119.57 mph
Pole position: J. P. Jabouille
    (Renault)

South African GP

1 March: Kyalami
320 km / 199 miles
1 R. Arnoux   Renault
    198.25 kph / 123.19 mph
2 J. Laffite   Ligier-Ford
3 D. Pironi   Ligier-Ford
4 N. Piquet   Brabham-Ford
5 C. Reutemann   Williams-Ford
6 J. Mass   Arrows-Ford
Fastest lap: R. Arnoux
    201.97 kph / 125.50 mph
Pole position: J. P. Jabouille
    (Renault)

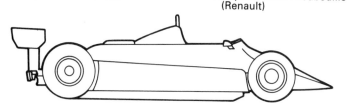

1980 Williams FW07

United States GP (West)

30 March: Long Beach
262 km / 163 miles
1 N. Piquet   Brabham-Ford
   142.35 kph / 88.45 mph
2 R. Patrese   Arrows-Ford
3 E. Fittipaldi   Fittipaldi-Ford
4 J. Watson   McLaren-Ford
5 J. Scheckter   Ferrari
6 D. Pironi   Ligier-Ford
Fastest lap: N. Piquet
   146.61 kph / 91.10 mph
Pole position: N. Piquet

Belgian GP

4 May: Zolder
307 km / 191 miles
1 D. Pironi   Ligier-Ford
   186.40 kph / 115.82 mph
2 A. Jones   Williams-Ford
3 C. Reutemann   Williams-Ford
4 R. Arnoux   Renault
5 J. P. Jarier   Tyrrell-Ford
6 G. Villeneuve   Ferrari
Fastest lap: J. Laffite (Ligier-Ford)
   189.70 kph / 117.88 mph
Pole position: A. Jones

Monaco GP

18 May: Monte Carlo
252 km / 156 miles
1 C. Reutemann   Williams-Ford
   130.68 kph / 81.20 mph
2 J. Laffite   Ligier-Ford
3 N. Piquet   Brabham-Ford
4 J. Mass   Arrows-Ford
5 G. Villeneuve   Ferrari
6 E. Fittipaldi   Fittipaldi-Ford
Fastest lap: R. Patrese (Arrows-Ford)
   138.55 kph / 86.09 mph
Pole position: D. Pironi (Ligier-Ford)

French GP

29 June: Paul Ricard
314 km / 195 miles
1 A. Jones   Williams-Ford
   203.02 kph / 126.15 mph
2 D. Pironi   Ligier-Ford
3 J. Laffite   Ligier-Ford
4 N. Piquet   Brabham-Ford
5 R. Arnoux   Renault
6 C. Reutemann   Williams-Ford
Fastest lap: A. Jones
   206.17 kph / 128.11 mph
Pole position: J. Laffite

British GP

13 July: Brands Hatch
320 km / 199 miles
1 A. Jones   Williams-Ford
   202.28 kph / 125.69 mph
2 N. Piquet   Brabham-Ford
3 C. Reutemann   Williams-Ford
4 D. Daly   Tyrrell-Ford
5 J. P. Jarier   Tyrrell-Ford
6 A. Prost   McLaren-Ford
Fastest lap: D. Pironi (Ligier-Ford)
   209.24 kph / 130.02 mph
Pole position: D. Pironi

German GP

10 August: Hockenheim
306 km / 190 mph
1 J. Laffite   Ligier-Ford
   220.83 kph / 137.22 mph
2 C. Reutemann   Williams-Ford
3 A. Jones   Williams-Ford
4 N. Piquet   Brabham-Ford
5 B. Giacomelli   Alfa Romeo
6 G. Villeneuve   Ferrari
Fastest lap: A. Jones
   225.25 kph / 139.96 mph
Pole position: A. Jones

Austrian GP

17 August: Osterreichring
321 km / 199 miles
1 J. P. Jabouille   Renault
   223.20 kph / 138.69 mph
2 A. Jones   Williams-Ford
3 C. Reutemann   Williams-Ford
4 J. Laffite   Ligier-Ford
5 N. Piquet   Brabham-Ford
6 E. de Angelis   Lotus-Ford
Fastest lap: R. Arnoux (Renault)
   231.20 kph / 143.66 mph
Pole position: R. Arnoux

Dutch GP

31 August: Zandvoort
306 km / 190 miles
1 N. Piquet   Brabham-Ford
   186.98 kph / 116.19 mph
2 R. Arnoux   Renault
3 J. Laffite   Ligier-Ford
4 C. Reutemann   Williams-Ford
5 J. P. Jarier   Tyrrell-Ford
6 A. Prost   McLaren-Ford
Fastest lap: R. Arnoux
   192.91 kph / 119.87 mph
Pole position: R. Arnoux

Italian GP

14 September: Imola
300 km / 186 miles
1 N. Piquet   Brabham-Ford
   183.44 kph / 113.98 mph
2 A. Jones   Williams-Ford
3 C. Reutemann   Williams-Ford
4 E. de Angelis   Lotus-Ford
5 K. Rosberg   Fittipaldi-Ford
6 D. Pironi   Ligier-Ford
Fastest lap: A. Jones
   187.33 kph / 116.40 mph
Pole position: R. Arnoux (Renault)

Canadian GP

28 September: Montreal
309 km / 192 miles
1 A. Jones   Williams-Ford
   177.03 kph / 110.00 mph
2 C. Reutemann   Williams-Ford
3 D. Pironi   Ligier-Ford
4 J. Watson   McLaren-Ford
5 G. Villeneuve   Ferrari
6 H. Rebaque   Brabham-Ford
Fastest lap: D. Pironi
   178.85 kph / 111.13 kph
Pole position: N. Piquet
   (Brabham-Ford)

United States GP

5 October: Watkins Glen
321 km / 199 miles
1 A. Jones   Williams-Ford
   203.37 kph / 126.37 mph
2 C. Reutemann   Williams-Ford
3 D. Pironi   Ligier-Ford
4 E. de Angelis   Lotus-Ford
5 J. Laffite   Ligier-Ford
6 M. Andretti   Lotus-Ford
Fastest lap: A. Jones
   207.99 kph / 129.24 mph
Pole position: B. Giacomelli
   (Alfa Romeo)

World Drivers' Championship

Pts	Driver	Wins	
67	Alan Jones (AUS)	5	Argentine GP, French GP, British GP, Canadian GP, United States GP
54	Nelson Piquet (BRA)	3	United States GP (West), Dutch GP, Italian GP
42	Carlos Reutemann (ARG)	1	Monaco GP
34	Jacques Laffite (FRA)	1	German GP
32	Didier Pironi (FRA)	1	Belgian GP
29	Rene Arnoux (FRA)	2	Brazilian GP, South African GP
13	Elio de Angelis (ITA)	–	
9	Jean-Pierre Jabouille (FRA)	1	Austrian GP
7	Riccardo Patrese (ITA)	–	
6	Keke Rosberg (FIN)	–	
6	Derek Daly (IRE)	–	
6	John Watson (GB)	–	
6	Jean-Pierre Jarier (FRA)	–	
6	Gilles Villeneuve (CAN)	–	
5	Emerson Fittipaldi (BRA)	–	
5	Alain Prost (FRA)	–	
4	Jochen Mass (FRG)	–	
4	Bruno Giacomelli (ITA)	–	
2	Jody Scheckter (SAF)	–	
1	Hector Rebaque (MEX)	–	
1	Mario Andretti (USA)	–	

Points scoring: First six drivers in each race to score. Points as follows: 9–6–4–3–2–1. Best five results from first seven races plus the best five results from the remaining seven races.

Constructors' Cup

Pts	Manufacturer	Wins	
120	Williams-Ford	6	Argentine GP, Monaco GP, French GP, British GP, Canadian GP, United States GP
66	Ligier-Ford	2	Belgian GP, German GP
55	Brabham-Ford	3	United States GP (West), Dutch GP, Italian GP
38	Renault	3	Brazilian GP, South African GP, Austrian GP
14	Lotus-Ford	–	
12	Tyrrell-Ford	–	
11	Arrows-Ford	–	
11	Fittipaldi-Ford	–	
11	McLaren-Ford	–	
8	Ferrari	–	
4	Alfa Romeo	–	

Points scoring: First six cars in each race to score, results from all 14 rounds counted. Points: 9–6–4–3–2–1.

Australian Alan Jones captured the world title for the Williams team in 1980. (The Goodyear Tyre & Rubber Co. Ltd.)

1981

United States GP (West)

15 March: Long Beach
262 km / 163 miles
1 A. Jones   Williams-Ford
   140.98 kph / 87.60 mph
2 C. Reutemann   Williams-Ford
3 N. Piquet   Brabham-Ford
4 M. Andretti   Alfa Romeo
5 E. Cheever   Tyrrell-Ford
6 P. Tambay   Theodore-Ford
Fastest lap: A. Jones
   144.66 kph / 89.89 mph
Pole position: R. Patrese
   (Arrows-Ford)

Brazilian GP

29 March: Rio de Janeiro
312 km / 194 miles
1 C. Reutemann   Williams-Ford
   155.45 kph / 96.60 mph
2 A. Jones   Williams-Ford
3 R. Patrese   Arrows-Ford
4 M. Surer   Ensign-Ford
5 E. de Angelis   Lotus-Ford
6 J. Laffite   Talbot-Matra
Fastest lap: M. Surer
   158.45 kph / 98.46 mph
Pole position: N. Piquet
   (Brabham-Ford)

Argentine GP

12 April: Buenos Aires
316 km / 196 miles
1 N. Piquet   Brabham-Ford
   200.63 kph / 124.67 mph
2 C. Reutemann   Williams-Ford
3 A. Prost   Renault
4 A. Jones   Williams-Ford
5 R. Arnoux   Renault
6 E. de Angelis   Lotus-Ford
Fastest lap: N. Piquet
   204.07 kph / 126.81 mph
Pole position: N. Piquet

San Marino GP

3 May: Imola
302 km / 188 miles
1 N. Piquet   Brabham-Ford
   162.87 kph / 101.21 mph
2 R. Patrese   Arrows-Ford
3 C. Reutemann   Williams-Ford
4 H. Rebaque   Brabham-Ford
5 D. Pironi   Ferrari
6 A. de Cesaris   McLaren-Ford
Fastest lap: G. Villeneuve (Ferrari)
   167.90 kph / 104.33 mph
Pole position: G. Villeneuve

Belgian GP

17 May: Zolder
230 km / 143 miles
1 C. Reutemann   Williams-Ford
   180.45 kph / 112.13 mph
2 J. Laffite   Talbot-Matra
3 N. Mansell   Lotus-Ford
4 G. Villeneuve   Ferrari
5 E. de Angelis   Lotus-Ford
6 E. Cheever   Tyrrell-Ford
Fastest lap: C. Reutemann
   184.19 kph / 114.45 mph
Pole position: C. Reutemann

Monaco GP

31 May: Monte Carlo
252 km / 157 miles
1 G. Villeneuve   Ferrari
   132.03 kph / 82.04 mph
2 A. Jones   Williams-Ford
3 J. Laffite   Talbot-Matra
4 D. Pironi   Ferrari
5 E. Cheever   Tyrrell-Ford
6 M. Surer   Ensign-Ford
Fastest lap: A. Jones
   136.31 kph / 84.70 mph
Pole position: N. Piquet
   (Brabham-Ford)

Spanish GP

21 June: Jarama
265 km / 165 miles
1 G. Villeneuve   Ferrari
   149.10 kph / 92.65 mph
2 J. Laffite   Talbot-Matra
3 J. Watson   McLaren-Ford
4 C. Reutemann   Williams-Ford
5 E. de Angelis   Lotus-Ford
6 N. Mansell   Lotus-Ford
Fastest lap: A. Jones (Williams-Ford)
   153.22 kph / 95.21 mph
Pole position: J. Laffite

French GP

5 July: Dijon-Prenois
304 km / 189 miles
1 A. Prost   Renault
   190.39 kph / 118.31 mph
2 J. Watson   McLaren-Ford
3 N. Piquet   Brabham-Ford
4 R. Arnoux   Renault
5 D. Pironi   Ferrari
6 E. de Angelis   Lotus-Ford
Fastest lap: A. Prost
   197.86 kph / 122.95 mph
Pole position: R. Arnoux

British GP

18 July: Silverstone
321 km / 199 miles
1 J. Watson   McLaren-Ford
   221.51 kph / 137.65 mph
2 C. Reutemann   Williams-Ford
3 J. Laffite   Talbot-Matra
4 E. Cheever   Tyrrell-Ford
5 H. Rebaque   Brabham-Ford
6 S. Borgudd   ATS-Ford
Fastest lap: R. Arnoux (Renault)
   226.29 kph / 140.62 mph
Pole position: R. Arnoux

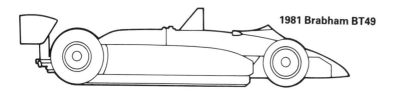

1981 Brabham BT49

● Lella Lombardi's co-driver in the 1980 Le Mans 24-Hour race was Mark Thatcher, the Prime Minister's son.

German GP

2 August: Hockenheim
306 km / 190 miles
1 N. Piquet   Brabham-Ford
   213.29 kph / 132.54 mph
2 A. Prost   Renault
3 J. Laffite   Talbot-Matra
4 H. Rebaque   Brabham-Ford
5 E. Cheever   Tyrrell-Ford
6 J. Watson   McLaren-Ford
Fastest lap: A. Jones (Williams-Ford)
   217.37 kph / 135.07 mph
Pole position: A. Prost

Austrian GP

16 August: Osterreichring
315 km / 196 miles
1 J. Laffite   Talbot-Matra
   215.70 kph / 134.03 mph
2 R. Arnoux   Renault
3 N. Piquet   Brabham-Ford
4 A. Jones   Williams-Ford
5 C. Reutemann   Williams-Ford
6 J. Watson   McLaren-Ford
Fastest lap: J. Laffite
   219.14 kph / 136.17 mph
Pole position: R. Arnoux

Dutch GP

30 August: Zandvoort
306 km / 190 miles
1 A. Prost   Renault
   183.00 kph / 113.72 mph
2 N. Piquet   Brabham-Ford
3 A. Jones   Williams-Ford
4 H. Rebaque   Brabham-Ford
5 E. de Angelis   Lotus-Ford
6 E. Salazar   Ensign-Ford
Fastest lap: A. Jones
   187.06 kph / 116.24 mph
Pole position: A. Prost

Italian GP

13 September: Monza
302 km / 188 miles
1 A. Prost   Renault
   209.00 kph / 129.87 mph
2 A. Jones   Williams-Ford
3 C. Reutemann   Williams-Ford
4 E. de Angelis   Lotus-Ford
5 D. Pironi   Ferrari
6 N. Piquet   Brabham-Ford
Fastest lap: C. Reutemann
   214.09 kph / 133.04 mph
Pole position: R. Arnoux (Renault)

Canadian GP

27 September: Montreal
278 km / 173 miles
1 J. Laffite   Talbot-Matra
   137.29 kph / 85.31 mph
2 J. Watson   McLaren-Ford
3 G. Villeneuve   Ferrari
4 B. Giacomelli   Alfa Romeo
5 N. Piquet   Brabham-Ford
6 E. de Angelis   Lotus-Ford
Fastest lap: J. Watson
   145.02 kph / 90.12 mph
Pole position: N. Piquet

Las Vegas GP

17 October: Las Vegas
273 km / 170 miles
1 A. Jones   Williams-Ford
   157.55 kph / 97.90 mph
2 A. Prost   Renault
3 B. Giacomelli   Alfa Romeo
4 N. Mansell   Lotus-Ford
5 N. Piquet   Brabham-Ford
6 J. Laffite   Talbot-Matra
Fastest lap: D. Pironi (Ferrari)
   163.93 kph / 101.87 mph
Pole position: C. Reutemann
   (Williams-Ford)

Constructors' Cup

Pts	Manufacturer	Wins	
95	Williams-Ford	4	United States GP (West), Brazilian GP, Belgian GP, Las Vegas GP
61	Brabham-Ford	3	Argentine GP, San Marino GP, German GP
54	Renault	3	French GP, Dutch GP, Italian GP
44	Talbot Ligier-Matra	2	Austrian GP, Canadian GP
34	Ferrari	2	Monaco GP, Spanish GP
28	McLaren-Ford	1	British GP
22	Lotus-Ford	–	
10	Arrows-Ford	–	
10	Alfa Romeo	–	
10	Tyrrell-Ford	–	
5	Ensign-Ford	–	
1	Theodore-Ford	–	
1	ATS-Ford	–	

Points scoring: First six cars in each race to score, results from all 15 rounds counted. Points: 9–6–4–3–2–1.

World Drivers' Championship

Pts	Driver	Wins	
50	Nelson Piquet (BRA)	3	Argentine GP, San Marino GP, German GP
49	Carlos Reutemann (ARG)	2	Brazilian GP, Belgian GP
46	Alan Jones (AUS)	2	United States GP (West), Las Vegas GP
44	Jacques Laffite (FRA)	2	Austrian GP, Canadian GP
43	Alain Prost (FRA)	3	French GP, Dutch GP, Italian GP
27	John Watson (GB)	1	British GP
25	Gilles Villeneuve (CAN)	2	Monaco GP, Spanish GP
14	Elio de Angelis (ITA)	–	
11	Rene Arnoux (FRA)	–	
11	Hector Rebaque (MEX)	–	
10	Riccardo Patrese (ITA)	–	
10	Eddie Cheever (USA)	–	
9	Didier Pironi (FRA)	–	
8	Nigel Mansell (GB)	–	
7	Bruno Giacomelli (ITA)	–	
4	Marc Surer (SWI)	–	
3	Mario Andretti (USA)	–	
1	Patrick Tambay (FRA)	–	
1	Andrea de Cesaris (ITA)	–	
1	Slim Borgudd (SWE)	–	
1	Eliseo Salazar (CHI)	–	

Points scoring: First six drivers in each race to score. Points as follows: 9–6–4–3–2–1. Best ten results from 15 rounds to count.

This is how Nelson Piquet's Brabham ended up in the 1981 British Grand Prix at Silverstone. (Michelin Tyre Co. Ltd.)

1982

South African GP

23 January: Kyalami
316 km / 197 miles
1 A. Prost   Renault
   205.70 kph / 127.82 mph
2 C. Reutemann   Williams-Ford
3 R. Arnoux   Renault
4 N. Lauda   McLaren-Ford
5 K. Rosberg   Williams-Ford
6 J. Watson   McLaren-Ford
Fastest lap: A. Prost
   216.39 kph / 134.46 mph
Pole position: R. Arnoux

Brazilian GP

21 March: Rio de Janeiro
317 km / 197 miles
1 N. Piquet*   Brabham-Ford
   183.00 kph / 113.72 mph
2 K. Rosberg*   Williams-Ford
3 A. Prost   Renault
4 J. Watson   McLaren-Ford
5 N. Mansell   Lotus-Ford
6 M. Alboreto   Tyrrell-Ford
* Subsequently disqualified
Fastest lap: N. Piquet (Brabham-Ford)
   187.52 kph / 116.52 mph
Pole position: A. Prost

United States GP (West)

4 April: Long Beach
258 km / 160 miles
1 N. Lauda   McLaren-Ford
   131.00 kph / 81.40 mph
2 K. Rosberg   Williams-Ford
3 G. Villeneuve*   Ferrari
4 R. Patrese   Brabham-Ford
5 M. Alboreto   Tyrrell-Ford
6 E. de Angelis   Lotus-Ford
* subsequently disqualified
Fastest lap: N. Lauda
   135.86 kph / 84.42 mph
Pole position: A. de Cesaris
   (Alfa Romeo)

San Marino GP

25 April: Imola
302 km / 188 miles
1 D. Pironi   Ferrari
   187.77 kph / 117.30 mph
2 G. Villeneuve   Ferrari
3 M. Alboreto   Tyrrell-Ford
4 J. P. Jarier   Osella-Ford
5 E. Salazar   ATS-Ford
only five classified
Fastest lap: D. Pironi
   190.92 kph / 118.64 mph
Pole position: R. Arnoux (Renault)

Belgian GP

9 May: Zolder
298 km / 185 miles
1 J. Watson   McLaren-Ford
   188.09 kph / 116.88 mph
2 K. Rosberg   Williams-Ford
3 N. Lauda*   McLaren-Ford
4 E. Cheever   Talbot-Matra
5 E. de Angelis   Lotus-Ford
6 N. Piquet   Brabham-BMW
* Subsequently disqualified
Fastest lap: J. Watson
   192.39 kph / 119.55 mph
Pole position: A. Prost (Renault)

Monaco GP

23 May: Monte Carlo
252 km / 157 miles
1 R. Patrese   Brabham-Ford
   132.30 kph / 82.21 mph
2 D. Pironi   Ferrari
3 A. de Cesaris   Alfa Romeo
4 N. Mansell   Lotus-Ford
5 E. de Angelis   Lotus-Ford
6 D. Daly   Williams-Ford
Fastest lap: R. Patrese
   139.67 kph / 85.79 mph
Pole position: R. Arnoux (Renault)

Detroit GP

6 June: Detroit
312 km / 194 miles
1 J. Watson   McLaren-Ford
   125.85 kph / 78.20 mph
2 E. Cheever   Talbot-Matra
3 D. Pironi   Ferrari
4 K. Rosberg   Williams-Ford
5 D. Daly   Williams-Ford
6 J. Laffite   Talbot-Matra
Fastest lap: A. Prost (Renault)
   130.80 kph / 81.28 mph
Pole position: A. Prost

Canadian GP

13 June: Montreal
309 km / 192 miles
1 N. Piquet   Brabham-BMW
   173.70 kph / 107.94 mph
2 R. Patrese   Brabham-Ford
3 J. Watson   McLaren-Ford
4 E. de Angelis   Lotus-Ford
5 M. Surer   Arrows-Ford
6 A. de Cesaris   Alfa Romeo
Fastest lap: D. Pironi (Ferrari)
   179.75 kph / 111.70 mph
Pole position: D. Pironi

Dutch GP

3 July: Zandvoort
306 km / 190 miles
1 D. Pironi   Ferrari
   187.30 kph / 116.39 mph
2 N. Piquet   Brabham-BMW
3 K. Rosberg   Williams-Ford
4 N. Lauda   McLaren-Ford
5 D. Daly   Williams-Ford
6 M. Baldi   Arrows-Ford
Fastest lap: D. Warwick
   (Toleman-Hart)
   191.87 kph / 119.23 mph
Pole position: R. Arnoux (Renault)

British GP

18 July: Brands Hatch
320 km / 199 miles
1 N. Lauda   McLaren-Ford
   200.69 kph / 124.71 mph
2 D. Pironi   Ferrari
3 P. Tambay   Ferrari
4 E. de Angelis   Lotus-Ford
5 D. Daly   Williams-Ford
6 A. Prost   Renault
Fastest lap: B. Henton (Tyrrell-Ford)
   207.35 kph / 128.85 mph
Pole position: K. Rosberg
   (Williams-Ford)

French GP

25 July: Paul Ricard
302 km / 188 miles
1 R. Arnoux   Renault
   201.20 kph / 125.03 mph
2 A. Prost   Renault
3 D. Pironi   Ferrari
4 P. Tambay   Ferrari
5 K. Rosberg   Williams-Ford
6 M. Alboreto   Tyrrell-Ford
Fastest lap: R. Patrese
   (Brabham-BMW)
   209.01 kph / 129.88 mph
Pole position: R. Arnoux

German GP

8 August: Hockenheim
306 km / 190 miles
1 P. Tambay   Ferrari
   209.90 kph / 130.43 mph
2 R. Arnoux   Renault
3 K. Rosberg   Williams-Ford
4 M. Alboreto   Tyrrell-Ford
5 B. Giacomelli   Alfa Romeo
6 M. Surer   Arrows-Ford
Fastest lap: N. Piquet
   (Brabham-BMW)
   214.58 kph / 133.34 mph
Pole position: D. Pironi (Ferrari)
   did not start

Austrian GP

15 August: Osterreichring
315 km / 196 miles
1 E. de Angelis   Lotus-Ford
   222.10 kph / 138.01 mph
2 K. Rosberg   Williams-Ford
3 J. Laffite   Talbot-Matra
4 P. Tambay   Ferrari
5 N. Lauda   McLaren-Ford
6 M. Baldi   Arrows-Ford
Fastest lap: N. Piquet
   (Brabham-BMW)
   228.32 kph / 141.88 mph
Pole position: N. Piquet

Swiss GP

29 August: Dijon-Prenois
304 km / 189 miles
1 K. Rosberg   Williams-Ford
   196.80 kph / 122.29 mph
2 A. Prost   Renault
3 N. Lauda   McLaren-Ford
4 N. Piquet   Brabham-BMW
5 R. Patrese   Brabham-BMW
6 E. de Angelis   Lotus-Ford
Fastest lap: A. Prost
   202.74 kph / 125.98 mph
Pole position: A. Prost

Italian GP

12 September: Monza
302 km / 188 miles
1 R. Arnoux   Renault
   219.50 kph / 136.40
2 P. Tambay   Ferrari
3 M. Andretti   Ferrari
4 J. Watson   McLaren-Ford
5 M. Alboreto   Tyrrell-Ford
6 E. Cheever   Talbot-Matra
Fastest lap: R. Arnoux
   223.03 kph / 138.59 mph
Pole position: M. Andretti

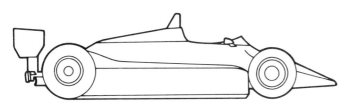

1982 Williams FW08

Las Vegas GP

25 September: Las Vegas
274 km / 170 miles
1 M. Alboreto   Tyrrell-Ford
     161.09 kph / 100.10 mph
2 J. Watson   McLaren-Ford
3 E. Cheever   Talbot-Matra
4 A. Prost   Renault
5 K. Rosberg   Williams-Ford
6 D. Daly   Williams-Ford
Fastest lap: M. Alboreto
     164.99 kph / 102.52 mph
Pole position: A. Prost

World Drivers' Championship

Pts	Driver	Wins	
44	Keke Rosberg (FIN)	1	Swiss GP
39	John Watson (GB)	2	Belgian GP, Detroit GP
39	Didier Pironi (FRA)	2	San Marino GP, Dutch GP
34	Alain Prost (FRA)	2	South African GP, Brazilian GP
30	Niki Lauda (AUT)	2	United States GP (West), British GP
28	Rene Arnoux (FRA)	2	French GP, Italian GP
25	Michele Alboreto (ITA)	1	Las Vegas GP
25	Patrick Tambay (FRA)	1	German GP
23	Elio de Angelis (ITA)	1	Austrian GP
21	Riccardo Patrese (ITA)	1	Monaco GP
20	Nelson Piquet (BRA)	1	Canadian GP
15	Eddie Cheever (USA)	–	
8	Derek Daly (IRE)	–	
7	Nigel Mansell (GB)	–	
6	Carlos Reutemann (ARG)	–	
6	Gilles Villeneuve (CAN)	–	
5	Andrea de Cesaris (ITA)	–	
5	Jacques Laffite (FRA)	–	
4	Mario Andretti (USA)	–	
3	Jean-Pierre Jarier (FRA)	–	
3	Marc Surer (SWI)	–	
2	Manfred Winkelhock (FRG)	–	
2	Eliseo Salazar (CHI)	–	
2	Bruno Giacomelli (ITA)	–	
2	Mauro Baldi (ITA)	–	
1	Chico Serra (BRA)	–	

Points scoring: First six drivers in each race to score.
Points as follows: 9–6–4–3–2–1. All scores from 16 rounds to count.

Above left The first of Elio de Angelis's two Grand Prix wins was in a Lotus-Ford at the Osterreichring in 1982. (The Goodyear Tyre & Rubber Co. Ltd.)

Above Keke Rosberg (FIN) won the world championship in 1982 despite only winning one race, the Swiss Grand Prix at Dijon-Prenois in France. (The Goodyear Tyre & Rubber Co. Ltd.)

Constructors' Cup

Pts	Manufacturer	Wins	
74	Ferrari	3	San Marino GP, Dutch GP, German GP
67	McLaren-Ford	4	United States GP (West), Belgian GP, Detroit GP, British GP
62	Renault	4	South African GP, Brazilian GP, French GP, Italian GP
58	Williams-Ford	1	Swiss GP
30	Lotus-Ford	1	Austrian GP
25	Tyrrell-Ford	1	Las Vegas GP
22	Brabham-BMW	1	Canadian GP
20	Talbot Ligier-Matra	–	
19	Brabham-Ford	1	Monaco GP
7	Alfa Romeo	–	
5	Arrows-Ford	–	
4	ATS-Ford	–	
3	Osella-Ford	–	
1	Fittipaldi-Ford	–	

Points scoring: First six cars in each race to score, results from all 16 rounds counted. Points: 9–6–4–3–2–1.

Jack Brabham

When 40-year-old Australian Jack Brabham won the World Championship in 1966, he became the first man to win the title in a car manufactured by himself and it reaped the rewards of a gamble he took five years earlier when he left Cooper to develop his own Grand Prix car.

John Arthur Brabham was the son of a Sydney greengrocer, born in 1926. He had a love of cars at a very early age and after serving as an engineer in the Royal Australian Air Force during the war, he started racing midget cars in his home country, winning the Australian Midget Car Champion-ship in the five years between 1947–51. He then turned to road racing in a Cooper and continued his run of success.

He toured Britain in 1955 and competed in the British Grand Prix at Aintree but had to retire after 34 laps in his Cooper-Bristol that was just not up to the task of Formula One racing against the likes of Moss and Fangio's Mercedes.

Unperturbed by the experience, Brabham saw his future in England and returned with his wife in 1957 to set up home. Naturally, he joined the Cooper Grand Prix team and he was to spearhead their revolutionary rear-engined attack on the World Champion-ship. Not only did he bring his delightful driving skills to the team but also his vast engineering knowledge and the two combined to make Cooper one of the leading forces in Grand Prix racing for several years.

Brabham's first Grand Prix success came in the 1959 Monaco Grand Prix, followed by another win in the British Grand Prix at Aintree. This, plus a season of consistent driving gave Brabham the world title and Cooper the

Brabham, as he is best remembered — with the determination showing in his face. He is behind the wheel of a Cooper-Climax in the 1960 Portuguese Grand Prix, which the Australian won by nearly a minute from team-mate Bruce McLaren. (National Motor Museum)

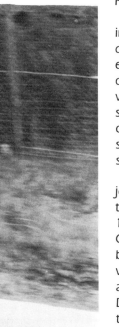

Constructors' Championship. They repeated the performance in 1960 when Brabham won five consecutive races in Holland, Belgium, France, England and Portugal.

Brabham has maintained his high level of a success as a manufacturer and Nelson Piquet (BRA) was the team's last world champion in 1981 and 1983

He only collected four points in the 1961 championship and decided to leave Cooper at the end of the season to develop his own Grand Prix car. The decision was bold, but Brabham was a shrewd businessman and he could adequately back his decision with his own engineering skills.

Fellow Australian Ron Tauranac joined him as chief designer and the first Brabham car was ready in 1962. It made its debut at the German Grand Prix at the Nurburgring with Jack behind the wheel, but he was forced to retire after nine laps. Two years later Dan Gurney (USA) provided the team with its first victory when he won the French Grand Prix with Brabham himself in third place. Brabham eventually had his first success in his own car in the 1966 French Grand Prix, shortly before which he had been awarded the OBE for his services to the sport. He went on to win the British, Dutch and German Grands Prix to clinch that season's championship by 14 points from John Surtees (GB).

Brabhams dominated the sport in 1967, with New Zealander Denny Hulme winning the world title and Brabham five points behind in second place. Since then Nelson Piquet (Bra) has provided the team with further World Championships, in 1981 and 1983.

Brabham, the quiet, shy Australian, who was the first man from the Antipodes to break into Grand Prix racing, retired from driving in 1970 with 123 Formula One Grand Prix starts to his credit and 14 victories.

1983

Brazilian GP

13 March: Rio de Janeiro
317 km / 197 miles
1 N. Piquet   Brabham-BMW
   175.30 kph / 108.93 mph
2 K. Rosberg*   Williams-Ford
3 N. Lauda   McLaren-Ford
4 J. Laffite   Williams-Ford
5 P. Tambay   Ferrari
6 M. Surer   Arrows-Ford
* Subsequently disqualified
Fastest lap: N. Piquet
   181.43 kph / 112.74 mph
Pole position: K. Rosberg

United States GP (West)

27 March: Long Beach
246 km / 153 miles
1 J. Watson   McLaren-Ford
   129.79 kph / 80.65 mph
2 N. Lauda   McLaren-Ford
3 R. Arnoux   Ferrari
4 J. Laffite   Williams-Ford
5 M. Surer   Arrows-Ford
6 J. Cecotto   Theodore-Ford
Fastest lap: N. Lauda
   133.48kph / 82.94 mph
Pole position: P. Tambay (Ferrari)

French GP

17 April: Paul Ricard
314 km / 195 miles
1 A. Prost   Renault
   199.87 kph / 124.20 mph
2 N. Piquet   Brabham-BMW
3 E. Cheever   Renault
4 P. Tambay   Ferrari
5 K. Rosberg   Williams-Ford
6 J. Laffite   Williams-Ford
Fastest lap: A. Prost
   203.67 kph / 126.57 mph
Pole position: A. Prost

San Marino GP

1 May: Imola
302 km / 188 miles
1 P. Tambay   Ferrari
   185.48 kph / 115.26 mph
2 A. Prost   Renault
3 R. Arnoux   Ferrari
4 K. Rosberg   Williams-Ford
5 J. Watson   McLaren-Ford
6 M. Surer   Arrows-Ford
Fastest lap: R. Patrese
   (Brabham-BMW)
   192.13 kph / 119.39 mph
Pole position: R. Arnoux

Monaco GP

15 May: Monte Carlo
252 km / 156 miles
1 K. Rosberg   Williams-Ford
   129.59 kph / 80.52 mph
2 N. Piquet   Brabham-BMW
3 A. Prost   Renault
4 P. Tambay   Ferrari
5 D. Sullivan   Tyrrell-Ford
6 M. Baldo   Alfa Romeo
Fastest lap: N. Piquet
   136.61 kph / 84.89 mph
Pole position: A. Prost

Belgian GP

22 May: Spa
278 km / 172 miles
1 A. Prost   Renault
   191.73 kph / 119.14 mph
2 P. Tambay   Ferrari
3 E. Cheever   Renault
4 N. Piquet   Brabham-BMW
5 K. Rosberg   Williams-Ford
6 J. Laffite   Williams-Ford
Fastest lap: A. de Cesaris
   (Alfa Romeo)
   196.22 kph / 121.93 mph
Pole position: A. Prost

Detroit GP

5 June: Detroit
241 km / 154 miles
1 M. Alboreto   Tyrrell-Ford
   130.41 kph / 81.04 mph
2 K. Rosberg   Williams-Ford
3 J. Watson   McLaren-Ford
4 N. Piquet   Brabham-BMW
5 J. Laffite   Williams-Ford
6 N. Mansell   Lotus-Ford
Fastest lap: J. Watson
   134.53 kph / 83.60 mph
Pole position: R. Arnoux (Ferrari)

Canadian GP

12 June: Montreal
309 km / 192 miles
1 R. Arnoux   Ferrari
   170.66 kph / 106.05 mph
2 E. Cheever   Renault
3 P. Tambay   Ferrari
4 K. Rosberg   Williams-Ford
5 A. Prost   Renault
6 J. Watson   McLaren-Ford
Fastest lap: P. Tambay
   174.75 kph / 108.59 mph
Pole position: R. Arnoux

British GP

16 July: Silverstone
316 km / 196 miles
1 A. Prost   Renault
   224.05 kph / 139.22 mph
2 N. Piquet   Brabham-BMW
3 P. Tambay   Ferrari
4 N. Mansell   Lotus-Renault
5 R. Arnoux   Ferrari
6 N. Lauda   McLaren-Ford
Fastest lap: A. Prost
   228.90 kph / 142.24 mph
Pole position: R. Arnoux

German GP

7 August: Hockenheim
306km / 190 miles
1 R. Arnoux   Ferrari
   210.52 kph / 130.82 mph
2 A. de Cesaris   Alfa Romeo
3 R. Patrese   Brabham-BMW
4 A. Prost   Renault
5 N. Lauda   McLaren-Ford
6 J. Watson   McLaren-Ford
Fastest lap: R. Arnoux
   214.76 kph / 133.45 mph
Pole position: P. Tambay (Ferrari)

Austrian GP

14 August: Osterreichring
315 km / 196 miles
1 A. Prost   Renault
   223.49 kph / 138.88 mph
2 R. Arnoux   Ferrari
3 N. Piquet   Brabham-BMW
4 E. Cheever   Renault
5 N. Mansell   Lotus-Renault
6 N. Lauda   McLaren-Ford
Fastest lap: A. Prost
   227.66 kph / 141.47 mph
Pole position: P. Tambay (Ferrari)

Dutch GP

28 August: Zandvoort
306 km / 190 miles
1 R. Arnoux   Ferrari
   186.10 kph / 115.64 mph
2 P. Tambay   Ferrari
3 J. Watson   McLaren-Ford
4 D. Warwick   Toleman-Hart
5 M. Baldi   Alfa Romeo
6 M. Alboreto   Tyrrell-Ford
Fastest lap: R. Arnoux
   191.67 kph / 119.10 mph
Pole position: N. Piquet
   (Brabham-BMW)

Italian GP

11 September: Monza
302 km / 187 miles
1 N. Piquet   Brabham-BMW
   217.55 kph / 135.19 mph
2 R. Arnoux   Ferrari
3 E. Cheever   Renault
4 P. Tambay   Ferrari
5 E. de Angelis   Lotus-Renault
6 D. Warwick   Toleman-Hart
Fastest lap: N. Piquet
   221.11 kph / 137.40 mph
Pole position: R. Patrese
   (Brabham-BMW)

European GP

25 September: Brands Hatch
320 km / 199 miles
1 N. Piquet   Brabham-BMW
   198.21 kph / 123.17 mph
2 A. Prost   Renault
3 N. Mansell   Lotus-Renault
4 A. de Cesaris   Alfa Romeo
5 D. Warwick   Toleman-Hart
6 B. Giacomelli   Toleman-Hart
Fastest lap: N. Mansell
   203.68 kph / 126.57 mph
Pole position: E. de Angelis
   (Lotus-Renault)

South African GP

16 October: Kyalami
316 km / 196 miles
1 R. Patrese   Brabham-BMW
   202.94 kph / 126.11
2 A. de Cesaris   Alfa Romeo
3 N. Piquet   Brabham-BMW
4 D. Warwick   Toleman-Hart
5 K. Rosberg   Williams-Honda
6 E. Cheever   Renault
Fastest lap: N. Piquet
   211.22 kph / 131.25 mph
Pole position: P. Tambay (Ferrari)

Constructors' Cup

Pts	Manufacturer		Wins	
89	Ferrari		4	San Marino GP, Canadian GP, German GP, Dutch GP
79	Renault		4	French GP, Belgian GP, British GP, Austrian GP
72	Brabham-BMW		4	Brazilian GP, Italian GP, European GP, South African GP
36	Williams-Ford		1	Monaco GP
34	McLaren-Ford		1	Long Beach GP
18	Alfa Romeo		–	
12	Tyrrell-Ford		1	Detroit GP
11	Lotus-Renault		–	
10	Toleman-Hart		–	
4	Arrows-Ford		–	
2	Williams-Honda		–	
1	Theodore-Ford		–	
1	Lotus-Ford		–	

Points scoring: First six cars in each race to score, results from all 15 rounds counted. Points: 9–6–4–3–2–1.

World Drivers' Championship

Pts	Driver		Wins	
59	Nelson Piquet (BRA)		3	Brazilian GP, Italian GP, European GP
57	Alain Prost (FRA)		4	French GP, Belgian GP, British GP, Austrian GP
49	Rene Arnoux (FRA)		3	Canadian GP, German GP, Dutch GP
40	Patrick Tambay (FRA)		1	San Marino GP
27	Keke Rosberg (FIN)		1	Monaco GP
22	John Watson (GB)		1	Long Beach GP
22	Eddie Cheever (USA)		–	
15	Andrea de Cesaris (ITA)		–	
13	Riccardo Patrese (ITA)		1	South African GP
12	Niki Lauda (AUT)		–	
11	Jacques Laffite (FRA)		–	
10	Michele Alboreto (ITA)		1	Detroit GP
10	Nigel Mansell (GB)		–	
9	Derek Warwick (GB)		–	
4	Marc Surer (SWI)		–	
3	Mauro Baldi (ITA)		–	
2	Elio de Angelis (ITA)		–	
2	Danny Sullivan (USA)		–	
1	Johnny Cecotto (VEN)		–	
1	Bruno Giacomelli (ITA)		–	

Points scoring: First six drivers in each race to score. Points as follows: 9–6–4–3–2–1. Points from 15 rounds to count.

1983 Brabham BT52

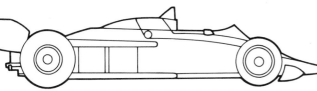

1984

Brazilian GP

25 March: Rio de Janeiro
307 km / 191 miles
1 A. Prost   McLaren-Porsche
   179.51 kph / 111.55 mph
2 K. Rosberg   Williams-Honda
3 E. de Angelis   Lotus-Renault
4 E. Cheever   Alfa Romeo
5 M. Brundle   Tyrrell-Ford
6 P. Tambay   Renault
Fastest lap: A. Prost
   187.69 mph / 116.63 mph
Pole position: E. de Angelis

South African GP

7 April: Kyalami
308 km / 191 miles
1 N. Lauda   McLaren-Porsche
   206.59 kph / 128.38 mph
2 A. Prost   McLaren-Porsche
3 D. Warwick   Renault
4 R. Patrese   Alfa Romeo
5 A. de Cesaris   Ligier-Renault
6 A. Senna   Toleman-Hart
Fastest lap: P. Tambay (Renault)
   214.49 kph / 133.28 mph
Pole position: N. Piquet
   (Brabham-BMW)

Belgian GP

29 April: Zolder
298 km / 185 miles
1 M. Alboreto   Ferrari
   185.43 kph / 115.23 mph
2 D. Warwick   Renault
3 R. Arnoux   Ferrari
4 K. Rosberg   Williams-Honda
5 E. de Angelis   Lotus-Renault
6 S. Bellof   Tyrrell-Ford
Fastest lap: R. Arnoux
   193.50 kph / 120.24 mph
Pole position: M. Alboreto

San Marino GP

6 May: Imola
302 km / 188 miles
1 A. Prost   McLaren-Porsche
   187.25 kph / 116.36 mph
2 R. Arnoux   Ferrari
3 E. de Angelis   Lotus-Renault
4 D. Warwick   Renault
5 S. Bellof   Tyrrell-Ford
6 T. Boutsen   Arrows-Ford
Fastest lap: N. Piquet
   (Brabham-BMW)
   194.52 kph / 120.87 mph
Pole position: N. Piquet

French GP

20 May: Dijon-Prenois
307 km / 191 miles
1 N. Lauda   McLaren-Porsche
   202.02 kph / 125.54 mph
2 P. Tambay   Renault
3 N. Mansell   Lotus-Renault
4 R. Arnoux   Ferrari
5 E. de Angelis   Lotus-Renault
6 K. Rosberg   Williams-Honda
Fastest lap: A. Prost
   (McLaren-Porsche)
   214.43 kph / 133.25 mph
Pole position: P. Tambay

Monaco GP

3 June: Monte Carlo
103 km / 64 miles
1 A. Prost   McLaren-Porsche
   100.78 kph / 62.62 mph
2 A. Senna   Toleman-Hart
3 S. Bellof   Tyrrell-Ford
4 R. Arnoux   Ferrari
5 K. Rosberg   Williams-Honda
6 E. de Angelis   Lotus-Renault
shortened race, only half points at stake
Fastest lap: A. Senna
   104.28 kph / 64.80 mph
Pole position: A. Prost

Canadian GP

17 June: Montreal
309 km / 192 miles
1 N. Piquet   Brabham-BMW
   174.09 kph / 108.18 mph
2 N. Lauda   McLaren-Porsche
3 A. Prost   McLaren-Porsche
4 E. de Angelis   Lotus-Renault
5 R. Arnoux   Ferrari
6 N. Mansell   Lotus-Renault
Fastest lap: N. Piquet
   178.86 kph / 111.14 mph
Pole position: N. Piquet

1984 McLaren MP4/2

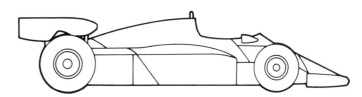

Detroit GP

24 June: Detroit
253 km / 157 miles
1 N. Piquet   Brabham-BMW
   131.45 kph / 81.68 mph
2 M. Brundle   Tyrrell-Ford
3 E. de Angelis   Lotus-Renault
4 T. Fabi   Brabham-BMW
5 A. Prost   McLaren-Porsche
6 J. Laffite   Williams-Honda
Fastest lap: D. Warwick (Renault)
   136.36 kph / 84.73 mph
Pole position: N. Piquet

Dallas GP

8 July: Fir Park
261 km / 162 miles
1 K. Rosberg   Williams-Honda
   129.22 kph / 80.30 mph
2 R. Arnoux   Ferrari
3 E. de Angelis   Lotus-Renault
4 J. Laffite   Williams-Honda
5 P. Ghinzani   Osella-Alfa
6 N. Mansell   Lotus-Renault
Fastest lap: N. Lauda
   (McLaren-Porsche)
   133.30 kph / 82.83 mph
Pole position: N. Mansell

British GP

22 July: Brands Hatch
299 km / 186 miles
1 N. Lauda   McLaren-Porsche
   200.21 kph / 124.41 mph
2 D. Warwick   Renault
3 A. Senna   Toleman-Hart
4 E. de Angelis   Lotus-Renault
5 M. Alboreto   Ferrari
6 R. Arnoux   Ferrari
Fastest lap: N. Lauda
   206.83 kph / 128.52 mph
Pole position: N. Piquet
   (Brabham-BMW)

German GP

5 August: Hockenheim
299 km / 186 miles
1 A. Prost   McLaren-Porsche
   211.80 kph / 131.61 mph
2 N. Lauda   McLaren-Porsche
3 D. Warwick   Renault
4 N. Mansell   Lotus-Renault
5 P. Tambay   Renault
6 R. Arnoux   Ferrari
Fastest lap: A. Prost
   215.52 kph / 133.92 mph
Pole position: A. Prost

Austrian GP

19 August: Osterreichring
303 km / 188 miles
1 N. Lauda   McLaren-Porsche
   223.88 kph / 139.12 mph
2 N. Piquet   Brabham-BMW
3 M. Alboreto   Ferrari
4 T. Fabi   Brabham-BMW
5 T. Boutsen   Arrows-BMW
6 M. Surer   Arrows-BMW
Fastest lap: N. Lauda
   230.31 kph / 143.11 mph
Pole position: N. Piquet

Dutch GP

26 August: Zandvoort
302 km / 188 miles
1 A. Prost   McLaren-Porsche
   186.05 kph / 115.61 mph
2 N. Lauda   McLaren-Porsche
3 N. Mansell   Lotus-Renault
4 E. de Angelis   Lotus-Renault
5 T. Fabi   Brabham-BMW
6 P. Tambay   Renault
Fastest lap: R. Arnoux (Ferrari)
   192.63 kph / 119.70 mph
Pole position: A. Prost

Italian GP

9 September: Monza
296 km / 184 miles
1 N. Lauda   McLaren-Porsche
   220.51 kph / 137.02 mph
2 M. Alboreto   Ferrari
3 R. Patrese   Alfa Romeo
4 S. Johansson   Toleman-Hart
5 J. Gartner   Osella-Alfa
6 G. Berger   ATS-BMW
Fastest lap: N. Lauda
   227.17 kph / 141.16 mph
Pole position: N. Piquet
   (Brabham-BMW)

European GP

7 October: Nurburgring
304 km / 189 miles
1 A. Prost   McLaren-Porsche
   191.75 kph / 119.15 mph
2 M. Alboreto   Ferrari
3 N. Piquet   Brabham-BMW
4 N. Lauda   McLaren-Porsche
5 R. Arnoux   Ferrari
6 R. Patrese   Alfa Romeo
Fastest lap: N. Piquet
   196.66 kph / 122.20 mph
Pole position: N. Piquet

Portuguese GP

21 October: Estoril
298 km / 186 miles
1 A. Prost   McLaren-Porsche
   180.54 kph / 112.19 mph
2 N. Lauda   McLaren-Porsche
3 A. Senna   Toleman-Hart
4 M. Alboreto   Ferrari
5 E. de Angelis   Lotus-Renault
6 N. Piquet   Brabham-BMW
Fastest lap: N. Lauda
   188.68 kph / 117.25 mph
Pole position: N. Piquet

World Drivers' Championship

Pts	Driver	Wins
72	Niki Lauda (AUT)	5 South African GP, French GP, British GP, Austrian GP, Italian GP
71½	Alain Prost (FRA)	7 Brazilian GP, San Marino GP, Monaco GP*, German GP, Dutch GP, European GP, Portuguese GP
34	Elio de Angelis (ITA)	–
30½	Michele Alboreto (ITA)	1 Belgian GP
29	Nelson Piquet (BRA)	2 Canadian GP, Detroit GP
27	Rene Arnoux (FRA)	–
23	Derek Warwick (GB)	–
20½	Keke Rosberg (FIN)	1 Dallas GP
13	Nigel Mansell (GB)	–
13	Ayrton Senna (BRA)	–
11	Patrick Tambay (FRA)	–
9	Teo Fabi (ITA)	–
8	Riccardo Patrese (ITA)	–
5	Jacques Laffite (FRA)	–
5	Thierry Boutsen (BEL)	–
3	Eddie Cheever (USA)	–
3	Andrea de Cesaris (ITA)	–
3	Stefan Johansson (SWE)	–
2	Piercarlo Ghinzani (ITA)	–
1	Marc Surer (SWI)	–

* Only half points awarded
Points scoring: First six drivers in each race to score. Points as follows: 9–6–4–3–2–1. Scores from 16 rounds to count.

Constructors' Cup

Pts	Manufacturer	Wins
143½	McLaren-Porsche	12 Brazilian GP, South African GP, San Marino GP, French GP, Monaco GP*, British GP, German GP, Austrian GP, Dutch GP, Italian GP, European GP, Portuguese GP
57½	Ferrari	1 Belgian GP
47	Lotus-Renault	–
38	Brabham-BMW	2 Canadian GP, Detroit GP
34	Renault	–
25½	Williams-Honda	1 Dallas GP
16	Toleman-Hart	–
11	Alfa Romeo	–
5	Arrows-BMW	–
3	Ligier-Renault	–
2	Osella-Alfa	–
1	Arrows-Ford	–

* Half points only awarded
Points scoring: First six cars in each race to score, results from all 16 rounds counted. Points: 9–6–4–3–2–1.

Lauda v Prost

Not since the early days of the World Championship, when Alfa Romeo and Ferrari dominated, has the championship been dominated by one team as in 1984, when the Marlboro-McLaren pair of Niki Lauda (Aut) and Alain Prost (Fra) monopolized the 16-race series.

Between them they won 12 of the races and no fewer than four times did they occupy the first two places. There were only two occasions, at Zolder and Dallas, where neither driver picked up a championship point.

It all started in Brazil on 25 March when Prost was the first of the two to register a win. Lauda picked up no points but had a win to Prost's second in the next race at Kyalami. After a fruitless race at Zolder, Prost pulled away from his team-mate with a win at Imola but at Dijon it was Lauda's turn for a victory and he closed the gap once more. But Prost, who joined the team as a replacement for Britain's John Watson at the end of 1983, was looking for his first world title after narrowly losing to Nelson Piquet in his last season with Renault, and he extended his championship lead over Lauda to 10½ points after winning at Monte Carlo, when only half points were awarded after the race was stopped because of bad weather.

After the next two races, in Montreal and Detroit, Prost still led Lauda by 10½ points with half the championship gone.

Neither picked up points in the next race at Dallas but then Lauda won the British Grand Prix at Brands Hatch with the Frenchman not scoring, and so the gap was down to 1½ points. Prost held on to beat Lauda into second place at Hockenheim and gain three

Prost leads the Dutch Grand Prix at Zandvoort. He went on to win the race with Lauda second to register the team's ninth win of the season, and their third 1–2. (McLaren International)

points on the Austrian but Lauda then took the lead for the first time in the championship, when he won at the Osterreichring after Prost spun off on the 41st lap. Prost got back to winning ways at Zandvoort, but by finishing second, Lauda still held on to a slim 1½ point lead.

At Monza, Lauda won his fifth race of the season while Prost was again out of the points and, with just two races remaining, Lauda was favourite to win his third title. Prost won at the New Nurburgring with Lauda fourth and with one race left Lauda had 66 points to Prost's 61½. But, just before the final race of the season at Estoril, F.I.S.A. added one point to Prost's total after the disqualification of Martin Brundle in the Detroit Grand Prix, four months earlier. Therefore, going into the final race Prost was 3½ points behind. A win for the Frenchman would give him nine points and, provided Lauda finished third or worse, thus collecting no more than four points, the title would be Prost's.

Prost was on the front row of the grid at Estoril, alongside the Brabham of Piquet—the man who pipped him for the 1983 title in the final race. Lauda was struggling on the sixth row of the grid.

Prost got the lead when he went past the Williams of Keke Rosberg on lap 9, and he was to remain at the head of the field for the remaining 61 laps. The championship was in the hands of Lauda. He kept on picking off opponent after opponent and on lap 33 went into third place. But he still needed to move up another place and when Nigel Mansell (GB) went into the pits on lap 51, Lauda moved into second place. Prost was aware of what was happening behind him but was powerless to do anything. The Frenchman won the race, and the determined Austrian finished second to win his third title by the smallest of margins, half a point.

The triumph of both drivers was a testament to the great team, particularly manager Ron Dennis and designer John Bernard, who had worked so well together since 1979. Their efforts and hard work had produced machines for two men, both capable of winning the world title. Sadly for McLaren, and Prost, there had to be a runner-up.

The Honda Dream

After dominating the world of international motor cycling in the early 60s, Honda president Soichiro Honda decided to build Formula One racing cars. The competition, however, was much fiercer than that of the motor bike world and their dream only lasted for five seasons.

The first Honda-designed car was a sleek model with a transverse mounting of a V12 engine that had 12 small carburettors and was capable of producing 210 b.h.p. at 12 500 r.p.m. The car was assembled at the company's British headquarters at Slough, and the first Honda car was seen at the Nurburgring in 1964 with American Sports Car exponent Ron Bucknum behind the wheel. The car spun out of the race on the 11th lap, largely because of Bucknum's lack of experience of Formula One cars.

The following year saw a significant improvement when they switched to a fuel-injected engine and also recruited the experienced Richie Ginther (USA) as team-leader. Ginther got the car on the front row of the starting grid several times during the 1965 season and, following sixth placings in the Belgian and Dutch Grands Prix he provided the team with its first win in the final race of the season in Mexico, with Bucknum in fifth place. Ironically, it was to be the final race under the old 1½ litre formula, and Honda started to fall behind the rest of the Formula One manufacturers with the introduction of the 3-litre formula.

Their new car was not seen until the 1966 season was nearly four months old and they made little impact on the championship. In 1967 they recruited the experience of John Surtees and he

scored a surprise win in the Italian Grand Prix at Monza, driving the new Eric Broadley-designed RA300.

Surtees remained with the team in 1968 but a troubled year caused them to pull out of Formula One.

They had introduced their new V8 3-litre car at the French Grand Prix at Rouen and entrusted Frenchman Jo Schlesser with the drive. His inexperience was apparent early on, and on lap three he lost control of the car as it spun off the track, hit a bank and exploded. Schlesser was killed and they never introduced another V8. Surtees completed the season by finishing joint seventh in the championship but at the end of the season the competitive world of Formula One racing had proved too much for the ambitious Japanese manufacturer.

Honda also pulled out of Grand Prix motor cycle racing in 1968. They did return to the two-wheel branch of motor sport and later provided their reliable

It was hoped that the redesigned Honda RA301 would provide success for Honda and team-leader John Surtees in 1968 but their best result was second in the French Grand Prix at Rouen. (National Motor Museum)

engines for Formula Two and Formula Three cars before returning to Formula One in 1983, when they supplied engines for the successful Williams team.

1985

Brazilian GP

7 April: Rio de Janeiro
307 km / 191 miles
1 A. Prost   McLaren-Porsche
   181.53 kph / 112.80 mph
2 M. Alboreto   Ferrari
3 E. de Angelis   Lotus-Renault
4 R. Arnoux   Ferrari
5 P. Tambay   Renault
6 J. Laffite   Ligier-Renault
Fastest lap: A. Prost
   187.29 kph / 116.38 mph
Pole position: M. Alboreto

Portuguese GP

21 April: Estoril
285 km / 181 miles
1 A. Senna   Lotus-Renault
   145.16 kph / 90.20 mph
2 M. Alboreto   Ferrari
3 P. Tambay   Renault
4 E. de Angelis   Lotus-Renault
5 N. Mansell   Williams-Honda
6 S. Bellof   Tyrrell-Ford
Fastest lap: A. Senna
   150.40 kph / 93.46 mph
Pole position: A. Senna

San Marino GP

5 May: Imola
302 km / 188 miles
1 E. de Angelis   Lotus-Renault
   191.80 kph / 119.18 mph
2 T. Boutsen   Arrows-BMW
3 P. Tambay   Renault
4 N. Lauda   McLaren-Porsche
5 N. Mansell   Williams-Honda
6 S. Johansson   Ferrari
Fastest lap: M. Alboreto (Ferrari)
   199.47 kph / 123.95 mph
Pole position: A. Senna
   (Lotus-Renault)

Monaco GP

19 May: Monte Carlo
258 km / 161 miles
1 A. Prost   McLaren-Porsche
   138.43 kph / 86.02 mph
2 M. Alboreto   Ferrari
3 E. de Angelis   Lotus-Renault
4 A. de Cesaris   Ligier-Renault
5 D. Warwick   Renault
6 J. Laffite   Ligier-Renault
Fastest lap: M. Alboreto
   144.28 kph / 89.66 mph
Pole position: A. Senna
   (Lotus-Renault)

Canadian GP

17 June: Montreal
309 km / 192 miles
1 M. Alboreto   Ferrari
   174.69 kph / 108.55 mph
2 S. Johansson   Ferrari
3 A. Prost   McLaren-Porsche
4 K. Rosberg   Williams-Honda
5 E. de Angelis   Lotus-Renault
6 N. Mansell   Williams-Honda
Fastest lap: A. Senna (Lotus-Renault)
   181.55 kph / 112.82 mph
Pole position: E. de Angelis

Detroit GP

23 June: Detroit
253 km / 161 miles
1 K. Rosberg   Williams-Honda
   131.49 kph / 81.71 mph
2 S. Johansson   Ferrari
3 M. Alboreto   Ferrari
4 S. Bellof   Tyrrell-Ford
5 E. de Angelis   Lotus-Renault
6 N. Piquet   Brabham-BMW
Fastest lap: A. Senna (Lotus-Renault)
   137.13 kph / 85.21 mph
Pole position: A. Senna

French GP

7 July: Paul Ricard
308 km / 191 miles
1 N. Piquet   Brabham-BMW
   201.32 kph / 125.10 mph
2 K. Rosberg   Williams-Honda
3 A. Prost   McLaren-Porsche
4 S. Johansson   Ferrari
5 E. de Angelis   Lotus-Renault
6 P. Tambay   Renault
Fastest lap: K. Rosberg
   209.34 kph / 130.08 mph
Pole position: K. Rosberg

British GP

21 July: Silverstone
307 km / 191 miles
1 A. Prost   McLaren-Porsche
   235.40 kph / 146.28 mph
2 M. Alboreto   Ferrari
3 J. Laffite   Ligier-Renault
4 N. Piquet   Brabham-BMW
5 D. Warwick   Renault
6 M. Surer   Brabham-BMW
Fastest lap: A. Prost
   243.07 kph / 151.04 mph
Pole position: K. Rosberg
   (Williams-Honda)

German GP

4 August: Nurburgring
304 km / 187 miles
1 M. Alboreto   Ferrari
   191.15 kph / 118.78 mph
2 A. Prost   McLaren-Porsche
3 J. Laffite   Ligier-Renault
4 T. Boutsen   Arrows-BMW
5 N. Lauda   McLaren-Porsche
6 N. Mansell   Williams-Honda
Fastest lap: N. Lauda
   197.46 kph / 122.70 mph
Pole position: T. Fabi (Toleman-Hart)

Austrian GP

18 August: Osterreichring
309 km / 193 miles
1 A. Prost   McLaren-Porsche
   231.13 kph / 143.62 mph
2 A. Senna   Lotus-Renault
3 M. Alboreto   Ferrari
4 S. Johansson   Ferrari
5 E. de Angelis   Lotus-Renault
6 M. Surer   Brabham-BMW
Fastest lap: A. Prost
   239.70 kph / 148.95 mph
Pole position: A. Prost

Dutch GP

25 August: Zandvoort
298 km / 185 miles
1 N. Lauda   McLaren-Porsche
   193.09 kph / 119.99 mph
2 A. Prost   McLaren-Porsche
3 A. Senna   Lotus-Renault
4 M. Alboreto   Ferrari
5 E. de Angelis   Lotus-Renault
6 N. Mansell   Williams-Honda
Fastest lap: A. Prost
   199.99 kph / 124.27 mph
Pole position: N. Piquet
   (Brabham-BMW)

The Arrows Racing team made their Formula One debut in 1978 and have still to win a Grand Prix. Thierry Boutsen, however, came close when he finished second in the 1985 San Marino Grand Prix. (Arrows Racing Team Ltd.)

Italian GP

8 September: Monza
296 km / 184 miles
1 A. Prost   McLaren-Porsche
   227.57 kph / 141.41 mph
2 N. Piquet   Brabham-BMW
3 A. Senna   Lotus-Renault
4 M. Surer   Brabham-BMW
5 S. Johansson   Ferrari
6 E. de Angelis   Lotus-Renault
Fastest lap: N. Mansell
   (Williams-Honda)
   236.51 kph / 146.97 mph
Pole position: A. Senna

Belgian GP

15 September: Spa
296 km / 186 miles
1 A. Senna   Lotus-Renault
   189.81 kph / 117.95 mph
2 N. Mansell   Williams-Honda
3 A. Prost   McLaren-Porsche
4 K. Rosberg   Williams-Honda
5 N. Piquet   Brabham-BMW
6 D. Warwick   Renault
Fastest lap: A. Prost
   205.24 kph / 127.54 mph
Pole position: A. Prost

European GP

6 October: Brands Hatch
316 km / 196 miles
1 N. Mansell   Williams-Honda
   203.63 kph / 126.54 mph
2 A. Senna   Lotus-Renault
3 K. Rosberg   Williams-Honda
4 A. Prost   McLaren-Porsche
5 E. de Angelis   Lotus-Renault
6 T. Boutsen   Arrows-BMW
Fastest lap: J. Laffite (Ligier-Renault)
   211.73 kph / 131.57 mph
Pole position: A. Senna

South African GP

19 October: Kyalami
308 km / 191 miles
1 N. Mansell   Williams-Honda
   208.96 kph / 129.85 mph
2 K. Rosberg   Williams-Honda
3 A. Prost   McLaren-Porsche
4 S. Johansson   Ferrari
5 G. Berger   Arrows-BMW
6 T. Boutsen   Arrows-BMW
Fastest lap: K. Rosberg
   216.80 kph / 134.72 mph
Pole position: N. Mansell

Australian GP

3 November: Adelaide
310 km / 193 miles
1 K. Rosberg   Williams-Honda
   154.03 kph / 95.71 mph
2 J. Laffite   Ligier-Renault
3 P. Streiff   Ligier-Renault
4 I. Capelli   Tyrrell-Renault
5 S. Johansson   Ferrari
6 G. Berger   Arrows-BMW
Fastest lap: K. Rosberg
   162.38 kph / 100.90 mph
Pole position: A. Senna
   (Lotus-Renault)

World Drivers' Championship

Pts	Driver	Wins	
73	Alain Prost (FRA)	5	Brazilian GP, Monaco GP, British GP, Austrian GP, Italian GP
53	Michele Alboreto (ITA)	2	Canadian GP, German GP
40	Keke Rosberg (FIN)	2	Detroit GP, Australian GP
38	Ayrton Senna (BRA)	2	Portuguese GP, Belgian GP
33	Elio de Angelis (ITA)	1	San Marino GP
31	Nigel Mansell (GB)	2	European GP, South African GP
26	Stefan Johansson (SWE)	–	
21	Nelson Piquet (BRA)	1	French GP
16	Jacques Laffite (FRA)	–	
14	Niki Lauda (AUT)	1	Dutch GP
11	Patrick Tambay (FRA)	–	
11	Thierry Boutsen (BEL)	–	
5	Derek Warwick (GB)	–	
5	Marc Surer (SWI)	–	
4	Stefan Bellof (FRG)	–	
4	Philippe Streiff (FRA)	–	
3	Rene Arnoux (FRA)	–	
3	Andrea de Cesaris (ITA)	–	
3	Gerhard Berger (AUT)	–	
3	Ivan Capelli (ITA)	–	

Points scoring: First six drivers in each race to score. Points as follows: 9–6–4–3–2–1. Scores from 16 rounds to count.

A full house at Brands Hatch for the 1985 European Grand Prix. (Michelin Tyre Co. Ltd.)

Constructors' Cup

Pts	Manufacturer	Wins	
90	McLaren-TAG	6	Brazilian GP, Monaco GP, British GP, Austrian GP, Dutch GP, Italian GP
82	Ferrari	2	Canadian GP, German GP
71	Williams-Honda	4	Detroit GP, European GP, South African GP, Australian GP
71	Lotus-Renault	3	Portuguese GP, San Marino GP, Belgian GP
26	Brabham-BMW	1	French GP
23	Ligier-Renault	–	
16	Renault	–	
14	Arrows-BMW	–	
4	Tyrrell-Ford	–	
3	Tyrrell-Renault	–	

Points scoring: First six cars in each race to score, results from all 16 rounds counted. Points: 9–6–4–3–2–1.

● The first known female racing driver was Mme. Labrouse of Paris who competed in the Tour de France in 1899.

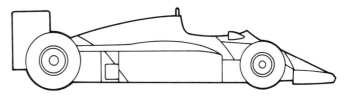

1985 McLaren MP4/2B

1986

Brazilian GP

23 March: Rio de Janeiro
307 km / 191 miles
1 N. Piquet   Williams-Honda
  184.97 kph / 114.94 mph
2 A. Senna   Lotus-Renault
3 J. Laffite   Ligier-Renault
4 R. Arnoux   Ligier-Renault
5 M. Brundle   Tyrrell-Renault
6 G. Berger   Benetton-BMW
Fastest lap: N. Piquet
  193.74 kph / 120.39 mph
Pole position: A. Senna

Spanish GP

13 April: Montjuich
319 km / 189 miles
1 A. Senna   Lotus-Renault
  167.48 kph / 104.07 mph
2 N. Mansell   Williams-Honda
3 A. Prost   McLaren-TAG
4 K. Rosberg   McLaren-TAG
5 T. Fabi   Benetton-BMW
6 G. Berger   Benetton-BMW
Fastest lap: N. Mansell
  174.17 kph / 108.23 mph
Pole position: A. Senna

San Marino GP

27 April: Imola
302 km / 188 miles
1 A. Prost   McLaren-TAG
  196.20 kph / 121.92 mph
2 N. Piquet   Williams-Honda
3 G. Berger   Benetton-BMW
4 S. Johansson   Ferrari
5 K. Rosberg   McLaren-TAG
6 R. Patrese   Brabham-BMW
Fastest lap: N. Piquet
  199.47 kph / 123.95 mph
Pole position: A. Senna
  (Lotus-Renault)

Monaco GP

11 May: Monte Carlo
261 km / 162 miles
1 A. Prost   McLaren-TAG
  134.56 kph / 83.66 mph
2 K. Rosberg   McLaren-TAG
3 A. Senna   Lotus-Renault
4 N. Mansell   Williams-Honda
5 R. Arnoux   Ligier-Renault
6 J. Laffite   Ligier-Renault
Fastest lap: A. Prost
  138.34 kph / 85.96 mph
Pole position: A. Prost

Belgian GP

25 May: Spa
299 km / 186 miles
1 N. Mansell   Williams-Honda
  206.75 kph / 126.48 mph
2 A. Senna   Lotus-Renault
3 S. Johansson   Ferrari
4 M. Alboreto   Ferrari
5 J. Laffite   Ligier-Renault
6 A. Prost   McLaren-TAG
Fastest lap: A. Prost
  209.44 kph / 130.15 mph
Pole position: N. Piquet
  (Williams-Honda)

Canadian GP

15 June: Montreal
305 km / 190 miles
1 N. Mansell   Williams-Honda
  179.26 kph / 111.39 mph
2 A. Prost   McLaren-TAG
3 N. Piquet   Williams-Honda
4 K. Rosberg   McLaren-TAG
5 A. Senna   Lotus-Renault
6 R. Arnoux   Ligier-Renault
Fastest lap: N. Piquet
  186.88 kph / 116.13 mph
Pole position: N. Mansell

Detroit GP

22 June: Detroit
254 km / 158 miles
1 A. Senna   Lotus-Renault
  136.75 kph / 84.97 mph
2 J. Laffite   Ligier-Renault
3 A. Prost   McLaren-TAG
4 M. Alboreto   Ferrari
5 N. Mansell   Williams-Honda
6 R. Patrese   Brabham-BMW
Fastest lap: N. Piquet
  (Williams-Honda)
  143.07 kph / 88.90 mph
Pole position: A. Senna

French GP

6 July: Paul Ricard
307 km / 191 miles
1 N. Mansell   Williams-Honda
  189.15 kph / 117.54 mph
2 A. Prost   McLaren-TAG
3 N. Piquet   Williams-Honda
4 K. Rosberg   McLaren-TAG
5 R. Arnoux   Ligier-Renault
6 J. Laffite   Ligier-Renault
Fastest lap: N. Mansell
  197.25 kph / 122.57 mph
Pole position: A. Senna
  (Lotus-Renault)

British GP

13 July: Brands Hatch
315 km / 196 miles
1 N. Mansell   Williams-Honda
  208.85 kph / 129.78 mph
2 N. Piquet   Williams-Honda
3 A. Prost   McLaren-TAG
4 R. Arnoux   Ligier-Renault
5 M. Brundle   Tyrrell-Renault
6 P. Streiff   Tyrrell-Renault
Fastest lap: N. Mansell
  217.60 kph / 135.22 mph
Pole position: N. Piquet

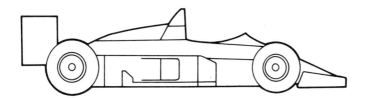

1986 Williams FW11

German GP

27 July: Hockenheim
301 km / 187 miles
1 N. Piquet   Williams-Honda
   219.72 kph / 136.54 mph
2 A. Senna   Lotus-Renault
3 N. Mansell   Williams-Honda
4 R. Arnoux   Ligier-Renault
5 K. Rosberg   McLaren-TAG
6 A. Prost   McLaren-TAG
Fastest lap: G. Berger
   (Benetton-BMW)
   230.86 kph / 143.46 mph
Pole position: K. Rosberg

Hungarian GP

10 August: Budapest
306 km / 190 miles
1 N. Piquet   Williams-Honda
   151.81 kph / 94.33 mph
2 A. Senna   Lotus-Renault
3 N. Mansell   Williams-Honda
4 S. Johansson   Ferrari
5 J. Dumfries   Lotus-Renault
6 M. Brundle   Tyrrell-Renault
Fastest lap: N. Piquet
   158.79 kph / 98.67 mph
Pole position: A. Senna

Austrian GP

17 August: Osterreichring
309 km / 192 miles
1 A. Prost   McLaren-TAG
   227.80 kph / 141.56 mph
2 M. Alboreto   Ferrari
3 S. Johansson   Ferrari
4 A. Jones   Lola-Ford
5 P. Tambay   Lola-Ford
6 C. Danner   Arrows-BMW
Fastest lap: G. Berger
   (Benetton-BMW)
   238.90 kph / 148.46 mph
Pole position: T. Fabi
   (Benetton-BMW)

Italian GP

7 September: Monza
296 km / 184 miles
1 N. Piquet   Williams-Honda
   228.35 kph / 141.90 mph
2 N. Mansell   Williams-Honda
3 S. Johansson   Ferrari
4 K. Rosberg   McLaren-TAG
5 G. Berger   Benetton-BMW
6 A. Jones   Lola-Ford
Fastest lap: T. Fabi (Benetton-BMW)
   236.99 kph / 147.27 mph
Pole position: T. Fabi

Portuguese GP

21 September: Estoril
305 km / 189 miles
1 N. Mansell   Williams-Honda
   187.64 kph / 116.60 mph
2 A. Prost   McLaren-TAG
3 N. Piquet   Williams-Honda
4 A. Senna   Lotus-Renault
5 M. Alboreto   Ferrari
6 S. Johansson   Ferrari
Fastest lap: N. Mansell
   193.43 kph / 120.22 mph
Pole position: A. Senna

Mexican GP

12 October: Mexico City
301 km / 187 miles
1 G. Berger   Benetton-BMW
   193.34 kph / 120.14 mph
2 A. Prost   McLaren-TAG
3 A. Senna   Lotus-Renault
4 N. Piquet   Williams-Honda
5 N. Mansell   Williams-Honda
6 P. Alliot   Ligier-Renault
Fastest lap: N. Piquet
   200.50 kph / 124.60 mph
Pole position: A. Senna

Australian GP

26 October: Adelaide
310 km / 193 miles
1 A. Prost   McLaren-TAG
   163.55 kph / 101.63 mph
2 N. Piquet   Williams-Honda
3 S. Johansson   Ferrari
4 M. Brundle   Tyrrell-Renault
5 P. Streiff   Tyrrell-Renault
6 J. Dumfries   Lotus-Renault
Fastest lap: N. Piquet
   168.34 kph / 104.60 mph
Pole position: N. Mansell

World Drivers' Championship

Pts	Drivers	Wins	
72	Alain Prost (FRA)	4	San Marino GP, Monaco GP, Austrian GP, Australian GP
70	Nigel Mansell (GB)	5	Belgian GP, Canadian GP, French GP, British GP, Portuguese GP
69	Nelson Piquet (BRA)	4	Brazilian GP, German GP, Hungarian GP, Italian GP
55	Ayrton Senna (BRA)	2	Spanish GP, Detroit GP
23	Stefan Johansson (SWE)	–	
22	Keke Rosberg (FIN)	–	
17	Gerhard Berger (AUT)	1	Mexican GP
14	Michele Alboreto (ITA)	–	
14	Rene Arnoux (FRA)	–	
14	Jacques Laffite (FRA)	–	
8	Martin Brundle (GB)	–	
4	Alan Jones (AUS)	–	
3	Johnny Dumfries (GB)	–	
3	Philippe Streiff (FRA)	–	
2	Teo Fabi (ITA)	–	
2	Patrick Tambay (FRA)	–	
2	Riccardo Patrese (ITA)	–	
1	Christian Danner (FRG)	–	
1	Philippe Alliot (FRA)	–	

Points scoring: First six drivers in each race to score. Points as follows: 9–6–4–3–2–1. Best eleven results from 16 rounds to count.

Constructors' Cup

Pts	Manufacturer	Wins	
141	Williams-Honda	9	Brazilian GP, Belgian GP, Canadian GP, French GP, British GP, German GP, Hungarian GP, Italian GP, Portuguese GP
96	McLaren-TAG	4	San Marino GP, Monaco GP, Austrian GP, Australian GP
60	Lotus-Renault	2	Spanish GP, Detroit GP
37	Ferrari	–	
29	Ligier-Renault	–	
19	Benetton-BMW	1	Mexican GP
11	Tyrrell-Renault	–	
6	Lola-Ford	–	
2	Brabham-BMW	–	
1	Arrows-BMW	–	

Points scoring: First six cars in each race to score, results from all 16 rounds counted. Points: 9–6–4–3–2–1.

● Graham Hill (GB) won the award as Best After Dinner Speaker of 1971, presented to him in London by the Guild of Professional Toastmasters.

● The 1986 Indianapolis 500 was put back seven days because of adverse weather conditions. It was the longest delay in the long history of the race.

Drivers' Records

Most World Titles

No. Titles	Driver	Year
5	Juan Manuel Fangio (ARG)	1951, 1954–57
3	Jack Brabham (AUS)	1959–60, 1966
3	Jackie Stewart (GB)	1969, 1971, 1973
3	Niki Lauda (AUT)	1975, 1977, 1984
2	Jim Clark (GB)	1963, 1965
2	Alberto Ascari (ITA)	1952–53
2	Graham Hill (GB)	1962, 1968
2	Emerson Fittipaldi (BRA)	1972, 1974
2	Nelson Piquet (BRA)	1981, 1983
2	Alain Prost (FRA)	1985–86
1	Giuseppe Farina (ITA)	1950
1	Mike Hawthorn (GB)	1958
1	Phil Hill (USA)	1961
1	John Surtees (GB)	1964
1	Denny Hulme (NZ)	1967
1	Jochen Rindt (AUT)	1970
1	James Hunt (GB)	1976
1	Mario Andretti (USA)	1978
1	Jody Scheckter (SAF)	1979
1	Alan Jones (AUS)	1980
1	Keke Rosberg (FIN)	1982

The only man to win world titles on two and four wheels, John Surtees (GB). Judging by the action, there was no way he was going to be an outstanding sportsman in a third sport! (National Motor Museum)

Below left
Mario Andretti became only the second North American world champion in 1978 – 17 years after the first, Phil Hill

Below Giuseppe Farina (ITA), the first world champion in 1950. Before he started racing, Farina completed his studies and obtained a doctorate degree. (National Motor Museum)

Race Winners   Complete list of drivers who have won World Championship races

Driver	Wins	First Grand Prix Win	Last Grand Prix Win
Alboreto, Michele (ITA)	5	1982 Las Vegas GP (Tyrrell-Ford)	1985 German GP (Ferrari)
Andretti, Mario (USA)	12	1971 South African GP (Ferrari)	1978 Dutch GP (Lotus-Ford)
Arnoux, Rene (FRA)	7	1980 Brazilian GP (Renault)	1983 Dutch GP (Ferrari)
Ascari, Alberto (ITA)	13	1951 German GP (Ferrari)	1953 Swiss GP (Ferrari)
Baghetti, Giancarlo (ITA)	1	1961 French GP (Ferrari)	–
Brabham, Jack (AUS)	14	1959 Monaco GP (Cooper-Climax)	1970 S. African GP (Brabham-Ford)
Bandini, Lorenzo (ITA)	1	1964 Austrian GP (Ferrari)	–
Beltoise, Jean-Pierre (FRA)	1	1972 Monaco GP (BRM)	–
Berger, Gerhardt (AUT)	1	1986 Mexican GP (Benetton-BMW)	–
Brambilla, Vittorio (ITA)	1	1975 Austrian GP (March-Ford)	–
Bonnier, Jo (SWE)	1	1959 Dutch GP (BRM)	–
Brooks, Tony (GB)	6	1957 British GP* (Vanwall)	1959 German GP (Ferrari)
Bryan, Jimmy (USA)	1	1958 Indianapolos 500 (Belond Exhaust)	–
Cevert, Francois (FRA)	1	1971 United States GP (Tyrrell-Ford)	–
Clark, Jim (GB)	25	1962 Belgian GP (Lotus-Climax)	1968 S. African GP (Lotus-Ford)
Collins, Peter (GB)	3	1956 Belgian GP (Lancia-Ferrari)	1958 British GP (Ferrari)
De Angelis, Elio (ITA)	2	1982 Austrian GP (Lotus-Ford)	1985 San Marino GP (Lotus-Renault)
Depailler, Patrick (FRA)	2	1978 Monaco GP (Tyrrell-Ford)	1979 Spanish GP (Ligier-Ford)
Fagioli, Luigi (ITA)	1	1951 French GP* (Alfa Romeo)	–
Fangio, Juan Manuel (ARG)	24	1950 Monaco GP (Alfa Romeo)	1957 German GP (Maserati)
Farina, Giuseppe (ITA)	5	1950 British GP (Alfa Romeo)	1953 German GP (Ferrari)
Fittipaldi, Emerson (BRA)	14	1970 United States GP (Lotus-Ford)	1975 British GP (McLaren-Ford)
Flaherty, Pat (USA)	1	1956 Indianapolis 500 (John Zink)	–
Gethin, Peter (GB)	1	1971 Italian GP (BRM)	–
Ginther, Richie (USA)	1	1965 Mexican GP (Honda)	–
Gonzalez, Jose Froilan (ARG)	2	1951 British GP (Ferrari)	1954 British GP (Ferrari)
Gurney, Dan (USA)	4	1962 French GP (Porsche)	1967 Belgian GP (Eagle-Weslake)
Hanks, Sam (USA)	1	1957 Indianapolis 500 (Belond Exhaust)	–
Hawthorn, Mike (GB)	3	1953 French GP (Ferrari)	1958 French GP (Ferrari)
Hill, Graham (GB)	14	1962 Dutch GP (BRM)	1969 Monaco GP (Lotus-Ford)
Hill, Phil (USA)	3	1960 Italian GP (Ferrari)	1961 Italian GP (Ferrari)
Hulme, Denny (NZ)	8	1967 Monaco GP (Brabham-Repco)	1974 Argentine GP (McLaren-Ford)
Hunt, James (GB)	10	1975 Dutch GP (Hesketh-Ford)	1977 Japanese GP (McLaren-Ford)
Ickx, Jacky (BEL)	8	1968 French GP (Ferrari)	1972 German GP (Ferrari)
Ireland, Innes (GB)	1	1961 United States GP (Lotus-Climax)	–
Jabouille, Jean-Pierre (FRA)	2	1979 French GP (Renault)	1980 Austrian GP (Renault)
Jones, Alan (AUS)	12	1977 Austrian GP (Shadow-Ford)	1981 Las Vegas GP (Williams-Ford)
Laffite, Jacques (FRA)	6	1977 Swedish GP (Ligier-Matra)	1981 Canadian GP (Talbot-Matra)
Lauda, Niki (AUT)	25	1974 Spanish GP (Ferrari)	1985 Dutch GP (McLaren-Porsche)
McLaren, Bruce (NZ)	4	1959 United States GP (Cooper-Climax)	1968 Belgian GP (McLaren-Ford)
Mansell, Nigel (GB)	7	1985 European GP (Williams-Honda)	1986 Portuguese GP (Williams-Honda)
Mass, Jochen (FRG)	1	1975 Spanish GP (McLaren-Ford)	–
Moss, Stirling (GB)	16	1955 British GP (Mercedes-Benz)	1961 German GP (Lotus-Climax)
Nilsson, Gunnar (SWE)	1	1977 Belgian (Lotus-Ford)	–
Pace, Carlos (BRA)	1	1975 Brazilian (Brabham-Ford)	–
Parsons, Johnny (USA)	1	1950 Indianapolis 500 (Wynn's F.P.)	–
Patrese, Riccardo (ITA)	2	1982 Monaco GP (Brabham-Ford)	1983 South African GP (Brabham-BMW)
Peterson, Ronnie (SWE)	10	1973 French GP (Lotus-Ford)	1978 Austrian GP (Lotus-Ford)
Pironi, Didier (FRA)	3	1980 Belgian GP (Ligier-Ford)	1982 Dutch GP (Ferrari)
Piquet, Nelson (BRA)	17	1980 United States (West) GP (Brabham-Ford)	1986 Italian GP (Williams-Honda)
Prost, Alain (FRA)	25	1981 French GP (Renault)	1986 Australian GP (McLaren-TAG)
Rathmann, Jim (USA)	1	1960 Indianapolis 500 (Ken Paul)	–
Regazzoni, Clay (SWI)	5	1970 Italian GP (Ferrari)	1979 British GP (Williams-Ford)
Reutemann, Carlos (ARG)	12	1974 South African GP (Brabham-Ford)	1981 Belgian GP (Williams-Ford)
Revson, Peter (USA)	2	1973 British GP (McLaren-Ford)	1973 Canadian GP (McLaren-Ford)
Rindt, Jochen (AUT)	6	1969 United States GP (Lotus-Ford)	1970 German GP (Lotus-Ford)
Rodriguez, Pedro (MEX)	2	1967 S. African GP (Cooper-Maserati)	1970 Belgian GP (BRM)
Rosberg, Keke (FIN)	5	1982 Swiss GP (Williams-Ford)	1985 Australian GP (Williams-Honda)
Ruttman, Troy (USA)	1	1952 Indianapolis 500 (Agajanian)	–
Scarfiotti, Ludovico (ITA)	1	1966 Italian GP (Ferrari)	–
Scheckter, Jody (SAF)	10	1974 Swedish GP (Tyrrell-Ford)	1979 Italian GP (Ferrari)
Senna, Ayrton (BRA)	4	1985 Portuguese GP (Lotus-Renault)	1986 Detroit GP (Lotus-Renault)
Siffert, Jo (SWI)	2	1968 British GP (Lotus-Ford)	1971 Austrian GP (BRM)
Stewart, Jackie (GB)	27	1965 Italian GP (BRM)	1973 German GP (Tyrrell-Ford)
Surtees, John (GB)	6	1963 German GP (Ferrari)	1967 Italian GP (Honda)
Sweikert, Bob (USA)	1	1955 Indianapolis 500 (John Zink)	–
Tambay, Patrick (FRA)	2	1982 German GP (Ferrari)	1983 San Marino GP (Ferrari)
Taruffi, Piero (ITA)	1	1952 Swiss GP (Ferrari)	–
Trintignant, Maurice (FRA)	2	1955 Monaco GP (Ferrari)	1958 Monaco GP (Cooper-Climax)
Villeneuve, Gilles (CAN)	6	1978 Canadian GP (Ferrari)	1981 Spanish GP (Ferrari)
Von Trips, Wolfgang (FRG)	2	1961 Dutch GP (Ferrari)	1961 British GP (Ferrari)
Vukovich, Bill (USA)	2	1953 Indianapolis 500 (Fuel Injection)	1954 Indianapolis 500 (Fuel Injection)
Wallard, Lee (USA)	1	1951 Indianapolis 500 (Belanger)	–
Ward, Rodger (USA)	1	1959 Indianapolis 500 (Leader Card)	–
Watson, John (GB)	5	1976 Austrian GP (Penske-Ford)	1983 Long Beach GP (McLaren-Ford)

* Indicates shared drive

Leading Points Scorers

Points	Driver
420½	Niki Lauda (AUT)
360	Jackie Stewart (GB)
355½	Alain Prost (FRA)
310	Carlos Reutemann (ARG)
305	Nelson Piquet (BRA)
289	Graham Hill (GB)
281	Emerson Fittipaldi (BRA)
277½	Juan Manuel Fangio (ARG)
274	Jim Clark (GB)
261	Jack Brabham (AUS)
255	Jody Scheckter (SAF)
248	Denny Hulme (NZ)
212	Clay Regazzoni (SWI)
212	Jacques Laffite (FRA)
206	Ronnie Peterson (SWE)
206	Alan Jones (AUS)

Because of the changing format season by season, comparisons between the various champion drivers would be unfair and unrealistic.

Most Starts

Complete list of drivers that have started 100 World Championship Grand Prix races or more.

176	Graham Hill (GB)
176	Jacques Laffite (FRA)
171	Niki Lauda (AUT)
152	John Watson (GB)
146	Carlos Reutemann (ARG)
144	Emerson Fittipaldi (BRA)
144	Riccardo Patrese (ITA)
136	Jean-Pierre Jarier (FRA)
132	Clay Regazzoni (SWI)
128	Mario Andretti (USA)
126	Jack Brabham (AUS)
126	Nelson Piquet (BRA)
123	Ronnie Peterson (SWE)
116	Jacky Ickx (BEL)
116	Alan Jones (AUS)
114	Keke Rosberg (FIN)
114	Patrick Tambay (FRA)
112	Rene Arnoux (FRA)
112	Jody Scheckter (SAF)
111	John Surtees (GB)
108	Elio de Angelis (ITA)
105	Jochen Mass (FRG)
105	Alain Prost (FRA)
102	Jo Bonnier (SWE)
102	Denny Hulme (NZ)
101	Bruce McLaren (NZ)

Above Three great world champions, with nine titles between them: Britain's Jim Clark (left), Argentina's Juan Manuel Fangio (centre) and Graham Hill (GB). This formidable trio won 63 Grands Prix between them. (National Motor Museum)

Left Scottish-born Jackie Stewart won a record 27 Grand Prix races between 1965–73. He surpassed Jim Clark's record of 25 when he won the 1973 Dutch Grand Prix at Zandvoort. (National Motor Museum)

Below Frenchman Jacques Laffite equalled Graham Hill's record of 176 Grand Prix starts in the 1986 British Grand Prix. Laffite, however, was forced off the track at the start and suffered serious leg and pelvis injuries which caused him to miss the remainder of the season, and thus miss out on the opportunity to claim the record outright. (National Motor Museum)

Most Wins

27	Jackie Stewart (GB)	1965–73
25	Jim Clark (GB)	1962–68
25	Niki Lauda (AUT)	1974–85
25	Alain Prost (FRA)	1981–86
24	Juan Manuel Fangio (ARG)	1950–57
17	Nelson Piquet (BRA)	1980–86
16	Stirling Moss (GB)	1955–61
14	Graham Hill (GB)	1962–69
14	Jack Brabham (AUS)	1959–70
14	Emerson Fittipaldi (BRA)	1970–75
13	Alberto Ascari (ITA)	1951–53
12	Mario Andretti (USA)	1971–78
12	Carlos Reutemann (ARG)	1974–81
12	Alan Jones (AUS)	1977–81
10	James Hunt (GB)	1975–77
10	Ronnie Peterson (SWE)	1973–78
10	Jody Scheckter (SAF)	1974–79

Winners of their first Grand Prix

Only two drivers have won their first ever World Championship Grand Prix.
Giuseppe Farina (ITA)   1950 British GP (The first World Championship race)
Giancarlo Baghetti (ITA)
1961 French GP

Juan Manuel Fangio

Motor racing, like other sports, often poses the question: 'Who was the greatest?' There are plenty of candidates: Italy's Tazio Nuvolari was certainly the outstanding driver before the war, and post-war candidates include Britain's Jim Clark and Jackie Stewart, and Austria's Niki Lauda. But none of their records compare with that of the Argentinian Juan Manuel Fangio who won the world driver's title a record five times.

Even more remarkable, compared to the modern-day heroes, Fangio was aged 39 when the World Championship was introduced in 1950 and 46 when he won his fifth, and final, title in 1957.

Born at Balcarce, near Buenos Aires, in 1911 he was first introduced to the sport as a 17-year-old when he travelled as an accompanying mechanic in the long-distance races in his home country. It was not until 1933 that he started driving. Initially he used to race Model A Fords before later joining the Chevrolet team, after which he went on to win Argentina's top event, the Gran Premio Nacional.

He came to Europe in 1948 and returned again the following year when his familiar blue and yellow Maserati was a regular sight at Grands Prix on the continent. While he was good enough to win races, quite often his car was not. But, when Alfa Romeo returned to racing for the first World Championship in 1950, he was invited to join their team and he finished second in the inaugural championship, having won the Monaco, Belgian and French Grands Prix.

His first world title came the following year when his Alfa

enabled him to register three more wins and a six-point win over Ascari in the championship. When Alfa pulled out of racing in 1952, Fangio returned to Maserati but a bad accident at Monza, in which he broke his neck, put him in plaster for five months.

The brave Argentinian, nicknamed 'Cheuco'—meaning Bandy Legs—was back with a vengeance in 1953 and pushed his Maserati to second place in the championship. In 1954, he

joined Mercedes, who had made a welcome return to racing, and his second championship followed. He was with them when he won the title again in 1955 and his hat-trick was completed a year later after joining the Ferrari team.

While his Lancia-Ferrari D50 was a winning machine, Fangio spent an unhappy year with the Italian manufacturer and returned to Maserati for the 1957 season. He won the championship for a

record fifth time and in winning the German Grand Prix at the Nurburgring he not only won his 24th, and last, World Championship Grand Prix, but he enjoyed one of the best races of his career.

The strong Ferrari team decided to run the entire race non-stop without pit stops for refuelling or tyre changes, while Maserati, and Fangio, decided to run on half fuel, and then refill. He cleverly made use of the lowering fuel

weight and bedding in of new tyres, to outwit his British challengers, Hawthorn and Collins. The Argentinian trailed by 45 seconds just after the half-way stage as a result of his pit stop but then broke the lap record with each lap before snatching a last-gasp victory. He lowered the lap record by a staggering 11 seconds.

Still with Maserati in 1958 and still world champion, he announced his retirement after the French Grand Prix. He competed in 51 World Championship races and started in pole position in 29 of them, winning 24.

Above Juan Manuel Fangio was the first of the great post-war drivers. He is seen here (right) talking to Ferrari director Guglielmo Dei at Silverstone in 1961. (National Motor Museum)

Fangio (No. 50) is lying third behind the Ferrari duo of Farina and Ascari (both Italy) in the 1953 Italian Grand Prix at Monza. But it was the Argentinian who took the honours in his Maserati, with Farina second. (National Motor Museum)

Carlos Reutemann (ARG) being congratulated by the Duke of Kent after winning the 1978 British Grand Prix. Reutemann obtained 310 championship points during his career, one of only five men to top the 300-mark. (Michelin Tyre Co. Ltd.)

Least Successful Drivers

Complete list of drivers who have taken part in 50 or more Grands Prix without registering a win.

Races	Driver	Years
136	Jean-Pierre Jarier (FRA)	1971–83
96	Chris Amon (NZ)	1963–76
88	Andrea de Cesaris (ITA)	1980–86
86	Eddie Cheever (USA)	1978–86
82	Marc Surer (SWI)	1979–86
74	Hans-Joachim Stuck (FRG)	1974–79
69	Bruno Giacomelli (ITA)	1977–83
69	Derek Warwick (GB)	1981–86
57	Arturo Merzario (ITA)	1972–79
57	Thierry Boutsen (BEL)	1983–86
56	Henri Pescarolo (FRA)	1968–76
55	Harry Schell (USA)	1950–60
53	Rolf Stommelen (FRG)	1970–78
52	Jeannot Behra (FRA)	1952–59
50	Mike Hailwood (GB)	1963–74
50	Jackie Oliver (GB)	1967–77
50	Piercarlo Ghinzani (ITA)	1981–86

Winners of the most Grands Prix year by year

Year	GP	Driver	Car	
1950	3	Giuseppe Farina (ITA)	6	Alfa Romeo
	3	Juan Manuel Fangio (ARG)		
1951	3	Juan Manuel Fangio (ARG)	4	Alfa Romeo
1952	6	Alberto Ascari (ITA)	7	Ferrari
1953	5	Alberto Ascari (ITA)	7	Ferrari
1954	6	Juan Manuel Fangio (ARG)	4	Mercedes-Benz
1955	4	Juan Manuel Fangio (ARG)	5	Mercedes-Benz
1956	3	Juan Manuel Fangio (ARG)	5	Lancia-Ferrari
1957	4	Juan Manuel Fangio (ARG)	4	Maserati
1958	4	Stirling Moss (GB)	6	Vanwall
1959	2	Jack Brabham (AUS)	5	Cooper-Climax
	2	Tony Brooks (GB)		
	2	Stirling Moss (GB)		
1960	5	Jack Brabham (AUS)	6	Cooper-Climax
1961	2	Phil Hill (USA)	5	Ferrari
	2	Wolfgang Von Trips (FRG)		
	2	Stirling Moss (GB)		
1962	4	Graham Hill (GB)	4	BRM
1963	7	Jim Clark (GB)	7	Lotus-Climax
1964	3	Jim Clark (GB)	3	Ferrari
			3	Lotus-Climax
1965	6	Jim Clark (GB)	6	Lotus-Climax
1966	4	Jack Brabham (AUS)	4	Brabham-Repco

Year	GP	Driver	Car	
1967	4	Jim Clark (GB)	4	Brabham-Repco
			4	Lotus-Ford
1968	3	Graham Hill (GB)	5	Lotus-Ford
	3	Jackie Stewart (GB)		
1969	6	Jackie Stewart (GB)	6	Matra-Ford
1970	5	Jochen Rindt (AUT)	6	Lotus-Ford
1971	6	Jackie Stewart (GB)	6	Tyrrell-Ford
1972	5	Emerson Fittipaldi (BRA)	5	Lotus-Ford
1973	5	Jackie Stewart (GB)	7	Lotus-Ford
1974	3	Emerson Fittipaldi (BRA)	4	McLaren-Ford
	3	Ronnie Peterson (SWE)		
	3	Carlos Reutemann (ARG)		
1975	5	Niki Lauda (AUT)	6	Ferrari
1976	6	James Hunt (GB)	6	Ferrari
			6	McLaren-Ford
1977	4	Mario Andretti (USA)	5	Lotus-Ford
1978	6	Mario Andretti (USA)	8	Lotus-Ford
1979	4	Alan Jones (AUS)	6	Ferrari
1980	5	Alan Jones (AUS)	6	Williams-Ford
1981	3	Nelson Piquet (BRA)	4	Williams-Ford
	3	Alain Prost (FRA)		
1982	2	John Watson (GB)	4	McLaren-Ford
	2	Didier Pironi (FRA)	4	Renault
	2	Alain Prost (FRA)		
	2	Niki Lauda (AUT)		
	2	Rene Arnoux (FRA)		
1983	4	Alain Prost (FRA)	4	Ferrari
			4	Renault
			4	Brabham-BMW
1984	7	Alain Prost (FRA)	12	McLaren-Porsche
1985	5	Alain Prost (FRA)	6	McLaren-TAG
1986	5	Nigel Mansell (GB)	9	Williams-Honda

Left Alain Prost (FRA) seen here celebrating his second successive world title after winning the 1986 Australian Grand Prix. Prost shares with Jim Clark the record for winning the most races in a season — seven, in 1984

Right Juan Manuel Fangio (ARG), shown at the wheel of a Ferrari in 1956, and Britain's Jim Clark, are the only men to have won three or more successive races on three occasions. (National Motor Museum)

Most successive Grand Prix wins

Note: The Indianapolis 500 race is ignored for the purpose of compiling these statistics because the race was generally restricted to American drivers who did not compete in any European Grands Prix, and vice versa.

Wins	Driver	Race
9	Alberto Ascari (ITA)	1952 – Belgian, French, British, German, Dutch, Italian: 1953 – Argentine, Dutch, Belgian GPs
5	Jack Brabham (AUS)	1960 – Dutch, Belgian, French, British, Portuguese GPs
5	Jim Clark (GB)	1965 – Belgian, French, British, Dutch, German GPs
4	Juan Manuel Fangio (ARG)	1953 – Italian: 1954 – Argentine, Belgian, French GPs
4	Jim Clark (GB)	1963 – Belgian, Dutch, French, British GPs
4	Jack Brabham (AUS)	1966 – French, British, Dutch, German GPs
4	Jochen Rindt (AUT)	1970 – Dutch, French, British, German GPs
3	Juan Manuel Fangio (ARG)	1954 – German, Swiss, Italian GPs
3	Stirling Moss (GB)	1957 – Pescara, Italian: 1958 – Argentine GPs
3	Juan Manuel Fangio (ARG)	1957 – Argentine, Monaco, French GPs
3	Jim Clark (GB)	1967 – United States, Mexican: 1968 – South African GPs
3	Jackie Stewart (GB)	1969 – Dutch, French, British GPs
3	Jackie Stewart (GB)	1971 – French, British, German GPs
3	Niki Lauda (AUT)	1975 – Monaco, Belgian, Swedish GPs
3	Niki Lauda (AUT)	1975 – United States: 1976 – Brazilian, South African GPs
3	Alan Jones (AUS)	1979 – German, Austrian, Dutch GPs
3	Alan Jones (AUS)	1980 – Canadian, United States: 1981 – United States (West) GPs
3	Alain Prost (FRA)	1984 – European, Portuguese: 1985 – Brazilian GPs

Fastest Laps

Largest number of fastest laps

27	Jim Clark (GB)	
25	Niki Lauda (AUT)	
23	Juan Manuel Fangio (ARG)	(Including 1 shared)
20	Stirling Moss (GB)	(Including 3 shared)
19	Nelson Piquet (BRA)	
18	Alain Prost (FRA)	
15	Jackie Stewart (GB)	
15	Clay Regazzoni (SWI)	(Including 1 shared)
14	Jacky Ickx (BEL)	(Including 2 shared)
13	Alan Jones (AUS)	
12	Alberto Ascari (ITA)	(Including 4 shared)
11	Jack Brabham (AUS)	(Including 3 shared)
11	John Surtees (GB)	(Including 1 shared)
11	Rene Arnoux (FRA)	
10	Graham Hill (GB)	
10	Mario Andretti (USA)	

Most Grand Prix wins in a season

Wins	Driver	Year
7	Jim Clark (GB)	1963*
7	Alain Prost (FRA)	1984
6	Alberto Ascari (ITA)	1952*
6	Juan Manuel Fangio (ARG)	1954*
6	Jim Clark (GB)	1965*
6	Jackie Stewart (GB)	1969*
6	Jackie Stewart (GB)	1971*
6	James Hunt (GB)	1976*
6	Mario Andretti (USA)	1978*

* Indicates that season's world champion

Wins	Car	Year
12	McLaren-Porsche	1984
8	Lotus-Ford	1978
7	Ferrari	1952
7	Ferrari	1953
7	Lotus-Climax	1963
7	Tyrrell-Ford	1971
7	Lotus-Ford	1973

Fastest 'Fastest Laps'

Speed kph	mph	Driver	Car	Race
247.02	153.49	H. Pescarolo (FRA)	March-Ford	1971 Italian GP (Monza)
244.74	152.08	C. Amon (NZ)	March-Ford	1970 Belgian GP (Spa)
243.07	151.04	A. Prost (FRA)	McLaren-Porsche	1985 British GP (Silverstone)
242.96	150.97	J. P. Beltoise (FRA)	Matra-Ford	1969 Italian GP (Monza)
242.96	150.97	C. Regazzoni (SWI)	Ferrari	1970 Italian GP (Monza)
241.14	149.84	J. Surtees (GB)	Honda	1968 Belgian GP (Spa)
239.97	149.14	C. A. S. Brooks (GB)	Ferrari	1959 German GP (Avus)
239.70	148.95	A. Prost (FRA)	McLaren-Porsche	1985 Austrian GP (Osterreichring)
239.55	148.85	D. Gurney (USA)	Eagle-Weslake	1967 Belgian GP (Spa)
239.31	148.70	J. Oliver (GB)	Lotus-Ford	1968 Italian GP (Monza)

Pole Positions

The following drivers have all been in pole position on ten or more occasions

33	Jim Clark (GB)	1962–68
28	Juan Manuel Fangio (ARG)	1950–58
24	Niki Lauda (AUT)	1974–78
20	Nelson Piquet (BRA)	1980–86
18	Mario Andretti (USA)	1968–82
18	Rene Arnoux (FRA)	1979–83
17	Jackie Stewart (GB)	1969–73
16	Stirling Moss (GB)	1955–61
16	Alain Prost (FRA)	1981–86
15	Ayrton Senna (BRA)	1985–86
14	Alberto Ascari (ITA)	1951–54
14	Ronnie Peterson (SWE)	1973–78
14	James Hunt (GB)	1976–78
13	Jack Brabham (AUS)	1959–70
13	Graham Hill (GB)	1962–68
13	Jacky Ickx (BEL)	1968–72
10	Jochen Rindt (AUT)	1968–70

Most consecutive pole positions

(Indianapolis 500 excluded)

6	Stirling Moss (GB)	1959 – Portuguese, Italian, US
		1960 – Argentine, Monaco, Dutch
5	Juan Manuel Fangio (ARG)	1950 – French, Italian
5	Alberto Ascari (ITA)	1951 – Swiss, Belgian, French
		1952 – German, Dutch, Italian
		1953 – Argentine, Dutch
5	Juan Manuel Fangio (ARG)	1955 – Italian
		1956 – Argentine, Monaco, Belgian, French
5	Phil Hill (USA)	1961 – Dutch, Belgian, French, British, German

Oldest and Youngest

OLDEST GP DRIVERS

Years	Months	Driver	Last Race	
55	8	Louis Chiron (MC)	1955	Monaco GP
55	6	Phillipe Etancelin (FRA)	1952	French GP
53	1	Luigi Fagioli (ITA)	1951	French GP

(Oldest Briton: Bill Aston 52yr 4mth, 1952 German GP)

YOUNGEST DRIVERS

Years	Months	Driver	First Race	
19	6	Mike Thackwell (NZ)	1980	Canadian GP
19	7	Ricardo Rodriguez (MEX)	1961	Italian GP
19	11	Chris Amon (NZ)	1963	Belgian GP

(Youngest Briton: Peter Collins 20yr 7mth, 1952 Swiss GP)

OLDEST GP WINNERS

Years	Months	Driver	Last Win	
53	1	Luigi Fagioli (ITA)	1951	French GP
46	9	Giuseppe Farina (ITA)	1953	German GP
46	1	Juan Manuel Fangio (ARG)	1957	German GP

(Oldest Briton: Graham Hill 40yr 3mth, 1969 Monaco GP)

YOUNGEST GP WINNERS

Years	Months	Driver	First Win	
22	3	Troy Ruttman (USA)	1952	Indianapolis 500
22	3	Bruce McLaren (NZ)	1959	United States GP
23	6	Jacky Ickx (BEL)	1968	French GP

(Youngest Briton: Mike Hawthorn 24yr 3mth, 1953 French GP)

OLDEST WORLD CHAMPIONS

Years	Months	Driver	Season
46	2	Juan Manuel Fangio (ARG)	1957
43	11	Giuseppe Farina (ITA)	1950
40	6	Jack Brabham (AUS)	1966

When Italy's Luigi Fagioli won the 1951 French Grand Prix at Rheims, he became the oldest winner of a Formula One Grand Prix at the age of 53 years 1 month. (National Motor Museum)

At 19 years 6 months New Zealand's Mike Thackwell became the youngest ever Grand Prix driver when he drove a Tyrrell-Ford in the Canadian Grand Prix at Montreal on 28 September 1980.

Brazilian Emerson Fittipaldi is seen celebrating his win in the 1975 British Grand Prix. Three years earlier he was the youngest ever world champion at the age of 25 years 8 months

YOUNGEST WORLD CHAMPIONS

Years	Months	Driver	Season
25	8	Emerson Fittipaldi (BRA)	1972
26	8	Niki Lauda (AUT)	1975
27	7	Jim Clark (GB)	1963

OLDEST POINTS SCORERS

Years	Months	Driver	Race
53	8	Phillipe Etancelin (FRA)	1950 Italian GP (5th)
53	1	Luigi Fagioli (ITA)	1951 French GP (1st)
50	9	Louis Chiron (MC)	1950 Monaco GP (3rd)

(Oldest Briton: 45yr 4mth Graham Hill, 1975 Swedish GP (6th))

YOUNGEST POINTS SCORERS

Years	Months	Driver	Race
20	4	Ricardo Rodriguez (MEX)	1962 Belgian GP (4th)
20	10	Chris Amon (NZ)	1964 Dutch GP (5th)
21	6	Elio de Angelis (ITA)	1979 US GP (4th)

(Youngest Briton: Tony Brise 23yr 2mth, 1975 Swedish GP (6th))

Drivers who have won Grands Prix in their own country

The following drivers have all won World Championship Grand Prix races on home soil. The Indianapolis 500 winners are excluded because, during the period 1950–60, when the race counted towards the Championship, all winners were American.

Giuseppe Farina (ITA)	1950 Italian GP
Alberto Ascari (ITA)	1951–54 Italian GP
Juan Manuel Fangio (ARG)	1954–57 Argentine GP
Stirling Moss (GB)	1955, 1957 British GP
Tony Brooks (GB)	1957 British GP
Peter Collins (GB)	1958 British GP
Jim Clark (GB)	1962–65, 1967 British GP
Ludovico Scarfiotti (ITA)	1966 Italian GP
Jackie Stewart (GB)	1969, 1971 British GP
Emerson Fittipaldi (BRA)	1973–74 Brazilian GP
Carlos Pace (BRA)	1975 Brazilian GP
Jody Scheckter (SAF)	1975 South African GP
Mario Andretti (USA)	1977 United States GP (West)
James Hunt (GB)	1977 British GP
Gilles Villeneuve (CAN)	1978 Canadian GP
Jean-Pierre Jabouille (FRA)	1979 French GP
Alain Prost (FRA)	1981, 1983 French GP
John Watson (GB)	1981 British GP
Rene Arnoux (FRA)	1982 French GP
Nelson Piquet (BRA)	1983, 1986 Brazilian GP
Niki Lauda (AUT)	1984 Austrian GP
Elio de Angelis (ITA)	1985 San Marino GP
Nigel Mansell (GB)	1985 European GP (Brands Hatch), 1986 British GP

Longest Careers

Years	Months	Driver	First Grand Prix	Last Grand Prix
16	8	Graham Hill (GB)	18 May 1958, Monaco GP	26 Jan 1975, Brazilian GP
15	3	Jack Brabham (AUS)	16 Jul 1955, British GP	18 Oct 1970, Mexican GP
14	4	Maurice Trintignant (FRA)	21 May 1950, Monaco GP	6 Sep 1964, Italian GP
14	2	Niki Lauda (AUT)	15 Aug 1971, Austrian GP	3 Nov 1985, Australian GP
14	2	Jo Bonnier (SWE)	20 Jul 1957, British GP	3 Oct 1971, United States GP
13	11	Mario Andretti (USA)	6 Oct 1968, United States GP	25 Sep 1982, Las Vegas GP
13	2	Chris Amon (NZ)	9 Jun 1963, Belgian GP	1 Aug 1976, German GP
13		Andre Pilette (BEL)	17 Jun 1951, Belgian GP	14 Jun 1964, Belgian GP

Maurice Trintignant (FRA) enjoyed a Formula One Grand Prix career lasting more than 14 years between 1950–64. He is seen enjoying himself behind the wheel of a famous Type 35 Bugatti at Silverstone in 1960. (National Motor Museum)

● While lying joint third in the 1979 World Drivers' Championship, Frenchman Patrick Depailler put himself out of action for the rest of the season by breaking both his legs in a hang-gliding accident.

Manufacturers' Records

The 2½-litre Vanwall that won the first Constructors' Championship in 1958. (National Motor Museum)

Most World Titles

The following cars have won the Constructors' Cup.

8	Ferrari	1961, 1964, 1975–77, 1979, 1982–83
5	Lotus-Ford	1968, 1970, 1972–73, 1978
2	Cooper-Climax	1959–60
2	Lotus-Climax	1963, 1965
2	Brabham-Repco	1966–67
2	Williams-Ford	1980–81
1	Vanwall	1958
1	BRM	1962
1	Matra-Ford	1969
1	Tyrrell-Ford	1971
1	McLaren-Ford	1974
1	McLaren-Porsche	1984
1	McLaren-TAG	1985
1	Williams-Honda	1986

Winning Cars

The following manufacturers have all won World Championship Grand Prix races. Indianapolis 500 winners are excluded.

Wins	Manufacturer	Years	First Grand Prix Win
91	FERRARI	1951–85	1951 British GP (F. Gonzalez)
86	Ferrari		
5	Lancia-Ferrari		
77	LOTUS	1960–86	1960 Monaco GP (S. Moss)
47	Lotus-Ford		
24	Lotus-Climax		
5	Lotus-Renault		
1	Lotus-BRM		
52	McLAREN	1968–86	1968 Belgian GP (B. McLaren)
30	McLaren-Ford		
12	McLaren-Porsche		
10	McLaren-TAG		

Wins	Manufacturer	Years	First Grand Prix Win
35	BRABHAM	1964–85	1964 French GP (D. Gurney)
15	Brabham-Ford		
8	Brabham-Repco		
8	Brabham-BMW		
2	Brabham-Climax		
2	Brabham-Alfa Romeo		
31	WILLIAMS	1979–86	1979 British GP (C. Regazzoni)
17	Williams-Ford		
14	Williams-Honda		
23	TYRRELL	1971–83	1971 Spanish GP (J. Stewart)
23	Tyrrell-Ford		

Wins	Manufacturer	Years	First Grand Prix Win
17	BRM	1959–72	1959 Dutch GP (J. Bonnier)
16	COOPER	1958–67	1958 Argentine GP (S. Moss)
	14 Cooper-Climax		
	2 Cooper-Maserati		
15	RENAULT	1979–83	1979 French GP (J-P. Jabouille)
10	ALFA ROMEO	1950–51	1950 British GP (G. Farina)
9	MERCEDES-BENZ	1954–55	1954 French GP (J. M. Fangio)
9	VANWALL	1957–58	1957 British GP (C. A. S. Brooks/ S. Moss)
9	MATRA	1968–69	1968 Dutch GP (J. Stewart)
	9 Matra-Ford		
9	MASERATI	1953–57	1953 Italian GP (J. M. Fangio)
8	LIGIER	1977–81	1977 Swedish GP (J. Laffite)
	5 Ligier-Ford		
	3 Ligier-Matra		
3	WOLF	1977	1977 Argentine GP (J. Scheckter)
	3 Wolf-Ford		
3	MARCH	1970–76	1970 Spanish GP (J. Stewart)
	3 March-Ford		
2	HONDA	1965–67	1965 Mexican GP (R. Ginther)
1	PORSCHE	1962	1962 French GP (D. Gurney)

Wins	Manufacturer	Years	First Grand Prix Win
1	EAGLE	1967	1967 Belgian GP (D. Gurney)*
1	PENSKE	1976	1976 Austrian GP (J. Watson)
1	HESKETH	1975	1975 Dutch GP (J. Hunt)
	1 Hesketh-Ford		
1	SHADOW	1977	1977 Austrian GP (A. Jones)
	1 Shadow-Ford		
1	BENETTON	1986	1986 Mexican GP (G. Berger)
	1 Benetton-BMW		

* Dan Gurney (USA) drove three cars to their first GP success – the Porsche in 1962, Brabham in 1964 and Eagle in 1967
* Stirling Moss (GB) drove the first winning Cooper in 1958 and the first Lotus to victory in 1960, he also shared the winning drive with Tony Brooks (GB) in Vanwall's first success in 1957.
* Jackie Stewart was behind the wheel when Matra (1968), March (1970) and Tyrrell (1971) all registered their first wins.

Most successive Grand Prix wins

(Indianapolis 500 excluded)

14	Ferrari	1952 Swiss GP to 1953 Swiss GP
9	Alfa Romeo	1950 British GP to 1951 French GP
8	McLaren-Porsche	1984 British GP to 1985 Brazilian GP
5	Cooper-Climax	1960 Dutch GP to Portuguese GP
5	Lotus-Climax	1965 Belgian GP to German GP
5	Lotus-Ford	1967 United States GP to 1968 Monaco GP
5	Ferrari	1975 Italian GP to 1976 United States (West) GP

Left Frank Williams with his highly successful Williams-Honda that won the 1986 Constructors' Championship with nine victories

Left, below Ferrari have won the Constructors' Championship a record eight times. Frenchman Rene Arnoux helped them to their last triumph in 1983

Below Jackie Stewart (GB) in the cockpit of the Matra MS10, waiting for the start of the 1968 French Grand Prix. Two weeks earlier Stewart had piloted the car to its first ever Grand Prix success, at Zandvoort. (National Motor Museum)

Manufacturers who won their first ever Grand Prix

Alfa Romeo	1950 British GP (G. Farina) (the first World Championship GP)
Mercedes-Benz	1954 French GP (J. M. Fangio)
Wolf-Ford	1977 Argentine GP (J. Scheckter)

The Wolf car of Jody Scheckter on its way to registering its second world championship win, at Monaco in 1977. Their first win was in the opening race of the season at Buenos Aires — the car's first ever race. Scheckter was also behind the wheel on that occasion. (National Motor Museum)

Races in which the same car occupied first and second places

Year	Grand Prix	Car	First	Second
1950	British GP	Alfa Romeo*	G. Farina	L. Fagioli
1950	Swiss GP	Alfa Romeo	G. Farina	L. Fagioli
1950	Belgian GP	Alfa Romeo	J. M. Fangio	L. Fagioli
1950	French GP	Alfa Romeo	J. M. Fangio	L. Fagioli
1951	Italian GP	Ferrari	A. Ascari	F. Gonzalez
1951	Spanish GP	Ferrari	J. M. Fangio	F. Gonzalez
1952	Swiss GP	Ferrari	P. Taruffi	R. Fischer
1952	Belgian GP	Ferrari	A. Ascari	G. Farina
1952	French GP	Ferrari*	A. Ascari	G. Farina
1952	British GP	Ferrari	A. Ascari	P. Taruffi
1952	German GP	Ferrari†	A. Ascari	G. Farina
1952	Dutch GP	Ferrari*	A. Ascari	G. Farina
1953	Argentine GP	Ferrari	A. Ascari	L. Villoresi
1953	Dutch GP	Ferrari	A. Ascari	G. Farina
1953	Belgian GP	Ferrari	A. Ascari	L. Villoresi
1953	Swiss GP	Ferrari*	A. Ascari	G. Farina
1954	French GP	Mercedes-Benz	J. M. Fangio	K. Kling
1954	British GP	Ferrari	F. Gonzalez	M. Hawthorn
1955	Belgian GP	Mercedes-Benz	J. M. Fangio	S. Moss
1955	Dutch GP	Mercedes-Benz	J. M. Fangio	S. Moss
1955	British GP	Mercedes-Benz†	S. Moss	J. M. Fangio
1955	Italian	Mercedes-Benz	J. M. Fangio	P. Taruffi
1956	Belgian GP	Lancia-Ferrari	P. Collins	P. Frere
1956	French GP	Lancia-Ferrari	P. Collins	E. Castellotti
1956	British GP	Lancia-Ferrari	J. M. Fangio	A de Portago/ P. Collins
1957	Argentine GP	Maserati†	J. M. Fangio	J. Behra
1958	British GP	Ferrari	P. Collins	M. Hawthorn
1959	French GP	Ferrari	C. A. S. Brooks	P. Hill
1959	German GP	Ferrari*	C. A. S. Brooks	D. Gurney
1959	Portuguese GP	Cooper-Climax	S. Moss	M. Gregory
1959	United States GP	Cooper-Climax	B. McLaren	M. Trintignant
1960	Belgian GP	Cooper-Climax*	J. Brabham	B. McLaren
1960	French GP	Cooper-Climax†	J. Brabham	O. Gendebien
1960	Portuguese GP	Cooper-Climax	J. Brabham	B. McLaren
1960	Italian GP	Ferrari*	P. Hill	R. Ginther
1960	United States GP	Lotus-Climax	S. Moss	I. Ireland
1961	Dutch GP	Ferrari	W. Von Trips	P. Hill
1961	Belgian GP	Ferrari†	P. Hill	W. Von Trips
1961	British GP	Ferrari*	W. Von Trips	P. Hill
1962	Italian GP	BRM	G. Hill	R. Ginther
1963	Monaco GP	BRM	G. Hill	R. Ginther
1963	United States GP	BRM	G. Hill	R. Ginther
1964	Monaco GP	BRM	G. Hill	R. Ginther
1965	Italian GP	BRM	J. Stewart	G. Hill
1966	British GP	Brabham-Repco	J. Brabham	D. Hulme
1966	Italian GP	Ferrari	L. Scarfiotti	M. Parkes
1967	French GP	Brabham-Repco	J. Brabham	D. Hulme
1967	German GP	Brabham-Repco	D. Hulme	J. Brabham
1967	Canadian GP	Brabham-Repco	J. Brabham	D. Hulme
1967	United States GP	Lotus-Ford	J. Clark	G. Hill
1968	South African GP	Lotus-Ford	J. Clark	G. Hill
1968	Canadian GP	McLaren-Ford	D. Hulme	B. McLaren
1969	French GP	Matra-Ford	J. Stewart	J-P. Beltoise
1969	Canadian GP	Brabham-Ford	J. Ickx	J. Brabham
1970	Austrian GP	Ferrari	J. Ickx	C. Regazzoni
1970	Canadian GP	Ferrari	J. Ickx	C. Regazzoni
1970	Mexican GP	Ferrari	J. Ickx	C. Regazzoni
1971	French GP	Tyrrell-Ford	J. Stewart	F. Cevert
1971	German GP	Tyrrell-Ford	J. Stewart	F. Cevert
1972	German GP	Ferrari	J. Ickx	C. Regazzoni
1972	United States GP	Tyrrell-Ford	J. Stewart	F. Cevert
1973	Belgian GP	Tyrrell-Ford	J. Stewart	F. Cevert
1973	Dutch GP	Tyrrell-Ford	J. Stewart	F. Cevert

Year	Grand Prix	Car	First	Second
1973	German GP	Tyrrell-Ford	J. Stewart	F. Cevert
1973	Italian GP	Lotus-Ford	R. Peterson	E. Fittipaldi
1974	Spanish GP	Ferrari	N. Lauda	C. Regazzoni
1974	Swedish GP	Tyrrell-Ford	J. Scheckter	P. Depailler
1974	Dutch GP	Ferrari	N. Lauda	C. Regazzoni
1974	United States GP	Brabham-Ford	C. Reutemann	C. Pace
1976	United States (West) GP	Ferrari	C. Regazzoni	N. Lauda
1976	Belgian GP	Ferrari	N. Lauda	C. Regazzoni
1976	Swedish	Tyrrell-Ford	J. Scheckter	P. Depailler
1978	Belgian GP	Lotus-Ford	M. Andretti	R. Peterson
1978	Spanish GP	Lotus-Ford	M. Andretti	R. Peterson
1978	French GP	Lotus-Ford	M. Andretti	R. Peterson
1978	Dutch GP	Lotus-Ford	M. Andretti	R. Peterson
1978	Italian GP	Brabham-Alfa Romeo	N. Lauda	J. Watson
1979	Brazilian GP	Ligier-Ford	J. Laffite	P. Depailler
1979	South African GP	Ferrari	G. Villeneuve	J. Scheckter
1979	United States (West) GP	Ferrari	G. Villeneuve	J. Scheckter
1979	German GP	Williams-Ford	A. Jones	C. Regazzoni
1979	Italian GP	Ferrari	J. Scheckter	G. Villeneuve
1980	Canadian GP	Williams-Ford	A. Jones	C. Reutemann
1980	United States GP	Williams-Ford	A. Jones	C. Reutemann
1981	United States (West) GP	Williams-Ford	A. Jones	C. Reutemann
1981	Brazilian	Williams-Ford	C. Reutemann	A. Jones
1982	San Marino GP	Ferrari	D. Pironi	G. Villeneuve

Year	Grand Prix	Car	First	Second
1982	French GP	Renault	R. Arnoux	A. Prost
1983	Long Beach GP	McLaren-Ford	J. Watson	N. Lauda
1983	Dutch GP	Ferrari	R. Arnoux	P. Tambay
1984	South African GP	McLaren-Porsche	N. Lauda	A. Prost
1984	German GP	McLaren-Porsche	A. Prost	N. Lauda
1984	Dutch GP	McLaren-Porsche	A. Prost	N. Lauda
1984	Portuguese GP	McLaren-Porsche	A. Prost	N. Lauda
1985	Canadian GP	Ferrari	M. Albereto	S. Johansson
1985	Dutch GP	McLaren-Porsche	N. Lauda	A. Prost
1985	South African GP	Williams-Honda	N. Mansell	K. Rosberg
1986	Monaco GP	McLaren-TAG	A. Prost	K. Rosberg
1986	British GP	Williams-Honda	N. Mansell	N. Piquet
1986	Italian GP	Williams-Honda	N. Piquet	N. Mansell

The same car has occupied the first four places on the following occasions:
1952 German GP, Ferrari (Ferrari also sixth place)
1955 British GP, Mercedes
1957 Argentine GP, Maserati
1960 French GP, Cooper-Climax
1961 Belgian GP, Ferrari
In the 1951 German GP, Ferrari occupied five of the top six places – only Fangio's second placing in an Alfa Romeo prevented total domination.
* Indicates car also occupied third place
† Indicates car also occupied third and fourth places

Niki Lauda and Alain Prost on their way to filling first and second places in the 1985 Dutch Grand Prix. The previous season they occupied the first two places four times. (McLaren International)

Jackie Stewart

Jackie Stewart was easily recognizable on the starting grid before a race. Not because he was generally on the front of the grid, but because of the distinguishable Stewart tartan band across his helmet.

Scottish, and very proud of it, just as Scotland is proud of him, John Young Stewart was born near Dumbarton, Strathclyde in 1939 and went on to become the most dominant Formula One driver between 1969 and his retirement in 1973.

The son of a Jaguar dealer, motoring ran through the family's

Below If he had not taken up racing, Jackie Stewart could well have been a world clay pigeon shooting champion . . . . (National Motor Museum)

Jackie Stewart still keeps a close watch on what is happening in the motor racing world

veins. Jackie's brother, Jimmy, was the first to take up racing but he quit after an accident. Despite pleas from his mother, Jackie was next to try his hand at the sport. His first race was at Oulton Park in 1962 when he was behind the wheel of a Porsche.

One of the greatest partnerships in motor racing was formed in 1964 when Stewart and Ken Tyrrell teamed up. Stewart was signed up to race Tyrrell's Formula Three Coopers and he won his first race at Snetterton. Furthermore, he won virtually every Formula Three event he entered. With Tyrrell he also picked up valuable Formula Two experience and it was not long before Formula One manufacturers were after his signature. Stewart joined BRM in 1965 where he replaced American Richie Ginther as Graham Hill's new

stablemate. He finished sixth in his first Grand Prix, the South African, but enjoyed his first win later in the season when he won the Italian Grand Prix at Monza, and eventually finished the championship in third place.

In 1966 he won the opening round of the championship at Monte Carlo but, after a bad crash at Spa in the next race, he failed to win again that season, or the season after. His fortune took a turn for the better in 1968, however, when he teamed up with Tyrrell again who had entered the world of Formula One with the Matra MS10. Stewart gave the car its first win at Zandvoort, and victories at the Nurburgring, by a staggering four minutes, and at Watkins Glen ensured him of second place in the championship to his former team-mate Hill.

The Matra-Ford proved even more reliable the following season, as car and driver swept the board with six wins which gave Stewart the first of his three world titles, winning by 26 points from Jacky Ickx (Bel). Tyrrell ran the March team in 1970 but the car was not good enough for a driver of Stewart's calibre so Tyrrell decided to build and run one under his own name for Stewart. In 1971 the glory days returned as Stewart won six of the eleven rounds of the championship on his way to winning his second title.

Early-season mechanical problems with his car in 1972 were too big a handicap, despite his late-season burst, for him to win his third title but another title came in 1973 when he won five races and surpassed the all-time records of Juan Manuel Fangio (Arg) and Jim Clark (GB). Stewart had announced he was retiring at the end of that season but his retirement happened earlier than anticipated.

He was scheduled to compete in his 100th, and last, Grand Prix at Watkins Glen but he pulled out of the race in respect for his team-mate Francois Cevert who was killed in practice.

Despite numerous offers to return to Grand Prix racing, in-

The unmistakable Jackie Stewart with his distinguishable Stewart tartan band around his helmet. (National Motor Museum)

cluding a staggering £1 million from the Brabham team in 1981, Stewart never returned to the sport. But he has remained in contact with motor racing as a broadcaster and interviewer.

When not attending a race meeting, Stewart can often be seen enjoying his favourite pastime, clay-pigeon shooting, a sport at which he gained international honours and came close to Olympic selection.

Circuits

Complete list of World Championship Circuits

Circuit	Country	First Used	Last Used	No of Times Used
Adelaide	Australia	1985	1986	2
Ain-Diab	Morocco	1958	–	1
Aintree	Great Britain	1955	1962	5
Anderstorp	Sweden	1973	1978	6
Avus	West Germany	1959	–	1
Brands Hatch	Great Britain	1964	1986	14
Bremgarten	Switzerland	1950	1954	5
Budapest	Hungary	1986	–	1
Buenos Aires	Argentina	1953	1981	16
Caesar's Palace	United States	1981	1982	2
Clermont-Ferrand	France	1965	1972	4
Dallas	United States	1984	–	1
Detroit	United States	1982	1986	5
Dijon-Prenois	France	1974	1984	6
East London	South Africa	1962	1965	3
Estoril	Portugal	1984	1986	3
Fuji	Japan	1976	1977	2
Hockenheim	West Germany	1970	1986	10
Imola	Italy	1982	1986	5
Indianapolis	United States	1950	1960	11
Interlagos	Brazil	1973	1980	7
Jarama	Spain	1968	1981	10
Kyalami	South Africa	1967	1985	7
Le Mans	France	1967	–	1
Long Beach	United States	1976	1983	7
Mexico City	Mexico	1963	1986	9
Monsanto	Portugal	1959	–	1
Monte Carlo	Monaco	1950	1986	33
Montjuich	Spain	1969	1986	5
Montreal	Canada	1978	1986	9
Monza	Italy	1950	1986	36
Mosport	Canada	1967	1977	8
Nivelles	Belgium	1972	1974	2
Nurburgring (New)	West Germany	1984	1985	2
Nurburgring (Old)	West Germany	1951	1976	22
Oporto	Portugal	1958	1960	2
Osterreichring	Austria	1970	1986	17
Paul Ricard	France	1971	1986	10
Pedralbes	Spain	1951	1954	2
Pescara	Italy	1957	–	1
Rheims	France	1950	1966	11
Rio de Janeiro	Brazil	1978	1986	7
Riverside	United States	1960	–	1
Rouen	France	1952	1968	5
St. Jovite	Canada	1968	1970	2
Sebring	United States	1959	–	1
Silverstone	Great Britain	1950	1985	20
Spa	Belgium	1950	1986	21
Watkins Glen	United States	1961	1980	20
Zandvoort	Holland	1952	1985	30
Zeltweg	Austria	1964	–	1
Zolder	Belgium	1973	1984	11

Longest

Circuit	Length	First used
Pescara, Italy	25.57 km / 15.89 miles	1957
Nurburgring, W. Germany	22.83 km / 14.19 miles	1951
Spa, Belgium	14.12 km / 8.77 miles	1950
Monza, Italy	10.00 km / 6.21 miles	1955
Sebring, USA	8.37 km / 5.20 miles	1959
Rheims, France	8.35 km / 5.19 miles	1953
Avus, W. Germany	8.30 km / 5.16 miles	1959
Clermont-Ferrand, France	8.05 km / 5.01 miles	1965

Because circuits have been modified over the years, the greatest length of a particular course has been taken into consideration.

Shortest

Circuit	Length	First used
Monte Carlo, Monaco	3.14 km / 1.95 miles	1955
Zeltweg, Austria	3.20 km / 1.99 miles	1964
Long Beach, USA	3.25 km / 2.02 miles	1976
Dijon-Prenois, France	3.29 km / 2.04 miles	1974
Jarama, Spain	3.31 km / 2.06 miles	1981

Because circuits have been modified over the years, the shortest length of a particular course only has been taken into consideration.

Fastest

The fastest circuits, based on the Grand Prix winner's average speed, have been:

Circuit	Winner's Avge Speed	Year
Monza, Italy	242.62 kph / 150.75 mph	1971
Spa, Belgium	241.31 kph / 149.94 mph	1970
Avus, W. Germany	236.04 kph / 146.67 mph	1959
Silverstone, GB	235.40 kph / 146.28 mph	1985
Osterreichring, Austria	231.13 kph / 143.62 mph	1985

Note: Monza and Spa had other races that would have figured in the above list, but the fastest race over the circuit only is included.

Slowest

Because of its nature the Monaco Grand Prix, through the streets of Monte Carlo, is regarded as the slowest of all Grands Prix and indeed nine of the ten all-time slowest World Championship Grand Prix races have been over the circuit. The following is a list of the slowest race at Monte Carlo, plus other notably slow races:

Circuit	Winner's Avge Speed	Year
Monte Carlo, Monaco	98.68 kph / 61.33 mph	1950
Buenos Aires, Argentine	112.84 kph / 70.13 mph	1954
Detroit, USA	125.85 kph / 78.20 mph	1982
Rouen, France	128.94 kph / 80.14 mph	1952
Dallas, USA	129.22 kph / 80.30 mph	1984
Nurburgring, W. Germany	129.30 kph / 80.35 mph	1962
Long Beach, USA	129.79 kph / 80.65 mph	1983

Note: Buenos Aires had other races that would have figured in the above list, but the slowest race over the circuit only is included.

Tight bends like this help make the Monaco Grand Prix the slowest on the Grand Prix calendar

Above One of the great long-distance circuits — the old Nurburgring. (National Motor Museum)

The Indianapolis Speedway filled to capacity. Between 1950–60 the 'Indy 500' was part of the Formula One World Championship. (National Motor Museum)

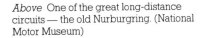

South Curve

AVUS

One of the least imaginative of all the 52 circuits that have staged world championship races. The Avus circuit in West Berlin was two stretches of motorway joined together by two banked curves. It was only used once, in 1959 and Tony Brooks' winning speed of 236.04 kph (146.67 mph) was the fastest winning speed in a Grand Prix until Pedro Rodriguez won at Spa in 1970.

SILVERSTONE (*Right*)

Silverstone has been staging British Grands Prix since the introduction of the world championship in 1950. Its length was increased from 4.7105 km (2.927 miles) to 4.7185 km (2.932 miles) in 1975 with the addition of the chicane at Woodcote.

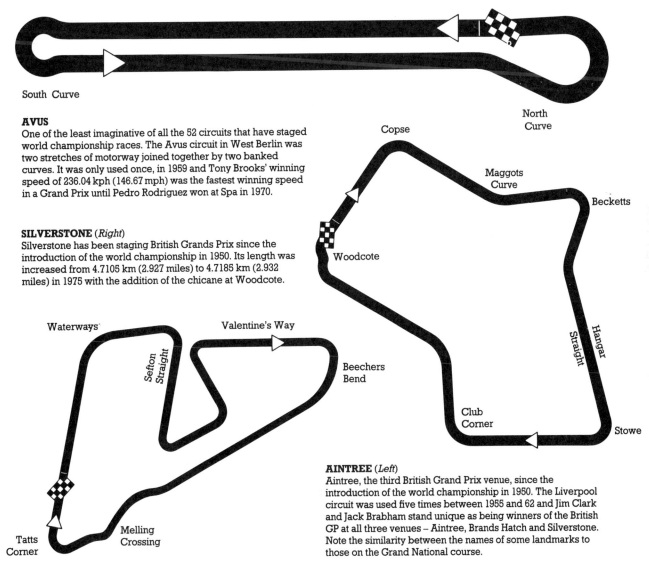

North Curve

Copse

Maggots Curve

Becketts

Woodcote

Hangar Straight

Waterways

Sefton Straight

Valentine's Way

Beechers Bend

Club Corner

Stowe

Tatts Corner

Melling Crossing

AINTREE (*Left*)

Aintree, the third British Grand Prix venue, since the introduction of the world championship in 1950. The Liverpool circuit was used five times between 1955 and 62 and Jim Clark and Jack Brabham stand unique as being winners of the British GP at all three venues – Aintree, Brands Hatch and Silverstone. Note the similarity between the names of some landmarks to those on the Grand National course.

MONTE CARLO

The Monaco Grand Prix has provided both the shortest and slowest races. This circuit measured just 3.145 km (1.954 miles) and was used between 1955–72. It was modified in 1973 with the inclusion of a longer, more modern tunnel.

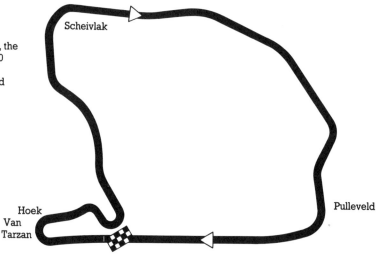

Virage de
Sainte Devote

Virages
Mirabeau

Casino
Square

La
Rascasse

Tunnel

ZANDVOORT

Third only to Monza and Monte Carlo, the Zandvoort circuit has been used for 30 world championship races. The 4.193 km (2.605 miles) circuit was used for the first time in 1952.

Scheivlak

Pulleveld

Hoek
Van
Tarzan

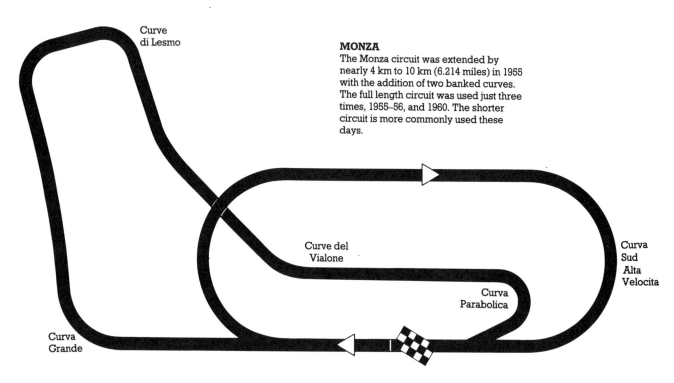

Curve
di Lesmo

MONZA

The Monza circuit was extended by nearly 4 km to 10 km (6.214 miles) in 1955 with the addition of two banked curves. The full length circuit was used just three times, 1955–56, and 1960. The shorter circuit is more commonly used these days.

Curve del
Vialone

Curva
Sud
Alta
Velocita

Curva
Parabolica

Curva
Grande

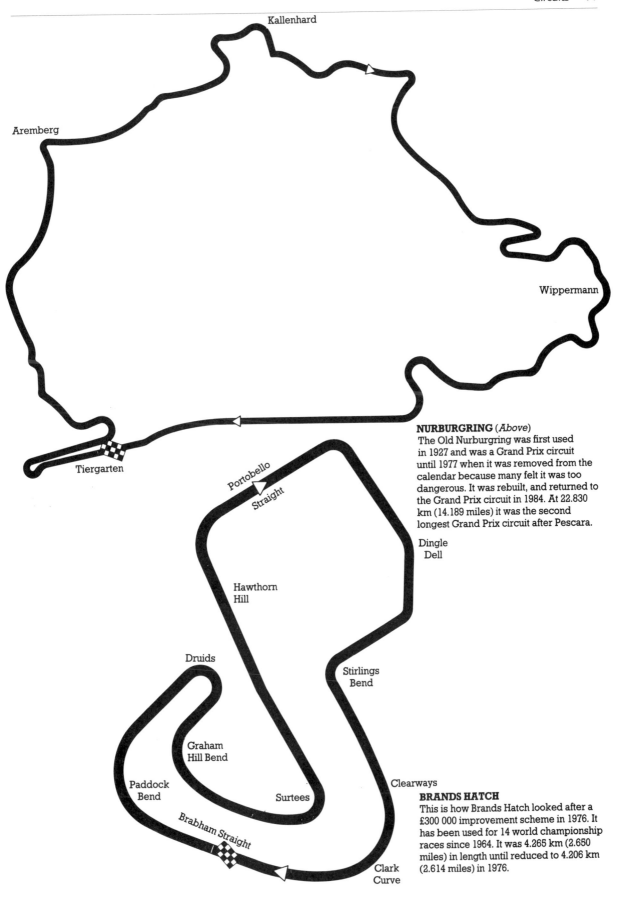

Kallenhard

Aremberg

Wippermann

Tiergarten

NURBURGRING (*Above*)
The Old Nurburgring was first used
in 1927 and was a Grand Prix circuit
until 1977 when it was removed from the
calendar because many felt it was too
dangerous. It was rebuilt, and returned to
the Grand Prix circuit in 1984. At 22.830
km (14.189 miles) it was the second
longest Grand Prix circuit after Pescara.

Portobello
Straight

Dingle
Dell

Hawthorn
Hill

Druids

Stirlings
Bend

Graham
Hill Bend

Clearways

Paddock
Bend

Surtees

BRANDS HATCH
This is how Brands Hatch looked after a
£300 000 improvement scheme in 1976. It
has been used for 14 world championship
races since 1964. It was 4.265 km (2.650
miles) in length until reduced to 4.206 km
(2.614 miles) in 1976.

Brabham Straight

Clark
Curve

SPA

The current Spa circuit, in the Ardennes, south of Liege in Belgium, bears little resemblance to the one illustrated as it was completely rebuilt in 1983. The circuit (right) was the 14.120 km (8.774 miles) one used for the 1950 Belgian Grand Prix. The Virage de la Source is one of the few original landmarks that can still be found on the new circuit.

Virage de la Source

Virage de Burnenville

Virage de Stavelot

An all-too-familiar sight these days, the Marlboro-McLaren team occupying first and second place

PESCARA

The Pescara road circuit was used for just one Grand Prix, in 1957. Its 25.579 km (15.890 miles) route up into the Abruzzi mountains made it the longest ever circuit used for a world championship race.

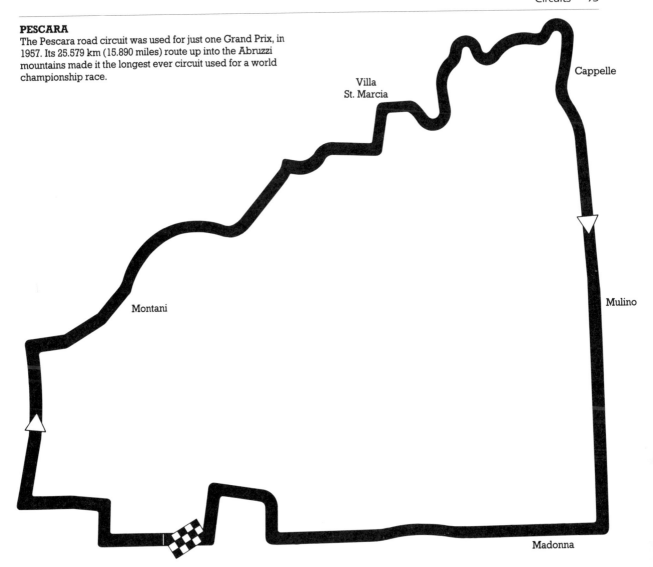

Races

Fastest

Winner's Avge
Speed

kph	mph	Race	Circuit
242.62	150.75	1971 Italian GP	Monza
241.31	149.94	1970 Belgian GP	Spa
236.80	147.14	1968 Belgian GP	Spa
236.70	147.08	1970 Italian GP	Monza
236.52	146.97	1969 Italian GP	Monza
236.04	146.67	1959 German GP	Avus
235.40	146.28	1985 British GP	Silverstone
234.95	145.99	1967 Belgian GP	Spa
234.02	145.41	1968 Italian GP	Monza
231.13	143.62	1985 Austrian GP	Osterreichring
228.35	141.90	1986 Italian GP	Monza
227.80	141.56	1986 Austrian GP	Osterreichring
227.57	141.41	1985 Italian GP	Monza
226.12	140.50	1967 Italian GP	Monza

Slowest

Winner's Avge
Speed

kph	mph	Race	Circuit
98.68	61.33	1950 Monaco GP	Monte Carlo
100.78	62.62	1984 Monaco GP	Monte Carlo
102.76	63.85	1972 Monaco GP	Monte Carlo
104.16	64.72	1957 Monaco GP	Monte Carlo
104.51	64.94	1956 Monaco GP	Monte Carlo
105.91	65.81	1955 Monaco GP	Monte Carlo
107.36	66.71	1959 Monaco GP	Monte Carlo
108.60	67.48	1960 Monaco GP	Monte Carlo
109.41	67.99	1958 Monaco GP	Monte Carlo
112.84	70.13	1954 Argentine GP	Buenos Aires

Longest

Distance	Race	Year
805 km / 500 miles	Indianapolis 500	1951–60
602 km / 374 miles	French GP (Rheims)	1951
555 km / 345 miles	Indianapolis 500	1950 (shortened race)
508 km / 316 miles	Belgian GP (Spa)	1951–56

Fatalities

The following drivers all lost their lives either competing in, or practising for, a Formula One World Championship Grand Prix.

Onofre Marimon (ARG)	1954 German GP, Nurburgring (P)
Luigi Musso (ITA)	1958 French GP, Rheims
Peter Collins (GB)	1958 German GP, Nurburgring
Stuart Lewis-Evans (GB)	1958 Moroccan GP, Casablanca
Chris Bristow (GB)	1960 Belgian GP, Spa
Alan Stacey (GB)	1960 Belgian GP, Spa
Wolfgang von Trips (FRG)	1961 Italian GP, Monza
Carel Godin de Beaufort (HOL)	1964 German GP, Nurburgring (P)
John Taylor (GB)	1966 German GP, Nurburgring
Lorenzo Bandini (ITA)	1967 Monaco GP, Monte Carlo
Jo Schlesser (FRA)	1968 French GP, Rouen
Piers Courage (GB)	1970 Dutch GP, Zandvoort
Jochen Rindt (AUT)	1970 Italian GP, Monza (P)
Roger Williamson (GB)	1973 Dutch GP, Zandvoort
Francois Cevert (FRA)	1973 United States GP, Watkins Glen (P)
Helmuth Koinigg (AUT)	1974 United States GP, Watkins Glen
Mark Donohue (USA)	1975 Austrian GP, Osterreichring
Tom Pryce (GB)	1977 South African GP, Kyalami
Ronnie Peterson (SWE)	1978 Italian GP, Monza
Gilles Villeneuve (CAN)	1982 Belgian GP, Zolder (P)
Ricardo Paletti (ITA)	1982 Canadian GP, Montreal
Manfred Winkelhock (FRG)	1985 Canadian GP, Montreal

(P) Indicates killed during practice

Germany's Wolfgang von Trips lost his life when his Ferrari flew off the track during the 1961 Italian Grand Prix at Monza. Von Trips was killed, along with 11 spectators. (National Motor Museum)

The popular Italian Elio de Angelis died in 1986 when his Brabham lost control during a testing session at the Paul Ricard circuit in France

The last driver to lose his life during a Formula One Grand Prix was Manfred Winkelhock (FRG) during the 1985 Canadian GP at Montreal

World Sports Car Championship

Endurance racing has remained one of the most popular forms of motor racing and, apart from the Formula One World Championship, the Sports Car World Championship is the longest surviving World Championship event, although it has appeared under different guises since first seen in 1953.

It was known as the Sports Car World Championship from 1953–61 and the title went to the leading manufacturer. A 3-litre capacity limit was introduced in 1958. The championship ended in 1961 and the F.I.A. introduced a championship for Grand Touring (GT) cars and strictly speaking the Sports Car World Championship ceased, although the organizers of the Targa Florio, Le Mans, Nurburgring and Sebring races offered the Challenge Mondiale de Vitesse for Prototype cars. The Daytona race became part of the 'Championship' in 1965 and in 1967 a total of eight races made up the Prototype competition. From 1968 the F.I.A. introduced a new World Sports Car Manufacturers' Championship for both Competition Sports Cars (Group 4) and Prototypes (Group 6). This championship, like all others before it, was for manufacturers only, and not for drivers.

With the distinction between Competition Sports Cars and Prototypes disappearing, a new championship was introduced in 1972 which was called the World Championship for Makes for Prototype Sports Cars (Group 5) and GT Cars (Group 4). From 1976 the championship was open to Group 5 cars only.

In 1981, however, sports car drivers had a World Championship for the first time, when the championship was again renamed the World Endurance Championship and from 1982 the championship was for the new Group C cars.

The championship was renamed yet again in 1986 when it became The Sports-Prototype World Championship, for both drivers and teams.

Results

• John Watson (GB) and McLaren team-mate Niki Lauda (Aut) finished first and second in the 1983 Long Beach Grand Prix. Remarkably, they were 22nd and 23rd on the starting grid. Watson had won the previous year's Detroit Grand Prix from 17th position on the grid.

1953

Sebring, United States
1 J. Fitch/P. Walters   Cunningham
   120.60 kph / 74.94 mph
2 R. Parnell/
   G. Abecassis   Aston Martin
3 C. Johnston/Wilder   Jaguar

Mille Miglia, Italy
1 G. Marzotto/Crosaro   Ferrari
   142.32 kph / 88.45 mph
2 J. M. Fangio/Sala   Alfa Romeo
3 F. Bonetto/Peruzzi   Lancia

Le Mans, France
1 M. A. Rolt/
   D. Hamilton   Jaguar
   170.30 kph / 105.82 mph
2 S. Moss/P. Walker   Jaguar
3 P. Walters/J. Fitch   Cunningham

Spa, Belgium
1 G. Farina/
   M. Hawthorn   Ferrari
   152.72 kph / 94.90 mph
2 J. Scott-Douglas/
   G. Gale   Jaguar
3 H. Roosdorp/
   T. Ulmen   Jaguar

Nurburgring, West Germany
1 A. Ascari/G. Farina   Ferrari
   120.30 kph / 74.75 mph
2 I. Stewart/
   R. Salvadori   Jaguar
3 A. Brudes/
   F. Hammernick   Borgward

Dundrod, Northern Ireland
1 P. Collins/P. Griffiths   Aston Martin
   131.45 kph / 81.68 mph
2 R. Parnell/
   E. Thompson   Aston Martin
3 K. Wharton/C. Robb   Frazer Nash

Carrera Panamericana, Mexico
1 J. M. Fangio/
   G. Bronzoni   Lancia
   170.16 kph / 105.74 mph
2 P. Taruffi/L. Maggio   Lancia
3 E. Castellotti/
   C. Luoni   Lancia

Final Championship Standing
1 Ferrari   30 pts
2 Jaguar   27 pts
3 Aston Martin   16 pts

1954

Buenos Aires, Argentina

1 G. Farina/U. Maglioli   Ferrari
  150.40 kph / 93.46 mph
2 H. Schell/A. de
  Portago   Ferrari
3 P. Collins/
  P. Griffiths   Aston Martin

Sebring, United States

1 S. Moss/W. Lloyd   Osca
  118.30 kph / 73.51 mph
2 G. Valenzano/
  P. Rubirosa   Lancia
3 L. Macklin/
  G. Huntoon   Austin-Healey

Mille Miglia, Italy

1 A. Ascari   Lancia
  139.61 kph / 86.77 mph
2 V. Marzotto   Ferrari
3 L. Musso/Zocca Maserati

Le Mans, France

1 J. F. Gonzalez/
  M. Trintignant Ferrari
  169.19 kph / 105.13 mph
2 A. Rolt/J. Hamilton   Jaguar
3 W. Spear/S. Johnson   Cunningham

Dundrod, Northern Ireland

1 P. Armagnac/
  G. Loreau   Panhard
  138.50 kph / 86.06 mph
2 M. Hawthorn/
  M. Trintignant Ferrari
3 L. Musso/
  S. Mantovani   Maserati

Carrera Panamericana, Mexico

1 U. Maglioli   Ferrari
  173.70 kph / 107.94 mph
2 P. Hill   Ferrari
3 H. Herrmann   Porsche

Final Championship Standing

1 Ferrari   38 pts
2 Lancia   20 pts
3 Jaguar   10 pts

1955

Buenos Aires, Argentina

1 E. S. Valiente/
  J. M. Ibanez   Ferrari
  150.87 kph / 93.75 mph
2 C. Najurieta/
  O. Ribera   Ferrari
3 R. Grandio/J. Faraoni   Maserati

Sebring, United States

1 M. Hawthorn/
  P. Walters   Jaguar
  126.58 kph / 78.66 mph
2 P. Hill/C. Shelby   Ferrari
3 W. Spear/
  S. Johnston   Maserati

Mille Miglia, Italy

1 S. Moss/
  D. Jenkinson   Mercedes-
                  Benz
  157.62 kph / 97.96 mph
2 J. M. Fangio   Mercedes-
                  Benz
3 U. Maglioli   Ferrari

Le Mans, France

1 M. Hawthorn/
  I. Bueb   Jaguar
  172.28 kph / 107.05 mph
2 P. Collins/P. Frere   Aston Martin
3 J. Claes/J. Swaters   Jaguar

Dundrod, Northern Ireland

1 S. Moss/J. Fitch   Mercedes-
                     Benz
  142.16 kph / 88.34 mph
2 J. M. Fangio/
  K. Kling   Mercedes-
                  Benz
3 A. Simon/
  W. von Trips/
  K. Kling   Mercedes-
                  Benz

Targa Florio, Italy

1 S. Moss/P. Collins   Mercedes-
                       Benz
  95.90 kph / 59.60 mph
2 J. M. Fangio/K. Kling   Mercedes-
                          Benz
3 E. Castellotti/
  R. Manzon   Ferrari

Final Championship Standing

1 Mercedes-Benz   24 pts
2 Ferrari   23 pts
3 Jaguar   16 pts

1956

Buenos Aires, Argentina

1 S. Moss/
  G. Menditeguy   Maserati
  158.68 kph / 98.60 mph
2 O. Gendebien/
  P. Hill   Ferrari
3 J. F. Gonzalez/
  J. Behra   Maserati

Sebring, United States

1 J. M. Fangio/
  E. Castellotti Ferrari
  135.30 kph / 84.08 mph
2 L. Musso/H. Schell   Ferrari
3 R. Sweikert/J. Ensley   Jaguar

Mille Miglia, Italy

1 E. Castellotti   Ferrari
  137.41 kph / 85.40 mph
2 P. Collins/
  L. Klementaski Ferrari
3 L. Musso   Ferrari

Nurburgring, West Germany

1 S. Moss/J. Behra/
  P. Taruffi/H. Schell   Maserati
  129.70 kph / 80.60 mph
2 J. M. Fangio/
  E. Castellotti Ferrari
3 O. Gendebien/A. de
  Portago/P. Hill   Ferrari

Kristianstad, Sweden

1 P. Hill/M. Trintignant   Ferrari
  152.39 kph / 94.70 mph
2 P. Collins/W. von
  Trips   Ferrari
3 M. Hawthorn/
  A. de Portago/
  J. Hamilton   Ferrari

Final Championship Standing

1 Ferrari   36 pts
2 Maserati   18 pts
3 Jaguar   7 pts

1957

Buenos Aires, Argentina

1 M. Gregory/C.
  Perdisa/L. Musso/
  E. Castellotti Ferrari
  162.18 kph / 100.78 mph
2 J. Behra/S. Moss/
  C. Menditeguy   Maserati
3 E. Castellotti/A. de
  Portago/W. von
  Trips/P. Collins   Ferrari

Sebring, United States

1 J. M. Fangio/J. Behra   Maserati
  137.40 kph / 85.38 mph
2 S. Moss/H. Schell   Maserati
3 M. Hawthorn/I. Bueb   Jaguar

Mille Miglia, Italy

1 P. Taruffi   Ferrari
  152.60 kph / 94.84 mph
2 W. von Trips   Ferrari
3 Wascher/
  O. Gendebien   Ferrari

Nurburgring, West Germany

1 C. A. S. Brooks/
  N. Cunningham-
  Reid   Aston Martin
  132.60 kph / 82.40 mph
2 P. Collins/
  O. Gendebien   Ferrari
3 M. Trintignant/
  M. Hawthorn   Ferrari

Le Mans, France

1 R. Flockhart/I. Bueb   Jaguar
  183.18 kph / 113.83 mph
2 N. Sanderson/
  J. Lawrence   Jaguar
3 J. Lucas/
  'Jean-Marie'   Jaguar

Jody Scheckter, the 1979 world champion by four points from Canadian Gilles Villeneuve, to become the first South African to win the title. (Michelin Tyre Co. Ltd.)

John Watson keeping the sun off him before the start of the 1982 British Grand Prix at Brands Hatch. (Michelin Tyre Co. Ltd.)

Renault were responsible for the introduction of the turbo engine in 1977 when they introduced the RS01. The above engine was the RS12. (Michelin Tyre Co. Ltd.)

Just another side of the costly business of running a Formula One team – the huge stock of tyres. (Michelin Tyre Co. Ltd.)

The German-based Zakspeed team entered the world of Formula One racing in 1985. Mechanics are seen here tending to Dutchman Huub Rothengatter's car at Imola. (Ferdi Kraling)

The 1980 Williams FW07 that won the Constructors' Championship. (Michelin Tyre Co. Ltd.)

Britain's Graham Hill on his way to winning his second successive Monaco Grand Prix in 1964. Hill went on to win the race a record five times, winning again in 1965, to complete the hat-trick. He also won in 1968 and 1969. (National Motor Museum)

Left Brazil has produced two world champions, Emerson Fittipaldi and Nelson Piquet. Will Ayrton Senna be the third? (The Goodyear Tyre & Rubber Co. Ltd.)

World champion Emerson Fittipaldi used to race karts – he shows he never lost the technique, although somebody should have told him that the helmet goes on his head!

Winning can be sweet, but how bitter defeat can be . . . mind you the latter is the exception rather than the rule for Alain Prost (Fra)

Britain's Nigel Mansell, who came close to winning the 1986 world championship, only being deprived by a blown tyre in the final race of the season at Adelaide, Austrualia. (The Goodyear Tyre & Rubber Co. Ltd.)

There's more to a racing car than meets the eye . . .

One of the sport's great ambassadors, Jack Brabham (AUS). He is seen here during the 1964 Monaco Grand Prix (National Motor Museum)

The impressive sight of a procession of sports cars at Silverstone with the Lancia-Martini team occupying first and second places. (National Motor Museum)

Elio de Angelis (ITA) during the 1984 British Grand Prix at Brands Hatch, showing how well supported Grand Prix racing is. (Michelin Tyre Co. Ltd.)

Left The backdrop on Monte Carlo makes the Monaco Grand Prix one of the most dramatic settings on the Formula One calendar

The 24 hours at Le Mans is more than just a race, it is a day-long carnival and, as darkness falls, the other features, like the fairground, attract the thousands of fans. (All Sport)

Below A clever shot of the Marlboro-McLaren MP4/2 with Austrian Niki Lauda behind the wheel

Stirling Moss must surely be the best driver *never* to have won the World Drivers' Championship. He was runner-up four years in succession 1955–8, to Fangio three times and to fellow Briton Mike Hawthorn once. (All Sport)

Oh to be a photographer! (All Sport)

Today, 14 years after his retirement, Jackie Stewart (GB) still holds the record for the most Grand Prix wins in a career, 27, but Frenchman Alain Prost is capable of overtaking him in 1987 as he needs just three more wins for the record. (All Sport)

Kristianstad, Sweden

1 S. Moss/J. Behra Maserati
 157.53 kph / 97.89 mph
2 P. Collins/P. Hill Ferrari
3 J. Bonnier/
 G. Scarlatti/S. Moss/
 H. Schell Maserati

Caracas, Venezuela

1 P. Collins/P. Hill Ferrari
 153.77 kph / 95.55 mph
2 L. Musso/
 M. Hawthorn Ferrari
3 W. Seidel/W. von
 Trips Ferrari

Final Championship Standing

1 Ferrari 41 pts
2 Maserati 28 pts
3 Jaguar 17 pts

1958

Buenos Aires, Argentina

1 P. Collins/P. Hill Ferrari
 158.40 kph / 98.43 mph
2 O. Gendebien/
 W. von Trips/
 L. Musso Ferrari
3 S. Moss/J. Behra Porsche

Sebring, United States

1 P. Hill/P. Collins Ferrari
 139.48 kph / 86.67 mph
2 O. Gendebien/
 L. Musso Ferrari
3 W. Seidel/H. Schell Porsche

Targa Florio, Italy

1 O. Gendebien/
 L. Musso Ferrari
 94.79 kph / 58.71 mph
2 J. Behra/G. Scarlatti Porsche
3 M. Hawthorn/
 W. von Trips Ferrari

Nurburgring, West Germany

1 S. Moss/J. Brabham Aston Martin
 135.76 kph / 84.36 mph
2 M. Hawthorn/
 P. Collins Ferrari
3 O. Gendebien/
 W. von Trips Ferrari

Le Mans, France

1 P. Hill/O. Gendebien Ferrari
 170.88 kph / 106.18 mph
2 A. Whitehead/
 P. Whitehead Aston Martin
3 H. Herrmann/
 J. Behra Porsche

Goodwood, England

1 S. Moss/
 C. A. S. Brooks Aston Martin
 142.12 kph / 88.31 mph
2 R. Salvadori/
 J. Brabham Aston Martin
3 C. Shelby/S. Lewis-
 Evans Aston Martin

Final Championship Standing

1 Ferrari 38 pts
2 Porsche 20 pts
3 Aston Martin 18pts

1959

Sebring, United States

1 O. Gendebien/
 D. Gurney/P. Hill/
 C. Daigh Ferrari
 131.11 kph / 81.47 mph
2 C. Allison/J. Behra Ferrari
3 J. Bonnier/W. von
 Trips Porsche

Targa Florio, Italy

1 E. Barth/W. Seidel Porsche
 91.29 kph / 56.74 mph
2 E. Mahle/D. Strahle/
 H. Linge Porsche
3 A. Pucci/H. von
 Hanstein Porsche

Nurburgring, West Germany

1 S. Moss/J. Fairman Aston Martin
 132.80 kph / 82.52 mph
2 O. Gendebien/P. Hill Ferrari
3 C. A. S. Brooks/
 J. Behra Ferrari

Le Mans, France

1 R. Salvadori/
 C. Shelby Aston Martin
 181.13 kph / 112.55 mph
2 M. Trintignant/
 P. Frere Aston Martin
3 'Buerlys'/'Elde' Ferrari

Goodwood, England

1 J. Fairman/C. Shelby/
 S. Moss Aston Martin
 143.89 kph / 89.41 mph
2 J. Bonnier/W. von
 Trips Porsche
3 O. Gendebien/P. Hill/
 C. Allison/C. A. S.
 Brooks Ferrari

Final Championship Standing

1 Aston Martin 24 pts
2 Ferrari 22 pts
3 Porsche 21 pts

1960

Buenos Aires, Argentina

1 C. Allison/P. Hill Ferrari
 159.78 kph / 99.29 mph
2 R. Ginther/W. von
 Trips Ferrari
3 C. Heins/C. Narberis Porsche

Sebring, United States

1 O. Gendebien/
 H. Herrmann Porsche
 136.68 kph / 84.93 mph
2 R. Holbert/Schlecter/
 Fowler Porsche
3 P. Lovely/
 J. Nethercutt Ferrari

Targa Florio, Italy

1 J. Bonnier/
 H. Herrmann Porsche
 95.32 kph / 59.24 mph
2 P. Hill/W. von Trips Ferrari
3 O. Gendebien/
 H. Herrmann Porsche

Nurburgring, West Germany

1 S. Moss/D. Gurney Maserati
 133.20 kph / 82.77 mph
2 J. Bonnier/
 O. Gendebien Porsche
3 P. Hill/C. Allison/
 W. Mairesse Ferrari

Le Mans, France

1 O. Gendebien/
 P. Frere Ferrari
 175.69 kph / 109.17 mph
2 A. Pilette/
 R. Rodriguez Ferrari
3 J. Clark/R. Salvadori Aston Martin

Final Championship Standing

1 Ferrari 30 pts
2 Porsche 26 pts
3 Maserati 11 pts

1961

Sebring, United States

1 O. Gendebien/P. Hill Ferrari
 145.50 kph / 90.41 mph
2 R. Ginther/W. von
 Trips Ferrari
3 P. Rodriguez/
 R. Rodriguez Ferrari

Targa Florio, Italy

1 O. Gendebien/
 W. von Trips Ferrari
 103.41 kph / 64.27 mph
2 J. Bonnier/
 D. Gurney Porsche
3 E. Barth/H. Herrmann Porsche

Nurburgring, West Germany

1 M. Gregory/L. Casner Maserati
 127.60 kph / 79.29 mph
2 P. Rodriguez/
 R. Rodriguez Ferrari
3 R. Ginther/
 W. von Trips/
 O. Gendebien Ferrari

Le Mans, France

1 O. Gendebien/P. Hill Ferrari
 186.48 kph / 115.88 mph
2 G. Mairesse/
 M. Parkes Ferrari
3 J. Guichet/P. Noblet Ferrari

Pescara, Italy

1 L. Bandini/
   G. Scarlatti   Ferrari
   143.22 kph / 89.00 mph
2 K. Orthuber/E. Barth Porsche
3 M. Boffa   Maserati

Final Championship Standing

1 Ferrari   24 pts
2 Maserati   14 pts
3 Porsche   11 pts

1962

Sebring, United States

1 L. Bianchi/J. Bonnier Ferrari
   143.43 kph / 89.14 mph
2 O. Gendebien/P. Hill   Ferrari
3 B. Jennings/F. Rand/
   W. Woesthoff   Porsche

Targa Florio, Italy

1 W. Mairesse/
   R. Rodriguez/
   O. Gendebien   Ferrari
   102.12 kph / 63.47 mph
2 G. Baghetti/
   L. Bandini   Ferrari
3 N. Vaccarella/
   J. Bonnier   Porsche

Nurburgring, West Germany

1 O. Gendebien/P. Hill Ferrari
   143.60 kph / 89.23 mph
2 M. Parkes/
   W. Mairesse   Ferrari
3 G. Hill/H. Herrmann Porsche

Le Mans, France

1 O. Gendebien/P. Hill Ferrari
   185.42 kph / 115.22 mph
2 J. Guichet/P. Noblet Ferrari
3 'Beurlys'/'Elde'   Ferrari

1963

Sebring, United States

1 L. Scarfiotti/
   J. Surtees   Ferrari
   145.75 kph / 90.57 mph
2 W. Mairesse/
   N. Vaccarella/
   L. Bandini   Ferrari
3 G. Hill/P. Rodriguez Ferrari

Targa Florio, Italy

1 J. Bonnier/C. Abate   Porsche
   103.89 kph / 65.57 mph
2 L. Bandini/
   L. Scarfiotti/
   W. Mairesse   Ferrari
3 H. Linge/E. Barth   Porsche

Nurburgring, West Germany

1 J. Surtees/
   W. Mairesse   Ferrari
   133.10 kph / 82.71 mph
2 P. Noblet/J. Guichet Ferrari
3 C. Abate/U. Maglioli Ferrari

Le Mans, France

1 L. Bandini/
   L. Scarfiotti   Ferrari
   190.02 kph / 118.08 mph
2 'Buerlys'/
   G. Langlois   Ferrari
3 M. Parkes/U. Maglioli Ferrari

1964

Sebring, United States

1 M. Parkes/
   U. Magliolo   Ferrari
   148.61 kph / 92.35 mph
2 L. Scarfiotti/
   N. Vaccarella   Ferrari
3 J. Surtees/L. Bandini Ferrari

Targa Florio, Italy

1 C. Davis/A. Pucci   Porsche
   100.21 kph / 62.28 mph
2 H. Linge/G. Balzarini Porsche
3 R. Bussinello/
   N. Todaro   Alfa Romeo

Nurburgring, West Germany

1 L. Scarfiotti/
   N. Vaccarella   Ferrari
   140.50 kph / 87.31 mph
2 M. Parkes/J. Guichet Ferrari
3 B. Pon/G. Koch   Porsche

Le Mans, France

1 J. Guichet/
   N. Vaccarella   Ferrari
   195.59 kph / 121.54 mph
2 G. Hill/J. Bonnier   Ferrari
3 J. Surtees/L. Bandini Ferrari

1965

Sebring, United States

1 J. Hall/H. Sharp   Chaparral
   136.40 kph / 84.76 mph
2 B. McLaren/K. Miles   Ford
3 A. Maggs/D. Piper   Ferrari

Targa Florio, Italy

1 L. Bandini/
   N. Vaccarella   Ferrari
   102.49 kph / 63.70 mph
2 C. Davis/G. Mitter   Porsche
3 H. Linge/U. Maglioli Porsche

Nurburgring, West Germany

1 L. Scarfiotti/
   J. Surtees   Ferrari
   145.90 kph / 90.66 mph
2 M. Parkes/J. Guichet Ferrari
3 J. Bonnier/J. Rindt   Porsche

Le Mans, France

1 M. Gregory/J. Rindt   Ferrari
   194.83 kph / 121.07 mph
2 P. Dumay/
   G. Gosselin   Ferrari
3 W. Mairesse/
   'Beurlys'   Ferrari

1966

Daytona, United States

1 K. Miles/L. Ruby   Ford
   173.83 kph / 108.02
2 D. Gurney/J. Grant   Ford
3 W. Hansgen/
   M. Donohue   Ford

Sebring, United States

1 K. Miles/L. Ruby   Ford
   158.73 kph / 98.63 mph
2 W. Hansgen/
   M. Donohue   Ford
3 P. Revson/S. Scott   Ford

Targa Florio, Italy

1 W. Mairesse/
   H. Muller   Porsche
   98.91 kph / 61.47 mph
2 J. Guichet/
   G. Baghetti   Ferrari
3 A. Pucci/V. Arena   Porsche

Nurburgring, West Germany

1 P. Hill/J. Bonnier   Chaparral
   143.80 kph / 89.36 mph
2 L. Bandini/
   L. Scarfiotti   Ferrari
3 P. Rodriguez/
   R. Ginther   Ferrari

Le Mans, France

1 B. McLaren/C. Amon   Ford
   201.75 kph / 125.37 mph
2 K. Miles/D. Hulme   Ford
3 R. Bucknum/
   R. Hutcherson   Ford

1967

Daytona, United States

1 L. Bandini/C. Amon   Ferrari
   170.11 kph / 105.71 mph
2 L. Scarfiotti/
   M. Parkes   Ferrari
3 P. Rodriguez/
   J. Guichet   Ferrari

Sebring, United States

1 M. Andretti/
   B. McLaren   Ford
   165.97 kph / 103.13 mph
2 A. J. Foyt/L. Ruby   Ford
3 G. Mitter/S. Patrick Porsche

Monza, Italy

1 L. Bandini/C. Amon   Ferrari
   196.93 kph / 122.37 mph
2 L. Scarfiotti/
   M. Parkes   Ferrari
3 J. Rindt/G. Mitter   Porsche

Spa, Belgium

1 J. Ickx/R. Thompson Ford
   193.90 kph / 120.49 mph
2 H. Herrmann/
   J. Siffert   Porsche
3 R. Attwood/
   L. Bianchi   Ferrari

Targa Florio, Italy

1 P. Hawkins/
 R. Stommelen Porsche
 108.78 kph / 67.61 mph
2 L. Cella/G. Biscaldi Porsche
3 J. Neerpasch/
 V. Elford Porsche

Nurburgring, West Germany

1 U. Schutz/J. Buzzetta Porsche
 145.50 kph / 90.41 mph
2 P. Hawkins/G. Koch Porsche
3 J. Neerpasch/
 V. Elford Porsche

Le Mans, France

1 A. J. Foyt/D. Gurney Ford
 217.99 kph / 135.46 mph
2 L. Scarfiotti/
 M. Parkes Ferrari
3 W. Mairesse/
 'Beurlys' Ferrari

Brands Hatch, England

1 P. Hill/M. Spence Chaparral
 149.87 kph / 93.13 mph
2 J. Stewart/C. Amon Ferrari
3 J. Siffert/B. McLaren Porsche

1968

Daytona, United States

1 V. Elford/J. Siffert/
 R. Stommelen/
 J. Neerpasch/
 H. Herrmann Porsche
 170.70 kph / 106.07 mph
2 J. Siffert/
 H. Herrmann Porsche
3 J. Buzzetta/
 J. Schlesser Porsche

Sebring, United States

1 H. Herrmann/
 J. Siffert Porsche
 164.97 kph / 102.51 mph
2 V. Elford/
 J. Neerpasch Porsche
3 M. Donohue/
 C. Fisher Chevrolet

Brands Hatch, England

1 B. Redman/J. Ickx Ford
 154.50 kph / 96.01 mph
2 G. Mitter/L. Scarfiotti Porsche
3 V. Elford/
 J. Neerpasch Porsche

Monza, Italy

1 P. Hawkins/D. Hobbs Ford
 190.33 kph / 118.27 mph
2 R. Stommelen/
 J. Neerpasch Porsche
3 P. Depailler/A. de
 Cortanze Alpine

Targa Florio, Italy

1 V. Elford/U. Maglioli Porsche
 111.09 kph / 69.04 mph
2 N. Galli/I. Giunti Alfa Romeo
3 M. Casoni/L. Bianchi Alfa Romeo

Nurburgring, West Germany

1 J. Siffert/V. Elford Porsche
 152.96 kph / 95.05 mph
2 H. Herrmann/
 R. Stommelen Porsche
3 J. Ickx/P. Hawkins Ford

Spa, Belgium

1 J. Ickx/B. Redman Ford
 196.51 kph / 122.11 mph
2 G. Mitter/
 J. Schlesser Porsche
3 H. Herrmann/
 R. Stommelen Porsche

Watkins Glen, United States

1 J. Ickx/L. Bianchi Ford
 162.45 kph / 100.95 mph
2 P. Hawkins/D. Hobbs Ford
3 R. Thompson/
 R. Heppenstall Howmet

Zeltweg, Austria

1 J. Siffert Porsche
 171.98 kph / 106.87 mph
2 H. Herrmann Porsche
3 P. Hawkins Ford
(Known as the Austrian GP and held
over 500 km, only half championship
points at stake)

Le Mans, France

1 P. Rodriguez/
 L. Bianchi Ford
 185.50 kph / 115.27 mph
2 G. Steinemann/
 D. Spoerry Porsche
3 R. Stommelen/
 J. Neerpasch Porsche

Final Championship Standing

1 Ford 45 pts
2 Porsche 42 pts
3 Alfa Romeo 15½ pts

The Mark IV Ford GT40 of Dan Gurney
and A. J. Foyt (both USA) on its way to
winning Le Mans in 1967. (National Motor
Museum)

1969

Daytona, United States
1 M. Donohue/
   C. Parsons   Lola
   159.91 kph / 99.37 mph
2 L. Motschenbacher/
   E. Leslie   Lola
3 J. Ward/J. Titus   Pontiac

Sebring, United States
1 J. Ickx/J. Oliver   Ford
   166.34 kph / 103.36 mph
2 C. Amon/M. Andretti   Ferrari
3 J. Buzzetta/
   R. Stommelen   Porsche

Brands Hatch, England
1 J. Siffert/B. Redman Porsche
   161.29 kph / 100.23 mph
2 V. Elford/R. Attwood Porsche
3 G. Mitter/U. Schutz   Porsche

Monza, Italy
1 J. Siffert/B. Redman Porsche
   206.34 kph / 128.22 mph
2 H. Herrmann/
   K. Ahrens   Porsche
3 G. Koch/H. Dechent   Porsche

Targa Florio, Italy
1 G. Mitter/U. Schutz   Porsche
   117.47 kph / 72.99 mph
2 V. Elford/U. Maglioli Porsche
3 H. Herrmann/
   R. Stommelen   Porsche

Spa, Belgium
1 J. Siffert/B. Redman Porsche
   227.24 kph / 141.21 mph
2 P. Rodriguez/
   D. Piper   Ferrari
3 V. Elford/K. Ahrens   Porsche

Nurburgring, West Germany
1 J. Siffert/B. Redman Porsche
   162.50 kph / 100.98 mph
2 H. Herrmann/
   R. Stommelen   Porsche
3 V. Elford/K. Ahrens   Porsche

Le Mans, France
1 J. Ickx/J. Oliver   Ford
   208.20 kph / 129.38 mph
2 H. Herrmann/
   G. Larrousse   Porsche
3 D. Hobbs/
   M. Hailwood   Ford

Watkins Glen, United States
1 J. Siffert/B. Redman Porsche
   178.94 kph / 111.19 mph
2 V. Elford/R. Attwood Porsche
3 J. Buzzetta/R. Lins   Porsche

Osterreichring, Austria
1 J. Siffert/K. Ahrens Porsche
   186.33 kph / 115.79 mph
2 J. Bonnier/H. Muller Lola
3 B. Redman/
   R. Attwood   Porsche

Final Championship Standing
1 Porsche   45 pts
2 Ford   25 pts
3 Lola   20 pts

1970

Daytona, United States
1 P. Rodriguez/
   L. Kinnunen   Porsche
   185.88 kph / 115.51 mph
2 J. Siffert/B. Redman Porsche
3 M. Andretti/J. Ickx/
   A. Merzario   Ferrari

Sebring, United States
1 M. Andretti/
   N. Vaccarella/
   I. Giunti   Ferrari
   172.69 kph / 107.31 mph
2 P. Revson/
   S. McQueen   Porsche
3 M. Gregory/
   T. Hezemans   Alfa Romeo

Brands Hatch, England
1 P. Rodriguez/
   L. Kinnunen   Porsche
   148.30 kph / 92.15 mph
2 V. Elford/D. Hulme   Porsche
3 R. Attwood/
   H. Herrmann   Porsche

Monza, Italy
1 P. Rodriguez/
   L. Kinnunen   Porsche
   232.65 kph / 144.57 mph
2 I. Giunti/C. Amon/
   N. Vaccarella   Ferrari
3 J. Surtees/P. Schetty Ferrari

Targa Florio, Italy
1 J. Siffert/B. Redman Porsche
   120.15 kph / 74.66 mph
2 P. Rodriguez/
   L. Kinnunen   Porsche
3 N. Vaccarella/I. Giunti Ferrari

Spa, Belgium
1 J. Siffert/B. Redman Porsche
   240.46 kph / 149.42 mph
2 J. Ickx/J. Surtees   Ferrari
3 V. Elford/K. Ahrens   Porsche

Nurburgring, West Germany
1 V. Elford/K. Ahrens   Porsche
   165.00 kph / 102.53 mph
2 H. Herrmann/
   R. Attwood   Porsche
3 J. Surtees/
   N. Vaccarella   Ferrari

Le Mans, France
1 H. Herrmann/
   R. Attwood   Porsche
   191.95 kph / 119.28 mph
2 G. Larrousse/
   W. Kauhsen   Porsche
3 R. Lins/H. Marko   Porsche

Watkins Glen, United States
1 P. Rodriguez/
   L. Kinnunen   Porsche
   189.59 kph / 117.81 mph
2 J. Siffert/B. Redman Porsche
3 M. Andretti/I. Giunti Ferrari

Osterreichring, Austria
1 J. Siffert/B. Redman Porsche
   195.72 kph / 121.62 mph
2 A. de Adamich/
   H. Pescarolo   Alfa Romeo
3 G. Larrousse/
   R. Lins   Porsche

Final Championship Standing
1 Porsche   63 pts
2 Ferrari   39 pts
3 Alfa Romeo   10 pts

1971

Buenos Aires, Argentina
1 J. Siffert/D. Bell   Porsche
   186.22 kph / 115.72 mph
2 P. Rodriguez/
   J. Oliver   Porsche
3 R. Stommelen/
   N. Galli   Alfa Romeo

Daytona, United States
1 P. Rodriguez/
   J. Oliver   Porsche
   175.74 kph / 109.20 mph
2 R. Bucknum/
   T. Adamowicz   Ferrari
3 M. Donohue/
   D. Hobbs   Ferrari

Sebring, United States
1 V. Elford/
   G. Larrousse   Porsche
   181.20 kph / 112.60 mph
2 R. Stommelen/
   N. Galli   Alfa Romeo
3 A. de Adamich/
   H. Pescarolo   Alfa Romeo

Brands Hatch, England
1 A. de Adamich/
   H. Pescarolo   Alfa Romeo
   155.47 kph / 96.61 mph
2 J. Ickx/C. Regazzoni Ferrari
3 J. Siffert/D. Bell   Porsche

Monza, Italy
1 P. Rodriguez/
   J. Oliver   Porsche
   235.83 kph / 146.54 mph
2 J. Siffert/D. Bell   Porsche
3 A. de Adamich/
   H. Pescarolo   Alfa Romeo

Spa, Belgium
1 P. Rodriguez/
   J. Oliver   Porsche
   249.07 kph / 154.77 mph
2 J. Siffert/D. Bell   Porsche
3 A. de Adamich/
   H. Pescarolo   Alfa Romeo

Targa Florio, Italy

1 N. Vaccarella/
   T. Hezemans   Alfa Romeo
   120.06 kph / 74.60 mph
2 A. de Adamich/
   G. van Lennep   Alfa Romeo
3 J. Bonnier/
   R. Attwood   Lola

Nurburgring, West Germany

1 G. Larrousse/
   V. Elford   Porsche
   171.40 kph / 106.51 mph
2 P. Rodriguez/
   J. Siffert   Porsche
3 G. van Lennep/
   H. Marko   Porsche

Le Mans, France

1 G. van Lennep/
   H. Marko   Porsche
   222.25 kph / 138.13 mph
2 R. Attwood/
   H. Muller   Porsche
3 S. Posey/
   T. Adamowicz   Ferrari

Osterreichring, Austria

1 P. Rodriguez/
   R. Attwood   Porsche
   198.06 kph / 123.07 mph
2 T. Hezemans/
   N. Vaccarella   Alfa Romeo
3 R. Stommelen/
   N. Galli   Alfa Romeo

Watkins Glen, United States

1 R. Peterson/
   A. de Adamich   Alfa Romeo
   181.45 kph / 112.75 mph
2 J. Siffert/
   G. van Lennep   Porsche
3 D. Bell/R. Attwood   Porsche

Final Championship Standing

1 Porsche   63 pts
2 Alfa Romeo   51 pts
3 Ferrari   26 pts

1972

Buenos Aires, Argentina

1 R. Peterson/
   T. Schenken   Ferrari
   173.89 kph / 108.06 mph
2 C. Regazzoni/
   B. Redman   Ferrari
3 G. Albert/C. Facetti/
   A. de Adamich   Alfa Romeo

Daytona, United States

1 J. Ickx/M. Andretti   Ferrari
   199.52 kph / 123.98 mph
2 R. Peterson/
   T. Schenken   Ferrari
3 V. Elford/H. Marko   Alfa Romeo

Sebring, United States

1 J. Ickx/M. Andretti   Ferrari
   178.41 kph / 110.86 mph
2 R. Peterson/
   T. Schenken   Ferrari
3 T. Hezemans/
   N. Vaccarella   Alfa Romeo

Brands Hatch, England

1 J. Ickx/M. Andretti   Ferrari
   169.17 kph / 105.12 mph
2 R. Peterson/
   T. Schenken   Ferrari
3 R. Stommelen/
   P. Revson   Alfa Romeo

Monza, Italy

1 J. Ickx/C. Regazzoni   Ferrari
   170.49 kph / 105.94 mph
2 R. Jost/G. Schueler   Porsche
3 R. Peterson/
   T. Schenken   Ferrari

Spa, Belgium

1 B. Redman/
   A. Merzario   Ferrari
   233.43 kph / 145.05 mph
2 J. Ickx/C. Regazzoni   Ferrari
3 J. Hine/J. Bridges   Chevron-
                     Cosworth

Targa Florio, Italy

1 A. Merzario/
   S. Munari   Ferrari
   122.54 kph / 76.15 mph
2 H. Marko/N. Galli   Alfa Romeo
3 T. Hezemans/
   A. de Adamich   Alfa Romeo

Nurburgring, West Germany

1 R. Peterson/
   T. Schenken   Ferrari
   166.68 kph / 103.57 mph
2 B. Redman/
   A. Merzario   Ferrari
3 H. Marko/
   A. de Adamich   Alfa Romeo

Le Mans, France

1 G. Hill/H. Pescarolo   Matra-Simca
   195.41 kph / 121.45 mph
2 F. Cevert/H. Ganley   Matra-Simca
3 R. Jost/M. Weber/
   M. Casoni   Porsche

Osterreichring, Austria

1 J. Ickx/B. Redman   Ferrari
   201.86 kph / 125.44 mph
2 H. Marko/C. Pace   Ferrari
3 R. Peterson/
   T. Schenken   Ferrari

Watkins Glen, United States

1 J. Ickx/M. Andretti   Ferrari
   176.01 kph / 109.37 mph
2 R. Peterson/
   T. Schenken   Ferrari
3 D. Bell/C. Pace   Gulf Mirage

Final Championship Standing

1 Ferrari   160 pts
2 Alfa Romeo   85 pts
3 Porsche   67 pts

Graham Hill (GB) at the wheel of a
Matra-Simca in the 1972 Le Mans. Hill and
his co-driver Henri Pescarolo (FRA) went
on to win the race for the first time.
Pescarolo also won in 1973–4 and 1984.
(National Motor Museum)

Jim Clark

Today, nearly 20 years after his death, Jim Clark is still remembered, and generally regarded as the greatest driver of the post-war era.

Born in Fife, Scotland in 1936, Clark was the son of a wealthy sheep farmer and he gave up his education at the age of 16 to work on the farm. He used to have a go at driving his father's Austin Seven around the farm at an early age, and later he became seriously interested in motor racing—not least because Mike Hawthorn winning the Leinster Trophy in 1951 had made a deep impression. He decided to try his hand in racing and in June 1956 the skills of Jim Clark were first seen at Crimond Airfield, near Aberdeen, when he made his racing debut in a DKW Saloon. It was apparent from that day that he had a natural talent that was waiting to be developed.

He first met Colin Chapman, boss of Lotus cars, at Brands Hatch in 1958 who was impressed with the youngster's driving. It was not until two years later, however, that Clark accepted Chapman's offer to join the team. Both Clark and his mentor developed one of those partnerships whose memory will last forever. Who could even forget the sight of Clark steering the famous green Lotus to Grand Prix success time and time again.

Clark made his Formula One debut for Lotus in the 1960 Dutch Grand Prix when team-mate John Surtees was contracted to a motor cycle race. Two years later Clark had the first of his 25 Grand Prix wins at Spa and ended up runner-up in the World Championship to Graham Hill.

In 1963, however, Clark was champion for the first time, after winning a record seven rounds, and at 27 he became the youngest-ever world champion. Two years later Clark was champion again after winning another six rounds of the championship and he also, in 1965, became the first Briton to win the coveted Indianapolis 500 title.

Motor racing was deprived of the rare talent of Jim Clark in April 1968 when he lost his life at Hockenheim. The motor racing world was stunned because, in a sport that flirts with death, there were many drivers who thought that if it could happen to Clark, it could happen to any of them.

Jim Clark, a bachelor, spent his entire Formula One career at Lotus. He took part in 72 Grands Prix, was on pole position 33 times and won 25 races—a record at the time. He was not a loser, as his record of just one second placing shows. Had it not been for the tragic accident at Hockenheim, Jim Clark's record would surely have been unsurpassable.

Right Clark (looking like a portable forest) celebrating his victory in the 1965 German Grand Prix at the Nurburgring. Graham Hill (GB-left) and Dan Gurney (USA) join in the celebrations. Victory assured Clark of his second world title with three races remaining. (National Motor Museum)

Far right Jim Clark (left) with mentor Colin Chapman — the greatest partnership, in the history of motor racing? (National Motor Museum)

Jim Clark with his Lotus team at the Indianapolis speedway. (National Motor Museum)

1973

Daytona, United States

1 P. Gregg/
   H. Haywood   Porsche
  171.00 kph / 106.26 mph
2 M. Minter/F. Migault Ferrari
3 D. Heinz/R. McClure   Chevrolet

Vallelunga, Italy

1 H. Pescarolo/
   G. Larrousse/
   F. Cevert   Matra-Simca
  154.94 kph / 96.28 mph
2 C. Reutemann/
   T. Schenken   Ferrari
3 J. Ickx/B. Redman   Ferrari

Dijon, France

1 H. Pescarolo/
   G. Larrousse   Matra-Simca
  179.53 kph / 111.56 mph
2 J. Ickx/B. Redman   Ferrari
3 F. Cevert/
   J-P. Beltoise   Matra-Simca

Monza, Italy

1 J. Ickx/B. Redman   Ferrari
  242.47 kph / 150.67 mph
2 C. Reutemann/
   T. Schenken   Ferrari
3 H. Pescarolo/
   G. Larrousse   Matra-Simca

Spa, Belgium

1 D. Bell/M. Hailwood Mirage-
                        Cosworth
  244.44 kph / 151.90 mph
2 M. Hailwood/
   V. Schuppan/   Mirage-
   H. Ganley   Cosworth
3 H. Pescarolo/
   C. Amon/
   G. Larrousse   Matra-Simca

Targa Florio, Italy

1 H. Muller/
   G. van Lennep Porsche
  114.69 kph / 71.27 mph
2 S. Munari/
   J. C. Andruet   Lancia
3 L. Kinnunen/
   C. Haldi   Porsche

Nurburgring, West Germany

1 J. Ickx/B. Redman   Ferrari
  178.94 kph / 111.19 mph
2 A. Merzario/C. Pace Ferrari
3 J. Burton/J. Bridges Chevron-
                        Ford

Le Mans, France

1 H. Pescarolo/
   G. Larrousse   Matra-Simca
  202.20 kph / 125.67 mph
2 A. Merzario/
   C. Pace   Ferrari
3 J-P. Jaussaud/
   J-P. Jabouille   Matra-Simca

Mike Hailwood (GB) trying his hand at
Sports Car racing at Vallelunga, Italy in
1973. He is seen driving a Gulf-Mirage.
(National Motor Museum)

Osterreichring, Austria

1 H. Pescarolo/
   G. Larrousse   Matra-Simca
  208.63 kph / 129.64 mph
2 J-P. Beltoise/
   F. Cevert   Matra-Simca
3 J. Ickx/B. Redman   Ferrari

Watkins Glen, United States

1 H. Pescarolo/
   G. Larrousse   Matra-Simca
  180.00 kph / 111.85 mph
2 J. Ickx/B. Redman   Ferrari
3 A. Merzario/C. Pace Ferrari

Final Championship Standing

1 Matra-Simca   124 pts
2 Ferrari   115 pts
3 Porsche   82 pts

1974

Monza, Italy

1 A. Merzario/
   M. Andretti   Alfa Romeo
  210.66 kph / 130.90 mph
2 J. Ickx/R. Stommelen Alfa Romeo
3 C. Facetti/
   A. de Adamich Alfa Romeo

Spa, Belgium

1 J. Ickx/J-P. Jarier   Matra-Simca
  238.44 kph / 148.17 mph
2 M. Hailwood/D. Bell Gulf-
                        Cosworth
3 H. Muller/
   G. van Lennep Porsche

Nurburgring, West Germany

1 J-P. Jarier/
   J-P. Beltoise   Matra-Simca
  182.75 kph / 113.56 mph
2 R. Stommelen/
   C. Reutemann Alfa Romeo
3 C. Facetti/
   A. de Adamich Alfa Romeo

Imola, Italy

1 H. Pescarolo/
   G. Larrousse   Matra-Simca
  160.90 kph / 99.98 mph
2 R. Stommelen/
   C. Reutemann Alfa Romeo
3 C. Facetti/
   A. de Adamich Alfa Romeo

Le Mans, France

1 H. Pescarolo/
   G. Larrousse   Matra-Simca
  191.91 kph / 119.27 mph
2 H. Muller/
   G. van Lennep Porsche
3 J-P. Jabouille/
   F. Migault   Matra-Simca

Osterreichring, Austria

1 H. Pescarolo/
   G. Larrousse   Matra-Simca
  206.95 kph / 128.60 mph
2 C. Facetti/
   A. de Adamich Alfa Romeo
3 J-P. Jarier/
   J-P. Beltoise   Matra-Simca

Watkins Glen, United States

1 J-P. Jarier/
   J-P. Beltoise   Matra-Simca
  174.07 kph / 108.17 mph
2 H. Muller/
   G. van Lennep Porsche
3 P. Gregg/
   H. Haywood   Porsche

Paul Ricard, France

1 J-P. Jarier/
  · J-P. Beltoise   Matra-Simca
  180.56 kph / 112.20 mph
2 H. Pescarolo/
  G. Larrousse   Matra-Simca
3 D. Bell/J. Ickx   Gulf-
                     Cosworth

Brands Hatch, England

1 J-P. Jarier/
  J-P. Beltoise   Matra-Simca
  173.02 kph / 107.51 mph
2 H. Pescarolo/
  G. Larrousse   Matra-Simca
3 D. Bell/D. Hobbs   Gulf-
                      Cosworth

Kayalami, South Africa

1 H. Pescarolo/
  G. Larrousse   Matra-Simca
  160.74 kph / 99.88 mph
2 J-P. Jarier/
  J-P. Beltoise   Matra-Simca
3 D. Bell/D. Hobbs   Gulf-
                      Cosworth

Final Championship Standing

1 Matra-Simca   140 pts
2 Alfa Romeo   71 pts
3 Porsche   68 pts

1975

Daytona, United States

1 P. Gregg/
  H. Haywood   Porsche
  174.66 kph / 108.53 mph
2 M. Keyser/
  A. Contreras/
  B. Sprowls   Porsche
3 C. Kemp/C. Baird   Porsche

Mugello, Italy

1 J-P. Jabouille/   Alpine-
  G. Larrousse   Renault
  164.15 kph / 102.00 mph
2 A. Merzario/J. Ickx   Alfa Romeo
3 H. Muller/
  G. van Lennep   Porsche

Dijon, France

1 A. Merzario/
  J. Laffite   Alfa Romeo
  180.75 kph / 112.32 mph
2 R. Joest/M. Casoni   Porsche
3 J. Hine/I. Grob   Chevron-
                     Ford

Monza, Italy

1 A. Merzario/
  J. Laffite   Alfa Romeo
  212.58 kph / 132.10 mph
2 R. Joest/M. Casoni   Porsche
3 G. Larrousse/   Alpine-
  J-P. Jabouille   Renault

Spa, Belgium

1 H. Pescarolo/
  D. Bell   Alfa Romeo
  214.81 kph / 133.48 mph
2 A. Merzario/J. Ickx   Alfa Romeo
3 A. Peltier/S. Muller   BMW-CSL

Enna, Italy

1 A. Merzario/J. Mass   Alfa Romeo
  197.02 kph / 122.43 mph
2 H. Pescarolo/D. Bell   Alfa Romeo
3 R. Joest/M. Casoni   Porsche

Nurburgring, West Germany

1 A. Merzario/
  J. Laffite   Alfa Romeo
  176.70 kph / 109.80 mph
2 T. Schenken/   Gulf-
  H. Ganley   Cosworth
3 H. Muller/
  L. Kinnunen   Porsche

Osterreichring, Austria

1 H. Pescarolo/D. Bell   Alfa Romeo
  170.02 kph / 105.65 mph
2 A. Merzario/
  V. Brambilla   Alfa Romeo
3 R. Joest/M. Casoni   Porsche

Watkins Glen, United States

1 H. Pescarolo/
  D. Bell   Alfa Romeo
  137.15 kph / 85.23 mph
2 A. Merzario/
  M. Andretti   Alfa Romeo
3 J-P. Jabouille/   Alpine-
  G. Larrousse   Renault

Final Championship Standing

1 Alfa Romeo   140 pts
2 Porsche   98 pts
3 Alpine-Renault   54 pts

1976

Mugello, Italy

1 J. Mass/J. Ickx   Porsche
  151.72 kph / 94.28 mph
2 R. Wollek/H. Heyer   Porsche
3 L. Kinnunen/
  E. Evertz   Porsche

Vallelunga, Italy

1 J. Mass/J. Ickx   Porsche
  143.76 kph / 89.33 mph
2 H. Grohs/S. Posey/
  H. de Fierlant   BMW
3 K. Simonsen/K. Leim   Porsche

Silverstone, England

1 T. Walkinshaw/
  J. Fitzpatrick   BMW
  170.81 kph / 106.14 mph
2 R. Wollek/H. Heyer   Porsche
3 L. Kinnunen/
  E. Evertz   Porsche

Nurburgring, West Germany

1 D. Quester/A. Krebs   BMW
  161.66 kph / 100.46 mph
2 T. Hezemans/
  T. Schenken   Porsche
3 D. Bell/R. Stenzel/
  G. Stekkonig   Porsche

Osterreichring, Austria

1 D. Quester/
  G. Nilsson   BMW
  184.10 kph / 114.40 mph
2 T. Walkinshaw/
  J. Fitzpatrick   BMW
3 C. Haldi/P. Zbinden   Porsche

Watkins Glen, United States

1 R. Stommelen/
  M. Schurti   Porsche
  157.41 kph / 97.81 mph
2 T. Hezemans/E.
  Evertz/L. Kinnunen   Porsche
3 J. Mass/J. Ickx   Porsche

Dijon, France

1 J. Mass/J. Ickx   Porsche
  169.93 kph / 105.59 mph
2 R. Wollek/H. Heyer   Porsche
3 R. Stommelen/
  M. Schurti   Porsche

Final Championship Standing

1 Porsche   95 pts
2 BMW   85 pts
3 Ford   8 pts

1977

Daytona, United States

1 J. Graves/
  H. Haywood/
  D. Helmick   Porsche
  175.10 kph / 108.81 mph
2 M. Finotto/C. Facetti/
  R. Camathias   Porsche
3 R. Wollek/R. Joest/
  A. Krebs   Porsche

Mugello, Italy

1 R. Stommelen/
  M. Schurti   Porsche
  140.66 kph / 87.41 mph
2 M. Finotto/C. Facetti/
  R. Camathias   Porsche
3 V. Coggiola/
  P. Monticone   Porsche

Silverstone, England

1 J. Mass/J. Ickx   Porsche
  180.89 kph / 112.41 mph
2 R. Wollek/
  J. Fitzpatrick   Porsche
3 R. Stommelen/
  T. Hezemans   Porsche

• James Hunt (GB) came fourth in the World Steam-Roller championship in 1977, at an average speed of just 7 mph (11.3 kph).

Nurburgring, West Germany

1 R. Stommelen/
   T. Hezemans/
   T. Schenken   Porsche
   168.15 kph / 104.49 mph
2 R. Wollek/
   J. Fitzpatrick   Porsche
3 M. Winkelhock/
   M. Surer   BMW

Watkins Glen, United States

1 J. Mass/J. Ickx   Porsche
   155.28 kph / 96.49 mph
2 G. Follmer/B. Lunger Porsche
3 H. Haywood/
   B. Hagestad   Porsche

Mosport, Canada

1 P. Gregg/R. Wollek   Porsche
   160.34 kph / 99.64 mph
2 L. Heimrath/
   P. Miller   Porsche
3 G. Villeneuve/
   E. Cheever   BMW

Brands Hatch, England

1 J. Mass/J. Ickx   Porsche
   157.22 kph / 97.70 mph
2 M. Schurti/E. Doren   Porsche
3 R. Joest/R. Wollek/
   F. Konrad   Porsche

Hockenheim, West Germany

1 R. Wollek/
   J. Fitzpatrick   Porsche
   186.69 kph / 116.00 mph
2 C. Ballot-Lena/
   J. L. Lafosse   Porsche
3 M. Surer/E. Cheever   BMW

Vallelunga, Italy

1 L. Moreschi/'Dino'   Porsche
   132.76 kph / 82.50 mph
2 P. Monticone/'Victor' Porsche
3 M. Micangeli/
   P. Pietromarchi   De Tomaso

Final Championship Standing

1 Porsche   140 pts
2 BMW   37 pts
3 De Tomaso   12 pts

1978_____

Daytona, United States

1 R. Stommelen/
   T. Hezemans/
   P. Gregg   Porsche
   174.93 kph / 108.70 mph
2 J. Rutherford/
   M. Schurti/
   R. Barbour   Porsche
3 A. Poole/
   D. Feoles   Porsche

Mugello, Italy

1 T. Hezemans/
   H. Heyer/
   J. Fitzpatrick   Porsche
   153.08 kph / 95.12 mph
2 F. Konrad/V. Merl/
   R. Joest   Porsche
3 D. Quester/D. Bell   BMW

Dijon, France

1 R. Wollek/
   H. Pescarolo   Porsche
   159.93 kph / 99.38 mph
2 T. Hezemans/
   H. Heyer/
   J. Fitzpatrick   Porsche
3 E. Cheever/G. Francis BMW

Silverstone, England

1 J. Mass/J. Ickx   Porsche
   184.93 kph / 114.92 mph
2 R. Wollek/
   H. Pescarolo   Porsche
3 H. Grohs/E. Joosen   BMW

Nurburgring, West Germany

1 T. Hezemans/
   H. Heyer/
   K. Ludwig   Porsche
   169.44 kph / 105.29 mph
2 J. Ickx/M. Schurti   Porsche
3 R. Wollek/
   H. Pescarolo   Porsche

Misano, Italy

1 R. Wollek/
   H. Pescarolo   Porsche
   151.33 kph / 94.04 mph
2 V. Coggiola/
   P. Monticone   Porsche
3 F. Konrad/V. Merl   Porsche

Watkins Glen, United States

1 T. Hezemans/
   P. Gregg/
   J. Fitzpatrick   Porsche
   131.55 kph / 81.75 mph
2 R. Stommelen/
   M. Schurti/
   R. Barbour   Porsche
3 H. Stuck/D. Quester   BMW

Vallelunga, Italy

1 R. Wollek/
   H. Pescarolo   Porsche
   142.01 kph / 88.25 mph
2 T. Hezemans/
   H. Heyer/
   J. Fitzpatrick   Porsche
3 K. Ludwig/
   T. Hezemans/
   J. Fitzpatrick   Porsche

Final Championship Standing

1 Porsche   120 pts
2 BMW   44 pts
3 Chevrolet   4 pts

1979_____

Daytona, United States

1 D. Ongais/
   H. Haywood/
   E. Field   Porsche
   176.13 kph / 109.45 mph
2 J. Morton/
   A. Adamowicz   Ferrari
3 R. Mears/B. Canepa/
   M. Shelton   Porsche

Mugello, Italy

1 J. Fitzpatrick/
   M. Schurti/
   R. Wollek   Porsche
   137.52 kph / 85.45 mph
2 R. Wollek/M. Schurti/
   J. Ickx   Porsche
3 C. Facetti/
   M. Finotto   Porsche

Dijon, France

1 R. Joest/V. Merl/
   M. Ketterer   Porsche
   161.47 kph / 100.34 mph
2 R. Wollek/J. Ickx/
   M. Schurti   Porsche
3 D. Shornstein/
   E. Doren   Porsche

Silverstone, England

1 J. Fitzpatrick/
   R. Wollek/H. Heyer   Porsche
   179.83 kph / 111.75 mph
2 A. de Cadenet/   De Cadenet-
   F. Migault   Cosworth
3 D. Schornstein/
   E. Doren   Porsche

Nurburgring, West Germany

1 J. Fitzpatrick/
   R. Wollek/
   M. Schurti   Porsche
   168.59 kph / 104.76 mph
2 K. Ludwig/
   A. Plankenhorn   Porsche
3 H. Pescarolo/
   B. Redman   Porsche

Enna, Italy

1 Sig. L. Lombardi/
   E. Grimaldi   Osella-BMW
   151.13 kph / 93.91 mph
2 R. Patrese/
   C. Facetti   Lancia
3 A. Pallavicini/
   M. Vanoli   Porsche

● Apart from the first season of
the Formula One World Championship, Keke Rosberg is the only
man to have won the title the
season after failing to gain a single
championship point. His best
placing in 1981 was ninth in the
Brazilian Grand Prix. The following season he was world champion.

Watkins Glen, United States

1 D. Whittington/
  K. Ludwig/
  W. Whittington   Porsche
  158.44 kph / 98.45 mph
2 R. Stommelen/
  R. Barbour/
  P. Newman   Porsche
3 R. McFarlin/R. Akin/
  R. Woods   Porsche

Brands Hatch, England

1 R. Joest/V. Merl   Porsche
  161.90 kph / 100.60 mph
2 K. Ludwig/
  A. Plankenhorn   Porsche
3 A. Charnell/   Chevron-
  M. Raymond   Ford

Vallelunga, Italy

1 Sig. L. Lombardi/
  G. Francia   Osella-BMW
  141.21 kph / 87.75 mph
2 E. Coloni/
  P. Barberio/
  G. Vatielli   Osella-BMW
3 'Gero'/'Robin Hood' Osella-Ford

Final Championship Standing

1 Porsche   140 pts
2 Lancia   50 pts
3 BMW   32 pts

1980

Daytona, United States

1 R. Joest/
  R. Stommelen/
  V. Merl   Porsche
  183.95 kph / 114.31 mph
2 J. Paul/A. Holbert/
  P. Henn   Porsche
3 D. Ongais/E. Field Porsche

Brands Hatch, England

1 R. Patrese/W. Rohrl Lancia
  159.93 kph / 99.38 mph
2 E. Cheever/
  M. Alboreto   Lancia
3 A. de Cadenet/   De Cadenet-
  Mrs. D. Wilson   Cosworth

Mugello, Italy

1 R. Patrese/E. Cheever Lancia
  154.24 kph / 95.84 mph
2 M. Alboreto/
  W. Rohrl   Lancia
3 'Gimax'/M. Gallo   Osella-BMW

Monza, Italy

1 A. de Cadenet/   De Cadenet-
  Mrs. D. Wilson   Cosworth
  176.34 kph / 109.58 mph
2 H. Pescarolo/
  J. Barth   Porsche
3 R. Patrese/
  W. Rohrl   Lancia

Silverstone, England

1 A. de Cadenet/   De Cadenet-
  Mrs. D. Wilson   Cosworth
  184.43 kph / 114.60 mph
2 S. Brunn/J. Barth   Porsche
3 B. Redman/
  J. Paul, Snr   Porsche

Nurburgring, West Germany

1 R. Stommelen/
  J. Barth   Porsche
  171.14 kph / 106.35 mph
2 J. Fitzpatrick/
  D. Barbour/
  A. Plankenhorn   Porsche
3 H. Stuck/N. Piquet BMW

Le Mans, France

1 J. Rondeau/   Rondeau-
  J-P. Jaussaud   Cosworth
  191.84 kph / 119.23 mph
2 J. Ickx/R. Joest/
  M. Leclere   Porsche
3 G. Spice/J. Martin/ Rondeau-
  P. Martin   Cosworth

Watkins Glen, United States

1 R. Patrese/H. Heyer Lancia
  125.12 kph / 77.75 mph
2 E. Cheever/
  M. Alboreto   Lancia
3 B. Redman/
  J. Fitzpatrick   Porsche

Mosport, Canada

1 B. Redman/
  J. Fitzpatrick   Porsche
  161.50 kph / 100.36 mph
2 J. Paul, Snr/
  J. Paul, Jnr   Porsche
3 D. Ongais/E. Field Porsche

Vallelunga, Italy

1 G. Francia/R. Marazzi Osella-BMW
  144.04 kph / 89.51 mph
2 D. Bell/S. Brunn   Porsche
3 R. Patrese/
  E. Cheever   Lancia

Dijon, France

1 H. Pescarolo/J. Barth Porsche
  155.39 kph / 96.56 mph
2 C. Haldi/B. Beguin   Porsche
3 C. Justice/V. Chelli Chevron-
                       Ford

Final Championship Standing

1 Lancia   160 pts
2 Porsche   160 pts
3 BMW   49 pts

1981

Daytona, United States

1 B. Redman/R. Rahal/
  R. Garretson   Porsche
  184.30 kph / 114.52 mph
2 D. Bell/R. Aiken/
  C. Siebert   Porsche
3 W. Koll/J. Kline/
  R. McFarlin   Porsche

Sebring, United States

1 H. Haywood/B.
  Levin/A. Holbert   Porsche
  170.68 kph / 106.06 mph
2 R. Cooke/R. Woods/
  S. McKitterick   Porsche
3 M. Minter/M. Hinze/
  W. Whittington   Porsche

Mugello, Italy

1 Sig. L. Lombardi/
  G. Francia   Osella-BMW
  154.55 kph / 96.04 mph
2 J. Cooper/D. Wood   Porsche
3 A. Fischaber/
  M. Ketterer   BMW

Monza, Italy

1 E. Doren/J. Lassig/
  G. Holup   Porsche
  152.87 kph / 94.99 mph
2 Sig. L. Lombardi/
  G. Francia   Osella-BMW
3 'Gimax'/L. Moreschi Osella-BMW

Silverstone, England

1 H. Grohs/W. Rohrl/
  D. Schornstein   Porsche
  161.49 kph / 100.35 mph
2 D. Bell/D. Hobbs/
  S. O'Rourke   BMW
3 S. Brunn/E. Jordan Porsche

Nurburgring, West Germany

1 H. Stuck/N. Piquet BMW
  170.20 kph / 105.76 mph
2 J. Mass/R. Joest   Porsche
3 R. Wollek/P. Henn/
  A. Smith   Porsche

Le Mans, France

1 J. Ickx/D. Bell   Porsche
  201.06 kph / 124.94 mph
2 J. Haran/
  J. Schlesser/   Rondeau-
  P. Streiff   Cosworth
3 G. Spice/F. Migault Rondeau-
                       Cosworth

Enna, Italy

1 G. Edwards/   Lola-
  E. de Villota   Cosworth
  166.26 kph / 103.31 mph
2 Sig. L. Lombardi/
  G. Francia   Osella-BMW
3 'Gimax'/L. Moreschi Osella-BMW

Daytona, United States

1 H. Haywood/
  M. de Narvaez   Porsche
  175.15 kph / 108.84 mph
2 D. Cowart/K. Miller BMW
3 J. Paul, Snr/
  J. Paul, Jnr   Porsche

● Film Star Paul Newman came
close to fulfilling a lifetime ambi-
tion when he finished second in
the 1979 Le Mans 24-Hour race.

Watkins Glen, United States

1 M. Alboreto/
  R. Patrese   Lancia
  148.81 kph / 92.47 mph
2 H. Pescarolo/
  A. de Cesaris   Lancia
3 R. Garretson/
  J. Rutherford/
  R. Mears   Porsche

Spa, Belgium

1 P. Dieudonne/
  T. Walkinshaw   Mazda
  132.73 kph / 82.48 mph
2 J. C. Andruet/
  E. Joosen   BMW
3 V. Woodman/
  J. Buncombe/
  P. Clark   Ford

Mosport, Canada

1 R. Stommelen/
  H. Meister/
  H. Grohs   Porsche
  150.73 kph / 93.66 mph
2 B. Redman/   Lola-
  E. Wietzes   Chevrolet
3 E. Field/
  W. Whittington   Porsche

Road America, United States

1 R. Stommelen/
  H. Grohs   Porsche
  169.64 kph / 105.41 mph
2 B. Redman/S. Posey Lola-
                      Chevrolet
3 C. Cord/J. Adams   Lola-
                      Chevrolet

Brands Hatch, England

1 G. Edwards/   Lola-
  E. de Villota   Cosworth
  180.80 kph / 112.35 mph
2 R. Garretson/
  R. Rahal   Porsche
3 C. Craft/D. Bell   BMW

Final Championship Standing (Drivers)

1 Bob Garretson
  United States   123 pts
2 Harold Grohs
  West Germany   113½ pts
3 Bobby Rahal
  United States   110 pts

Final Championship Standing (Manufacturers)

1 Porsche   100 pts
2 BMW   52 pts
3 Ferrari   18 pts
Lancia's were Group 6 cars and not
eligible for championship points.)

● In 1970 Jack Brabham (Aus)
topped a poll among Australian
people who were asked to iden-
tify more than 20 Australian
heroes. Nearly 97 per cent of the
poll recognized Brabham.

1982

Monza, Italy

1 H. Pescarolo/
  J. Rondeau/   Rondeau-
  G. Francia   Cosworth
  181.29 kph / 112.65 mph
2 R. Stommelen/
  E. Field   Porsche
3 G. Cuiti/
  M. Benusiglio/
  G. Piazzi   Osella-BMW

Silverstone, England

1 R. Patrese/
  M. Alboreto   Lancia
  188.61 kph / 117.20 mph
2 J. Ickx/D. Bell   Porsche
3 J. Martin/P. Martin/
  R. Wollek   Porsche

Nurburgring, West Germany

1 R. Patrese/
  M.Alboreto/T. Fabi Lancia
  170.21 kph / 105.77 mph
2 H. Pescarolo/   Rondeau-
  R. Stommelen   Cosworth
3 H. Kelleners/
  U. Grano/
  E. Calderari   BMW

Le Mans, France

1 J. Ickx/D. Bell   Porsche
  204.13 kph / 126.85 mph
2 J. Mass/V. Schuppan Porsche
3 H. Haywood/
  A. Holbert/J. Barth Porsche

Spa, Belgium

1 J. Ickx/J. Mass   Porsche
  164.65 kph / 102.31 mph
2 D. Bell/V. Schuppan Porsche
3 R. Patrese/T. Fabi Lancia

Mugello, Italy

1 M. Alboreto/
  P. Ghinzani   Lancia
  158.74 kph / 98.64 mph
2 C. Fabi/A. Nannini Lancia
3 R. Wollek/
  H. Pescarolo/
  H. Heyer   Porsche

Fuji, Japan

1 J. Ickx/J. Mass   Porsche
  189.00 kph / 117.44 mph
2 R. Patrese/T. Fabi Lancia
3 M. Nakamura/   March-
  K. Misaki   Toyota

Brands Hatch, England

1 J. Ickx/D. Bell   Porsche
  158.94 kph / 98.77 mph
2 R. Patrese/T. Fabi Lancia
3 J. Fitzpatrick/
  D.Hobbs/R.Wollek   Porsche

Final Championship Standing (Drivers)

1 Jacky Ickx
  Belgium   95 pts
2 Riccardo Patrese
  Italy   87 pts
3 Derek Bell
  Great Britain   70 pts

Final Championship Standing (Manufacturers)

1 Porsche   75 pts
2 Rondeau-Cosworth   62 pts
3 Nimrod-
  Aston Martin   5 pts
(Lancia's were Group 6 cars and not
eligible for championship points)

1983

Monza, Italy

1 R. Wollek/T. Boutsen Porsche
  192.89 kph / 119.86 mph
2 J. Ickx/J. Mass   Porsche
3 R. Stommelen/
  H. Heyer/
  C. Schickentanz   Porsche

Silverstone, England

1 D. Bell/S. Bellof   Porsche
  198.27 kph / 123.20 mph
2 R. Wollek/
  S. Johansson   Porsche
3 J. Lammers/
  T. Boutsen   Porsche

Nurburgring, West Germany

1 J. Ickx/J. Mass   Porsche
  168.40 kph / 104.64 mph
2 R. Wollek/
  S. Johansson   Porsche
3 J. Lammers/J.
  Palmer/K. Rosberg   Porsche

Le Mans, France

1 V. Schuppan/
  H. Haywood/
  A. Holbert   Porsche
  210.33 kph / 130.70 mph
2 J. Ickx/D. Bell   Porsche
3 M. Andretti, Snr/
  P. Alliot/
  M. Andretti, Jnr   Porsche

Spa, Belgium

1 J. Ickx/J. Mass   Porsche
  174.25 kph / 108.28 mph
2 D. Bell/S. Bellof   Porsche
3 J. Fitzpatrick/
  D. Hobbs   Porsche

Brands Hatch, England

1 J. Fitzpatrick/
  D. Warwick   Porsche
  162.17 kph / 100.77 mph
2 J. Ickx/J. Mass   Porsche
3 D. Bell/S. Bellof   Porsche

Fuji, Japan

1 D. Bell/S. Bellof   Porsche
   197.91 kph / 122.98 mph
2 J. Ickx/J. Mass   Porsche
3 V. Schuppan/
      N. Fujita   Porsche

Kyalami, South Africa

1 D. Bell/S. Bellof   Porsche
   174.59 kph / 108.49 mph
2 R. Patrese/A. Nannini   Lancia
3 J. Ickx/J. Mass   Porsche

Final Championship Standing (Drivers)

1 Jacky Ickx
      Belgium   97 pts
2 Derek Bell
      Great Britain   94 pts
3 Jochen Mass
      West Germany   82 pts

Final Championship Standing (Manufacturers)

1 Porsche   140 pts
2 Lancia   32 pts
3 BMW   6 pts

1984

Monza, Italy

1 D. Bell/S. Bellof   Porsche
   195.90 kph / 121.73 mph
2 J. Ickx/J. Mass   Porsche
3 H. Stuck/H. Grohs/
      W. Brun   Porsche

Silverstone, England

1 J. Ickx/J. Mass   Porsche
   196.55 kph / 122.14 mph
2 K. Ludwig/
      H. Pescarolo   Porsche
3 R. Keegan/
      G. Edwards   Porsche

Le Mans, France

1 K. Ludwig/
      H. Pescarolo   Porsche
   204.18 kph / 126.88 mph
2 P. Henn/J. Paul, Jnr/
      J. Rondeau   Porsche
3 D. Hobbs/P. Streiff/
      S. van der Merwe   Porsche

Nurburgring, West Germany

1 D. Bell/S. Bellof   Porsche
   156.38 kph / 97.17 mph
2 D. Hobbs/T. Boutsen   Porsche
3 P. Barilla/S. Nannini/
      R. Patrese   Lancia

Brands Hatch, England

1 J. Palmer/
      J. Lammers   Porsche
   175.74 kph / 109.20 mph
2 J. Mass/H. Pescarolo   Porsche
3 T. Boutsen/
      R. Keegan/
      G. Edwards   Porsche

Mosport, Canada

1 J. Ickx/J. Mass   Porsche
   166.55 kph / 130.49 mph
2 D. Hobbs/R. Keegan/
      F. Konrad   Porsche
3 A. Coppelli/G. Dacco   Alba-
                              Giannini

Spa, Belgium

1 D. Bell/S. Bellof   Porsche
   169.73 kph / 105.74 mph
2 J. Ickx/J. Mass   Porsche
3 H. Stuck/H. Grohs/
      W. Brun   Porsche

Fuji, Japan

1 S. Bellof/J. Watson   Porsche
   181.21 kph / 112.60 mph
2 J. Ickx/J. Mass   Porsche
3 H. Stuck/
      V. Schuppan   Porsche

● Davina Galica was the first British woman to compete in a Formula One race—the 1977 Race of Champions at Brands Hatch.

Kyalami, South Africa

1 R. Patrese/S. Nannini   Lancia
   177.62 kph / 110.37 mph
2 R. Wollek/P. Barilla   Lancia
3 G. Santana/
      E. Shearsby/
      H. van der Linde   Nissan

Sandown Park, Australia

1 D. Bell/S. Bellof   Porsche
   133.13 kph / 82.74 mph
2 J. Ickx/J. Mass   Porsche
3 J. Palmer/
      J. Lammers   Porsche

Final Championship Standing (Drivers)

1 Stefan Bellof
      West Germany   138 pts
2 Jochen Mass
      West Germany   127 pts
3 Jacky Ickx
      Belgium   104 pts

Final Championship Standing (Manufacturers)

1 Porsche   120 pts
2 Lancia   57 pts
3 Alba-Giannini   12 pts

The Porsche 956 of Jacky Ickx (BEL) and Jochen Mass (FRG) on its way to winning the 1000 km race at Silverstone in 1984. It was a good year for the team who won the Constructors' Championship. (National Motor Museum)

Stefan Bellof (FRG) won seven world championship races with Britain's Derek Bell in 1983–4 but the partnership came to an end when the German lost his life at Spa, Belgium in 1985.

1985

Mugello, Italy

1 J. Ickx/J. Mass   Porsche
  166.15 kph / 103.25 mph
2 M. Winkelhock/
  M. Surer   Porsche
3 S. Belloff/T. Boutsen   Porsche

Monza, Italy

1 M. Winkelhock/
  M. Surer   Porsche
  196.26 kph / 121.96 mph
2 D. Bell/H. Stuck   Porsche
3 R. Patrese/
  A. Nannini   Lancia

Silverstone, England

1 J. Ickx/J. Mass   Porsche
  204.11 kph / 126.83 mph
2 D. Bell/H. Stuck   Porsche
3 R. Patrese/
  A. Nannini   Lancia

Le Mans, France

1 K. Ludwig/P. Barilla/
  'J. Winter'   Porsche
  212.02 kph / 131.75 mph
2 J. Palmer/R. Lloyd/
  J. Weaver   Porsche
3 D. Bell/H. Stuck   Porsche

Hockenheim, West Germany

1 D. Bell/H. Stuck   Porsche
  185.60 kph / 115.33 mph
2 O. Larrauri/
  M. Sigala   Porsche
3 K. Ludwig/P. Barilla   Porsche

Mosport, Canada

1 D. Bell/H. Stuck   Porsche
  168.92 kph / 104.97 mph
2 J. Ickx/J. Mass   Porsche
3 J-L. Schlesser/
  M. Brundle/
  M. Thackwell   Jaguar

Spa, Belgium

1 R. Wollek/M. Baldi/
  R. Patrese   Lancia
  169.12 kph / 105.09 mph
2 D. Bell/H. Stuck   Porsche
3 K. Ludwig/P. Barilla   Porsche

Brands Hatch, England

1 D. Bell/H. Stuck   Porsche
  179.59 kph / 111.60 mph
2 J. Ickx/J. Mass   Porsche
3 R. Wollek/M. Baldi/
  A. de Cesaris   Lancia

Fuji, Japan

1 K. Hoshino   March-
  135.38 kph / 84.13 mph Nissan
2 O. Nakako   Nissan
3 S. Nakajima   Dome-
                          Toyota

Selangor, Malaysia

1 J. Ickx/J. Mass   Porsche
  145.13 kph / 90.18 mph
2 M. Thackwell/
  J. Nielsen/
  J. Lammers   Jaguar
3 V. Schuppan/
  J. Weaver   Porsche

Final Championship Standing (Drivers)

1 Derek Bell
  Great Britain   117 pts
  Hans-Joachim
  Stuck
  West Germany   117 pts
3 Jochen Mass
  West Germany   101 pts
  Jacky Ickx
  Belgium   101 pts

Final Championship Standing (Teams)

1 Rothmans-Porsche   107 pts
2 Martini-Lancia   58 pts
3 NewMan Joest Racing   50 pts

1986

Monza, Italy

1 H. Stuck/D. Bell   Porsche
  201.70 kph / 125.36 mph
2 A. de Cesaris/
  S. Nannini   Lancia
3 M. Sigala/W. Brun   Porsche

Silverstone, England

1 D. Warwick/
  E. Cheever   Jaguar
  207.69 kph / 129.08 mph
2 D. Bell/H. Stuck   Porsche
3 J. Gartner/T. Needell   Porsche

Le Mans, France

1 H. Stuck/D. Bell/
  A. Holbert   Porsche
  207.20 kph / 128.75 mph

2 O. Larrauri/
  J. Gouhier/
  J. Pareja   Porsche
3 G. Follmer/
  J. Morton/
  K. Miller   Porsche

Norisring, West Germany

1 K. Ludwig   Porsche
  163.51 kph / 101.62 mph
2 E. Cheever   Jaguar
3 D. Warwick   Jaguar

Brands Hatch, England

1 R. Wollek/M. Baldi   Porsche
  168.33 kph / 104.62 mph
2 D. Bell/H. Stuck   Porsche
3 T. Boutsen/
  F. Jelinski   Porsche

Jerez, Spain

1 O. Larrauri/J. Pareja   Porsche
  147.25 kph / 91.50 mph
2 F. Jelinski/W. Brun   Porsche
3 D. Warwick/
  J. Lammers   Jaguar

Nurburgring, West Germany

1 M. Thackwell/
  H. Pescarolo   Mercedes
  148.04 kph / 91.99 mph
2 M. Baldi/
  K. Niedwiedz   Porsche
3 E. de Villota/F. Velez Porsche

Spa, Belgium

1 T. Boutsen/
  F. Jelinski   Porsche
  180.76 kph / 112.32 mph
2 D. Warwick/
  J. Lammers   Jaguar
3 D. Bell/H. Stuck   Porsche

Fuji, Japan

1 P. Barilla/
  P. Ghinzani   Porsche
  182.77 kph / 113.57 mph
2 F. Jelinski/
  S. Dickens   Porsche
3 E. Cheever/
  D. Warwick   Jaguar

Final Championship Standing (Drivers)

1 Derek Bell
  Great Britain   82 pts
  Hans-Joachim Stuck
  West Germany   82 pts
3 Derek Warwick
  Great Britain   81 pts

Final Championship Standing (Teams)

1 Brun Motorsport   52 pts
2 Joest Racing   48 pts
3 Rothmans-Porsche   47 pts
  Silk Cut-Jaguar   47 pts

The Le Mans Disaster

The 1955 Le Mans was to be the fastest ever and the two Mercedes of Stirling Moss (GB) and Juan Manuel Fangio (Arg) were expected to dominate the race. But it was the Mercedes, driven by Pierre Levagh, that was the centre of attraction—for the wrong reasons.

At 4.00 p.m. on Saturday 11 June the drivers engaged in their traditional sprint start to their cars for the 23rd Le Mans, scheduled to cover more than 4000 km (2500 miles). Less than two and a half hours later, Le Mans was to be the scene of the worst disaster in motor racing history.

On the 42nd lap Levagh came up the straight between the grandstand and pits in his silver Mercedes at about 240 kph (150 mph) and was being followed by Fangio. In front of Levagh was the Austin Healey of Lance Macklin (GB), travelling at about 210 kph (130 mph). Levagh put his hand up to indicate to Fangio that he was about to overtake; Macklin then braked, Levagh caught Macklin's car and somersaulted over the safety barrier and into the crowd. The Mercedes burst

into flames and broke up with the burning wreckage being thrown among the spectators. Levagh was killed, as were numerous fans. The full extent of the tragedy was impossible to assess at first, but it soon became apparent that the number who were killed instantly was in excess of 70.

The race went on, and the other two Mercedes cars stayed in the race. The extent of the disaster was kept from the remaining drivers, particularly Levagh's team-mates Moss and Fangio but at two o'clock in the morning, orders were received by the Mercedes team-manager Alfred Neubauer, direct from the German factory, to pull all their cars out of the race. At that point the full impact of the devastation hit the two favoured drivers. With the Mercedes contingent out of the race, it paved the way for Mike Hawthorn (GB) and Ivor Bueb (GB) to go on and win in their Jaguar.

Many thought the race should have been stopped immediately, while others believed the Mercedes policy to keep racing was wrong. But both decisions were

at the request of the race organizers who felt any cancellation or withdrawal may have resulted in a mass exodus of spectators from the circuit which would have hindered rescue operations. At dawn the death toll rose still further in the worst disaster since 1952, when 13 people were killed after a car left the track at Weyberg, Rhineland, Germany. The Le Mans officials were blameless as their safety measures were found to be more than adequate, and the speed at which the injured were taken to hospital was also exemplary. The tragedy did, naturally, have its consequences, as many races were cancelled throughout Europe that year and the sport was banned completely in Spain, Switzerland and Mexico. It was even banned in France until such time as the rules were revised.

The final toll was 83 dead and more than 100 injured, many seriously, but Le Mans still went ahead the following year—with the memory of 1955 still very fresh in everybody's mind.

(BBC Hulton Pic. Lib.)

Alberto Ascari

Italian Alberto Ascari was not a spectacular driver but a consistent winner as his World Championship Grand Prix record of 13 successes from 31 races shows.

Born in 1918 he pursued the sport chosen by his father, much to his mother's annoyance because Alberto's father, Antonio, lost his life at Montlhery, France in 1925 when Alberto was just seven. Despite his mother's displeasure the youngster started motor cycle racing before turning to four wheels.

He drove a Ferrari in the 1940 Mille Miglia and after the war joined the Maserati team. In 1949 he returned to Ferrari and teamed up with his friend Luigi Villoresi (Ita). When the World Championship was introduced in 1950 Ascari was expected to mastermind Ferrari's challenge while the Alfa Romeos of Farina (Ita) and Fangio (Arg) were seen as the biggest rivals. But the best Ascari could offer was a couple of second places, including one in his first World Championship Grand Prix at Monaco. Farina and Fangio finished first and second in the championship with Ascari fifth.

Ascari was runner-up to Fangio the following year, after wins in the German Grand Prix at Nurburgring and the Italian Grand Prix at Monza. He served notice that he was ready to take the world title and in 1952 when Formula Two was adopted for the championship this suited the Ferrari 500 and Ascari swept the board with wins in all six championship races he entered. With Formula Two still in force the following year, Ascari again dominated with five wins out of the nine that counted towards the championship.

Lancia tempted the Italian star to their team for 1954 but their cars were not ready until the end of the season and Ascari did not get a drive with them until the final race, the Spanish Grand Prix. Their sports car, however, was ready for him to compete in that

These three men dominated the early years of the Formula One World Championship. Ascari (left) Farina (right) and Fangio won every title from 1950–7. (National Motor Museum)

year's Mille Miglia, a race Ascari never particularly enjoyed, but he still went on to win at an average speed of 139.61 kph (86.77 mph).

Ascari was involved in two inexplicable incidents in 1955. First, shortly after taking the lead at Monaco, his car went wide at the chicane, flew over the straw bales and into the harbour. Ascari escaped to the rescue boat unharmed. Four days later, on 26 May, while testing a Ferrari (the car with which he had enjoyed so much success) at Monza, it flew out of control and the Italian was killed.

For some unknown reason Ascari was not wearing a crash helmet that fateful day. He was aged 36 at the time of his death and left a wife and two small children, just as his father had done 30 years earlier.

Drivers' Records

Most Wins

34 Jacky Ickx (BEL)
21 Henri Pescarolo (FRA)
20 Derek Bell (GB)
17 Jochen Mass (FRG)
16 Brian Redman (GB)
14 Jo Siffert (SWI)
13 Phil Hill (USA)

Most Points in a Season

(Since introduction of World
Endurance Championship in 1981)
138 Stefan Bellof (FRG) 1984
127 Jochen Mass (FRG) 1984
123 Bob Garretson (USA) 1981
117 Derek Bell (GB)/Hans Stuck
    (FRG) 1985

Fastest Races

Spa 1971	Winner's average speed: 249.07 kph / 154.77 mph
	Pedro Rodriguez (MEX)/Jackie Oliver (GB)
Spa 1973	Winner's average speed: 244.44 kph / 151.90 mph
	Derek Bell (GB)/Mike Hailwood (GB)
Monza 1973	Winner's average speed: 242.47 kph / 150.67 mph
	Jacky Ickx (BEL)/Brian Redman (GB)

Fastest, other than Spa or Monza:

Le Mans 1971	Winner's average speed: 222.25 kph / 138.13 mph
	Gijs van Lennep (HOL)/Helmut Marko (AUT)

Most Consecutive Wins

4 Jacky Ickx (BEL) 1972 Daytona,
Sebring, Brands Hatch, Monza

Formula One World Champions who have won races

13 Phil Hill (USA)
7 Mario Andretti (USA)
3 Juan Manuel Fangio (ARG)
3 Giuseppe Farina (ITA)
3 Mike Hawthorn (GB)
3 John Surtees (GB)
2 Alberto Ascari (ITA)
1 Jack Brabham (AUS)
1 Graham Hill (GB)
1 Jochen Rindt (AUT)
1 Nelson Piquet (BRA)

Most Wins Season by Season

1953	3	Giuseppe Farina (ITA)
1954	2	Umberto Maglioli (ITA)
1955	3	Stirling Moss (GB)
1956	2	Stirling Moss (GB), Eugenio Castellotti (ITA)
1957	2	Jean Behra (FRA)
1958	3	Phil Hill (USA)
1959	2	Stirling Moss (GB), Jack Fairman (GB), Carroll Shelby (GB)
1960	2	Olivier Gendebien (BEL), Hans Hermann (FRG)
1961	3	Olivier Gendebien (BEL)
1962	3	Olivier Gendebien (BEL)
1963	2	John Surtees (GB), Ludovico Scarfiotti (ITA)
1964	2	Nino Vaccarella (ITA)
1965	1	eight drivers each had one win
1966	2	Ken Miles (GB), Lloyd Ruby (USA)
1967	2	Lorenzo Bandini (ITA), Chris Amon (NZ)
1968	4	Jo Siffert (SWI)
1969	6	Jo Siffert (SWI)
1970	4	Pedro Rodriguez (MEX), Leo Kinnunen (FIN)
1971	4	Pedro Rodriguez (MEX)
1972	6	Jacky Ickx (BEL)
1973	5	Henri Pescarolo (FRA), Gerard Larrousse (FRA)
1974	5	Jean-Pierre Jarier (FRA)
1975	4	Arturo Merzario (ITA)
1976	3	Jacky Ickx (BEL), Jochen Mass (FRG)
1977	3	Jacky Ickx (BEL), Jochen Mass (FRG)
1978	4	Toine Hezemans (HOL)
1979	3	John Fitzpatrick (GB), Bob Wollek (FRA)
1980	3	Riccardo Patrese (ITA)
1981	3	Harald Grohs (FRG)
1982	4	Jacky Ickx (BEL)
1983	3	Stefan Bellof (FRG), Derek Bell (GB)
1984	5	Stefan Bellof (FRG)
1985	3	Jacky Ickx (BEL), Derek Bell (GB), Hans Stuck (FRG), Jochen Mass (FRG)
1986	2	Derek Bell (GB), Hans Stuck (FRG)

Rolf Stommelen (FRG) enjoyed a long
and successful Sports Car career until he
lost his life at Riverside, United States in
1983. He is seen here at the controls of a
ski-bob . . . somewhat slower than his Alfa
Romeo! (National Motor Museum)

Manufacturers' Records

Most Wins

116 Porsche
52 Ferrari
15 Matra-Simca
13 Ford
11 Lancia
11 Alfa Romeo

Consecutive Wins

24 Porsche (1976–79)
18 Porsche (1982–84)
11 Porsche (1970–71)
9 Matra-Simca (1974)
8 Ferrari (1972)

Most Wins Season by Season

Year	Wins	Manufacturer	Year	Wins	Manufacturer
1953	3	Ferrari	1970	9	Porsche
1954	3	Ferrari	1971	8	Porsche
1955	3	Mercedes-Benz	1972	10	Ferrari
1956	3	Ferrari	1973	5	Matra-Simca
1957	3	Ferrari	1974	9	Matra-Simca
1958	4	Ferrari	1975	7	Alfa Romeo
1959	3	Aston Martin	1976	4	Porsche
1960	2	Ferrari, Porsche	1977	9	Porsche
1961	4	Ferrari	1978	8	Porsche
1962	4	Ferrari	1979	7	Porsche
1963	3	Ferrari	1980	4	Porsche
1964	3	Ferrari	1981	8	Porsche
1965	3	Ferrari	1982	4	Porsche
1966	3	Ford	1983	8	Porsche
1967	3	Ford	1984	9	Porsche
1968	5	Ford, Porsche	1985	8	Porsche
1969	7	Porsche	1986	7	Porsche

Lancia have 11 world championship wins to their credit and have won the Constructors' Championship twice, in 1980 and 1981. (National Motor Museum)

Le Mans

Any mention of Sports Car racing immediately brings to mind the Le Mans 24-Hour race. While many Le Mans results have been included in the foregoing pages, the race holds such a special place in motor racing history that it deserves inclusion in its own right.

The Le Mans Grand Prix d'Endurance, to give it its full and correct name, is not only one of the most famous motor races in the world, but also an institution in France.

The first Le Mans was held in 26/27 May 1923 and won by Andre Lagache and Rene Leonard in their 3-litre Chenard & Walcker. All subsequent races have been held in June with the exception of 1956 (July) and 1968 (September). Because 24 hours is a long time for spectators to stand and watch a race, many attractions were added to the occasion to provide a gala atmosphere, including the famous fun fair.

One feature of Le Mans was the famous race across the track by the drivers to their unstarted cars. Sadly, that great sight disappeared in 1970, when the cars lined up in front of the pits at the commencement of the race.

The original Le Mans circuit measured 17.26 km (10.73 miles) which was reduced to 16.34 km (10.15 miles) and in 1932 it was shortened considerably to 13.64 km (8.48 miles). All subsequent races have been held over that distance with minor fluctuations.

The Le Mans race has been a prominent part of the World Sports Car Championship since its inauguration in 1953 and formed a round in the championship every year with the exception of 1956 and 1975–79. For results of races in the championship see pages 95–110.

Opposite The great Le Mans tradition of the drivers racing across the track to start their cars disappeared in 1970, when a conventional line-up in front of the grandstand was adopted. This picture shows the drivers 'under starter's orders' at the commencement of the 1930 race. (National Motor Museum)

Results

(Figures in brackets indicate distance covered)

1923

	Car	Winning Speed
1 A. Lagache/R. Leonard (2209.06 km / 1372.94 miles)	Chenard & Walcker	92.04 kph / 57.21 mph
2 R. Bachmann/C. Dauvergne	Chenard & Walcker	
3 de Tornaco/P. Gros	Bignan	

1924

1 J. Duff/F. Clement (2078.89 km / 1290.80 miles)	Bentley	86.53 kph / 53.78 mph
2 H. Stoffel/E. Brisson	La Lorraine	
3 G. de Courcelles/A. Rossignol	La Lorraine	

1925

1 G. de Courcelles/A. Rossignol (2233.50 km / 1388.13 miles)	La Lorraine	93.06 kph / 57.84 mph
2 J. Chassagne/S. C. Davis	Sunbeam	
3 H. Stalter/E. Brisson	La Lorraine	

1926

1 R. Bloch/A. Rossignol (2551.86 km / 1585.99 miles)	La Lorraine	106.33 kph / 66.08 mph
2 G. de Courcelles/M. Mongin	La Lorraine	
3 H. Stalter/E. Brisson	La Lorraine	

1927

1 J. Benjafield/S. C. Davis (2369.29 km / 1472.53 miles)	Bentley	98.72 kph / 61.35 mph
2 A. de Victor/J. Hasley	Salmson	
3 L. Desveaux/F. Vallon	SCAP	

● Nick Mason (GB), a member of the Pink Floyd pop group, entered his own Dome Car, which he drove with co-driver Chris Craft (GB) and Elisio Salazar (Chi), in the 1983 Le Mans 24-Hour race. They completed 75 laps and finished in 42nd place.

Refuelling and pit stops were somewhat different from the fast-action stops of today, as this picture from the 1928 Le Mans shows. (National Motor Museum)

	Car	Winning Speed
1928		
1 W. Barnato/B. Rubin	Bentley	111.20 kph / 69.11 mph
(2668.70 km / 1658.61 miles)		
2 E. Brisson/R. Bloch	Stutz	
3 H. Stoffel/A. Rossignol	Chrysler	
1929		
1 W. Barnato/H. Birkin	Bentley	118.47 kph / 73.63 mph
(2843.22 km / 1767.07 miles)		
2 J. Dunfee/G. Kidston	Bentley	
3 J. Benjafield/H. d'Erlanger	Bentley	
1930		
1 W. Barnato/G. Kidston	Bentley	122.08 kph / 75.88 mph
(2930.03 km / 1821.03 miles)		
2 F. Clement/R. Watney	Bentley	
3 B. E. Lewis/H. S. Eaton	Talbot	
1931		
1 E. Howe/H. Birkin	Alfa Romeo	125.71 kph / 78.13 mph
(3017.00 km / 1875.08 miles)		
2 B. Ivanowski/H. Stoffel	Mercedes-Benz	
3 T. Rose-Richards/A. Saunders-Davis	Talbot	
1932		
1 R. Sommer/L. Chinetti	Alfa Romeo	123.06 kph / 76.48 mph
(2953.40 km / 1835.55 miles)		
2 F. Cortese/G. Guidotti	Alfa Romeo	
3 B. E. Lewis/T. Rose-Richards	Talbot	
1933		
1 R. Sommer/T. Nuvolari	Alfa Romeo	130.97 kph / 81.40 mph
(3143.36 km / 1953.61 miles)		
2 L. Chinetti/P. Varent	Alfa Romeo	
3 B. E. Lewis/T. Rose-Richards	Alfa Romeo	
1934		
1 L. Chinetti/P. Etancelin	Alfa Romeo	120.26 kph / 74.74 mph
(2886.31 km / 1793.86 miles)		
2 J. Sebilleau/G. Delaroche	Riley	
3 F. Dixon/C. Paul	Riley	

1935	Car	*Winning Speed*
1 J. S. Hindmarsh/L. Fontes	Lagonda	125.26 kph / 77.85 mph
(3006.15 km / 1868.33 miles)		
2 M. Helde/H. Stoffel	Alfa Romeo	
3 C. E. Martin/C. Brackenbury	Aston Martin	

1936

Not held

1937

1 J-P. Wimille/R. Benoist	Bugatti	136.97 kph / 85.13 mph
(3283.23 km / 2043.03 miles)		
2 J. Paul/M. Mongin	Delahaye	
3 R. Dreyfus/H. Stoffel	Delahaye	

1938

1 E. Chaboud/J. Tremoulet	Delahaye	132.51 kph / 82.36 mph
(3180.25 km / 1976.54 miles)		
2 G. Seraud/Y. Giraud-Cabantous	Delahaye	
3 J. Prenant/A. Morel	Lago-Talbot	

1939

1 J-P. Wimille/P. Veyron	Bugatti	139.75 kph / 86.86 mph
(3354.04 km / 2084.55 miles)		
2 L. Gerard/G. Monneret	Delage	
3 A. Dobson/C. Brackenbury	Lagonda	

1940–48

Not held

1949

1 L. Chinetti/Lord Selsdon	Ferrari	132.40 kph / 82.28 mph
(3177.61 km / 1974.90 miles)		
2 H. Louveau/J. Jover	Delage	
3 N. Culpan/H. Aldington	Frazer-Nash	

1950

1 L. Rosier/J-L. Rosier	Lago-Talbot	144.35 kph / 89.71 mph
(3764.37 km / 2153.12 miles)		
2 P. Meyrat/G. Mairesse	Lago-Talbot	
3 S. Allard/T. Cole	Allard	

1951

1 P. Whitehead/P. Walker	Jaguar	150.43 kph / 93.50 mph
(3610.41 km / 2243.89 miles)		
2 P. Meyrat/G. Mairesse	Lago-Talbot	
3 L. Macklin/E. Thompson	Aston Martin	

1952

1 H. Lang/F. Riess	Mercedes-Benz	155.54 kph / 96.67 mph
(3732.99 km / 2320.07 miles)		
2 T. Helfrich/N. Niedermayr	Mercedes-Benz	
3 N. Johnson/T. Wisdom	Nash-Healey	

1953–55

See Sports Car World Championship results

1956

1 R. Flockhart/N. Sanderson	Jaguar	168.08 kph / 104.47 mph
(4034.06 km / 2507.18 miles)		
2 S. Moss/P. Collins	Aston Martin	
3 O. Gendebien/M. Trintignant	Ferrari	

1957–74

See Sports Car World Championship results

One of motor racing's great sights, the Le Mans 24-Hour race at night. This picture was taken during the 1965 race won by Masten Gregory (USA) and Jochen Rindt (Aut). (National Motor Museum)

	Car	Winning Speed
1975		
1 D. Bell/J. Ickx	Gulf-Cosworth	191.44 kph / 118.98 mph
(4594.58 km / 2855.55 miles)		
2 J. L. Lafosse/G. Chasseuil	Ligier-Cosworth	
3 V. Schuppan/J-P. Jaussaud	Gulf-Cosworth	
1976		
1 J. Ickx/G. van Lennep	Porsche	198.70 kph / 123.49 mph
(4768.90 km / 2963.89 miles)		
2 J. L. Lafosse/F. Migault	Mirage-Cosworth	
3 A. de Cadenet/C. Craft	Lola-Porsche	
1977		
1 J. Ickx/J. Barth/H. Haywood	Porsche	194.61 kph / 120.95 mph
(4670.62 km / 2902.81 miles)		
2 V. Schuppan/J-P. Jarier	Mirage-Renault	
3 C. Ballot-Lena/P. Gregg	Porsche	
1978		
1 D. Pironi/J-P. Jaussaud	Renault-Alpine	210.19 kph / 130.60 mph
(5044.43 km / 3134.46 miles)		
2 R. Wollek/J. Ickx/J. Barth	Porsche	
3 R. Joest/P. Gregg/H. Haywood	Porsche	
1979		
1 D. Whittington/K. Ludwig/W. Whittington	Porsche	173.93 kph / 108.10 mph
(4168.81 km / 2590.93 miles)		
2 R. Stommelen/R. Barbour/P. Newman	Porsche	
3 L. Ferrier/F. Servanin/F. Trisconi	Porsche	

1980–86

See Sports Car World Championship results

Drivers' Records

Most Wins

6 Jacky Ickx (BEL) 1969, 1975, 1976, 1977, 1981, 1982
4 Olivier Gendebien (BEL) 1958, 1960, 1961, 1962
4 Henri Pescarolo (FRA) 1972, 1973, 1974, 1984
4 Derek Bell (GB) 1975, 1981, 1982, 1986
3 Woolf Barnato (GB) 1928, 1929, 1930
3 Luigi Chinetti (ITA/USA) 1932, 1934, 1949
3 Phil Hill (USA) 1958, 1961, 1962

Most Successive Wins

3 Woolf Barnato (GB) 1928–30
3 Olivier Gendebien (BEL) 1960–62
3 Henri Pescarolo (FRA) 1972–74
3 Jacky Ickx (BEL) 1975–77

Most Successful Combination

3 wins Olivier Gendebien (BEL)/Phil Hill (USA) 1958, 1961, 1962
3 wins Jacky Ickx (BEL)/Derek Bell (GB) 1975, 1981, 1982

Fastest Races

222.25 kph / 138.13 mph Helmut Marko (AUT)/Gijs van Lennep (HOL) 1971 (over the 13.47 / 8.37 mile circuit)
217.99 kph / 135.48 mph Dan Gurney (USA)/A. J. Foyt (USA) 1967 (over the 13.46 / 8.36 mile circuit)
212.02 kph / 131.75 mph Klaus Ludwig (FRG)/'John Winter' (FRG)/Paulo Barilla (ITA) 1985 (over the 13.64 km / 8.48 mile circuit)

Greatest Distances Covered

5333.72 km / 3314.22 miles Helmut Marko (AUT)/Gijs van Lennep (HOL) 1971 (over the 13.47 / 8.37 mile circuit)
5088.51 km / 3162.00 miles Klaus Ludwig (FRG)/'John Winter' (FRG)/Paulo Barilla (ITA) 1985 (over the 13.64 km / 8.48 mile circuit)
5043.44 km / 3134.52 miles Jean-Pierre Jaussaud (FRA)/Didier Pironi (FRA) 1978 (over the 13.62 km / 8.47 mile circuit)

Britain's most successful driver in the Le Mans, Derek Bell. He won the great race four times, partnering Jacky Ickx (BEL) in 1975, 1981–2, and with Hans Stuck (FRG) and Al Holbert (USA) in 1986. (National Motor Museum)

Below The finest Sports Car driver of the modern era, Jacky Ickx (BEL) who won Le Mans six times, 1969–82. He is seen here in a different role, however, behind the wheel of the Ligier Formula One car. Ickx won eight Formula One races in addition to his record 34 Sports Car successes. (All Sport)

Manufacturers' Records

Most Wins

11	Porsche	1970, 1971, 1976, 1977, 1979, 1981, 1982, 1983, 1984, 1985, 1986
9	Ferrari	1949, 1954, 1958, 1960, 1961, 1962, 1963, 1964, 1965
5	Bentley	1924, 1927, 1928, 1929, 1930
5	Jaguar	1951, 1953, 1955, 1956, 1957
4	Alfa Romeo	1931, 1932, 1933, 1934
4	Ford	1966, 1967, 1968, 1969

Most Consecutive Wins

6 Ferrari 1960–65
6 Porsche 1981–86
4 Bentley 1927–30
4 Alfa Romeo 1931–34
4 Ford 1966–69

A historic collection of famous British cars that have won Le Mans over the years. Back, left: 4½-litre Bentley. Right: 'D' Type Jaguar. Front, left: Aston Martin DBR1 and, right: Gulf Ford GT40. (National Motor Museum)

European Formula Two Championship

Formula Two was introduced in 1947 to enable young drivers, who could not get into Formula One teams, to compete internationally. The F.I.A. introduced a new Formula Two in 1967 and that same season saw the birth of the European Formula Two Championships with the first meeting at Snetterton on 24 March when the late Jochen Rindt (Austria) won the Guards Trophy over 174.5 km (108 miles).

The championships ended in 1984 and were replaced by the new Formula 3000 Championship.

1967

24 Mar: Snetterton, England *Average speed*
1 J. Rindt   Brabham-Cosworth 175.39 kph / 108.99 mph
2 G. Hill   Lotus-Cosworth
3 A. Rees   Brabham-Cosworth

27 Mar: Silverstone, England
1 J. Rindt   Brabham-Cosworth 187.74 kph / 116.66 mph
2 A. Rees   Brabham-Cosworth
3 J. Surtees Lola-Cosworth

23 Apr: Nurburgring, West Germany
1 J. Rindt   Brabham-Cosworth 145.50 kph / 90.41 mph
2 J. Surtees Lola-BMW
3 J. Ickx   Matra-Cosworth

11 Jun: Hockenheim, West Germany
1 R. Widdows Brabham-Cosworth 194.79 kph / 121.04 mph
2 C. Lambert Brabham-Cosworth
3 P. Gethin   Cooper-Cosworth

16 Jul: Langenlebarn, Austria
1 J. Rindt   Brabham-Cosworth 148.17 kph / 92.07 mph
2 J. Brabham Brabham-Cosworth
3 J-P. Beltoise Matra-Cosworth

23 Jul: Jarama, Spain
1 J. Clark   Lotus-Cosworth   131.50 kph / 81.71 mph
2 J. Stewart Matra-Cosworth
3 C. Irwin   Lola-Cosworth

30 Jul: Zandvoort, Holland
1 J. Ickx   Matra-Cosworth   168.77 kph / 104.87 mph
2 P. Courage McLaren-Cosworth
3 F. Gardner Brabham-Cosworth

20 Aug: Enna, Italy
1 J. Stewart Matra-Cosworth   229.59 kph / 142.67 mph
2 J-P. Beltoise Matra-Cosworth
3 J. Ickx   Matra-Cosworth

8 Oct: Vallelunga, Italy
1 J. Ickx   Matra-Cosworth   139.33 kph / 86.58 mph
2 J-P. Beltoise Matra-Cosworth
3 J. Servoz-
  Gavin   Matra-Cosworth

Final Championship Standing
1 Jacky Ickx   Belgium   41 pts
2 Frank Gardner   Australia   34 pts
3 Jean-Pierre
  Beltoise   France   27 pts

1968

7 Apr: Hockenheim, West Germany
                              Average speed
1 J-P. Beltoise Matra-Cosworth 189.60 kph / 117.82 mph
2 H. Pescarolo Matra-Cosworth
3 P. Courage   Brabham-Cosworth

15 Apr: Thruxton, England
1 J. Rindt   Brabham-Cosworth 176.09 kph / 109.42 mph
2 J-P. Beltoise Matra-Cosworth
3 D. Bell   Brabham-Cosworth

28 Apr: Jarama, Spain
1 J-P. Beltoise Matra-Cosworth   136.17 kph / 84.62 mph
2 J. Rindt   Brabham-Cosworth
3 K. Ahrens   Brabham-Cosworth

3 Jun: Crystal Palace, England
1 J. Rindt   Brabham-Cosworth 150.78 kph / 93.69 mph
2 B. Redman   Lola-Cosworth
3 C. Regazzoni Tecno-Cosworth

14 Jul: Langenlebarn, Austria
1 J. Rindt   Brabham-Cosworth 159.12 kph / 98.88 mph
2 J-P. Beltoise Matra-Cosworth
3 H. Pescarolo   Matra-Cosworth

25 Aug: Enna, Italy
1 J. Rindt   Brabham-Cosworth 229.64 kph / 142.70 mph
2 P. Courage   Brabham-Cosworth
3 E. Brambilla Ferrari

13 Oct: Hockenheim, West Germany
1 E. Brambilla Ferrari   198.50 kph / 123.35 mph
2 H. Pescarolo Matra-Cosworth
3 D. Bell   Ferrari

27 Oct: Vallelunga, Italy
1 E. Brambilla Ferrari   *
2 A. de
  Adamich   Ferrari
3 P. Gethin   Brabham-Cosworth
* Raced over two heats, aggregate time taken

Final Championship Standing

1 Jean-Pierre
   Beltoise   France   48 pts
2 Henri
   Pescarolo   France   30 pts
3 Ernesto
   Brambilla   Italy   26 pts

1969

7 Apr: Thruxton, England

Average speed

1 J. Rindt   Lotus-Cosworth   182.60 kph / 113.47 mph
2 J. Stewart   Matra-Cosworth
3 J-P. Beltoise Matra-Cosworth

13 Apr: Hockenheim, West Germany

1 J-P. Beltoise Matra-Cosworth   *
2 H. Hahne   Lola-BMW
3 P. Courage   Brabham-Cosworth

27 Apr: Nurburgring, West Germany

1 J. Stewart   Matra-Cosworth   167.70 kph / 104.21 mph
2 J. Siffert   BMW
3 J-P. Beltoise Matra-Cosworth

11 May: Jarama, Spain

1 J. Stewart   Matra-Cosworth   136.76 kph / 84.98 mph
2 J-P. Beltoise Matra-Cosworth
3 P. Courage   Brabham-Cosworth

12 Jul: Langenlebarn, Austria

1 J. Rindt   Lotus-Cosworth   163.94 kph / 101.87 mph
2 J. Stewart   Matra-Cosworth
3 G. Hill   Lotus-Cosworth

24 Aug: Enna, Italy

1 P. Courage   Brabham-Cosworth 228.91 kph / 142.24 mph
2 J. Servoz-
   Gavin   Matra-Cosworth
3 F. Cevert   Tecno-Cosworth

12 Oct: Vallelunga, Italy

1 J. Servoz-
   Gavin   Matra-Cosworth   145.78 kph / 90.59 mph
2 P. Westbury   Brabham-Cosworth
3 J. Miles   Lotus-Cosworth
* Raced over two heats, aggregate time taken

Final Championship Standing

1 Johnny
   Servoz-Gavin France   37 pts
2 Hubert Hahne   West Germany   28 pts
3 Francois Cevert France   21 pts

1970

30 Mar: Thruxton, England   *Average speed*

1 J. Rindt   Lotus-Cosworth   181.42 kph / 112.73 mph
2 J. Stewart   Brabham-Cosworth
3 D. Bell   Brabham-Cosworth

12 Apr: Hockenheim, West Germany

1 C. Regazzoni Tecno-Cosworth   198.10 kph / 123.10 mph
2 T. Ikuzawa   Lotus-Cosworth
3 D. Bell   Brabham-Cosworth

26 Apr: Barcelona, Spain

1 D. Bell   Brabham-Cosworth 141.40 kph / 87.87 mph
2 H. Pescarolo Brabham-Cosworth
3 E. Fittipaldi Lotus-Cosworth

28 Jun: Rouen, France

1 J. Siffert   BMW   190.90 kph / 118.63 mph
2 C. Regazzoni Tecno-Cosworth
3 E. Fittipaldi Lotus-Cosworth

23 Aug: Enna, Italy

1 C. Regazzoni Tecno-Cosworth   *
2 J. Siffert   BMW
3 J. Ickx   BMW

13 Sep: Langenlebarn, Austria

1 J. Ickx   BMW   *
2 J. Brabham   Brabham-Cosworth
3 F. Cevert   Tecno-Cosworth

27 Sep: Imola, Italy

1 C. Regazzoni Tecno-Cosworth   *
2 E. Fittipaldi Lotus-Cosworth
3 D. Bell   Brabham-Cosworth

11 Oct: Hockenheim, West Germany

1 D. Quester   BMW   186.17 kph / 115.69 mph
2 C. Regazzoni Tecno-Cosworth
3 R. Peterson   March-Cosworth
* Raced over two heats, aggregate time taken

Final Championship Standing

1 Clay Regazzoni   Switzerland   45 pts
2 Derek Bell   Great Britain 35 pts
3 Emerson Fittipaldi Brazil   23 pts

1971

4 Apr: Hockenheim, West Germany

Average speed

1 F. Cevert   Tecno   183.60 kph / 114.09 mph
2 G. Hill   Brabham-Cosworth
3 C. Reute-
   mann   Brabham-Cosworth

12 Apr: Thruxton, England

1 G. Hill   Brabham-Cosworth 182.02 kph / 113.11 mph
2 R. Peterson   March-Cosworth
3 D. Bell   March-Cosworth

2 May: Nurburgring, West Germany

1 F. Cevert   Tecno   170.60 kph / 106.01 mph
2 E. Fittipaldi Lotus-Cosworth
3 C. Reute-
   mann   Brabham-Cosworth

16 May: Jarama, Spain

1 E. Fittipaldi Lotus-Cosworth   136.60 kph / 84.88 mph
2 D. Quester   March-BMW
3 C. Reute-
   mann   Brabham-Cosworth

31 May: Crystal Palace, England

1 E. Fittipaldi Lotus-Cosworth   159.59 kph / 99.17 mph
2 T. Schenken   Brabham-Cosworth
3 R. Peterson   March-Cosworth

27 Jun: Rouen, France

1 R. Peterson	March-Cosworth	176.48 kph / 109.66 mph
2 D. Quester	March-BMW	
3 G. Hill	Brabham-Cosworth	

8 Aug: Mantorp, Sweden

1 R. Peterson	March-Cosworth	153.24 kph / 95.22 mph
2 T. Schenken	Brabham-Cosworth	
3 C. Reute- mann	Brabham-Cosworth	

12 Sep: Langenlebarn, Austria

1 R. Peterson	March-Cosworth	142.20 kph / 88.36 mph
2 T. Schenken	Brabham-Cosworth	
3 D. Quester	March-BMW	

26 Sep: Albi, France

1 E. Fittipaldi	Lotus-Cosworth	179.24 kph / 111.38 mph
2 C. Reute- mann	Brabham-Cosworth	
3 J-P. Jarier	March-Cosworth	

10 Oct: Vallelunga, Italy

1 R. Peterson	March-Cosworth	156.35 kph / 97.16 mph
2 D. Quester	March-BMW	
3 C. Reute- mann	Brabham-Cosworth	

17 Oct: Vallelunga, Italy

1 M. Beuttler	March-Cosworth	156.36 kph / 97.16 mph
2 D. Quester	March-BMW	
3 J-P. Jarier	March-Cosworth	

Final Championship Standing

1 Ronnie Peterson	Sweden	54 pts
2 Carlos Reutemann	Argentina	40 pts
3 Dieter Quester	Austria	31 pts

1972

12 Mar: Mallory Park, England

Average speed

1 D. Morgan	Brabham-Ford	174.87 kph / 108.66 mph
2 N. Lauda	March-Ford	
3 C. Reute- mann	Brabham-Ford	

3 Apr: Thruxton, England

1 R. Peterson	March-Ford	188.57 kph / 117.18 mph
2 F. Cevert	March-Ford	
3 N. Lauda	March-Ford	

16 Apr: Hockenheim, West Germany

1 J-P. Jaussaud	Brabham-Ford	190.80 kph / 118.56 mph
2 M. Beuttler	March-Ford	
3 R. Wollek	Brabham-Ford	

7 May: Pau, France

1 P. Gethin	Chevron-Ford	123.74 kph / 76.89 mph
2 P. Depailler	March-Ford	
3 D. Purley	March-Ford	

29 May: Crystal Palace, England

1 J. Scheckter	McLaren-Ford	161.56 kph / 100.39 mph
2 M. Hailwood	Surtees-Ford	
3 C. Reute- mann	Brabham-Ford	

11 Jun: Hockenheim, West Germany

1 E. Fittipaldi	Lotus-Ford	165.93 kph / 103.11 mph
2 J-P. Jaussaud	Brabham-Ford	
3 R. Peterson	March-Ford	

25 Jun: Rouen, France

1 E. Fittipaldi	Lotus-Ford	183.63 kph / 114.11 mph
2 M. Hailwood	Surtees-Ford	
3 C. Reute- mann	Brabham-Ford	

9 Jul: Osterreichring, Austria

1 E. Fittipaldi	Lotus-Ford	203.07 kph / 126.19 mph
2 M. Hailwood	Surtees-Ford	
3 C. Reute- mann	Brabham-Ford	

23 Jul: Imola, Italy

1 J. Surtees	Surtees-Ford	191.29 kph / 118.87 mph
2 R. Wollek	Brabham-Ford	
3 N. Lauda	March-Ford	

6 Aug: Mantorp, Sweden

1 M. Hailwood	Surtees-Ford	*
2 J-P. Jabouille	March-Ford	
3 J-P. Jaussaud	Brabham-Ford	

20 Aug: Enna, Italy

1 H. Pescarolo	Brabham-Ford	187.39 kph / 116.44 mph
2 P. Depailler	March-Ford	
3 C. Ruesch	Surtees-Ford	

3 Sep: Salzburg, Austria

1 M. Hailwood	Surtees-Ford	*
2 C. Pace	Surtees-Ford	
3 D. Morgan	Brabham-Ford	

24 Sep: Albi, France

1 J-P. Jaussaud	Brabham-Ford	184.25 kph / 114.49 mph
2 P. Depailler	March-Ford	
3 R. Wollek	Brabham-Ford	

1 Oct: Hockenheim, West Germany

1 T. Schenken	Brabham-Ford	193.40 kph / 120.18 mph
2 M. Hailwood	Surtees-Ford	
3 R. Peterson	March-Ford	

* Raced over two heats, aggregate time taken

Final Championship Standing

1 Mike Hailwood	Great Britain	52 pts
2 Jean-Pierre Jaussaud	France	37 pts
3 Patrick Depailler	France	27 pts

1973

11 Mar: Mallory Park, England

Average speed
1 J-P. Jarier   March-BMW   180.65 kph / 112.25 mph
2 M. Hailwood Surtees-Ford
3 D. McConnell Surtees-Ford

8 Apr: Hockenheim, West Germany

1 J-P. Jarier   March-BMW   197.60 kph / 122.78 mph
2 P. Depailler Elf-Ford
3 D. Bell   Surtees-Ford

23 Apr: Thruxton, England

1 H. Pescarolo Motul-Ford   184.19 kph / 114.45 mph
2 R. Wollek   Motul-Ford
3 M. Beuttler March-BMW

29 Apr: Nurburgring, West Germany

1 R. Wisell   GRD-Ford   149.90 kph / 93.06 mph
2 T. Schenken Motul-Ford
3 P. Depailler Elf-Ford

6 May: Pau, France

1 F. Cevert   Elf-Ford   127.63 kph / 79.30 mph
2 J-P. Jarier   March-BMW
3 T. Schenken Motul-Cosworth

20 May: Kinnekulle, Sweden

1 J. Mass   Surtees-Ford   151.05 kph / 93.88 mph
2 P. Depailler Elf-Ford
3 T. Schenken Motul-Cosworth

10 Jun: Nivelles, Belgium

1 J-P. Jarier   March-BMW   177.34 kph / 110.20 mph
2 J. Mass   Surtees-Ford
3 V. Brambilla March-BMW

17 Jun: Hockenheim, West Germany

1 J. Mass   Surtees-Ford   197.83 kph / 122.95 mph
2 C. Vandervell March-BMW
3 J. Coulon   March-BMW

24 Jun: Rouen, France

1 J-P. Jarier   March-BMW   177.08 kph / 110.03 mph
2 J. Mass   Surtees-Ford
3 T. Schenken Motul-Cosworth

29 Jun: Monza, Italy

1 R. William-
    son   March-BMW   200.60 kph / 124.65 mph
2 P. Depailler Elf-Ford
3 J. Coulon   March-BMW

29 Jul: Mantorp, Sweden

1 J-P. Jarier   March-BMW   173.13 kph / 107.60 mph
2 J. Mass   Surtees-Ford
3 J. Watson   Chevron-Ford

12 Aug: Karlskoga, Sweden

1 J-P. Jarier   March-BMW   145.82 kph / 90.63 mph
2 P. Gethin   Chevron-Ford
3 T. Palm   Surtees-Ford

26 Aug: Enna, Italy

1 J-P. Jarier   March-BMW   207.91 kph / 129.19 mph
2 V. Brambilla March-BMW
3 J. Mass   Surtees-Ford

2 Sep: Salzburg, Austria

1 V. Brambilla March-BMW   212.76 kph / 132.20 mph
2 P. Depailler Elf-Ford
3 J. Coulon   March-BMW

9 Sep: Norisring, West Germany

1 T. Schenken Motul-Ford   155.23 kph / 96.46 mph
2 T. Pryce   Motul-Ford
3 H. Pescarolo Motul-BMW

16 Sep: Albi, France

1 V. Brambilla March-BMW   187.96 kph / 116.82 mph
2 J-P. Jarier   March-BMW
3 J-P. Beltoise March-BMW

14 Oct: Vallelunga, Italy

1 J. Coulon   March-BMW   157.78 kph / 98.05 mph
2 V. Brambilla March-BMW
3 J. Vonian-
    then   GRD-Cosworth

Final Championship Standing

1 Jean-Pierre
    Jarier   France
2 Jochen Mass   West Germany   78 pts
3 Patrick Depailler France   41 pts
                                       38 pts

1974

24 Mar: Montjuich, Spain

Average speed
1 H. Stuck   March-BMW   156.75 kph / 97.40 mph
2 P. Depailler March-BMW
3 J-P.
    Jabouille Elf-BMW

7 Apr: Hockenheim, West Germany

1 H. Stuck   March-BMW   *
2 J. Watson   Surtees-Ford
3 M. Leclere   Elf-BMW

5 May: Pau, France

1 P. Depailler March-BMW   108.40 kph / 68.37 mph
2 J. Laffite   March-BMW
3 A. Sutcliffe   March-BMW

2 Jun: Salzburg, Austria

1 J. Laffite   March-BMW   210.13 kph / 130.57 mph
2 D. Purley   Chevron-BMW
3 J. Dolhem   Surtees-Ford

9 Jun: Hockenheim, West Germany

1 J-P.
    Jabouille Elf-BMW   198.76 kph / 123.51 mph
2 J. Laffite   March-BMW
3 H. Stuck   March-BMW

30 Jun: Rouen, France

1 H. Stuck   March-BMW   155.63 kph / 96.71 mph
2 D. Purley   Chevron-BMW
3 M. Leclere   Elf-BMW

14 Jul: Mugello, Italy

1 P. Depailler March-BMW   169.61 kph / 105.40 mph
2 J-P. Paoli March-BMW
3 T. Pryce Chevron-BMW

11 Aug: Karlskoga, Sweden

1 R. Peterson March-BMW   147.45 kph / 91.63 mph
2 P. Depailler March-BMW
3 J. Laffite March-BMW

25 Aug: Enna, Italy

1 H. Stuck March-BMW   208.81 kph / 129.75 mph
2 D. Purley Chevron-BMW
3 G. Serblin March-BMW

22 Sep: Nogaro, France

1 P. Tambay Elf-BMW   149.12 kph / 92.66 mph
2 T. Schenken Surtees-BMW
3 M. Leclere Elf-BMW

29 Sep: Hockenheim, West Germany

1 P. Depailler March-BMW   *
2 H. Stuck March-BMW
3 J-P.
   Jabouille Elf-BMW

13 Oct: Vallelunga, Italy

1 P. Depailler March-BMW   162.29 kph / 100.85 mph
2 H. Stuck March-BMW
3 J. Laffite March-BMW
* Raced over two heats, aggregate time taken

Final Championship Standing

1 Patrick Depailler France   54 pts
2 Hans Stuck West Germany   43 pts
3 Jacques Laffite France   31 pts

1975

9 Mar: Estoril, Portugal

Average speed

1 J. Laffite Martini-BMW   137.22 kph / 85.27 mph
2 J. Vonlan-
   then March-BMW
3 L. Leoni March-BMW

31 Mar: Thruxton, England

1 J. Laffite Martini-BMW   186.64 kph / 115.98 mph
2 P. Tambay March-BMW
3 G. Martini March-BMW

13 Apr: Hockenheim, West Germany

1 G. Larrousse Alpine-BMW   196.42 kph / 122.06 mph
2 H. Stuck March-BMW
3 B. Henton March-Ford

27 Apr: Nurburgring, West Germany

1 J. Laffite Martini-BMW   180.30 kph / 112.04 mph
2 P. Tambay March-BMW
3 H. Ertl Chevron-BMW

19 May: Pau, France

1 J. Laffite Martini-BMW   131.14 kph / 81.49 mph
2 J-P.
   Jabouille Elf-BMW
3 P. Depailler March-BMW

8 Jun: Hockenheim, West Germany

1 J. Laffite Martini-BMW   198.30 kph / 123.22 mph
2 C. Bour-
   goignie March-BMW
3 M. Flammini March-BMW

15 Jun: Salzburg, Austria

1 J-P.
   Jabouille Elf-BMW   210.67 kph / 130.91 mph
2 H. Binder March-BMW
3 G. Serblin March-BMW

29 Jun: Rouen, France

1 M. Leclere March-BMW   180.98 kph / 112.46 mph
2 P. Tambay March-BMW
3 C. Bour-
   goignie March-BMW

13 Jul: Mugello, Italy

1 M. Flammini March-BMW   166.61 kph / 103.53 mph
2 A. Pesenti-
   Rossi March-BMW
3 'Gianfranco' March-BMW

27 Jul: Enna, Italy

1 J. Laffite Martini-BMW   178.24 kph / 110.76 mph
2 G. Larrousse Alpine-BMW
3 G. Serblin March-BMW

31 Aug: Silverstone, England

1 M. Leclere March-BMW   199.11 kph / 123.73 mph
2 G. Larrousse Elf-BMW
3 B. Henton Wheatcroft-Ford

14 Sep: Zolder, Belgium

1 M. Leclere March-BMW   168.65 kph / 104.80 mph
2 P. Tambay March-BMW
3 M. Flammini March-BMW

28 Sep: Nogaro, France

1 P. Tambay March-BMW   150.71 kph / 93.65 mph
2 M. Leclere March-BMW
3 J-P.
   Jabouille Elf-BMW

12 Oct: Vallelunga, Italy

1 V. Bram-
   billa March-BMW   156.10 kph / 97.00 mph
2 J. Laffite Martini-BMW
3 M. Flammini March-BMW

Final Championship Standing

1 Jacques Laffite France   60 pts
2 Michel Leclere France   36 pts
   Patrick Tambay France   36 pts

1976

11 Apr: Hockenheim, West Germany

Average speed
199.25 kph / 123.81 mph

1 H. Stuck March-BMW
2 R. Arnoux Martini-Renault
3 P. Tambay Martini-Renault

19 Apr: Thruxton, England

1 M. Flammini　March-BMW
2 A. Ribeiro　　March-BMW
3 P. Tambay　　Martini-Renault

187.15 kph / 116.30 mph

9 May: Vallelunga, Italy

1 J-P.
　　Jabouille　Elf-Renault
2 P. Tambay　　Martini-Renault
3 A. Ribeiro　　March-BMW

159.89 kph / 99.36 mph

23 May: Salzburg, Austria

1 M. Leclere　　Elf-Renault
2 M. Flammini　March-BMW
3 P. Tambay　　Martini-Renault

197.49 kph / 122.72 mph

7 Jun: Pau, France

1 R. Arnoux　　Martini-Renault
2 J. Laffite　　　Chevron-BMW
3 J-P.
　　Jabouille　Elf-Renault

131.12 kph / 81.48 mph

20 Jun: Hockenheim, West Germany

1 H. Stuck　　　March-BMW
2 M. Leclere　　Elf-Renault
3 P. Tambay　　Martini-Renault

200.19 kph / 124.40 mph

27 Jun: Rouen, France

1 M. Flammini　March-BMW
2 J-P.
　　Jabouille　Elf-Renault
3 G. Martini　　March-BMW

180.57 kph / 112.21 mph

11 Jul: Mugello, Italy

1 J-P.
　　Jabouille　Elf-Renault
2 R. Arnoux　　Martini-Renault
3 P. Tambay　　Martini-Renault

170.25 kph / 105.79 mph

25 Jul: Enna, Italy

1 R. Arnoux　　Martini-Renault
2 A. Ribeiro　　March-BMW
3 E. Cheever　　March-Hart

185.24 kph / 115.11 mph

8 Aug: Estoril, Portugal

1 R. Arnoux　　Martini-Renault
2 J-P.
　　Jabouille　Elf-Renault
3 A. Ribeiro　　March-BMW

163.40 kph / 101.54 mph

19 Sep: Nogaro, France

1 P. Tambay　　Martini-Renault
2 J. Laffite　　　Chevron-Hart
3 M. Leclere　　Elf-Renault

151.69 kph / 94.26 mph

26 Sep: Hockenheim, West Germany

1 J-P.
　　Jabouille　Elf-Renault
2 M. Leclere　　Elf-Renault
3 R. Arnoux　　Martini-Renault

197.65 kph / 122.82 mph

Final Championship Standing

1 Jean-Pierre
　　Jabouille　　　France　　　　53 pts
2 Rene Arnoux　　　France　　　　52 pts
3 Patrick Tambay　　France　　　　39 pts

1977

6 Mar: Silverstone, England

Average speed

1 R. Arnoux　　Martini-Renault
2 R. Mallock　　Chevron-Hart
3 P. Neve　　　March-BMW

202.29 kph / 125.70 mph

11 Apr: Thruxton, England

1 B. Henton　　Boxer-Hart
2 E. Cheever　　Ralt-BMW
3 A. Ribeiro　　March-BMW

189.61 kph / 117.82 mph

17 Apr: Hockenheim, West Germany

1 J. Mass　　　March-BMW
2 R. Arnoux　　Martini-Renault
3 R. Patrese　　Chevron-BMW

200.29 kph / 124.46 mph

1 May: Nurburgring, West Germany

1 J. Mass　　　March-BMW
2 E. Cheever　　Ralt-BMW
3 K. Rosberg　　Chevron-Hart

184.91 kph / 114.90 mph

15 May: Vallelunga, Italy

1 B. Giacomelli　March-BMW
2 D. Pironi　　　Martini-Renault
3 E. Cheever　　Ralt-BMW

162.17 kph / 100.77 mph

30 May: Pau, France

1 R. Arnoux　　Martini-Renault
2 D. Pironi　　　Martini-Renault
3 R. Patrese　　Chevron-BMW

130.49 kph / 81.09 mph

19 Jun: Mugello, Italy

1 B. Giacomelli　March-BMW
2 R. Patrese　　Chevron-BMW
3 A. Colombo　　March-BMW

172.54 kph / 107.22 mph

26 Jun: Rouen, France

1 E. Cheever　　Ralt-BMW
2 R. Patrese　　Chevron-BMW
3 D. Pironi　　　Martini-Renault

184.21 kph / 114.47 mph

10 Jul: Nogaro, France

1 R. Arnoux　　Martini-Renault
2 R. Patrese　　Chevron-BMW
3 I. Hoffman　　Ralt-BMW

150.76 kph / 93.68 mph

24 Jul: Enna, Italy

1 K. Rosberg　　Chevron-Hart
2 R. Arnoux　　Martini-Renault
3 I. Hoffman　　Ralt-BMW

185.04 kph / 114.98 mph

7 Aug: Misano, Italy

1 L. Leoni　　　Chevron-Ferrari
2 E. Cheever　　Ralt-BMW
3 I. Hoffman　　Ralt-BMW

170.27 kph / 105.81 mph

2 Oct: Estoril, Portugal

1 D. Pironi　　　Martini-Renault
2 R. Arnoux　　Martini-Renault
3 E. Cheever　　Ralt-BMW

164.18 kph / 102.02 mph

30 Oct: Donington, England

1 B. Giacomelli　March-BMW
2 K. Rosberg　　Chevron-Hart
3 D. Pironi　　　Martini-Renault

166.12 kph / 103.23 mph

Final Championship Standing

1 Rene Arnoux   France   52 pts
2 Eddie Cheever   United States   40 pts
3 Didier Pironi   France   38 pts

24 Sep: Hockenheim, West Germany

1 B. Giacomelli   March-BMW   202.40 kph / 125.77 mph
2 M. Surer   March-BMW
3 M. Winkel-
   hock   March-BMW

Final Championship Standing

1 Bruno Giacomelli   Italy   78 pts
2 Marc Surer   Switzerland   48 pts
3 Derek Daly   Ireland   27 pts

1978

27 Mar: Thruxton, England   *Average speed*

1 B. Giacomelli   March-BMW   188.92 kph / 117.39 mph
2 M. Surer   March-BMW
3 R. Dougall   March-BMW

9 Apr: Hockenheim, West Germany

1 B. Giacomelli   March-BMW   202.71 kph / 125.96 mph
2 M. Surer   March-BMW
3 J-P. Jarier   March-BMW

30 Apr: Nurburgring, West Germany

1 A. Ribeiro   March-Hart   185.23 kph / 115.10 mph
2 K. Rosberg   Chevron-Hart
3 E. Cheever   March-BMW

15 May: Pau, France

1 B. Giacomelli   March-BMW   129.71 kph / 80.60 mph
2 E. Elgh   Chevron-Hart
3 M. Surer   March-BMW

28 May: Mugello, Italy

1 D. Daly   Chevron-Hart   174.69 kph / 108.55 mph
2 M. Surer   March-BMW
3 B. Giacomelli   March-BMW

4 Jun: Vallelunga, Italy

1 D. Daly   Chevron-Hart   161.65 kph / 100.45 mph
2 B. Giacomelli   March-BMW
3 P. Necchi   March-BMW

18 Jun: Rouen, France

1 B. Giacomelli   March-BMW   185.65 kph / 115.36 mph
2 E. Cheever   March-BMW
3 M. Surer   March-BMW

25 Jun: Donington, England

1 K. Rosberg   Chevron-Hart   168.27 kph / 104.56 mph
2 P. Necchi   March-BMW
3 M. Surer   March-BMW

9 Jul: Nogaro, France

1 B. Giacomelli   March-BMW   153.60 kph / 95.45 mph
2 M. Surer   March-BMW
3 D. Daly   Chevron-Hart

23 Jul: Enna, Italy

1 B. Giacomelli   March-BMW   189.99 kph / 118.06 mph
2 E. Cheever   March-BMW
3 D. Daly   Chevron-Hart

6 Aug: Misano, Italy

1 B. Giacomelli   March-BMW   170.25 kph / 105.79 mph
2 M. Surer   March-BMW
3 E. de Angelis   Chevron-Hart

1979

25 Mar: Silverstone, England *Average speed*

1 E. Cheever   Osella-BMW   183.51 kph / 114.03 mph
2 D. Daly   March-BMW
3 B. Henton   Ralt-Hart

8 Apr: Hockenheim, West Germany

1 K. Rosberg   March-BMW   202.50 kph / 125.83 mph
2 R. Dougall   March-Hart
3 A. Guerra   March-BMW

16 Apr: Thruxton, England

1 R. Dougall   March-Hart   194.99 kph / 121.17 mph
2 D. Daly   March-BMW
3 A. Colombo   March-BMW

29 Apr: Nurburgring, West Germany

1 M. Surer   March-BMW   169.40 kph / 105.27 mph
2 B. Henton   March-Hart
3 M. Winkel-
   hock   Ralt-BMW

13 May: Vallelunga, Italy

1 M. Surer   March-BMW   162.96 kph / 101.26 mph
2 S. Stohr   Chevron-BMW
3 M. Flammini   March-BMW

20 May: Mugello, Italy

1 B. Henton   Ralt-Hart   174.24 kph / 108.27 mph
2 B. Gabbiani   March-BMW
3 E. Elgh   March-BMW

3 Jun: Pau, France

1 E. Cheever   Osella-BMW   105.57 kph / 65.60 mph
2 S. Stohr   Chevron-BMW
3 M. Surer   March-BMW

10 Jun: Hockenheim, West Germany

1 S. South   March-BMW   201.29 kph / 125.08 mph
2 D. Daly   March-BMW
3 B. Gabbiani   March-BMW

15 Jul: Zandvoort, Holland

1 E. Cheever   Osella-BMW   182.07 kph / 113.14 mph
2 T. Fabi   March-BMW
3 M. Surer   March-BMW

29 Jul: Enna, Italy

1 E. Elgh   March-BMW   188.11 kph / 116.89 mph
2 D. Daly   March-BMW
3 S. South   March-BMW

5 Aug: Misano, Italy

1 B. Henton   Ralt-Hart   168.59 kph / 104.76 mph
2 B. Gabbiani   March-BMW
3 M. Surer   March-BMW

19 Aug: Donington, England

1 D. Daly   March-BMW   170.90 kph / 106.20 mph
2 M. Surer   March-BMW
3 S. South   March-BMW

Final Championship Standing

1 Marc Surer   Switzerland   38 pts
2 Brian Henton Great Britain   36 pts
3 Derek Daly   Ireland   33 pts

10 Aug: Misano, Italy

1 A. de Cesaris March-BMW   172.82 kph / 107.39 mph
2 B. Henton   Toleman-Hart
3 D. Warwick   Toleman-Hart

28 Sep: Hockenheim, West Germany

1 T. Fabi   March-BMW   204.74 kph / 127.23 mph
2 N. Mansell   Ralt-Honda
3 S. Stohr   Toleman-Hart

Final Championship Standing

1 Brian Henton   Great Britain   61 pts
2 Derek Warwick Great Britain   42 pts
3 Teo Fabi   Italy   38 pts

1980

7 Apr: Thruxton, England   *Average speed*

1 B. Henton   Toleman-Hart   194.97 kph / 121.15 mph
2 D. Warwick   Toleman-Hart
3 A. de Cesaris March-BMW

13 Apr: Hockenheim, West Germany

1 T. Fabi   March-BMW   201.83 kph / 125.42 mph
2 B. Henton   Toleman-Hart
3 A. Colombo   March-BMW

27 Apr: Nurburgring, West Germany

1 T. Fabi   March-BMW   180.91 kph / 112.42 mph
2 B. Henton   Toleman-Hart
3 D. Warwick   Toleman-Hart

11 May: Vallelunga, Italy

1 B. Henton   Toleman-Hart   164.35 kph / 102.13 mph
2 A. de Cesaris March-BMW
3 D. Warwick   Toleman-Hart

26 May: Pau, France

1 R. Dallest   AGS-BMW   128.52 kph / 79.86 mph
2 S. Stohr   Toleman-Hart
3 B. Henton   Toleman-Hart

8 Jun: Silverstone, England

1 D. Warwick   Toleman-Hart   210.18 kph / 130.61 mph
2 A. de Cesaris March-BMW
3 M. Thackwell   March-BMW

22 Jun: Zolder, Belgium

1 H. Rothen-
      gatter   Toleman-Hart   173.38 kph / 107.74 mph
2 B. Henton   Toleman-Hart
3 S. Stohr   Toleman-Hart

6 Jul: Mugello, Italy

1 B. Henton   Toleman-Hart   175.35 kph / 108.96 mph
2 D. Warwick   Toleman-Hart
3 T. Fabi   March-BMW

20 Jul: Zandvoort, Holland

1 R. Dallest   AGS-BMW   151.27 kph / 94.00 mph
2 D. Warwick   Toleman-Hart
3 T. Fabi   March-BMW

2 Aug: Enna, Italy

1 S. Stohr   Toleman-Hart   189.13 kph / 117.53 mph
2 B. Henton   Toleman-Hart
3 M. Winkel-
      hock   March-BMW

1981

29 Mar: Silverstone, England *Average speed*

1 M. Thackwell Ralt-Honda   186.15 kph / 115.67 mph
2 R. Paletti   March-BMW
3 C. Fabi   March-BMW

5 Apr: Hockenheim, West Germany

1 S. Johansson Toleman-Hart   201.83 kph / 125.42 mph
2 M. Winkel-
      hock   Ralt-BMW
3 M. Thackwell Ralt-Honda

20 Apr: Thruxton, England

1 R. Guerrero   Maurer-BMW   195.39 kph / 121.42 mph
2 E. Elgh   Maurer-BMW
3 R. Paletti   March-BMW

26 Apr: Nurburgring, West Germany

1 T. Boutsen   March-BMW   189.48 kph / 117.74 mph
2 E. Elgh   Maurer-BMW
3 C. Fabi   March-BMW

10 May: Vallelunga, Italy

1 E. Elgh   Maurer-BMW   164.16 kph / 102.01 mph
2 S. Johansson Toleman-Hart
3 T. Boutsen   March-BMW

24 May: Mugello, Italy

1 C. Fabi   March-BMW   175.41 kph / 109.00 mph
2 G. Lees   Ralt-Honda
3 P. Necchi   March-BMW

8 Jun: Pau, France

1 G. Lees   Ralt-Honda   129.66 kph / 80.57 mph
2 T. Boutsen   March-BMW
3 P. Necchi   March-BMW

26 Jul: Enna, Italy

1 T. Boutsen   March-BMW   190.48 kph / 118.36 mph
2 H. Rothen-
      gatter   March-BMW
3 M. Alboreto   Minardi-BMW

9 Aug: Spa, Belgium

1 G. Lees   Ralt-Honda   179.26 kph / 111.39 mph
2 T. Boutsen   March-BMW
3 E. Elgh   Maurer-BMW

16 Aug: Donington, England

1 G. Lees	Ralt-Honda	172.20 kph / 107.01 mph
2 C. Fabi	March-BMW	
3 M. Winkel-hock	Maurer-BMW	

6 Sep: Misano, Italy

1 M. Alboreto	Minardi-BMW	171.24 kph / 106.41 mph
2 G. Lees	Ralt-Honda	
3 M. Thackwell	Ralt-Honda	

20 Sep: Mantorp, Sweden

1 S. Johansson	Toleman-Hart	152.05 kph / 94.50 mph
2 G. Lees	Ralt-Honda	
3 K. Acheson	Toleman-Hart	

Final Championship Standing

1 Geoff Lees	Great Britain	51 pts
2 Thierry Boutsen	Belgium	37 pts
3 Eje Elgh	Sweden	35 pts

1982

21 Mar: Silverstone, England *Average speed*

1 S. Bellof	Maurer-BMW	185.19 kph / 115.08 mph
2 S. Nakajima	March-Honda	
3 G. Gabbiani	Maurer-BMW	

4 Apr: Hockenheim, West Germany

1 S. Bellof	Maurer-BMW	194.04 kph / 120.58 mph
2 T. Boutsen	Spirit-Honda	
3 C. Fabi	March-BMW	

12 Apr: Thruxton, England

1 J. Cecotto	March-BMW	196.05 kph / 121.83 mph
2 K. Acheson	Ralt-Honda	
3 T. Boutsen	Spirit-Honda	

25 Apr: Nurburgring, West Germany

1 T. Boutsen	Spirit-Honda	189.64 kph / 117.84 mph
2 C. Fabi	March-BMW	
3 J. Cecotto	March-BMW	

Italy's Corrado Fabi won the 1982 European Formula Two Championship by just one point from Venezuela's Johnny Cecotto. Fabi clinched the title with a victory in the final race of the season on home soil, at Misano. (Michelin Tyre Co. Ltd.)

9 May: Mugello, Italy

1 C. Fabi	March-BMW	177.26 kph / 110.17 mph
2 J. Cecotto	March-BMW	
3 S. Johansson	Spirit-Honda	

16 May: Vallelunga, Italy

1 C. Fabi	March-BMW	164.70 kph / 102.36 mph
2 P. Streiff	AGS-BMW	
3 P. Fabre	AGS-BMW	

31 May: Pau, France

1 J. Cecotto	March-BMW	132.84 kph / 82.55 mph
2 T. Boutsen	Spirit-Honda	
3 M. Thackwell	March-BMW	

13 Jun: Spa, Belgium

1 T. Boutsen	Spirit-Honda	165.06 kph / 102.57 mph
2 J. Cecotto	March-BMW	
3 M. Thackwell	March-BMW	

20 Jun: Hockenheim, West Germany

1 C. Fabi	March-BMW	193.97 kph / 120.53 mph
2 G. Gabbiani	Maurer-BMW	
3 S. Bellof	Maurer-BMW	

4 Jul: Donington, England

1 C. Fabi	March-BMW	174.76 kph / 108.60 mph
2 J. Cecotto	March-BMW	
3 J. Palmer	Ralt-Honda	

18 Jul: Mantorp, Sweden

1 J. Cecotto	March-BMW	155.27 kph / 96.50 mph
2 P. Streiff	AGS-BMW	
3 G. Gabbiani	Maurer-BMW	

1 Aug: Enna, Italy

1 T. Boutsen	Spirit-Honda	192.67 kph / 119.73 mph
2 S. Bellof	Maurer-BMW	
3 J. Cecotto	March-BMW	

7 Aug: Misano, Italy

1 C. Fabi	March-BMW	160.12 kph / 99.50 mph
2 A. Nannini	Minardi-BMW	
3 G. Gabbiani	Maurer-BMW	

Final Championship Standing

1 Corrado Fabi	Italy	57 pts
2 Johnny Cecotto	Venezuela	56 pts
3 Thierry Boutsen	Belgium	50 pts

1983

20 Mar: Silverstone, England *Average speed*

1 G. Gabbiani	March-BMW	194.22 kph / 120.69 mph
2 M. Thackwell	Ralt-Honda	
3 C. Danner	March-BMW	

4 Apr: Thruxton, England

1 G. Gabbiani	March-BMW	195.81 kph / 121.68 mph
2 M. Thackwell	Ralt-Honda	
3 J. Palmer	Ralt-Honda	

10 Apr: Hockenheim, West Germany

1 J. Palmer	Ralt-Honda	196.02 kph / 121.81 mph
2 C. Danner	March-BMW	
3 M. Thackwell	Ralt-Honda	

Dr Jonathan Palmer (GB) won the 1983 championship thanks to six wins, including a record five in succession. (The Goodyear Tyre & Rubber Co. Ltd.)

24 Apr: Nurburgring, West Germany

1	G. Gabbiani	March-BMW	191.40 kph / 118.94 mph
2	A. Nannini	Minardi-BMW	
3	C. Danner	Ralt-Honda	

8 May: Vallelunga, Italy

1	G. Gabbiani	March-BMW	166.42 kph / 103.41 mph
2	J. Palmer	Ralt-Honda	
3	M. Thackwell	Ralt-Honda	

23 May: Pau, France

1	J. Gartner	Spirit-BMW	114.98 kph / 71.45 mph
2	K. Acheson	Maurer-Heidegger	
3	J. Palmer	Ralt-Honda	

12 Jun: Jarama, Spain

1	M. Thackwell	Ralt-Honda	143.31 kph / 90.30 mph
2	S. Bellof	Maurer-BMW	
3	J. Palmer	Ralt-Honda	

26 June: Donington, England

1	J. Palmer	Ralt-Honda	172.60 kph / 107.25 mph
2	M. Thackwell	Ralt-Honda	
3	P. Streiff	AGS-BMW	

24 Jul: Misano, Italy

1	J. Palmer	Ralt-Honda	174.33 kph / 108.33 mph
2	P. Martini	Minardi-BMW	
3	R. Castello	March-BMW	

31 Jul: Enna, Italy

1	J. Palmer	Ralt-Honda	190.42 kph / 118.33 mph
2	P. Streiff	AGS-BMW	
3	M. Thackwell	Ralt-Honda	

21 Aug: Zolder, Belgium

1	J. Palmer	Ralt-Honda	177.68 kph / 110.41 mph
2	M. Thackwell	Ralt-Honda	
3	P. Streiff	AGS-BMW	

4 Sep: Mugello, Italy

1	J. Palmer	Ralt-Honda	176.30 kph / 109.55 mph
2	M. Thackwell	Ralt-Honda	
3	P. Streiff	AGS-BMW	

Final Championship Standing

1	Dr. Jonathan Palmer	Great Britain	68 pts
2	Mike Thackwell	New Zealand	61 pts
3	'Beppe' Gabbiani	Italy	39 pts

1984

1 Apr: Silverstone, England

Average speed

1	M. Thackwell	Ralt-Honda	217.89 kph / 135.40 mph
2	R. Moreno	Ralt-Honda	
3	M. Ferte	Martini-BMW	

8 Apr: Hockenheim, West Germany

1	R. Moreno	Ralt-Honda	198.22 kph / 123.17 mph
2	M. Thackwell	Ralt-Honda	
3	M. Ferte	Martini-BMW	

23 Apr: Thruxton, England

1	M. Thackwell	Ralt-Honda	197.98 kph / 123.02 mph
2	C. Danner	March-BMW	
3	P. Streiff	AGS-BMW	

13 May: Vallelunga, Italy

1	M. Thackwell	Ralt-Honda	164.23 kph / 102.05 mph
2	R. Moreno	Ralt-Honda	
3	C. Danner	March-BMW	

19 May: Mugello, Italy

1	M. Thackwell	Ralt-Honda	179.47 kph / 111.52 mph
2	M. Ferte	Martini-BMW	
3	C. Danner	March-BMW	

11 Jun: Pau, France

1	M. Thackwell	Ralt-Honda	134.84 kph / 83.79 mph
2	P. Streiff	AGS-BMW	
3	R. Moreno	Ralt-Honda	

24 June: Hockenheim, West Germany

1	P. Fabre	March-BMW	196.27 kph / 121.96 mph
2	T. Tassin	March-BMW	
3	M. Ferte	Martini-BMW	

21 Jul: Misano, Italy

1	M. Thackwell	Ralt-Honda	177.82 kph / 110.50 mph
2	P. Streiff	AGS-BMW	
3	P. Petit	March-BMW	

29 Jul: Enna, Italy

1	M. Thackwell	Ralt-Honda	193.92 kph / 120.50 mph
2	R. Moreno	Ralt-Honda	
3	A. Nannini	Minardi-BMW	

27 Aug: Donington, England

1	R. Moreno	Ralt-Honda	174.84 kph / 108.65 mph
2	E. Pirro	March-BMW	
3	C. Danner	March-BMW	

23 Sep: Brands Hatch, England

1	P. Streiff	AGS-BMW	171.39 kph / 106.52 mph
2	M. Ferte	Martini-BMW	
3	R. Moreno	Ralt-Honda	

Final Championship Standing

1	Mike Thackwell	New Zealand	72 pts
2	Roberto Moreno	Brazil	44 pts
3	Michel Ferte	France	29 pts

After finishing runner-up to Britain's Jonathan Palmer in the 1983 championship, New Zealand's Mike Thackwell gained some consolation by winning the final European Formula Two championship the following year, by a massive 28 points. (Michelin Tyre Co. Ltd.)

Drivers' Records

Most Individual Wins

11 J. Rindt (AUT)
11 B. Giacomelli (ITA)
9 M. Thackwell (NZ)
7 J-P. Jarier (FRA)
7 J. Laffite (FRA)
6 E. Fittipaldi (BRA)
6 R. Peterson (SWE)
6 R. Arnoux (FRA)
6 B. Henton (GB)
6 C. Fabi (ITA)
6 J. Palmer (GB)
6 H. Stuck (FRG)

Most individual wins season by season

1967 J. Rindt (AUT)
1968 J. Rindt (AUT)
1969 2 J. Stewart (GB), J. Rindt (AUT)
1970 3 C. Regazzoni* (SWI)
1971 4 R. Peterson* (SWE)
1972 3 E. Fittipaldi (BRA)
1973 7 J-P. Jarier* (FRA)
1974 4 P. Depailler* (FRA), H. Stuck (FRG)
1975 6 J. Laffite* (FRA)
1976 3 J-P. Jabouille* (FRA), R. Arnoux (FRA)
1977 3 R. Arnoux* (FRA), B. Giacomelli (ITA)
1978 8 B. Giacomelli* (ITA)
1979 3 E. Cheever (USA)
1980 3 B. Henton* (GB), T. Fabi (ITA)
1981 3 G. Lees* (GB)
1982 4 C. Fabi* (ITA)
1983 6 J. Palmer* (GB)
1984 7 M. Thackwell* (NZ)
* Indicates that season's champion driver

Most Points in a Season

78 J-P. Jarier (FRA) 1973
78 B. Giacomelli (ITA) 1978
72 M. Thackwell (NZ) 1984
68 J. Palmer (GB) 1983

Largest Championship-winning margin

37 pts J-P. Jarier (FRA) 1973
30 pts B. Giacomelli (ITA) 1978
28 pts M. Thackwell (NZ) 1984
24 pts J. Laffite (FRA) 1975

Most points by driver not winning the Championship

56 J. Cecotto (VEN) 1982

Most wins in a season by drivers not winning the Championship

4 J. Rindt (AUT) 1967
4 J. Rindt (AUT) 1968
4 H. Stuck (FRG) 1974
4 G. Gabbiani (ITA) 1983

Least wins in a season by the champion driver

1 J. Servoz-Gavin (FRA) 1969

Most Consecutive Wins

5 J. Palmer (GB) 1983 Donington, Misano, Enna, Zolder, Mugello
4 B. Giacomelli (ITA) 1978 Nogaro, Enna, Misano, Hockenheim
4 M. Thackwell (NZ) 1984 Thruxton, Vallelunga, Mugello, Pau

Formula One World Champions who have won races

J. Rindt (AUT)	11
E. Fittipaldi (BRA)	6
K. Rosberg (FIN)	3
J. Stewart (GB)	3
J. Clark (GB)	1
G. Hill (GB)	1
J. Scheckter (SAF)	1
J. Surtees (GB)	1

Former world motor cycling champion Johnny Cecotto (VEN) scored 56 points in the 1982 championship, but still lost the title by one point to Italian Corrado Fabi. (Michelin Tyre Co. Ltd.)

Enzo Ferrari

Italian Enzo Ferrari represents the biggest name in motor racing, and the Ferrari team can boast the most loyal following among all the manufacturers.

Ferrari himself was born at Modena in 1898. When ambitions to become an opera singer and then a sports writer failed, he turned to his third interest—car racing. He started racing for a small local manufacturer. Then he joined the Alfa Romeo team in 1920 and finished second in that year's Targa Florio. While his career as a driver was moderately successful, he was never out-standing. He then took his engineering skills into the Alfa factory where he soon discovered he enjoyed the organizing side of the sport more than racing. He also had the responsibility of re-

cruiting top men for the Alfa team and one of his biggest recruits was not a driver, but top designer Vittorio Jano from Fiat. Between them they turned Alfa Romeo into the biggest name in motor racing in the 1920s.

When Alfa pulled out of racing in 1929, Ferrari took over the racing division and moved his headquarters to his home town. There he produced cars under the Scuderia (Team) Ferrari banner but these were basically Alfa de-signed cars. The first true Ferrari was seen at Piacenza in 1947 and by the time the World Championship was introduced in 1950, Ferraris were soon gaining a reputation for being a reliable car. They competed in their first World Championship race at Monaco but had to wait until

Froilan Gonzalez (Arg) triumphed in the British Grand Prix at Silver-stone a year later for their first World Championship success. Alberto Ascari (Ita) and Gonzalez finished second and third in the 1951 World Championship but a year later Ascari won the title as Ferrari team-mates Farina (Ita), Taruffi (Ita) and Fischer (Swi) occu-pied second, third and fourth places.

Since then the Ferrari car has competed in over 400 World Championship Grand Prix races, and has registered nearly 100 victories. But Ferrari has also pro-duced cars to win Le Mans, the Mille Miglia and many other major races, as well as to dominate the Formula One scene.

While Enzo Ferrari always had the ability to attract the best

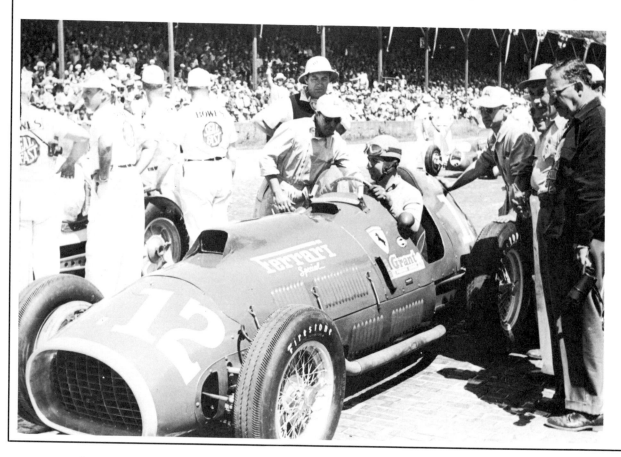

Frenchman Rene Arnoux in the Ferrari 126 at Brands Hatch during the 1983 European Grand Prix. (Michelin Tyre Co. Ltd.)

Right Ferrari occupying first and second place, by courtesy of Stefan Johansson and Michele Alboreto

Left Alberto Ascari (ITA) in the Ferrari Special before the start of the 1952 Indianapolis 500. Ascari was one of the first Europeans ever to take part in the race but he retired on lap 40 and was classified 31st out of 33. He went on to win the next six races in the World Drivers' Championship that year and beat fellow Italians Farina and Taruffi for the title. (National Motor Museum)

drivers in the world, including the one he regarded as the best of all—the legendary Italian Tazio Nuvolari—the one man he never managed to get was Britain's Stirling Moss. Had Moss joined the great Italian team, he could well have won the elusive World Championship.

Now aged 88 and based at his headquarters at Maranello, 100 miles from Monza, Ferrari no longer attends race meetings and has not been to one since the day his 25-year-old son Dino was killed in 1956. But he still remains very close to his business and, despite his age, still has ambitions . . . to see Ferrari's next win.

Manufacturers' Records

Most Wins

70 March-BMW
20 Ralt-Honda
12 Brabham-Cosworth
 9 Matra-Cosworth
 8 Martini-Renault
 8 Toleman-Hart
 7 Lotus-Cosworth

Most Consecutive Wins

12 Ralt-Honda	1983	Jarama, Donington, Misano, Enna, Zolder, Mugello
	1984	Silverstone, Hockenheim, Thruxton, Vallelunga, Mugello, Pau
6 March-BMW	1973	Rouen, Monza, Mantorp, Karl-skoga, Enna, Salzburg
6 March-BMW	1973	Albi, Vallelunga,
	1974	Montjuich, Hockenheim, Pau, Salzburg
6 March-BMW	1975	Silverstone, Zolder, Nolgaro, Vallelunga
	1976	Hockenheim, Thruxton

Most Wins season by season

1967	5	Brabham-Cosworth
1968	4	Brabham-Cosworth
1969	4	Matra-Cosworth
1970	3	Tecno-Cosworth, BMW
1971	5	March-Cosworth
1972	5	Brabham-Ford
1973	11	March-BMW
1974	10	March-BMW
1975	6	Martini-BMW, March-BMW
1976	4	Elf-Renault, Martini-BMW, March-BMW
1977	5	March-BMW
1978	8	March-BMW
1979	6	March-BMW
1980	6	Toleman-Hart
1981	4	Ralt-Honda
1982	8	March-BMW
1983	7	Ralt-Honda
1984	9	Ralt-Honda

Runner-up to Rene Arnoux (FRA) in the 1977 championship, Eddie Cheever (USA) won more races than any other driver in 1979 but still failed to finish in the first three in that year's championship

Formula 3000

A decision was taken in 1984 by F.I.S.A. at Pau to create Formula 3000 as a replacement for Formula Two. The first European Formula 3000 Championship was staged in 1985 and changed its name to the F.I.A. Formula 3000 International Championship in 1986.

Results

1985

24 Mar: Silverstone, England

			Average speed
1	M. Thackwell	Ralt-Judd	184.01 kph / 114.36 mph
2	J. Nielsen	Ralt-Judd	
3	M. Ferte	March-Mader	

7 Apr: Thruxton, England

1	E. Pirro	March-Peck	188.95 kph / 117.41 mph
2	M. Thackwell	Ralt-Judd	
3	M. Ferte	March-Mader	

21 Apr: Estoril, Portugal

1	J. Nielsen	Ralt-Judd	168.61 kph / 104.79 mph
2	M. Ferte	March-Mader	
3	G. Tarquini	March-Mader	

12 May: Vallelunga, Italy

1	E. Pirro	March-Peck	166.77 kph / 103.65 mph
2	J. Nielsen	Ralt-Judd	
3	C. Danner	March-Swindon	

26 May: Pau, France

1	C. Danner	March-Smith	131.78 kph / 81.89 mph
2	E. Pirro	March-Peck	
3	L. Leoni	Williams-Swindon	

2 Jun: Spa, Belgium

1	M. Thackwell	Ralt-Judd	166.80 kph / 104.91 mph
2	A. Ferte	March-Mader	
3	C. Danner	March-Smith	

30 Jun: Dijon, France

1	C. Danner	March-Smith	183.02 kph / 113.75 mph
2	M. Thackwell	Ralt-Judd	
3	J. Nielsen	Ralt-Judd	

28 Jul: Enna, Italy

1	M. Thackwell	Ralt-Judd	191.62 kph / 119.09 mph
2	E. Pirro	March-Peck	
3	C. Danner	March-Smith	

17 Aug: Osterreichring, Austria

1	I. Capelli	March-Mader	204.87 kph / 127.33 mph
2	J. Nielsen	Ralt-Judd	
3	L. Leoni	March-Mader	

24 Aug: Zandvoort, Holland

1	C. Danner	March-Smith	162.60 kph / 101.04 mph
2	M. Thackwell	Ralt-Judd	
3	P. Streiff	AGS-Mader	

22 Sep: Donington, England

1	C. Danner	March-Smith	162.80 kph / 101.18 mph
2	M. Hytten	March-Peck	
3	I. Capelli	March-Mader	

Final Championship Standing

1	Christian Danner	West Germany	51 pts
2	Mike Thackwell	New Zealand	45 pts
3	Emanuele Pirro	Italy	38 pts

1986

13 Apr: Silverstone, England *Average speed*

1	P. Fabre	Lola-Mader	191.00 kph / 118.71 mph
2	E. Pirro	March-Peck	
3	J. Nielsen	Ralt-Honda	

4 May: Vallelunga, Italy

1	I. Capelli	March-Mader	166.08 kph / 103.22 mph
2	P. Fabre	Lola-Mader	
3	E. Pirro	March-Peck	

19 May: Pau, France

1	M. Thackwell	Ralt-Honda	132.39 kph / 82.28 mph
2	E. Pirro	March-Peck	
3	M. Ferte	March-Mader	

25 May: Spa, Belgium

1	P. Alliot	March-Mader	188.93 kph / 117.42 mph
2	J. Nielsen	Ralt-Honda	
3	I. Capelli	March-Mader	

8 Jun: Imola, Italy

1	P. Martini	Ralt-Mader	180.22 kph / 112.01 mph
2	I. Capelli	March-Mader	
3	A. Ferte	March-Mader	

28 Jun: Mugello, Italy

1	P. Martini	Ralt-Mader	169.83 kph / 105.55 mph
2	M. Ferte	March-Mader	
3	I. Capelli	March-Mader	

20 Jul: Enna, Italy

1 L. Sala	Ralt-Mader	192.47 kph / 119.62mph
2 P. Martini	Ralt-Mader	
3 P. Fabre	Lola-Mader	

17 Aug: Osterreichring, Austria

1 I. Capelli	March-Mader	206.06 kph / 128.07 mph
2 J. Nielsen	Ralt-Honda	
3 G. Tarquini	March-Nicholson	

25 Aug: Birmingham, England

1 L. Sala	Ralt-Camosa	134.95 kph / 83.87 mph
2 P. Martini	Ralt-Mader	
3 M. Ferte	March-Mader	

28 Sep: Le Mans, France

1 E. Pirro	March-Peck	170.01 kph / 105.66 mph
2 M. Ferte	March-Peck	
3 P. H. Raphanel	March-Mader	

5 Oct: Jarama, Spain

1 E. Pirro	March-Peck	147.56 kph / 91.71 mph
2 M. Ferte	March-Mader	
3 I. Capelli	March-Mader	

Final Championship Standing

1 Ivan Capelli	Italy	39 pts
2 Emanuele Pirro	Italy	32 pts
3 Pierluigi Martini	Italy	27 pts

The excitement of motor racing came to the streets of Birmingham in 1986 when the Superprix was designated one of the rounds in the Formula 3000 championship. Sadly, the 'Gods' were not on the organisers' side as the 'heaven's opened' and the torrential rain brought a premature halt to the race. (National Motor Museum)

Ivan Capelli (ITA), the second Formula 3000 champion in 1986.

Drivers' Records

Most Individual Wins

4 Mike Thackwell (NZ)
4 Emanuele Pirro (ITA)
4 Christian Danner (FRG)

Most Points in a Season

51 Christian Danner (FRG) 1985

Largest Championship-winning margin

7 Ivan Capelli (ITA) 1986

Most Consecutive Wins

2 Christian Danner (ITA)   1985 Zandvoort, Donington
2 Pierluigi Martini (ITA)   1986 Imola, Mugello
2 Emanuele Pirro (ITA)   1986 Le Mans, Jarama

Most points by driver not winning the Championship

45 Mike Thackwell (NZ) 1985

Most individual wins season by season

1985 4 Christian Danner* (FRG)
1986 2 Emanuele Pirro (ITA)
         2 Pierluigi Martini (ITA)
         2 Luis Sala (SPA)
         2 Ivan Capelli* (ITA)
*Indicates that season's champion driver

Most wins in a season by a driver not winning the Championship

3 Mike Thackwell (NZ) 1985

Least wins in a season by the champion driver

2 Ivan Capelli (ITA) 1986

Manufacturers' Records

Most Wins

4 Ralt-Judd
4 March-Peck
4 March-Smith
4 March-Mader
3 Ralt-Mader

Most Consecutive Wins

3 Ralt-Mader   1986 Imola, Mugello, Enna
2 March-Smith 1985 Zandvoort, Donington
2 March-Peck   1986 Le Mans, Jarama

Most Wins season by season

1985 4 Ralt-Judd
1986 3 Ralt-Mader
         3 March-Mader

European Formula Three Championship

Following the success of the European Formula Two Championship the Formula Three Championship was started in 1975 under its initial banner of the F.I.A. Championship. Like its Formula Two counterpart it was removed from the international calendar at the end of 1984.

Results

1975

10 May: Monte Carlo, Monaco

			Average speed
1	R. Zorzi	GRD-Lancia	121.52 kph / 75.51 mph
2	P. Neve	Safir-Pinto	
3	U. Svensson	Brabham-Ford	

31 May: Nurburgring, West Germany

1	F. Kottu-linsky	Modus-BMW	169.43 kph / 105.28 mph
2	D. Kern	Alpine-Ford	
3	G. Nord-strom	Modus-Toyota	

7 Jun: Anderstorp, Sweden

1	C. Andersson	March-Toyota	148.40 kph / 92.22 mph
2	C. Ljungfeldt	March-Toyota	
3	C. Sigurds-son	Brabham-Toyota	

29 Jun: Monza, Italy

1	L. Perkins	Ralt-Ford	187.94 kph / 116.79 mph
2	F. Spreafico	GRD-Toyota	
3	A. Pesenti-Rossi	March-Toyota	

20 Jul: Croix-en-Ternois, France

1	L. Perkins	Ralt-Ford	120.86 kph / 75.10 mph
2	M. Gauden-ziot	March-Toyota	
3	A. Pesenti-Rossi	March-Toyota	

3 Aug: Djurslandring, Denmark

1	T. Perkins	Ralt-Ford	*
2	A. Olafsson	GRD-Toyota	
3	U. Svensson	Brabham-Ford	

* Raced over two heats, aggregate time taken

Final Championship Standing

1	Larry Perkins	Australia	18 pts
2	Conny Andersson	Sweden	14 pts
3	Renzo Zorzi	Italy	11 pts

Conny Andersson (SWE), runner-up in the inaugural championship in 1975, makes good use of his Brabham BT38! (National Motor Museum)

1976

2 Apr: Nurburgring, West Germany

Average speed

1 C.Andersson March-Toyota   163.00 kph / 101.29 mph
2 B. Schafer   Ralt-BMW
3 R. Patrese   Chevron-Toyota

19 Apr: Zandvoort, Holland

1 R. Patrese   Chevron-Toyota   *
2 M. Surer   March-BMW
3 W. Klein   March-Toyota

9 May: Mantorp, Sweden

1 G. Branca-
  telli   March-Toyota   162.07 kph / 101.21 mph
2 R. Patrese   Chevron-Toyota
3 C. Sigurds-
  son   Ralt-BMW

23 May: Avus, West Germany

1 C.Andersson March-Toyota   *
2 U. Svensson Ralt-Toyota
3 B. Schafer   Ralt-BMW

13 Jun: Enna, Italy

1 R. Patrese   Chevron-Toyota   162.68 kph / 101.09 mph
2 C.Andersson March-Toyota
3 P. Ghinzani March-Toyota

27 Jun: Monza, Italy

1 R. Patrese   Chevron-Toyota   181.09 kph / 112.53 mph
2 C.Andersson March-Toyota
3 B. Hayje   Ralt-Toyota

25 Jul: Croix-en-Ternois, France

1 C.Andersson March-Toyota   123.49 kph / 76.73 mph
2 G. Branca-
  telli   March-Toyota
3 R. Patrese   Chevron-Toyota

22 Aug: Kassel-Calden, West Germany

1 R. Patrese   Chevron-Toyota   *
2 G. Branca-
  telli   March-Toyota
3 C.Andersson March-Toyota

4 Sep: Knutsdorp, Sweden

1 C.Andersson March-Toyota   126.36 kph / 78.52 mph
2 J. Nelle-
  mann   Modus-Toyota
3 T. Thyrring Ralt-Toyota

3 Oct: Vallelunga, Italy

1 G. Branca-
  telli   March-Toyota   150.81 kph / 93.71 mph
2 R. Patrese   Chevron-Toyota
3 P. Ghinzani March-Toyota
* Raced over two heats, aggregate positions taken

Final Championship Standing

1 Riccardo Patrese   Italy   52 pts
2 Conny Andersson   Sweden   52 pts
3 Gianfranco
  Brancatelli   Italy   36 pts

1977

20 Mar: Paul Ricard, France   *Average speed*

1 B. Gabbiani Chevron-Toyota   147.37 kph / 91.58 mph
2 B. Schafer   Ralt-Toyota
3 P. Ghinzani March-Toyota

27 Mar: Nurburgring, West Germany

1 P. Ghinzani March-Toyota   143.07 kph / 88.90 mph
2 A. Olofsson Ralt-Toyota
3 U. Svensson Ralt-Toyota

11 Apr: Zandvoort, Holland

1 A. Olofsson Ralt-Toyota   177.22 kph / 110.14 mph
2 J. Nielsen   Ralt-Toyota
3 P. Ghinzani March-Toyota

24 Apr: Zolder, Belgium

1 P. Ghinzani March-Toyota   150.89 kph / 93.76 mph
2 P. Necchi   Chevron-Toyota
3 G. Lees   Chevron-Toyota

8 May: Osterreichring, Austria

1 A. Olofsson Ralt-Toyota   170.94 kph / 106.24 mph
2 P. Ghinzani March-Toyota
3 N. Piquet   March-Toyota

29 May: Imola, Italy

1 P. Ghinzani March-Toyota   161.88 kph / 100.59 mph
2 O. Pedersoli Ralt-Toyota
3 P. Necchi   Ralt-Toyota

12 Jun: Enna, Italy

1 O. Pedersoli Ralt-Toyota   173.68 kph / 107.92 mph
2 P. Ghinzani March-Toyota
3 M. Rosei   March-Toyota

26 Jun: Monza, Italy

1 E. de Angelis Ralt-Toyota   182.62 kph / 113.48 mph
2 B. Gabbiani Chevron-Toyota
3 P. Necchi   Ralt-Toyota

24 Jul: Croix-en-Ternois, France

1 D. Daly   Chevron-Toyota   124.44 kph / 77.34 mph
2 B. Gabbiani Chevron-Toyota
3 N. Piquet   Ralt-Toyota

7 Aug: Knutsdorp, Sweden

1 A. Olofsson Ralt-Toyota   128.66 kph / 79.96 mph
2 N. Piquet   Ralt-Toyota
3 B. Gabbiani Chevron-Toyota

21 Aug: Kassel-Calden, West Germany

1 N. Piquet   Ralt-Toyota   163.49 kph / 101.61 mph
2 D. Kennedy Argo-Toyota
3 A. Olofsson Ralt-Toyota

27 Aug: Donington, England

1 B. Riley   March-Toyota   157.94 kph / 98.14 mph
2 E. Elgh   Chevron-Toyota
3 D. Daly   Chevron-Toyota

18 Sep: Jarama, Spain

1 N. Piquet   Ralt-Toyota   137.23 kph / 85.27 mph
2 D. Kennedy Argo-Toyota
3 P. Ghinzani March-Toyota

9 Oct: Vallelunga, Italy
1 O. Pedersoli   Ralt-Toyota   151.65 kph / 94.25 mph
2 P. Necchi   Ralt-Toyota
3 P. Ghinzani   March-Toyota

Final Championship Standing
1 Piercarlo Ghinzani   Italy   58 pts
2 Anders Olofsson   Sweden   46 pts
3 Nelson Piquet   Brazil   33 pts

1978

27 Mar: Zandvoort, Holland   *Average speed*
1 J. Lammers   Ralt-Toyota   167.88 kph / 104.34 mph
2 M. Bleeke-
  molen   Chevron-Toyota
3 T. Fabi   March-Toyota

2 Apr: Nurburgring, West Germany
1 A. Olofsson   Ralt-Toyota   171.37 kph / 106.49 mph
2 T. Fabi   March-Toyota
3 D. Kennedy   Argo-Toyota

16 Apr: Osterreichring, Austria
1 A. Olofsson   Ralt-Toyota   183.22 kph / 113.87 mph
2 M. Bleeke-
  molen   Chevron-Toyota
3 P. Gaillard   Chevron-Toyota

23 Apr: Zolder, Belgium
1 T. Fabi   March-Toyota   158.73 kph / 98.63 mph
2 A. Olofsson   Ralt-Toyota
3 M. Bleeke-
  molen   Chevron-Toyota

14 May: Imola, Italy
1 P. Gaillard   Chevron-Toyota   164.07 kph / 101.97 mph
2 R. Campomi-
  nosi   Ralt-Toyota
3 A. Olofsson   Ralt-Toyota

28 May: Nurburgring, West Germany
1 P. Gaillard   Chevron-Toyota   173.26 kph / 107.66 mph
2 J. Lammers   Ralt-Toyota
3 R. Rahal   Wolf-Dallara

4 Jun: Dijon, France
1 T. Fabi   March-Toyota   167.37 kph / 104.00 mph
2 J. Lammers   Ralt-Toyota
3 A. Olofsson   Ralt-Toyota

25 Jun: Monza, Italy
1 J. Lammers   Ralt-Toyota   152.07 kph / 94.51 mph
2 P. Gaillard   Chevron-Toyota
3 M. Romano   March-Toyota

2 Jul: Enna, Italy
1 M. Bleeke-
  molen   Chevron-Toyota   176.40 kph / 109.61 mph
2 P. Gaillard   Chevron-Toyota
3 A. Olofsson   Ralt-Toyota

16 Jul: Magny Cours, France
1 J. Lammers   Ralt-Toyota   158.21 kph / 98.31 mph
2 P. Gaillard   Chevron-Toyota
3 T. Fabi   March-Toyota

6 Aug: Knutsdorp, Sweden
1 A. Olofsson   Ralt-Toyota   127.90 kph / 79.45 mph
2 J. Lammers   Ralt-Toyota
3 S. Borgudd   Ralt-Toyota

13 Aug: Karlskoga, Sweden
1 J. Lammers   Ralt-Toyota   139.92 kph / 86.96 mph
2 A. Olofsson   Ralt-Toyota
3 T. Fabi   March-Toyota

26 Aug: Donington, England
1 D. Warwick   Ralt-Toyota   159.86 kph / 99.34 mph
2 J. Lammers   Ralt-Toyota
3 D. Kennedy   Argo-Toyota

3 Sep: Kassel-Calden, West Germany
1 A. Olofsson   Ralt-Toyota   164.98 kph / 102.52 mph
2 J. Lammers   Ralt-Toyota
3 D. Albertin   Chevron-Toyota

17 Sep: Jarama, Spain
1 A. Prost   Martini-Renault 139.14 kph / 86.46 mph
2 A. Olofsson   Ralt-Toyota
3 D. Warwick   Ralt-Toyota

8 Oct: Vallelunga, Italy
1 T. Fabi   March-Toyota   153.93 kph / 95.65 mph
2 G. Pardini   Ralt-Toyota
3 M. Baldi   Ralt-Toyota

Final Championship Standing
1 Jan Lammers   Holland   71 pts
2 Anders Olofsson Sweden   71 pts
3 Patrick Gaillard France   48 pts

1979

18 Mar: Vallelunga, Italy   *Average speed*
1 A. Prost   Martini-Renault 153.07 kph / 95.11 mph
2 M. Baldi   Ralt-Toyota
3 C. Rossi   Ralt-Toyota

15 Apr: Osterreichring, Austria
1 A. Prost   Martini-Renault 187.40 kph / 116.45 mph
2 M. Bleeke-
  molen   Ralt-Toyota
3 S. Borgudd   Ralt-Toyota

22 Apr: Zolder, Belgium
1 A. Prost   Martini-Renault 159.19 kph / 98.91 mph
2 M. Alboreto   March-Toyota
3 H-G. Burger   Ralt-Toyota

1 May: Magny Cours, France
1 A. Prost   Martini-Renault 158.43 kph / 98.45 mph
2 A. Luyendijk   Argo-Toyota
3 S. Borgudd   Ralt-Toyota

20 May: Donington, England
1 B. Riley   March-Triumph   130.13 kph / 80.86 mph
2 F. Serra   March-Toyota
3 A. Prost   Martini-Renault

4 Jun: Zandvoort, Holland
1 A. Prost   Martini-Renault 168.05 kph / 104.42 mph
2 M. Baldi   March-Toyota
3 S. Borgudd   Ralt-Toyota

17 June: Enna, Italy

1 M. Bleeke-
   molen   March-Toyota   170.24 kph / 105.78 mph
2 M. Alboreto March-Toyota
3 M. Baldi   March-Toyota

24 Jun: Monza, Italy

1 M.Thackwell March-Toyota   183.59 kph / 114.08 mph
2 M. Baldi   March-Toyota
3 M. Alboreto March-Toyota

5 Aug: Knutsdorp, Sweden

1 A. Prost   Martini-Renault   128.94 kph / 80.12 mph
2 A. Olofsson Ralt-Toyota
3 M. Bleeke-
   molen   March-Toyota

12 Aug: Kinnekulle, Sweden

1 R. Dallest   Martini-Toyota   146.40 kph / 90.97 mph
2 M. Bleeke-
   molen   March-Toyota
3 S. Borgudd Ralt-Toyota

9 Sep: Jarama, Spain

1 A. Prost   Martini-Renault   138.85 kph / 86.28 mph
2 S. Saulnier Martini-Toyota
3 R. Dallest   Martini-Toyota

7 Oct: Kassel-Calden, West Germany

1 M. Korten   March-Toyota   162.98 kph / 101.27 mph
2 S. Borgudd Ralt-Toyota
3 D. Albertin Ralt-Toyota

Final Championship Standing

1 Alain Prost   France   67 pts
2 Michael
   Bleekemolen Holland   28 pts
3 Slim Borgudd Sweden   23 pts

1980

30 Mar: Nurburgring, West Germany

                          Average speed
1 T. Boutsen Martini-Toyota   170.54 kph / 105.99 mph
2 P. Alliot   Martini-Toyota
3 M. Alboreto March-Alfa Romeo

6 Apr: Osterreichring, Austria

1 M. Alboreto March-Alfa Romeo 187.71 kph / 116.66 mph
2 T. Boutsen Martini-Toyota
3 P. Alliot   Martini-Toyota

20 Apr: Zolder, Belgium

1 T. Boutsen Martini-Toyota   *
2 P. Alliot   Martini-Toyota
3 P. Fabre   Martini-Toyota

4 May: Magny Cours, France

1 T. Boutsen Martini-Toyota   158.82 kph / 98.69 mph
2 P. Alliot   Martini-Toyota
3 K. Thiim   Chevron-Toyota

26 May: Zandvoort, Holland

1 M. Baldi   Martini-Toyota   143.68 kph / 89.28 mph
2 T. Boutsen Martini-Toyota
3 C. Fabi   March-Alfa Romeo

1 Jun: La Chatre, France

1 M. Alboreto March-Alfa Romeo 127.93 kph / 79.51 mph
2 C. Fabi   March-Alfa Romeo
3 M. Baldi   Martini-Toyota

15 Jun: Mugello, Italy

1 C. Fabi   March-Alfa Romeo 162.35 kph / 100.90 mph
2 M. Alboreto March-Alfa Romeo
3 M. Baldi   Martini-Toyota

22 Jun: Monza, Italy

1 M. Alboreto March-Alfa Romeo 70.76 kph / 113.87 mph
2 E. Coloni   March-Toyota
3 C. Fabi   March-Alfa Romeo

27 Jul: Misano, Italy

1 M. Baldi   Martini-Toyota   159.76 kph / 99.27 mph
2 C. Fabi   March-Alfa Romeo
3 A. Ferte   Martini-Renault

10 Aug: Knutsdorp, Sweden

1 C. Fabi   March-Alfa Romeo 124.81 kph / 77.57 mph
2 T. Boutsen Martini-Toyota
3 K. Thiim   Chevron-Toyota

7 Sep: Silverstone, England

1 M. White   March-Toyota   192.73 kph / 119.76 mph
2 R. Wilson   Ralt-Toyota
3 M. Alboreto March-Alfa Romeo

21 Sep: Jarama, Spain

1 M. Baldi   Martini-Toyota   138.37 kph / 86.00 mph
2 A. Ferte   Martini-Renault
3 P. Alliot   Martini-Toyota

5 Oct: Kassel-Calden, West Germany

1 M. Alboreto March-Alfa Romeo 168.90 kph / 104.97 mph
2 C. Fabi   March-Alfa Romeo
3 P. Streiff   Martini-Toyota

12 Oct: Zolder, Belgium

1 P. Streiff   Martini-Toyota   163.13 kph / 101.37 mph
2 P. Alliot   Martini-Toyota
3 M. Alboreto March-Alfa Romeo
* Raced over two heats, aggregate time taken

Final Championship Standing

1 Michele Alboreto Italy   60 pts
2 Thierry Boutsen Belgium 54 pts
3 Corrado Fabi   Italy   50 pts

1981

15 Mar: Vallelunga, Italy   *Average speed*

1 M. Baldi   March-Alfa Romeo 154.85 kph / 96.24 mph
2 E. Coloni   Ralt-Toyota
3 A. Ferte   Martini-Alfa Romeo

29 Mar: Nurburgring, West Germany

1 O. Larrauri March-Toyota   157.87 kph / 98.10 mph
2 P. Alliot   Martini-Alfa Romeo
3 A. Ferte   Martini-Alfa Romeo

5 Apr: Donington, England

1 M. White   March-Alfa Romeo 162.22 kph / 100.80 mph
2 A. Ferte   Martini-Alfa Romeo
3 O. Larrauri March-Toyota

19 Apr: Osterreichring, Austria

1 M. Baldi   March-Alfa Romeo   191.73 kph / 119.14 mph
2 O.Larrauri   March-Toyota
3 P. Alliot   Martini-Alfa Romeo

26 Apr: Zolder, Belgium

1 M. Baldi   March-Alfa Romeo   165.62 kph / 102.92 mph
2 P. Streiff   Martini-Alfa Romeo
3 O.Larrauri   March-Toyota

3 May: Magny Cours, France

1 P. Alliot   Martini-Alfa Romeo 163.04 kph / 101.31 mph
2 M. Baldi   March-Alfa Romeo
3 A. Ferte   Martini-Alfa Romeo

24 May: La Chatre, France

1 P. Alliot   Martini-Alfa Romeo 129.60 kph / 80.53 mph
2 A. Ferte   Martini-Alfa Romeo
3 O. Larrauri   March-Toyota

8 Jun: Zandvoort, Holland

1 M. Baldi   March-Alfa Romeo   165.24 kph / 102.68 mph
2 A. Ferte   Martini-Alfa Romeo
3 P. Streiff   Martini-Alfa Romeo

21 Jun: Silverstone, England

1 R. Moreno   Ralt-Toyota   197.35 kph / 122.63 mph
2 M. Baldi   March-Alfa Romeo
3 J. Palmer   Ralt-Toyota

28 Jun: Croix-en-Ternois, France

1 M. Baldi   March-Alfa Romeo   125.45 kph / 77.95 mph
2 A. Ferte   Martini-Alfa Romeo
3 E. Pirro   Martini-Alfa Romeo

19 Jul: Misano, Italy

1 M. Baldi   March-Alfa Romeo   140.26 kph / 87.16 mph
2 A. Ferte   Martini-Alfa Romeo
3 J-L.
  Schlesser   Martini-Alfa Romeo

9 Aug: Knutsdorp, Sweden

1 M. Baldi   March-Alfa Romeo   128.78 kph / 80.02 mph
2 A. Ferte   Martini-Alfa Romeo
3 P. Streiff   Martini-Alfa Romeo

6 Sep: Jarama, Spain

1 A. Ferte   Martini-Alfa Romeo 139.77 kph / 86.87 mph
2 M. Baldi   March-Alfa Romeo
3 P. Alliot   Martini-Alfa Romeo

20 Sep: Imola, Italy

1 M. Baldi   March-Alfa Romeo   163.73 kph / 101.74 mph
2 P. Streiff   Martini-Alfa Romeo
3 A. Ferte   Martini-Alfa Romeo

4 Oct: Mugello, Italy

1 E. Pirro   Martini-Alfa Romeo 165.43 kph / 102.80 mph
2 K. Thiim   March-Alfa Romeo
3 P. Streiff   Martini-Alfa Romeo

Final Championship Standing

1 Mauro Baldi   Italy   94 pts
2 Alain Ferte   France   63 pts
3 Phillippe Alliot France   41 pts

1982

14 Mar: Mugello, Italy

                                     Average speed
1 O. Larrauri   Euro-Alfa Romeo   166.42 kph / 103.43 mph
2 E. Pirro   Euro-Alfa Romeo
3 D. Theys   Martini-Alfa Romeo

28 Mar: Nurburgring, West Germany

1 O. Larrauri   Euro-Alfa Romeo   158.47 kph / 98.49 mph
2 A. Ferte   Martini-Alfa Romeo
3 J. Nielsen   Ralt-VW

4 Apr: Donington, England

1 J. Weaver   Ralt-Toyota   162.38 kph / 100.90 mph
2 O. Larrauri   Euro-Alfa Romeo
3 D. Theys   Martini-Alfa Romeo

18 Apr: Zolder, Belgium

1 O. Larrauri   Euro-Alfa Romeo   163.62 kph / 101.67 mph
2 D. Theys   Martini-Alfa Romeo
3 A. Ferte   Martini-Alfa Romeo

2 May: Magny Cours, France

1 A. Ferte   Martini-Alfa Romeo 163.44 kph / 101.58 mph
2 O. Larrauri   Euro-Alfa Romeo
3 D. Theys   Martini-Alfa Romeo

16 May: Osterreichring, Austria

1 E. Pirro   Euro-Alfa Romeo   190.46 kph / 118.35 mph
2 O. Larrauri   Euro-Alfa Romeo
3 A. Ferte   Martini-Alfa Romeo

31 May: Zandvoort, Holland

1 O. Larrauri   Euro-Alfa Romeo   164.33 kph / 102.13 mph
2 P. Gian-   Ralt-Alfa Romeo
  grossi
3 D. Theys   Martini-Alfa Romeo

13 Jun: Silverstone, England

1 E. Pirro   Euro-Alfa Romeo   195.86 kph / 121.71 mph
2 J. Weaver   Ralt-Toyota
3 E. Mansilla   Ralt-Toyota

27 Jun: Monza, Italy

1 O. Larrauri   Euro-Alfa Romeo   186.08 kph / 115.63 mph
2 E. Pirro   Euro-Alfa Romeo
3 J. Nielsen   Ralt-VW

4 Jul: Enna, Italy

1 O. Larrauri   Euro-Alfa Romeo   178.58 kph / 110.97 mph
2 E. Pirro   Euro-Alfa Romeo
3 R. Ravaglia   Dallara-Alfa Romeo

18 Jul: La Chatre, France

1 P. Alliot   Martini-Alfa Romeo 130.57 kph / 81.14 mph
2 A. Ferte   Martini-Alfa Romeo
3 O. Larrauri   Euro-Alfa Romeo

8 Aug: Knutsdorp, Sweden

1 O. Larrauri   Euro-Alfa Romeo   128.91 kph / 80.12 mph
2 E. Pirro   Euro-Alfa Romeo
3 K. Thiim   March-Toyota

5 Sep: Nogaro, France

1 J. Weaver   Ralt-Toyota   147.95 kph / 91.94 mph
2 O. Larrauri   Euro-Alfa Romeo
3 P. Gian-
  grossi   Ralt-Alfa Romeo

12 Sep: Jarama, Spain

1 J. Weaver   Ralt-Toyota   139.35 kph / 86.59 mph
2 A. Ferte   Martini-Alfa Romeo
3 P. Alliot   Martini-Alfa Romeo

3 Oct: Kassel-Calden, West Germany

1 E. Pirro   Euro-Alfa Romeo   140.65 kph / 87.40 mph
2 J. Zeller   Ralt-Toyota
3 E. Benamo   Ralt-Toyota

Final Championship Standing

1 Oscar Larrauri   Argentine   87 pts
2 Emanuele Pirro   Italy   61 pts
3 Alain Ferte   France   42 pts

1983

13 Mar: Vallelunga, Italy   *Average speed*

1 E. Pirro   Ralt-Alfa Romeo   155.98 kph / 96.94 mph
2 J. Nielsen   Ralt-VW
3 P. Martini   Ralt-Alfa Romeo

17 Apr: Zolder, Belgium

1 E. Pirro   Ralt-Alfa Romeo   164.70 kph / 102.36 mph
2 D. Theys   Ralt-Alfa Romeo
3 G. Berger   Ralt-Alfa Romeo

1 May: Magny Cours, France

1 J. Nielsen   Ralt-VW   157.47 kph / 97.87 mph
2 F. Hesnault   Ralt-VW
3 M. Ferte   Martini-Alfa Romeo

22 May: Osterreichring, Austria

1 T. Byrne   Ralt-Toyota   192.07 kph / 119.35 mph
2 G. Berger   Ralt-Alfa Romeo
3 E. Pirro   Ralt-Alfa Romeo

5 Jun: La Chatre, France

1 R. Ravaglia   Ralt-Toyota   128.97 kph / 80.14 mph
2 D. Theys   Ralt-Alfa Romeo
3 P. Fabre   Martini-Alfa Romeo

12 Jun: Silverstone, England

1 M. Brundle   Ralt-Toyota   196.98 kph / 122.40 mph
2 T. Byrne   Ralt-Toyota
3 D. Theys   Ralt-Alfa Romeo

26 Jun: Monza, Italy

1 J. Nielsen   Ralt-VW   187.12 kph / 116.30 mph
2 R. Ravaglia   Ralt-Toyota
3 T. Byrne   Ralt-Toyota

10 Jul: Misano, Italy

1 T. Byrne   Ralt-Toyota   164.12 kph / 102.00 mph
2 P. Martini   Ralt-Alfa Romeo
3 R. Ravaglia   Ralt-Toyota

31 Jul: Zandvoort, Holland

1 J. Nielsen   Ralt-VW   163.62 kph / 101.67 mph
2 P. Martini   Ralt-Alfa Romeo
3 E. Pirro   Ralt-Alfa Romeo

7 Aug: Knutsdorp, Sweden

1 J. Nielsen   Ralt-VW   129.78 kph / 80.66 mph
2 G. Berger   Ralt-Alfa Romeo
3 E. Pirro   Ralt-Alfa Romeo

4 Sep: Nogaro, France

1 P. Martini   Ralt-Alfa Romeo   147.79 kph / 91.84 mph
2 E. Pirro   Ralt-Alfa Romeo
3 J. Nielsen   Ralt-VW

11 Sep: Jarama, Spain

1 P. Martini   Ralt-Alfa Romeo   138.35 kph / 85.97 mph
2 E. Pirro   Ralt-Alfa Romeo
3 J. Nielsen   Ralt-VW

25 Sep: Imola, Italy

1 P. Martini   Ralt-Alfa Romeo   167.09 kph / 103.85 mph
2 J. Nielsen   Ralt-VW
3 I. Capelli   Ralt-Alfa Romeo

9 Oct: Donington, England

1 M. Brundle   Ralt-Toyota   150.06 kph / 93.25 mph
2 P. Martini   Ralt-Alfa Romeo
3 J. Weaver   Ralt-VW

23 Oct: Croix-en-Ternois, France

1 P. Martini   Ralt-Alfa Romeo   128.19 kph / 79.67 mph
2 E. Pirro   Ralt-Alfa Romeo
3 R. Ravaglia   Ralt-Toyota

Final Championship Standing

1 Pierluigi Martini   Italy   66 pts
2 John Nielsen   Denmark   62 pts
3 Emanuele Pirro   Italy   52 pts

1984

25 Mar: Donington, England   *Average speed*

1 J. Dumfries   Ralt-VW   138.15 kph / 85.85 mph
2 T. Byrne   Anso-Alfa Romeo
3 C. Langes   Ralt-Toyota

15 Apr: Zolder, Belgium

1 J. Nielsen   Ralt-VW   165.60 kph / 102.90 mph
2 J. Dumfries   Ralt-VW
3 I. Capelli   Martin-Alfa Romeo

1 May: Magny Cours, France

1 I. Capelli   Martini-Alfa Romeo 165.00 kph / 102.53 mph
2 J. Nielsen   Ralt-VW
3 T. Byrne   Anson-Alfa Romeo

13 May: La Chatre, France

1 I. Capelli   Martini-Alfa Romeo 130.44 kph2 / 81.06 mph
2 J. Dumfries   Ralt-VW
3 G. Berger   Ralt-Alfa Romeo

27 May: Osterreichring, Austria

1 G. Berger   Ralt-Alfa Romeo   194.05 kph / 120.58 mph
2 C. Langes   Ralt-Toyota
3 J. Nielsen   Ralt-VW

10 Jun: Silverstone, England

1 J. Dumfries   Ralt-VW   200.23 kph / 124.42 mph
2 R. Spence   Ralt-VW
3 I. Capelli   Martini-Alfa Romeo

17 Jun: Nurburgring, West Germany

1 J. Dumfries　Ralt-VW　　　　　　166.90 kph / 103.71 mph
2 I. Capelli　　Martini-Alfa Romeo
3 G. Berger　　Ralt-Alfa Romeo

24 Jun: Monza, Italy

1 G. Berger　　Ralt-Alfa Romeo　　187.16 kph / 116.30 mph
2 C. Langes　　Ralt-Toyota
3 F. Forini　　Dallara-Toyota

8 Jul: Enna, Italy

1 I. Capelli　　Martini-Alfa Romeo　181.32 kph / 112.67 mph
2 C. Langes　　Ralt-Toyota
3 G. Berger　　Ralt-Alfa Romeo

16 Jul: Mugello, Italy

1 I. Cappeli　　Martini-Alfa Romeo　168.29 kph / 104.57 mph
2 G. Berger　　Ralt-Alfa Romeo
3 R. Melgrati　Ralt-Alfa Romeo

19 Aug: Knutsdorp, Sweden

1 C. Langes　　Ralt-Toyota　　　　128.63 kph / 79.93 mph
2 L. Sala　　　Ralt-Alfa Romeo
3 B. Santal　　Ralt-VW

16 Sep: Nogaro, France

1 J. Nielsen　　Ralt-VW　　　　　　151.91 kph / 94.40 mph
2 I. Capelli　　Martini-Alfa Romeo
3 G. Berger　　Ralt-Alfa Romeo

21 Oct: Jarama, Spain

1 J. Dumfries　Ralt-VW　　　　　　141.70 kph / 88.07 mph
2 J. Nielsen　　Ralt-VW
3 I. Capelli　　Martini-Alfa Romeo

Final Championship Standing

1 Ivan Capelli　　　Italy　　　　　　60 pts
2 Johnny Dumfries　Great Britain　　53 pts
3 Gerhard Berger　　Austria　　　　 46 pts

Drivers' Records

Most Individual Wins

11 Mauro Baldi (ITA)
8 Oscar Larrauri (ARG)
8 Alain Prost (FRA)
7 Anders Olofsson (SWE)
6 John Nielsen (DEN)
6 Emanuele Pirro (ITA)
5 Conny Andersson (SWE)
(Most successful British driver –
Johnny Dumfries, 4 wins)

Most points in a season

94 Mauro Baldi (ITA) 1981
87 Oscar Larrauri (ARG) 1982
71 Jan Lammers (HOL) 1978
71 Anders Olofsson (SWE) 1978

Largest Championship-winning margin

39 pts Alain Prost (FRA) 1979
31 pts Mauro Baldi (ITA) 1981
26 pts Oscar Larrauri (ARG) 1982

Most points by driver not winning the Championship

71 Anders Olofsson (SWE) 1978

Mauro Baldi (ITA), the 1981 European
Formula Three champion, won the title
with a record 94 points. His career total of
11 wins is also a championship record. He
is seen here driving the Spirit Formula
One car

Most individual wins season by season

1975	2	Larry Perkins* (AUS)
1976	4	Conny Andersson (SWE), Riccardo Patrese* (ITA)
1977	3	Piercarlo Ghinzani* (ITA), Anders Olofsson (SWE)
1978	4	Jan Lammers* (HOL), Anders Olofsson (SWE)
1979	6	Alain Prost* (FRA)
1980	4	Michele Alboreto* (ITA)
1981	8	Mauro Baldi* (ITA)
1982	7	Oscar Larrauri* (ARG)
1983	4	Pierluigi Martini* (ITA), John Nielsen (DEN)
1984	4	Ivan Capelli* (ITA), Johnny Dumfries (GB)

* Indicates that season's champion driver

Most wins in a season by drivers not winning the Championship

4 Conny Andersson (SWE) 1976
4 Anders Olofsson (SWE) 1978
4 John Nielsen (DEN) 1983
4 Johnny Dumfries (GB) 1984

Least wins in a season by the champion driver

2 Larry Perkins (AUS) 1975

Most Consecutive Wins

4 Alain Prost (FRA)1979 Vallelunga, Osterreichring, Zolder, Magny Cours
3 Mauro Baldi(ITA)1981 Croix-en-Ternois, Misano, Knutsdorp
3 Emanuele   1983 Kassel-Calden; 1983 Vallelunga, Pirro (ITA)   Zolder
3 Pierluigi
   Martini (ITA)   1983 Nogaro, Jarama, Imola

Formula One World Champions who have won races

Alain Prost (FRA) 8
Nelson Piquet (BRA) 2

Manufacturers' Records

Most Wins

27 Ralt-Toyota
19 March-Toyota
14 March-Alfa Romeo
10 Euro-Alfa Romeo
10 Ralt-VW

Most Consecutive Wins

5 Ralt-Toyota
   1977 Jarama, Vallelunga;
   1978 Zandvoort, Nurburgring, Osterreichring
5 Ralt-Toyota
   1978 Magny Cours, Knutsdorp, Karlskoga, Donington, Kassel-Calden
5 Euro-Alfa Romeo
   1982 Osterreichring, Zandvoort, Silverstone, Monza, Enna

Most wins season by season

1975	3	Ralt-Ford
1976	6	March-Toyota
1977	8	Ralt-Toyota
1978	9	Ralt-Toyota
1979	7	Martini-Renault
1980	8	Martini-Toyota
1981	9	March-Alfa Romeo
1982	10	Euro-Alfa Romeo
1983	6	Ralt-Alfa Romeo
1984	6	Ralt-VW

Martin Brundle (GB–left), the winner, with Tommy Byrne (IRE–centre) and Didier Theys (BEL) after the European Formula Three race at Silverstone in 1983

Colin Chapman– 'The Lotus Eater'

Genius, innovator, hard worker and self-made man were all accurate descriptions of Anthony Colin Bruce Chapman who died suddenly at the age of 54 at his Norfolk home in December 1982. Fortunately, Colin Chapman, the link between the motoring enthusiast and the glamour of Grand Prix racing, has left a legacy in his famous Lotus name.

Chapman studied engineering at London University just after the war. During his time at college he started modifying Austin Sevens and on 1 January 1952 his famous Lotus Engineering Company was registered, thanks to a loan of £25 from Hazel Williams, who later became his wife. The

company's first headquarters were at Hornsey, north London. The first of more than 100 different models to have since borne the Lotus name, was based on the plywood body on an Austin Seven chassis. These became not only very popular with enthusiasts but successful in 750 cc club events. It was apparent that a genius had been born.

Foreseeing a market with the DIY enthusiast, Chapman produced his famous Lotus in kit form. These and all his other cars became very popular, but Chapman had his heart set on entering the world of Formula One racing.

The first Lotus Grand Prix car, produced in 1958, was the Lotus

Colin Chapman, the man who turned Lotus into one of the most respected names in motoring, not just in the world of motor racing. (National Motor Museum)

12, designed by Frank Costin, formerly of Vanwall. Not surprisingly, the 12 looked like a Vanwall and was powered by a Coventry-Climax engine. The car made its debut at that year's Monaco Grand Prix with Cliff

Colin Chapman (left) with one of his five world champions, Emerson Fittipaldi (BRA). Jim Clark (GB), Graham Hill (GB), Jochen Rindt (AUT) and Mario Andretti (USA) all won the world title in one of Chapman's cars. (National Motor Museum)

Allison (GB) and Graham Hill (GB) behind the wheel of the two entered cars. Hill lasted 70 laps while Allison went on to finish sixth.

The first Grand Prix success for Lotus was not, ironically, for the Lotus team, but was by Stirling Moss (GB) in a privately entered rear-engined Lotus 18 in the 1960 Monaco Grand Prix, when he gave a superb display to beat New Zealander Bruce McLaren.

Jim Clark and Chapman teamed up in 1960 and one of the best relationships in Formula One Grand Prix racing soon developed. Clark, undoubtedly the best driver of his era, lifted the world title in the revolutionary Lotus 25, with its monocoque

Left One of Chapman's early cars, the Austin-Lotus III of 1951. (National Motor Museum)

Below A prototype of the first Lotus Formula One car, seen here in action at Crystal Palace in 1958. (National Motor Museum)

construction, in 1963 and 1965. But their partnership ended one sad April day in 1968, when Clark was inexplicably killed in a Formula Two race at Hockenheim. Graham Hill had already joined the Lotus team a year earlier and he helped lift the gloom by winning the world title in 1968. But tragedy struck again in 1970 when Jochen Rindt, Chapman's third world champion, was killed at Monza. He was that season's posthumous world champion.

Emerson Fittipaldi was the next Lotus world champion and,

just as it seemed the Midas touch was deserting Chapman, American Mario Andretti lifted the 1978 title in the lotus 78/79, with team-mate Ronnie Peterson (Swe) second.

There have been no Lotus world champions since then but Ayrton Senna (Bra) is hoping to join the long list of past champions. But, whether he does emerge as another champion or not, the name of Lotus will never be forgotten in the world of motoring and motor racing.

British Formula Three Championship

Formula Three racing has been popular in Great Britain since the early 1950s, when Formula Three cars were powered by 500 cc motor cycle engines. Various championships have been staged in Britain over the years, each with individual sponsors, and quite often with two or more championships running concurrently. But it was not until the introduction of the Vandervell British Formula Three Championship in 1979 that the Championship, as we know it today, was born.

Results

Major Formula Three Championships prior to 1979:

1966

Les Leston Championship

1	Harry Stiller	70 pts
2	Chris Lambert	50 pts
3	Jackie Oliver	34 pts

1967

Les Leston Championship

1	Harry Stiller	75 pts
2	John Miles	60 pts
3	Tony Lanfranchi	43 pts

1968

Lombank Championship

1	Tim Schenken	80 pts
2	Tony Lanfranchi	69 pts
3	Cyd Williams	53 pts

1969

Lombank Championship

1	Emerson Fittipaldi	57 pts
2	Alan Rollinson	49 pts
3	Bev Bond	39 pts

1970

Motor Sport/Shell Championship

1	Tony Trimmer	46 pts
2	Dave Walker	41 pts
3	Mike Beuttler	32 pts

Lombank Championship

1	Dave Walker	48 pts
2	Tony Trimmer	43 pts
3	Carlos Pace	43 pts

1971

Shell Super Oil Championship

1	Dave Walker	86 pts
2	Roger Williamson	56 pts
3	Bev Bond	48 pts

Lombard North Central Championship

1	Roger Williamson	90 pts
2	Colin Vandervell	63 pts
3	Jody Scheckter	28 pts

1972

Forward Trust Championship

1	Roger Williamson	50 pts
2	Rikki von Opel	48 pts
3	Mike Walker	46 pts

Lombard North Central Championship

1	Rikki von Opel	61 pts
2	Tony Brise	55 pts
3	Andy Sutcliffe	53 pts

Shell Championship

1	Roger Williamson	78 pts
2	Colin Vandervell	44 pts
3	Jacques Coulon	26 pts

1973

Forward Trust Championship

1	Ian Taylor	64 pts
2	Tony Brise	42 pts
3	Richard Robarts	32 pts

Lombard North Central Championship

1	Tony Brise	52 pts
2	Richard Robarts	52 pts
3	Mike Wilds	33 pts

John Player Championship

1	Tony Brise	123 pts
2	Alan Jones	121 pts
3	Russell Wood	119 pts

1974

Forward Trust Championship

1	Brian Henton	-
2	Tony Rouff	-
3	Jose Santo	-

Lombard North Central Championship

1	Brian Henton	78 pts
2	Alex Ribeiro	60 pts
3	Tony Rouff	54 pts

1975

BP Super Visco Championship

1	Gunnar Nilsson	74 pts
2	Alex Ribeiro	59 pts
3	Danny Sullivan	59 pts

1976

Shell Sport Championship

1	Bruno Giacomelli	79 pts
2	Rupert Keegan	62 pts
3	Geoff Lees	42 pts

BP Super Visco Championship

1	Rupert Keegan	74 pts
2	Bruno Giacomelli	71 pts
3	Geoff Lees	31 pts

1977

Vandervell Championship

1	Stephen South	75 pts
2	Brett Riley	58 pts
3	Derek Warwick	41 pts

BP Championship

1	Derek Daly	69 pts
2	Stephen South	56 pts
	Eje Elgh	56 pts

1978

Vandervell Championship

1	Derek Warwick	162 pts
2	Nelson Piquet	124 pts
3	Chico Serra	78 pts

BP Championship

1	Nelson Piquet	101 pts
2	Derek Warwick	72 pts
3	Chico Serra	72 pts

Results of all races since 1979:

1979

4 Mar: Silverstone

1 C. Serra   March-Toyota
  167.11 kph / 103.84 mph
2 M. Roe   Chevron-Toyota
3 A. de Cesaris   March-Toyota

11 Mar: Thruxton

1 A. de Cesaris   March-Toyota
  164.86 kph / 102.44 mph
2 N. Mansell   March-Triumph
3 C. Serra   March-Toyota

25 Mar: Silverstone

1 N. Mansell   March-Triumph
  170.82 kph / 106.14 mph
2 B. Riley   March-Triumph
3 A. de Cesaris   March-Toyota

1 Apr: Snetterton

1 C. Serra   March-Toyota
  152.29 kph / 94.63 mph
2 A. de Cesaris   March-Toyota
3 S. Johansson   Chevron-Toyota

8 Apr: Donington

1 C. Serra   March-Toyota
  141.46 kph / 87.90 mph
2 B. Devaney   Chevron-Toyota
3 S. Johansson   Chevron-Toyota

16 Apr: Thruxton

1 A. de Cesaris   March-Toyota
  178.75 kph / 111.07 mph
2 C. Serra   March-Toyota
3 B. Riley   March-Triumph

7 May: Brands Hatch

1 A. de Cesaris   March-Toyota
  153.68 kph / 95.49 mph
2 C. Serra   March-Toyota
3 M. Thackwell   March-Toyota

20 May: Donington

1 B. Riley   March-Triumph
  130.13 kph / 80.86 mph
2 C. Serra   March-Toyota
3 A. Prost   Martini-Renault

28 May: Silverstone

1 B. Devaney   Chevron-Toyota
  156.91 kph / 97.50 mph
2 M. Roe   Chevron-Toyota
3 M. Thackwell   March-Toyota

10 Jun: Brands Hatch

1 M. Thackwell   March-Toyota
  153.72 kph / 95.52 mph
2 A. de Cesaris   March-Toyota
3 S. Johansson   March-Toyota

17 Jun: Cadwell Park

1 A. de Cesaris   March-Toyota
  149.86 kph / 93.12 mph
2 C. Serra   March-Toyota
3 B. Riley   March-Triumph

1 Jul: Silverstone

1 A. de Cesaris   March-Toyota
  168.13 kph / 104.47 mph
2 S. Johansson   March-Toyota
3 C. Serra   March-Toyota

14 Jul: Silverstone

1 M. Thackwell   March-Toyota
  193.41 kph / 120.13 mph
2 C. Serra   March-Toyota
3 K. Acheson   March-Toyota

5 Aug: Snetterton

1 M. Thackwell   March-Toyota
  173.97 kph / 108.10 mph
2 C. Serra   March-Toyota
3 K. Acheson   March-Toyota

12 Aug: Mallory Park

1 C. Serra   March-Toyota
  152.53 kph / 94.78 mph
2 S. Johansson   March-Toyota
3 R. Wilson   March-Toyota

27 Aug: Silverstone

1 C. Serra   March-Toyota
  168.55 kph / 104.73 mph
2 S. Johansson   March-Toyota
3 M. Thackwell   March-Toyota

15 Sep: Oulton Park

1 M. Thackwell   March-Toyota
  162.27 kph / 100.83 mph
2 C. Serra   March-Toyota
3 K. Acheson   March-Toyota

30 Sep: Thruxton

1 A. de Cesaris   March-Toyota
  178.93 kph / 111.18 mph
2 K. Acheson   March-Toyota
3 E. Jordan   March-Toyota

7 Oct: Silverstone

1 S. Johansson   March-Toyota
  178.43 kph / 110.87 mph
2 M. Thackwell   March-Toyota
3 K. Acheson   March-Toyota

28 Oct: Thruxton

1 M. Thackwell   March-Toyota
  180.36 kph / 112.07 mph
2 K. Acheson   March-Toyota
3 B. Riley   March-Triumph

Final Championship Standing

1	Chico Serra	Brazil	103 pts
2	Andrea de Cesaris	Italy	90 pts
3	Mike Thackwell	New Zealand	71 pts

1980

2 Mar: Silverstone

1 S. Johansson   March-Toyota
  167.46 kph / 104.08 mph
2 K. Acheson   March-Toyota
3 M. Blanchet   Lola-Toyota

9 Mar: Thruxton

1 R. Guerrero   Argo-Toyota
  177.59 kph / 110.37 mph
2 M. Blanchet   Lola-Toyota
3 S. Johansson   March-Toyota

30 Mar: Brands Hatch

1 B. Riley   March-Toyota
  154.30 kph / 95.90 mph
2 K. Acheson   March-Toyota
3 S. Johansson   March-Toyota

7 Apr: Thruxton

1 K. Acheson   March-Toyota
  178.53 kph / 110.96 mph
2 R. Guerrero   Argo-Toyota
3 M. White   March-Toyota

20 Apr: Silverstone

1 K. Acheson   March-Toyota
  192.11 kph / 119.40 mph
2 T. Tassin   Argo-Toyota
3 R. Guerrero   Argo-Toyota

5 May: Thruxton

1 R. Guerrero   Argo-Toyota
  179.34 kph / 111.46 mph
2 T. Tassin   Argo-Toyota
3 S. Johansson   March-Toyota

11 May: Snetterton

1 K. Acheson   March-Toyota
  173.63 kph / 107.91 mph
2 R. Guerrero   Argo-Toyota
3 D. Sears   Argo-Toyota

26 May: Silverstone

1 S. Johansson   March-Toyota
  169.14 kph / 105.12 mph
2 K. Acheson   March-Toyota
3 R. Wilson   Ralt-Toyota

1 Jun: Cadwell Park

1 R. Guerrero   Argo-Toyota
  141.38 kph / 87.87 mph
2 S. Johansson   March-Toyota
3 T. Tassin   Argo-Toyota

8 Jun: Silverstone

1 K. Acheson   March-Toyota
  193.35 kph / 120.17 mph
2 R. Guerrero   Argo-Toyota
3 S. Johansson   March-Toyota

29 Jun: Brands Hatch

1 R. Guerrero   Argo-Toyota
  153.10 kph / 95.15 mph
2 T. Tassin   Argo-Toyota
3 K. Acheson   March-Toyota

6 Jul: Silverstone

1 T. Tassin   Argo-Toyota
  148.64 kph / 92.38 mph
2 R. Wilson   Ralt-Toyota
3 D. Sears   Argo-Toyota

13 Jul: Brands Hatch

1 K. Acheson   March-Toyota
  164.36 kph / 102.15 mph
2 S. Johansson   March-Toyota
3 B. Riley   March-
                   Alfa Romeo

19 Jul: Oulton Park

1 R. Guerrero   Argo-Toyota
  160.47 kph / 99.73 mph
2 S. Johansson   March-Toyota
3 R. Wilson   Ralt-Toyota

25 Aug: Silverstone

1 T. Tassin   Argo-Toyota
  169.27 kph / 105.20 mph
2 K. Acheson   March-Toyota
3 D. Albertin   Ralt-Toyota

7 Sep: Silverstone

1 M. White   March-Toyota
  192.69 kph / 119.76 mph
2 R. Wilson   Ralt-Toyota
3 M. Alboreto   March-
                   Alfa Romeo

28 Sep: Mallory Park

1 S. Johansson   Ralt-Toyota
  178.47 kph / 110.92 mph
2 M. White   March-Toyota
3 R. Guerrero   Argo-Toyota

5 Oct: Silverstone

1 S. Johansson   Ralt-Toyota
  193.71 kph / 120.39 mph
2 R. Wilson   Ralt-Toyota
3 K. Acheson   March-Toyota

18 Oct: Oulton Park

1 S. Johansson   Ralt-Toyota
  163.23 kph / 101.45 mph
2 K. Acheson   March-Toyota
3 R. Wilson   Ralt-Toyota

26 Oct: Thruxton

1 S. Johansson   Ralt-Toyota
  178.45 kph / 110.91 mph
2 R. Guerrero   Argo-Toyota
3 M. White   March-Toyota

Final Championship Standing

1 Stefan
  Johansson Sweden   97 pts
2 Kenneth
  Acheson   Great Britain 95 pts
3 Roberto
  Guerrero   Colombia   95 pts

1981

1 Mar: Silverstone

1 J. Palmer   Ralt-Toyota
  146.89 kph / 91.29 mph
2 M. White   March-
                   Alfa Romeo
3 R. Boesel   Ralt-Toyota

8 Mar: Thruxton

1 J. Palmer   Ralt-Toyota
  177.99 kph / 110.62 mph
2 D. Sears   Ralt-Toyota
3 M. Bleeke-
  molen   Ralt-Toyota

29 Mar: Silverstone

1 J. Palmer   Ralt-Toyota
  170.14 kph / 105.74 mph
2 K. Thiim   March-Toyota
3 R. Boesel   Ralt-Toyota

12 Apr: Mallory Park

1 J. Palmer   Ralt-Toyota
  178.95 kph / 111.22 mph
2 M. White   March-
                   Alfa Romeo
3 R. Boesel   Ralt-Toyota

20 Apr: Thruxton

1 T. Tassin   Ralt-Toyota
  182.67 kph / 113.53 mph
2 D. Leslie   Ralt-Toyota
3 R. Boesel   Ralt-Toyota

4 May: Thruxton

1 M. White   March-
                   Alfa Romeo
  180.56 kph / 112.22 mph
2 T. Tassin   Ralt-Toyota
3 D. Leslie   Ralt-Toyota

10 May: Snetterton

1 J. Weaver   Ralt-Toyota
  175.30 kph / 108.95 mph
2 J. Palmer   Ralt-Toyota
3 T. Tassin   Ralt-Toyota

25 May: Silverstone

1 T. Tassin   Ralt-Toyota
  150.76 kph 93.70 mph
2 R. Boesel   Ralt-Toyota
3 J. Palmer   Ralt-Toyota

14 Jun: Cadwell Park

1 J. Palmer   Ralt-Toyota
  153.00 kph / 95.09 mph
2 T. Tassin   Ralt-Toyota
3 R. Boesel   Ralt-Toyota

21 Jun: Silverstone

1 J. Palmer   Ralt-Toyota
  195.36 kph / 121.42 mph
2 R. Boesel   Ralt-Toyota
3 M. White   March-
                   Alfa Romeo

5 Jul: Silverstone

1 R. Boesel   Ralt-Toyota
  169.44 kph / 105.31 mph
2 J. Palmer   Ralt-Toyota
3 T. Tassin   Ralt-VW

12 Jul: Brands Hatch

1 T. Tassin   Ralt-Toyota
  155.43 kph / 96.60 mph
2 J. Palmer   Ralt-Toyota
3 D. Scott   Ralt-Toyota

18 Jul: Silverstone

1 T. Tassin   Ralt-Toyota
  195.72 kph / 121.64 mph
2 R. Boesel   Ralt-Toyota
3 J. Palmer   Ralt-Toyota

2 Aug: Mallory Park

1 R. Moreno   Ralt-Toyota
  179.26 kph / 111.41 mph
2 R. Boesel   Ralt-Toyota
3 M. White   March-
                   Alfa Romeo

15 Aug: Oulton Park

1 R. Boesel   Ralt-Toyota
  146.44 kph / 91.01 mph
2 J. Palmer   Ralt-Toyota
3 S. Sasaki   Ralt-Toyota

31 Aug: Silverstone

1 D. Scott   Ralt-Toyota
   170.67 kph / 106.07 mph
2 T. Tassin   Ralt-Toyota
3 J. Palmer   Ralt-Toyota

27 Sep: Oulton Park

1 J. Palmer   Ralt-Toyota
   138.07 kph / 85.81 mph
2 T. Tassin   Ralt-Toyota
3 R. Moreno   Ralt-Toyota

4 Oct: Silverstone

1 R. Boesel   Ralt-Toyota
   196.04 kph / 121.84 mph
2 J. Palmer   Ralt-Toyota
3 D. Scott   Ralt-Toyota

11 Oct: Snetterton

1 J. Palmer   Ralt-Toyota
   174.45 kph / 108.42 mph
2 R. Moreno   Ralt-Toyota
3 F. Krab   Ralt-Toyota

25 Oct: Thruxton

1 T. Tassin   Ralt-Toyota
   165.60 kph / 102.92 mph
2 B. Tragardh   Ralt-Toyota
3 D. Scott   Ralt-Toyota

Final Championship Standing

1 Jonathan Palmer   Great Britain   126 pts
2 Thierry Tassin   Belgium   91 pts
3 Raul Boesel   Brazil   80 pts

1982

7 Mar: Silverstone

1 T. Byrne   Ralt-Toyota
   171.34 kph / 106.49 mph
2 M. Brundle   Ralt-VW
3 D. Scott   Ralt-Toyota

14 Mar: Thruxton

1 T. Byrne   Ralt-Toyota
   181.30 kph / 112.68 mph
2 J. Weaver   Ralt-Toyota
3 E. Mansilla   Ralt-Toyota

21 Mar: Silverstone

1 D. Scott   Ralt-Toyota
   178.87 kph / 111.17 mph
2 J. Weaver   Ralt-Toyota
3 M. Brundle   Ralt-VW

12 Apr: Thruxton

1 T. Byrne   Ralt-Toyota
   181.87 kph / 113.03 mph
2 L. Schaffer   Ralt-Toyota
3 D. Scott   Ralt-Toyota

25 Apr: Mallory Park

1 T. Byrne   Ralt-Toyota
   179.63 kph / 111.64 mph
2 J. Weaver   Ralt-Toyota
3 E. Mansilla   Ralt-Toyota

2 May: Snetterton

1 T. Byrne   Ralt-Toyota
   177.41 kph / 110.26 mph
2 E. Mansilla   Ralt-Toyota
3 R. Moreno   Ralt-Toyota

31 May: Silverstone

1 R. Moreno   Ralt-Toyota
   169.89 kph / 105.59 mph
2 J. Weaver   Ralt-Toyota
3 D. Scott   Ralt-Toyota

13 Jun: Silverstone

1 E. Mansilla   Ralt-Toyota
   195.88 kph / 121.74 mph
2 R. Moreno   Ralt-Toyota
3 J-C. Abella   Ralt-VW

20 Jun: Cadwell Park

1 R. Moreno   Ralt-Alfa Romeo
   154.25 kph / 95.87 mph
2 E. Mansilla   Ralt-Toyota
3 J. Weaver   Ralt-Toyota

27 Jun: Silverstone

1 R. Morena   Ralt-Alfa Romeo
   170.01 kph / 105.66 mph
2 E. Mansilla   Ralt-Toyota
3 M. Brundle   Ralt-VW

18 Jul: Brands Hatch

1 T. Byrne   Ralt-Toyota
   175.70 kph / 109.20 mph
2 J. Weaver   Ralt-Toyota
3 R. Moreno   Ralt-Alfa Romeo

1 Aug: Mallory Park

1 E. Mansilla   Ralt-Toyota
   179.97 kph / 111.85 mph
2 D. Scott   Ralt-VW
3 T. Byrne   Ralt-Toyota

7 Aug: Oulton Park

1 E. Mansilla   Ralt-Toyota
   165.08 kph / 102.60 mph
2 D. Scott   Ralt-VW
3 M. White   Ralt-Toyota

15 Aug: Brands Hatch

1 D. Scott   Ralt-VW
   157.09 kph / 97.63 mph
2 M. Brundle   Ralt-VW
3 R. Trott   Ralt-Toyota

30 Aug: Silverstone

1 E. Mansilla   Ralt-Toyota
   152.10 kph / 94.53 mph
2 D. Sears   Ralt-Toyota
3 D. Scott   Ralt-VW

12 Sep: Snetterton

1 E. Mansilla   Ralt-Toyota
   175.83 kph / 109.28 mph
2 T. Byrne   Ralt-Toyota
3 D. Scott   Ralt-VW

26 Sep: Oulton Park

1 M. Brundle   Ralt-VW
   164.75 kph / 102.39 mph
2 D. Scott   Ralt-VW
3 E. Mansilla   Ralt-Toyota

13 Oct: Silverstone

1 T. Byrne   Ralt-Toyota
   194.35 kph / 120.79 mph
2 D. Scott   Ralt-VW
3 E. Mansilla   Ralt-Toyota

10 Oct: Brands Hatch

1 D. Scott   Ralt-VW
   156.80 kph / 97.45 mph
2 M. Brundle   Ralt-VW
3 E. Mansilla   Ralt-Toyota

24 Oct: Thruxton

1 M. Brundle   Ralt-VW
   169.65 kph / 105.44 mph
2 T. Byrne   Ralt-Toyota
3 E. Mansilla   Ralt-Toyota

Final Championship Standing

1 Tommy Byrne   Ireland   101 pts
2 Enrique Mansilla   Argentina   98 pts
3 Dave Scott   Great Britain   74 pts

1983

6 Mar: Silverstone

1 A. Senna   Ralt-Toyota
   171.39 kph / 106.50 mph
2 M. Brundle   Ralt-Toyota
3 D. Jones   Ralt-VW

13 Mar: Thruxton

1 A. Senna   Ralt-Toyota
   171.02 kph / 106.27 mph
2 M. Brundle   Ralt-Toyota
3 M. Hytten   Ralt-Toyota

20 Mar: Silverstone

1 A. Senna   Ralt-Toyota
   173.26 kph / 107.66 mph
2 M. Brundle   Ralt-Toyota
3 C. Fish   Ralt-VW

27 Mar: Donington

1 A. Senna   Ralt-Toyota
   161.61 kph / 100.42 mph
2 M. Brundle   Ralt-Toyota
3 D. Jones   Ralt-VW

4 Apr: Thruxton

1 A. Senna   Ralt-Toyota
   181.60 kph / 112.85 mph
2 M. Brundle   Ralt-Toyota
3 C. Fish   Ralt-VW

24 Apr: Silverstone

1 A. Senna   Ralt-Toyota
   172.07 kph / 106.92 mph
2 D. Jones   Ralt-VW
3 M. Brundle   Ralt-Toyota

2 May: Thruxton

1 A. Senna   Ralt-Toyota
  182.98 kph / 113.70 mph
2 M. Brundle   Ralt-Toyota
3 D. Jones   Ralt-VW

8 May: Brands Hatch

1 A. Senna   Ralt-Toyota
  133.90 kph / 83.21 mph
2 M. Brundle   Ralt-Toyota
3 D. Jones   Ralt-VW

30 May: Silverstone

1 A. Senna   Ralt-Toyota
  172.42 kph / 107.14 mph
2 M. Brundle   Ralt-Toyota
3 A. Berg   Ralt-Toyota

11 Jun: Silverstone

1 A. Berg   Ralt-Toyota
  191.94 kph / 119.29 mph
2 D. Jones   Ralt-VW
3 C. Fish   Ralt-VW

19 Jun: Cadwell Park

1 M. Brundle   Ralt-Toyota
  153.95 kph / 95.48 mph
2 C. Fish   Ralt-VW
3 D. Jones   Ralt-VW

3 Jul: Snetterton

1 M. Brundle   Ralt-Toyota
  177.17 kph / 110.09 mph
2 D. Jones   Ralt-VW
3 C. Fish   Ralt-VW

16 Jul: Silverstone

1 A. Senna   Ralt-Toyota
  195.31 kph / 121.37 mph
2 M. Brundle   Ralt-Toyota
3 C. Fish   Ralt-VW

24 Jul: Donington

1 M. Brundle   Ralt-Toyota
  161.29 kph / 100.23 mph
2 A. Senna   Ralt-Toyota
3 D. Jones   Ralt-VW

6 Aug: Oulton Park

1 C. Fish   Ralt-VW
  163.04 kph / 101.31 mph
2 D. Jones   Ralt-VW
3 A. Berg   Ralt-Toyota

29 Aug: Silverstone

1 A. Senna   Ralt-Toyota
  172.26 kph / 107.04 mph
2 M. Brundle   Ralt-Toyota
3 D. Jones   Ralt-VW

11 Sep: Oulton Park

1 M. Brundle   Ralt-Toyota
  162.66 kph / 101.08 mph
2 C. Fish   Ralt-VW
3 D. Leslie   Magnum-Toyota

18 Sep: Thruxton

1 M. Brundle   Ralt-Toyota
  180.58 kph / 112.21 mph
2 D. Jones   Ralt-VW
3 C. Fish   Ralt-VW

2 Oct: Silverstone

1 M. Brundle   Ralt-Toyota
  195.78 kph / 121.66 mph
2 A. Senna   Ralt-Toyota
3 D. Jones   Ralt-VW

23 Oct: Thruxton

1 A. Senna   Ralt-Toyota
  182.84 kph / 113.62 mph
2 D. Jones   Ralt-VW
3 M. Brundle   Ralt-Toyota

Final Championship Standing

1 Ayrton
  Senna   Brazil   132 pts
2 Martin
  Brundle   Great Britain   123 pts
3 Davy Jones   United States   77 pts

1984

4 Mar: Silverstone

1 J. Dumfries   Ralt-VW
  156.17 kph / 97.06 mph
2 A. Berg   Ralt-Toyota
3 R. Spence   Ralt-VW

11 Mar: Thruxton

1 J. Dumfries   Ralt-VW
  182.83 kph / 113.63 mph
2 A. Berg   Ralt-Toyota
3 A. Gilbert-Scott Ralt-VW

1 Apr: Silverstone

1 J. Dumfries   Ralt-VW
  191.52 kph / 119.03 mph
2 R. Spence   Ralt-VW
3 C. Abella   Ralt-Toyota

15 Apr: Zolder (Belgium)

1 R. Spence   Ralt-VW
  163.91 kph / 101.87 mph
2 J. Dumfries   Ralt-VW
3 A. Berg   Ralt-Toyota

23 Apr: Thruxton

1 J. Dumfries   Ralt-VW
  182.24 kph / 113.26 mph
2 M. Hytten   Ralt-VW
3 A. Gilbert-Scott Ralt-VW

7 May: Thruxton

1 J. Dumfries   Ralt-VW
  183.22 kph / 113.87 mph
2 M. Hytten   Ralt-VW
3 C. Abella   Ralt-Toyota

20 May: Donington

1 J. Dumfries   Ralt-VW
  160.42 kph / 99.70 mph
2 A. Berg   Ralt-Toyota
3 R. Spence   Ralt-VW

28 May: Silverstone

1 M. Hytten   Ralt-VW
  158.82 kph / 98.71 mph
2 T. Trevor   Ralt-VW
3 A. Berg   Ralt-Toyota

1 Jul: Snetterton

1 J. Dumfries   Ralt-VW
  177.54 kph / 110.34 mph
2 C. Abella   Ralt-Toyota
3 M. Hytten   Ralt-VW

8 Jul: Donington

1 R. Spence   Ralt-VW
  —
2 A. Berg   Ralt-Toyota
3 G. Evans   Ralt-Toyota

18 Aug: Oulton Park

1 R. Spence   Ralt-VW
  174.96 kph / 108.74 mph
2 D. Scott   Ralt-VW
3 C. Abella   Ralt-Toyota

27 Aug: Silverstone

1 J. Dumfries   Ralt-VW
  170.18 kph / 105.77 mph
2 A. Berg   Ralt-Toyota
3 M. Hytten   Ralt-VW

1 Sep: Spa (Belgium)

1 R. Cheever   Ralt-VW
  169.73 kph / 105.49 mph
2 A. Berg   Ralt-Toyota
3 D. Coyne   Ralt-VW

16 Sep: Zandvoort (Holland)

1 R. Cheever   Ralt-VW
  161.99 kph / 100.68 mph
2 R. Spence   Ralt-VW
3 A. Berg   Ralt-Toyota

23 Sep: Brands Hatch

1 R. Cheever   Ralt-VW
  176.73 kph / 109.84 mph
2 A. Berg   Ralt-Toyota
3 D. Scott   Ralt-VW

30 Sep: Thruxton

1 J. Dumfries   Ralt-VW
  —
2 R. Cheever   Ralt-VW
3 M. Hytten   Ralt-VW

7 Oct: Silverstone

1 J. Dumfries   Ralt-VW
  197.84 kph / 122.96 mph
2 A. Berg   Ralt-Toyota
3 A. Gilbert-Scott Ralt-VW

Final Championship Standing

1 Johnny
  Dumfries   Great Britain   106 pts
2 Allen Berg   Canada   67 pts
3 Russell
  Spence   Great Britain   64 pts

Niki Lauda

Niki Lauda displayed courage beyond all recognition in 1976 when, six weeks after being given the Last Rites, he was back behind the wheel of his Ferrari picking up points in the Italian Grand Prix at Monza. That was after his horrific accident at the Nurburgring on 1 August, when he was well clear in the World Championship and on his way to his second successive title. However, disaster struck at the German circuit and Lauda was pulled from his blazing car with multiple burns. He was scarred for life, but the accident had done nothing to dampen his competitive nature and just six weeks later he was finishing fourth at Monza. The accident had allowed Britain's James Hunt to close the gap in the championship, which he went on to win by just one point form Lauda.

Niklaus Andreas Lauda was born the son of a Viennese paper mill owner on 22 February 1949. He started racing in his home country in 1968 in a Mini Cooper. Three years later he had his first Formula One drive in a March 711 at at the Austrian Grand Prix, just six years after watching his first Grand Prix.

He was the John Player Formula Two champion in 1972 and then joined the BRM Formula One team the following season as the number three driver to Jean-Pierre Beltoise (Fra) and Clay Regazzoni (Swi). Despite having an unsuitable car at BRM, Lauda gave some superb performances which attracted the eye of Enzo Ferrari. It was after his move to the Italian manufacturer in 1974

that he enjoyed his first Grand Prix victory, at Jarama, in the Ferrari 312.

Lauda and Ferrari were supreme in 1975 and Lauda's five wins, including three in succession, were enough to take him on to his first world title, a title he would surely have retained had it not been for his accident at the Nurburgring. But his second title in three years came in 1977 when, after an intensely close battle in the first half of the season with South African Jody Scheckter and American Mario Andretti, Lauda pulled clear to win the title with 17 points to spare.

After a move to Brabham in 1978, Lauda made the shock announcement during practice for the following year's Canadian Grand Prix that he was retiring to concentrate on building up Lauda-Air, his own airline company. The retirement lasted two years, until McLaren tempted him back into the sport in 1982 and his old skills were soon apparent at Brands Hatch and Watkins Glen, where he returned to winning ways. He gradually built

A picture of Niki Lauda before his horrific accident at the Nurburgring in 1976, which scarred him for life

himself up to a third championship in 1984, when he emerged champion by just half a point from his McLaren team-mate Alain Prost in one of the sport's closest battles.

A second retirement followed in 1985 and it looks as though Lauda is going to stick to his word this time. If he does make another comeback though, it would not be surprising if he wins a fourth title because, if he can get back behind the wheel six weeks after being so close to death, there is no knowing what the courageous Austrian can do.

Niki Lauda has every reason to look elated as he celebrates his first win since his comeback, at Long Beach in 1982. (McLaren International)

Alain Prost

After finishing second in the World Championship in 1983 and 1984, Alain Prost lost the 'nearly man' tag in 1985 as he became the first Frenchman to win the title.

The likeable Frenchman, born in St. Chamond in 1955, could just as easily have established himself as a professional soccer player. However, he first gained recognition behind the wheel of a car in his native country in 1976, when he swept the board in the Formula Renault Championship, winning 12 of the 13 rounds. He won the European Formula Renault Championship the following year and then switched to Formula Three in 1978.

After lifting the European Formula Three crown in 1979, he was offered a position alongside John Watson in the McLaren For-

mula One team for 1980 and he picked up a point on his debut in the Argentine Grand Prix.

Prost joined the Renault team in 1981 as a replacement for Jean-Pierre Jabouille and had his first success in the rain-interrupted French Grand Prix at Dijon. He had two other wins that year, at Zandvoort and Monza, but his car let him down on other occasions when his excellent driving had put him in a race-winning situation.

Still with Renault in 1982 he won the opening two rounds in Argentina and Brazil, after the disqualification of Piquet and Rosberg, but, sadly, they turned out to be his only successes. However, it looked as though the talents of Prost were to be rewarded in 1983 when he went into the final race of the season at

Kyalami with four wins to his credit and a two-point lead over Nelson Piquet. Prost went out of the race on lap 36 and had to watch agonizingly as Piquet finished third to overhaul him and take the title by two points.

Prost lost the championship by an even smaller margin the following year when Niki Lauda, his new team-mate at McLaren, pipped him by a mere half a point despite the Frenchman winning seven rounds. But it all came good for Prost in 1985 when he won five championship races to win the title comfortably from Michele Alboreto (Ita).

Just as it looked as though he was going to be 'bridesmaid' again in 1986, he emerged from a tense season as champion for a third time, but it was not resolved until the very last race of the season once more.

The final round of the championship was the Australian Grand Prix at Adelaide and Prost won the race from Nelson Piquet (Bra) after the championship leader, Nigel Mansell (GB), spectacularly went out of the race on lap 63. Prost did to Mansell what Piquet had done to him in 1983, and in winning the title he became the first man since Jack Brabham (Aus) in 1960 to defend the title successfully and one of only four men to win it in successive years, joining two other greats, Alberto Ascari (Ita) and Juan Manuel Fangio (Arg).

Frenchman Alain Prost has not only rubbed noses with a bottle of champagne, but also with success which has made him a dual world champion. (Michelin Tyre Co. Ltd.)

Indianapolis 500

The Indianapolis 500 is the culmination of a day-long carnival at the Indianapolis Raceway, Indiana as part of the Memorial Day celebrations at the end of May each year. Crowds in excess of a quarter of a million flock to the raceway from all parts of America to share in the atmosphere.

The first 500-mile race over 200 laps of the 2.5-mile oval-shaped raceway was on 30 May 1911 and won by Ray Harroun in a Marmon Wasp.

Between 1950–60 the race was included in the World Drivers' Championship, and full results for those years can be found in the Grand Prix section, pages 12–25.

Results

1911

1 R. Harroun/
    C. Patschke   Marmon
    120.02 kph / 74.59 mph
2 R. Mulford   Lozier
3 D. Bruce-Brown Fiat

1912

1 J. Dawson/
    D. Herr   National
    126.66 kph / 78.72 mph
2 E. Teztlaff/
    C. Bragg   Fiat
3 H. Hughes   Mercer

1913

1 J. Goux   Peugeot
    122.17 kph / 75.93 mph
2 S. Wishart/
    R. de Palma   Mercer
3 C. Merz/
    E. Cooper   Stutz

1914

1 R. Thomas   Delage
    132.69 kph / 82.47 mph
2 A. Duray   Peugeot
3 A. Guyot   Delage

1915

1 R. de Palma   Mercedes
    144.55 kph / 89.84 mph
2 D. Resta   Peugeot
3 G. Anderson   Stutz

1916

1 D. Resta   Peugeot
    135.16 kph / 84.00 mph
2 W. d'Alene   Duesenberg
3 R. Mulford   Peugeot

1917

Not held

1918

Not held

1919

1 H. Wilcox   Peugeot
    141.67 kph / 88.05 mph
2 E. Hearne   Durant-Stutz
3 J. Goux   Peugeot

1920

1 G. Chevrolet   Monroe-
              Frontenac
    142.59 kph / 88.62 mph
2 R. Thomas   Ballot
3 T. Milton   Duesenberg

An aerial view of the famous Indianapolis Motor Speedway, but taken long before the development of raceway. (National Motor Museum)

Action from the third Indianapolis race, in 1913. The race was won by J. Goux in a Peugeot. This picture shows Mason, who finished ninth at an average speed of 63.47 kph (39.44 mph). (National Motor Museum)

1921

1 T. Milton   Frontenac
  144.20 kph / 89.62 mph
2 R. Sarles   Duesenberg
3 P. Ford/
  J. Ellingboe   Frontenac

1922

1 J. Murphy   Duesenberg-
                   Miller
  152.02 kph / 94.48 mph
2 H. C. Hartz   Duesenberg
3 E. Hearne   Ballot

1923

1 T. Milton/
  H. Wilcox   Miller
  146.34 kph / 90.95 mph
2 H. C. Hartz   Miller
3 J. Murphy   Miller

1924

1 L. Corum/
  J. Boyer   Duesenberg
  158.05 kph / 98.23 mph
2 E. Cooper   Studebaker-
                   Miller
3 J. Murphy   Miller

1925

1 P. De Paolo/
  N. K. Batten   Duesenberg
  162.72 kph / 101.13 mph
2 D. N. Lewis/
  B. Hill   Miller
3 P. Shafer/
  W. Morton   Duesenberg

1926

1 F. Lockhart   Miller
  154.32 kph / 95.91 mph
2 H. C. Hartz   Miller
3 C. Woodbury   Miller

1927

1 G. Souders   Duesenberg
  156.95 kph / 97.54 mph
2 E. Devore/
  Z. Myers   Miller
3 A. Gulotta/
  P. de Paolo   Miller

1928

1 L. Meyer   Miller
  160.06 kph / 99.48 mph
2 L. Moore/
  L. Schneider   Miller
3 G. Souders   Miller

1929

1 R. Keech   Miller
  157.01 kph / 97.59 mph
2 L. Meyer   Miller
3 J. Gleason/
  E. Triplett   Duesenberg

1930

1 W. Arnold   Miller
  161.62 kph / 100.45 mph
2 W. Cantlon   Miller
3 L. Schneider   Miller

1931

1 L. Schneider   Miller
  155.48 kph / 96.63 mph
2 F. Frame   Duesenberg
3 R. Hepburn/
  P. Kreis   Miller

1932

1 F. Frame   Miller
  167.56 kph / 104.14 mph
2 W. Wilcox   Miller
3 C. Bergere   Studebaker

1933

1 L. Meyer   Miller
  167.59 kph / 104.16 mph
2 W. Shaw   Miller
3 L. Moore   Miller

1934

1 B. Cummings   Miller
  168.43 kph / 104.86 mph
2 M. Rose   Miller
3 L. Moore   Miller

1935

1 K. Petillo   Miller
  170.94 kph / 106.24 mph
2 W. Shaw   Miller
3 B. Cummings   Miller

1936

1 L. Meyer   Miller
  175.49 kph / 109.07 mph
2 T. Horn   Miller
3 D. Mackenzie/
  K. Petillo   Miller

1937

1 W. Shaw   Gilmore-
                   Offenhauser
  182.75 kph / 113.58 mph
2 R. Hepburn   Miller
3 T. Horn   Miller

1938

1 F. Roberts   Miller
  188.57 kph / 117.20 mph
2 W. Shaw   Offenhauser
3 C. Miller   Offenhauser

1939

1 W. Shaw   Maserati
  185.07 kph / 115.04 mph
2 J. Snyder   Thorne-Sparks
3 C. Bergere   Offenhauser

1940

1 W. Shaw   Maserati
  183.86 kph / 114.82 mph
2 R. Mays   Bowes Seal Fast
3 M. Rose   Miller

1941

1 F. Davis/
  M. Rose   Noc-Out Hose
                   Clamp
  185.23 kph / 115.12 mph
2 R. Mays   Bowes Seal Fast
3 T. Horn   Thorne-Sparks

1942–45

Not held

1946

1 G. Robson   Thorne-Sparks
  184.75 kph / 114.82 mph
2 J. Jackson   Offenhauser
3 T. Horn   Maserati

1947

1 M. Rose   Blue Crown
  187.19 kph / 116.34 mph
2 W. Holland   Blue Crown
3 T. Horn   Maserati

1948

1 M. Rose   Blue Crown
  192.77 kph / 119.81 mph
2 W. Holland   Blue Crown
3 D. Nalon   Novi

1949

1 W. Holland   Blue Crown
  195.22 kph / 121.33 mph
2 J. Parsons   Kurtis-Kraft
3 G. Connor   Blue Crown

1950

1 J. Parsons   Wynn's Friction
                     Proof
  199.52 kph / 124.00 mph
2 W. Holland   Blue Crown
3 M. Rose   Howard Keck

1951

1 L. Wallard   Belanger
  203.12 kph / 126.24 mph
2 M. Nazaruk   Robbins
3 J. McGrath/
  M. Ayulo   Hinkle

1952

1 T. Ruttman   Agajanian
  207.43 kph / 128.92 mph
2 J. Rathmann   Grancor-Wynn
3 S. Hanks   Bardahl

1953

1 W. Vukovich   Fuel Injection
  207.14 kph / 128.74 mph
2 A. Cross   Springfield
                     Welding
3 S. Hanks/
  D. Carter   Bardahl

1954

1 W. Vukovich   Fuel Injection
  210.52 kph / 130.84 mph
2 J. Bryan   Dean Van Lines
3 J. McGrath   Hinkle

1955

1 B. Sweikert   John Zink
  206.29 kph / 128.21 mph
2 T. Bettenhausen/
  P. Russo   Chapman
3 J. Davies   Bardahl

1956

1 P. Flaherty   John Zink
  206.74 kph / 128.49 mph
2 S. Hanks   Jones & Maley
3 D. Freeland   Bob Estes

1957

1 S. Hanks   Belond Exhaust
  218.18 kph / 135.60 mph
2 J. Rathmann   Chiropractic
3 J. Bryan   Dean Van Lines

1958

1 J. Bryan   Belond Exhaust
  215.27 kph / 133.79 mph
2 G. Amick   Demler
3 J. Boyd   Bowes Seal Fast

1959

1 R. Ward   Leader Card
  218.60 kph / 135.86 mph
2 J. Rathmann   Simoniz
3 J. Thomson   Racing Associates

1960

1 J. Rathmann   Ken Paul
  223.28 kph / 138.77 mph
2 R. Ward   Leader Card
3 P. Goldsmith   Demler

1961

1 A. J. Foyt   Bowes Seal Fast
  223.86 kph / 139.13 mph
2 E. Sachs   Dean Van Lines
3 R. Ward   Del Webb Sun City

1962

1 R. Ward   Leader Card
  225.73 kph / 140.29 mph
2 L. Sutton   Leader Card
3 E. Sachs   Dean Autolite

1963

1 A. P. Jones   Agajanian
  230.31 kph / 143.14 mph
2 J. Clark   Lotus
3 A. J. Foyt   Thompson

By the mid-1920s the cars had started getting bigger as this Barber-Warnock-Ford Special shows. (National Motor Museum)

1964

1 A. J. Foyt   Sheraton
237.09 kph / 147.35 mph
2 R. Ward   Kaiser
3 L. Ruby   Forbes

1965

1 J. Clark   Lotus
242.46 kph / 150.69 mph
2 A. P. Jones   Lotus
3 M. Andretti   Brawner

1966

1 G. Hill   Lola
232.24 kph / 144.33 mph
2 J. Clark   Lotus
3 J. McElreath   Brabham

1967

1 A. J. Foyt   Coyote
243.30 kph / 151.21 mph
2 A. Unser   Lola
3 J. Leonard   Coyote

1968

1 R. Unser   Rislone
245.98 kph / 152.88 mph
2 D. Gurney   Eagle
3 M. Kenyon   Gerhardt

1969

1 M. Andretti   Hawk
252.40 kph / 156.86 mph
2 D. Gurney   Eagle
3 R. Unser   Lola

1970

1 A. Unser   Johnny Lightning
250.60 kph / 155.70 mph
2 M. Donohue   Lola
3 D. Gurney   Eagle

1971

1 A. Unser   Colt
253.79 kph / 157.73 mph
2 P. Revson   McLaren
3 A. J. Foyt   Coyote

1972

1 M. Donohue   McLaren
262.20 kph / 162.96 mph
2 A. Unser   Parnelli
3 J. Leonard   Parnelli

1973

1 G. Johncock   Eagle
255.90 kph / 159.04 mph
2 W. Vukovich   Eagle
3 R. McCluskey   McLaren

1974

1 J. Rutherford   McLaren
255.17 kph / 158.59 mph
2 B. Unser   Eagle
3 W. Vukovich   Eagle

1975

1 R. Unser   Eagle
240.08 kph / 149.21 mph
2 J. Rutherford   McLaren
3 A. J. Foyt   Coyote

1976

1 J. Rutherford   McLaren
238.28 kph / 148.73 mph
2 A. J. Foyt   Coyote
3 G. Johncock   Wildcat

1977

1 A. J. Foyt   Coyote
259.58 kph / 161.33 mph
2 T. Sneva   McLaren
3 A. Unser   Parnelli

1978

1 A. Unser   Lola
259.63 kph / 161.36 mph
2 T. Sneva   Penske
3 G. Johncock   Wildcat

1979

1 R. Mears   Penske
255.64 kph / 158.90 mph
2 A. J. Foyt   Parnelli
3 M. Moseley   Eagle

1980

1 J. Rutherford   Chaparral
229.86 kph / 142.86 mph
2 T. Sneva   McLaren
3 G. Betten-
  hausen   Wildcat

Mario Andretti, the 1969 winner, behind the wheel of his STP Oil Treatment Special (Hawk). Andretti won the race from his fellow Formula One colleague, Dan Gurney (National Motor Museum)

1981

1 R. Unser   Penske
   222.78 kph / 139.08 mph
2 M. Andretti   Wildcat
3 V. Schuppan   McLaren

1982

1 G. Johncock   Wildcat
   260.69 kph / 162.02 mph
2 R. Mears   Penske
3 P. Carter   March

1983

1 T. Sneva   March
   260.83 kph / 162.11 mph
2 A. Unser   Penske
3 R. Mears   Penske

1984

1 R. Mears   March
   263.25 kph / 163.61 mph
2 R. Guerrero   March
3 A. Unser   March

1985

1 D. Sullivan   March
   246.14 kph / 152.98 mph
2 M. Andretti   Lola
3 R. Guerrero   March

1986

1 B. Rahal   March
   274.69 kph / 170.72 mph
2 K. Cogan   March
3 R. Mears   March

Drivers' Records

Most Wins

4 A. J. Foyt (1961, 1964, 1967, 1977)
3 Louis Meyer (1928, 1933, 1936)
3 Mauri Rose (1941, 1947, 1948)
3 Bobby Unser (1968, 1975, 1981)
3 Al Unser (1970, 1971, 1978)
3 Johnny Rutherford (1974, 1976, 1980)

Consecutive Wins

Wilbur Shaw (1939–40)
Mauri Rose (1947–48)
Bill Vukovich (1953–54)
Al Unser (1970–71)

Fastest Winning Speeds

274.69 kph / 170.72 mph
   Bobby Rahal (March) 1986
263.25 kph / 163.61 mph
   Rick Mears (March) 1984
262.20 kph / 162.96 mph
   Mark Donohue (McLaren) 1972

First winner at an average speed of 100 mph

Peter de Paolo (Duesenberg) 1925
   (101.13 mph / 162.72 kph)

● In the 1950s the name of 'B. Bira' regularly figured among the list of Grand Prix drivers. 'B. Bira' was the pseudonym of Prince Birabongse Bhanuban of Siam (now Thailand). He retired after winning the 1955 New Zealand Grand Prix. A skilled pilot, he spent his latter years yacht racing in the Mediterranean. 'Bira' died in the winter of 1985, aged 71.

(National Motor Museum)

Miscellaneous

The Early Years

The Americans and French both lay claim to staging the first automobile race.

An Oshkosh steamer won a 323 km (201 miles) race from Green Bay to Madison, Wisconsin in 1878 but the French claim the first real race for automobiles was the 31 km (19.3 miles) race from Saint-James, Paris, along the Seine, to Neuilly in 1887. The race was organized by M. Fossier, editor of the French cycling magazine *La Velocipède* and won by Count Jules Felix Philippe Albert de Dion de Malfiance in his De Dion quadricycle.

That latter race was to be the forerunner of the great Paris races that started seven years later when continental manufacturers would use the races to show off their vehicles. The French capital was used as the starting point for all the races and the first, from Paris to Rouen, was organized by the Paris newspaper *Le Petit Journal* in 1894 with a £200 prize on offer.

The last Paris race was scheduled to go to Madrid but, by order of the government, it was halted at Bordeaux because of the high number of accidents involving pedestrians. Racing on open roads was subsequently banned and the great Paris races came to an end.

The following are the results of some of the major 'Paris Races' between 1894–1903.

1894 Paris–Rouen (127 km/79 miles)

			Average speed
1	Comte de Dion	De Dion	18.66 kph/11.60 mph
2	G. Lemaitre	Peugeot	
3	Doriot	Peugeot	

1895 Paris–Bordeaux–Paris (1178 km/732 miles)

1	E. Levasser	Panhard	24.54 kph/15.25 mph
2	Rigoulot	Peugeot	
3	Koechlin	Peugeot	

1896 Paris–Marseilles–Paris (1710 km/1063 miles)

1	Mayade	Panhard	25.26 kph/15.70 mph
2	Merkel	Panhard	
3	d'Hostingue	Panhard	

1898 Paris–Amsterdam–Paris (1430 km/889 miles)

over 400 kg class

1	F. Charron	Panhard	43.28 kph/26.90 mph
2	L. Girardot	Panhard	
3	E. Giraud	Bollee	

200–400 kg class

1	Corbiere	Decauville	26.87 kph/16.70 mph
2	L. Bollee	Leon Bollee	
3	Wilfred	Leon Bollee	

1899 Tour de France (2172 km/1350 miles)

over 400 kg class

1	R. de Knyff	Panhard	48.59 kph/30.20 mph
2	L. Girardot	Panhard	
3	Comte de Chasseloup-Laubat	Panhard	

200–400 kg class

1	F. Gabriel	Decauville	32.50 kph/20.20 mph
2	L. Thery	Decauville	
3	Aubin	Decauville	

1900 Paris–Toulouse–Paris (1347 km/837 miles)

over 400 kg class

1	'Levegh'	Mors	64.68 kph/40.20 mph
2	Pinson	Panhard	
3	Voigt	Panhard	

200–400 kg class

1	M. & L. Renault	Renault	30.25 kph/18.80 mph
2	Schrader	Renault-Aster	
3	Grus	Renault	

1901 Paris–Berlin (1105 km/687 miles)

over 650 kg class

1	H. Fournier	Mors	70.96 kph/44.10 mph
2	L. Girardot	Panhard	
3	R. de Knyff	Panhard	

650 kg class

1	E. Giraud	Panhard	57.12 kph/35.50 mph
2	G. Berteaux	Panhard	
3	Teste	Panhard	

400 kg class

1	L. Renault	Renault	59.37 kph/36.90 mph
2	Grus	Renault	
3	Morin	Corre	

1902 Paris–Vienna (990 km/615 miles)

1000 kg class

1	H. Farman	Panhard	61.79 kph/38.40 mph
2	Count Zborowski	Mercedes	
3	M. Farman	Panhard	

650 kg class

1 M. Renault	Renault	62.59 kph / 38.90 mph
2 Edmond	Darracq	
3 P. Baras	Darracq	

400 kg class

1 Guilleaume	Darracq	49.24 kph / 30.60 mph
2 Grus	Renault	
3 Cormier	Renault	

1903 Paris–Madrid (1014 km / 630 miles)

(race stopped at Bordeaux after 550 km / 342 miles)

1000 kg class

1 F. Gabriel	Mors	65.30 kph / 40.58 mph
2 Salleron	Mors	
3 C. Jarrott	de Dietrich	

650 kg class

1 L. Renault	Renault	62.30 kph / 38.71 mph
2 P. Baras	Darracq	
3 Page	Decauville	

400 kg class

1 Masson	Clement	47.20 kph / 29.33 mph
2 Barillier	Richard-Brasier	
3 L. Wagner	Darracq	

One of the greats of the early days of motor racing, Frenchman Leon Thery, who won the Gordon Bennett Cup in 1904 and 1905 — the last time it was contested. (National Motor Museum)

A cartoonist's impression of the 1898 Paris-Amsterdam race in which he depicts the eventual winner Charron in his Panhard. (National Motor Museum)

The giant engine of the De Dion that was seen in the first French Grand Prix at Le Mans in 1906. (National Motor Museum)

● The world's first 24-Hour Endurance race was the Endurance Derby at Point Breeze, Philadelphia, United States in May 1907. Messrs. Brown and Moyes won the race and covered 1273 km (791 miles) at an average speed of 53 kph (33 mph).

Gordon Bennett Races

After spending two years in Paris trying to establish a French edition of his newspaper, *New York Herald* owner James Gordon Bennett, as a result of watching the increasing popularity of motor racing, put up a magnificent trophy to be contested annually by national 'teams' in an effort to help promote the motor industry. The trophy became known as the Gordon Bennett Cup, although he preferred to call it the Coupe Internationale. The first race was from Paris to Lyons in 1900 and it remained an open road race until 1903 when it was held over the Athy circuit in Ireland.

Politics crept into the sport in 1905 and Bennett withdrew his sponsorship, turning his attention to flying instead. The French Grand Prix was born in 1906 but, although soon forgotten, the Gordon Bennett Cup was the foundation on which current Grand Prix racing was built.

A rare picture of the magnificent Gordon Bennett trophy that was motor racing's principal event between 1900–5. (National Motor Museum)

Below Jenatzy and his mechanic in their Mercedes that won the 1903 Gordon Bennett race at Athy. (National Motor Museum)

Opposite Competitors line up to weigh-in their cars before the start of the 1903 Gordon Bennett race at Athy, Ireland. (National Motor Museum)

1900 Paris–Lyons

1 F. Charron   Panhard
   62.11 kph / 38.60 mph
2 L. Girardot   Panhard
3 R. de Knyff   Panhard

1901 Paris–Bordeaux

1 L. Girardot   Panhard
   59.53 kph / 37.00 mph
   (only one finished)

1902 Paris–Innsbruck

1 S. F. Edge   Napier
   51.17 kph / 31.80 mph
   (only one finished)

1903 Athy, N. Ireland

1 C. Jenatzy   Mercedes
   79.16 kph / 49.20 mph
2 R. de Knyff   Panhard
3 H. Farman   Panhard

1904 Taunus, Germany

1 L. Thery   Richard-Brasier
   87.69 kph / 54.50 mph
2 C. Jenatzy   Mercedes
3 H. Rougier   Turcat-Mery

1905 Auvergne, France

1 L. Thery   Richard-Brasier
   77.88 kph / 48.40 mph
2 F. Nazzaro   F.I.A.T.
3 A. Cagno   F.I.A.T.

Pre-World Championship Grand Prix Racing

Grand Prix racing existed long before the formation of the World Championship in 1950, and goes back to 1906 when the first French Grand Prix was run. The following are the results of the major Grand Prix races prior to 1950.

BELGIAN GP

1925 Spa (known as the 'European Grand Prix')

			Average speed
1	A. Ascari (Snr)	Alfa Romeo	119.97 kph / 74.56 mph
2	G. Campari	Alfa Romeo	
(only two finished)			

1930 Spa (known as the 'European Grand Prix')

1	L. Chiron	Bugatti	116.01 kph / 72.10 mph
2	G. Bouriat	Bugatti	
3	A. Divo	Bugatti	

1931 Spa

1	Count Connelli/ W. Williams	Bugatti	131.95 kph / 82.01 mph
2	T. Nuvolari/B. Borzacchini	Alfa Romeo	
3	F. Minoia/ E. Minozzi	Alfa Romeo	

1933 Spa

1	T. Nuvolari	Maserati	132.31 kph / 89.23 mph
2	A. Varzi	Bugatti	
3	R. Dreyfus	Bugatti	

1934 Spa

1	R. Dreyfus	Bugatti	139.84 kph / 86.91 mph
2	A. Brivio	Bugatti	
3	R. Sommer	Maserati	

1935 Spa

1 R. Caraccioli	Mercedes-Benz	157.47 kph / 97.87 mph
2 M. von Brauchitsch/ L. Fagioli	Mercedes-Benz	
3 L. Chiron	Alfa Romeo	

1937 Spa

1 R. Hasse	Auto-Union	167.45 kph / 104.07 mph
2 H. Stuck	Auto-Union	
3 H. Lang	Mercedes-Benz	

1939 Spa

1 H. Lang	Mercedes-Benz	151.87 kph / 94.39 mph
2 R. Hasse	Auto-Union	
3 M. von Brauchitsch	Mercedes-Benz	

1947 Spa (known as the 'European Grand Prix')

1 J-P. Wimille	Alfa Romeo	153.31 kph / 95.28 mph
2 A. Varzi	Alfa Romeo	
3 C. Trossi	Alfa Romeo	

1949 Spa

1 L. Rosier	Talbot	155.99 kph / 96.95 mph
2 L. Villoresi	Ferrari	
3 A. Ascari (Jnr)	Ferrari	

1938 Donington (known as the 'Donington Grand Prix')

1 T. Nuvolari	Auto-Union	129.51 kph / 80.49 mph
2 H. Lang	Mercedes-Benz	
3 R. J. B. Seaman	Mercedes-Benz	

1948 Silverstone

1 L. Villoresi	Maserati	116.30 kph / 72.28 mph
2 A. Ascari (Jnr)	Maserati	
3 F. R. Gerard	ERA	

1949 Silverstone

1 E. de Graffenried	Maserati	124.39 kph / 77.31 mph
2 F. R. Gerard	ERA	
3 L. Rosier	Lago-Talbot	

DUTCH GP

1949 Zandvoort

1 L. Villoresi	Ferrari	124.05 kph / 77.10 mph
2 E. de Graffenreid	Maserati	
3 'B. Bira'	Maserati	

BRITISH GP

1926 Brooklands (known as the 'RAC Grand Prix')

1 R. Senechal/ L. Wagner	Delage	115.22 kph / 71.61 mph
2 M. Campbell	Bugatti	
3 R. Benoist/ A. Dubonnet	Delage	

1927 Brooklands (known as the 'RAC Grand Prix')

1 R. Benoist	Delage	137.71 kph / 85.59 mph
2 E. Bourlier	Delage	
3 A. Divo	Delage	

1935 Donington (known as the 'Donington Grand Prix')

1 R. Shuttleworth	Alfa Romeo	102.93 kph / 63.97 mph
2 Earl Howe	Bugatti	
3 C. Martin	Bugatti	

1936 Donington (known as the 'Donington Grand Prix')

1 H. Reusch/ R. J. B. Seaman	Alfa Romeo	111.39 kph / 69.23 mph
2 C. Martin	Alfa Romeo	
3 P. Whitehead/ P. Walker	ERA	

1937 Donington (known as the 'Donington Grand Prix')

1 R. Rosemeyer	Auto-Union	133.31 kph / 82.85 mph
2 M. von Brauchitsch	Mercedes-Benz	
3 R. Caracciola	Mercedes-Benz	

FRENCH GP

1906 Le Mans

1 F. Szisz	Renault	101.37 kph / 63.00 mph
2 F. Nazzaro	F.I.A.T.	
3 A. Clement	Clement-Bayard	

1907 Dieppe

1 F. Nazzaro	Fiat	113.43 kph / 70.50 mph
2 F. Szisz	Renault	
3 P. Baras	Brasier	

1908 Dieppe

1 C. Lautenschlager	Mercedes	111.02 kph / 69.00 mph
2 V. Hemery	Benz	
3 R. Hanriot	Benz	

1912 Dieppe

1 G. Boillot	Peugeot	110.14 kph / 68.45 mph
2 L. Wagner	Fiat	
3 V. Rigal	Sunbeam	

1913 Amiens

1 G. Boillot	Peugeot	115.28 kph / 71.65 mph
2 J. Goux	Peugeot	
3 J. Chassagne	Sunbeam	

1914 Lyons

1 C. Lautenschlager	Mercedes	105.15 kph / 65.35 mph
2 L. Wagner	Mercedes	
3 O. Salzer	Mercedes	

1921 Le Mans

1 J. Murphy	Duesenberg	125.66 kph / 78.10 mph
2 R. de Palma	Ballot	
3 J. Goux	Ballot	

Safety standards in the first grand prix, the 1906 French Grand Prix, were certainly no comparison to those of today . . . (National Motor Museum)

Action from the world's first grand prix, the 1906 French Grand Prix at Le Mans. (National Motor Museum)

1922 Strasbourg

1 F. Nazzaro	Fiat	127.43 kph / 79.20 mph
2 P. de Vizcaya	Bugatti	
3 P. Marco	Bugatti	

1923 Tours

1 H. O. Segrave	Sunbeam	121.16 kph / 75.30 mph
2 A. Divo	Sunbeam	
3 E. Freiderich	Bugatti	

1924 Lyons (known as the 'European Grand Prix')

1 G. Campari	Alfa Romeo	114.24 kph / 71.00 mph
2 A. Divo	Delage	
3 R. Benoist	Delage	

1925 Montlhery

1 R. Benoist/ A. Divo	Delage	112.15 kph / 69.70 mph
2 L. Wagner/ Torchy	Delage	
3 G. Masetti	Sunbeam	

1926 Miramas

1 J. Goux	Bugatti	109.70 kph / 68.20 mph
2 B. Constantini	Bugatti	
(only two finished)		

1927 Montlhery

1 R. Benoist	Delage	124.28 kph / 77.24 mph
2 E. Bourlier	Delage	
3 A. Morel	Delage	

1928 Comminges

1 W. Williams	Bugatti	136.54 kph / 84.86 mph
2 Rousseau	Salmson	
3 H. Brisson	Stutz	

1929 Le Mans

1 W. Williams	Bugatti	133.00 kph / 82.66 mph
2 A. Boillot	Peugeot	
3 C. Conelli	Bugatti	

1930 Pau

1 P. Etancelin   Bugatti   145.21 kph / 90.25 mph
2 H. R. Birkin   Bentley
3 J. Zanelli   Bugatti

1931 Montlhery

1 A. Varzi/
   L. Chiron   Bugatti   125.76 kph / 78.16 mph
2 B. Borzacchini/
   G. Campari   Alfa Romeo
3 C. Biondetti/
   G. Parenti   Maserati

1932 Rheims

1 T. Nuvolari   Alfa Romeo   148.45 kph / 92.26 mph
2 B. Borzacchini   Alfa Romeo
3 R. Caracciola   Alfa Romeo

1933 Montlhery

1 G. Campari   Maserati   131.17 kph / 81.52 mph
2 P. Etancelin   Alfa Romeo
3 G. Eyston   Alfa Romeo

1934 Montlhery

1 L. Chiron   Alfa Romeo   136.89 kph / 85.08 mph
2 A. Varzi   Alfa Romeo
3 C. Trossi/
   G. Moll   Alfa Romeo

1935 Montlhery

1 R. Caracciola   Mercedes-Benz 124.54 kph / 77.40 mph
2 M. von
   Brauchitsch   Mercedes-Benz
3 G. Zehender   Maserati

Bugatti was one of the biggest names in the sport in the 1920s
and 30s. This is a Type 37 that took part in a Vintage
Sports Car Club Rally at Oulton Park in 1961. (National Motor
Museum)

1936 Montlhery

1 J-P. Wimille/
   R. Sommer   Bugatti   125.26 kph / 77.85 mph
2 M. Paris/
   J. Mongin   Delahaye
3 R. Brunet/
   G. Zehender   Delahaye

1937 Montlhery

1 L. Chiron   Lago-Talbot   132.69 kph / 82.47 mph
2 G. Comotti   Lago-Talbot
3 A. Divo   Lago-Talbot

1938 Rheims

1 M. von
   Brauchitsch   Mercedes-Benz 162.99 kph / 101.30 mph
2 R. Caracciola   Mercedes-Benz
3 H. Lang   Mercedes-Benz

1939 Rheims

1 H. Muller   Auto-Union   169.35 kph / 105.25 mph
2 G. Meier   Auto-Union
3 R. Lebegue   Darracq

1947 Lyons

1 L. Chiron   Lago-Talbot   125.65 kph / 78.09 mph
2 H. Louveau   Maserati
3 E. Chaboud   Lago-Talbot

1948 Rheims

1 J-B. Wimille   Alfa Romeo   164.28 kph / 102.10 mph
2 C. Sanesi   Alfa Romeo
3 A. Ascari (Jnr)   Alfa Romeo

1949 Rheims

1 L. Chiron   Talbot   160.74 kph / 99.90 mph
2 'B. Bira'   Maserati
3 P. Whitehead   Ferrari

GERMAN GP

1926 Avus

1 R. Caracciola	Mercedes	134.98 kph / 83.89 mph
2 C. Reicken	N.A.G.	
3 W. Cleer	Alfa Romeo	

1927 Nurburgring

1 O. Merz	Mercedes-Benz	101.99 kph / 63.39 mph
2 C. Werner	Mercedes-Benz	
3 C. Walb	Mercedes-Benz	

1928 Nurburgring

1 R. Caracciola/ C. Werner	Mercedes-Benz	103.80 kph / 64.51 mph
2 O. Merz	Mercedes-Benz	
3 C. Walb/ C. Werner	Mercedes-Benz	

1929 Nurburgring

1 L. Chiron	Bugatti	106.81 kph / 66.38 mph
2 G. Philippe	Bugatti	
3 Count Arco/A. Momberger	Mercedes-Benz	

1931 Nurburgring

1 R. Caracciola	Mercedes-Benz	108.22 kph / 67.26 mph
2 L. Chiron	Bugatti	
3 A. Varzi	Bugatti	

1932 Nurburgring

1 R. Caracciola	Alfa Romeo	119.03 kph / 73.98 mph
2 T. Nuvolari	Alfa Romeo	
3 B. Borzacchini	Alfa Romeo	

Italy's Tazio Nuvolari enjoyed the same success between the wars that Fangio, Clark and Stewart enjoyed in the post-war era. He is seen here driving a 1750cc Alfa Romeo at the Ards circuit, Belfast. (National Motor Museum)

1934 Nurburgring

1 H. Stuck	Auto-Union	122.91 kph / 76.39 mph
2 L. Fagioli	Mercedes-Benz	
3 L. Chiron	Alfa Romeo	

1935 Nurburgring

1 T. Nuvolari	Alfa Romeo	121.06 kph / 75.24 mph
2 H. Stuck	Auto-Union	
3 R. Caracciola	Mercedes-Benz	

1936 Nurburgring

1 B. Rosemeyer	Auto-Union	131.65 kph / 81.82 mph
2 H. Stuck	Auto-Union	
3 A. Brivio	Alfa Romeo	

1937 Nurburgring

1 R. Caracciola	Mercedes-Benz	133.19 kph / 82.78 mph
2 M. von Brauchitsch	Mercedes-Benz	
3 B. Rosemeyer	Auto-Union	

1938 Nurburgring

1 R. J. B. Seaman	Mercedes-Benz	129.88 kph / 80.72 mph
2 R. Caracciola/ H. Lang	Mercedes-Benz	
3 H. Stuck	Auto-Union	

1939 Nurburgring

1 R. Caracciola	Mercedes-Benz	121.09 kph / 75.26 mph
2 H. Muller	Auto-Union	
3 P. Pietsch	Maserati	

ITALIAN GP

1921 Brescia

1 J. Goux	Ballot	144.71 kph / 89.94 mph
2 J. Chassagne	Ballot	
3 L. Wagner	Fiat	

1922 Monza

1 P. Bordino   Fiat   139.82 kph / 86.90 mph
2 F. Nazzaro   Fiat
3 P. de Vizcaya   Bugatti

1923 Monza (known as the 'European Grand Prix')

1 C. Salamano   Fiat   146.47 kph / 91.03 mph
2 F. Nazzaro   Fiat
3 J. Murphy   Miller

1924 Monza

1 A. Ascari (Snr)   Alfa Romeo 158.95 kph / 98.79 mph
2 L. Wagner   Alfa Romeo
3 G. Campari/
  E. Presenti   Alfa Romeo

1925 Monza

1 G. Brilli-Peri   Alfa Romeo 152.57 kph / 94.82 mph
2 G. Campari/
  G. Minozzi   Alfa Romeo
3 B. Constantini   Bugatti

1926 Monza

1 'Sabipa'   Bugatti   138.18 kph / 85.88 mph
2 B. Constantini   Bugatti
(Only two finished)

1927 Monza (known as the 'European Grand Prix')

1 R. Benoist   Delage   144.89 kph / 90.05 mph
2 O. Morandi   OM
3 P. Kreis/
  E. Cooper   Miller

1928 Monza

1 L. Chiron   Bugatti   159.87 kph / 99.36 mph
2 G. Campari/
  A. Varzi   Alfa Romeo
3 T. Nuvolari   Bugatti

1931 Monza (known as the 'European Grand Prix')

1 G. Campari/
  T. Nuvolari   Alfa Romeo 155.74 kph / 96.79 mph
2 F. Minoia/
  B. Borzacchini   Alfa Romeo
3 G. Bouriat/
  A. Divo   Bugatti

1932 Monza

1 G. Campari/
  T. Nuvolari   Alfa Romeo 167.48 kph / 104.09 mph
2 L. Fagioli/
  E. Maserati   Maserati
3 B. Borzacchini/
  R. Caracciola/
  A. Marinoni   Alfa Romeo

1933 Monza

1 L. Fagioli   Alfa Romeo 174.71 kph / 108.58 mph
2 T. Nuvolari   Maserati
3 G. Zehender   Maserati

1934 Monza

1 R. Caracciola/
  L. Fagioli   Mercedes-Benz 105.15 kph / 65.35 mph
2 Prince Zu
  Leiningen/
  H. Stuck   Auto-Union
3 G. Comotti/
  C. Trossi   Alfa Romeo

1935 Monza

1 H. Stuck   Auto-Union   137.05 kph / 85.18 mph
2 R. Dreyfus/
  T. Nuvolari   Alfa Romeo
3 P. Pietsch/B.
  Rosemeyer   Auto-Union

1936 Monza

1 B. Rosemeyer   Auto-Union   135.32 kph / 84.10 mph
2 T. Nuvolari   Alfa Romeo
3 E. von Delius   Auto-Union

1937 Leghorn

1 R. Caracciola   Mercedes-Benz 131.28 kph / 81.59 mph
2 H. Lang   Mercedes-Benz
3 B. Rosemeyer   Auto-Union

1938 Monza

1 T. Nuvolari   Auto-Union   155.69 kph / 96.76 mph
2 G. Farina   Alfa Romeo
3 M. von
  Brauchitsch/
  R. Caracciola   Mercedes-Benz

1947 Milan

1 C. Trossi   Alfa Romeo   113.18 kph / 70.34 mph
2 A. Varzi   Alfa Romeo
3 C. Sanesi   Alfa Romeo

1948 Turin

1 J-P. Wimille   Alfa Romeo   113.24 kph / 70.38 mph
2 L. Villoresi   Maserati
3 R. Sommer   Ferrari

1949 Monza (known as the 'European Grand Prix')

1 A. Ascari (Jnr)   Ferrari   169.09 kph / 105.09 mph
2 P. Etancelin   Talbot
3 'B. Bira'   Maserati

The cars may look different but the appeal of the Monaco Grand Prix seemed to be little different in 1932 from today's.
(I. Morrison)

Mille Miglia

In the Targa Florio and Mille Miglia, Italy was fortunate to stage two of the world's great endurance races. The Targa Florio started in 1906 but in 1923 the French introduced the Le Mans 24-Hour race which soon gained a reputation for being the world's premier long-distance event.

In an effort to restore some pride, and also to help pull their motor industry out of its depression, the Italians introduced the Mille Miglia. The idea was conceived by members of the Brescia Automobile Club and received the full blessing from Italian leader Mussolini.

The race was called the Mille Miglia because the distance of approximately 1000 miles was over the old Roman Mile. The first race was in 1927 and took in a circuit that started in Brescia, in the north of Italy, and weaved its way down to Rome and then back to Brescia. The Italian car industry received its much-needed boost in the first race when Messrs Minoia and Morandi beat off 76 other challengers to win in an Italian-made OM, who filled the first three places.

The cars used to set off at one-minute intervals, originally starting at 9.00 p.m. on a Saturday, but that was changed in 1949 to midnight. At the same time, cars were numbered in accordance with the time they set off so the thousands of spectators that lined the route could get some indication who was leading. A record 743 cars took part in 1950 which meant the last car away left Brescia about 12 hours after the first!

While the race covered approximately 1000 miles, the route varied over the years but maintained Brescia as its base. Following an accident in the 1938 race, however, the Mille Miglia was banned in Italy the following year and a race purporting to be the Mille Miglia was held between Tobruk and Tripoli in north Africa and won by Ercole Boratto (Ita), a former chauffeur of Mussolini. The race returned for one year in 1940 and was held over nine laps of a 100-mile circuit that took in Brescia–Cremona–Brescia and, while it was generally known as the Brescia Grand Prix, it still was accorded Mille Miglia status, unlike the 1939 event. After the war it returned to its original Brescia–Rome–Brescia route.

Stirling Moss (GB), in 1955, along with his co-driver Denis Jenkinson (GB), became one of only three non-Italians to win the great race and many regarded it as Moss's best-ever drive. His average speed of 157.62 kph (97.96 mph) was to remain an all-time record for the race over the full course.

The end of the Mille Miglia came in 1957, following an accident which resulted in the loss of 13 lives. A Ferrari driven by Spanish aristocrat Marquis de Portago and his co-driver Ed Nelson careered out of control and into a group of spectators. Portago, Nelson, five adults and six children were killed, and that was enough for officials to call a halt to the race.

For the next two years a smaller race around Brescia was held but the real Mille Miglia was gone for ever. It had certainly achieved one of its aims and revived the Italian car industry, as home-produced cars won every race with the exception of three when German manufacturers Mercedes (twice) and BMW broke their domination. Of the Italian manufacturers, Alfa Romeo dominated the pre-war races while Ferrari dominated the post-war era as Italy established itself as one of the leading motor racing nations.

For results see page 174–5.

The 'C' type Jaguar that was seen in post-war Mille Miglia races. Behind the wheel of this one is Prince Michael of Kent during the 1986 nostalgia race. (National Motor Museum)

Grand Prix motor racing
has been held at Monaco
since 1929 (West Zakspeed)

MONACO GP

1929 Monaco

1 W. Williams   Bugatti   80.77 kph / 50.20 mph
2 E. Bouriano   Bugatti
3 R. Caracciola   Mercedes-Benz

1930 Monaco

1 R. Dreyfus   Bugatti   89.46 kph / 55.60 mph
2 L. Chiron   Bugatti
3 G. Bouriat   Bugatti

1931 Monaco

1 L. Chiron   Bugatti   87.05 kph / 54.10 mph
2 L. Fagioli   Maserati
3 A. Varzi   Bugatti

1932 Monaco

1 T. Nuvolari   Alfa Romeo   89.80 kph / 55.81 mph
2 R. Caracciola   Alfa Romeo
3 L. Fagioli   Maserati

1933 Monaco

1 A. Varzi   Bugatti   91.39 kph / 57.00 mph
2 B. Borzacchini   Alfa Romeo
3 R. Dreyfus   Bugatti

1934 Monaco

1 G. Moll   Alfa Romeo   89.88 kph / 55.86 mph
2 L. Chiron   Alfa Romeo
3 R. Dreyfus   Bugatti

1935 Monaco

1 L. Fagioli   Mercedes-Benz   93.58 kph / 58.16 mph
2 R. Dreyfus   Alfa Romeo
3 A. Brivio   Alfa Romeo

1936 Monaco

1 R. Caracciola   Mercedes-Benz   83.17 kph / 51.69 mph
2 A. Varzi   Auto-Union
3 H. Stuck   Auto-Union

1937 Monaco

1 M. von Brauchitsch   Mercedes-Benz   101.79 kph / 63.26 mph
2 R. Caracciola   Mercedes-Benz
3 C. Kautz   Mercedes-Benz

1948 Monaco

1 G. Farina   Maserati   96.12 kph / 59.74 mph
2 L. Chiron   Lago-Talbot
3 E. de Graffen-ried   Maserati

PAU GP

1933 Pau

1 M. Lehoux   Bugatti   73.02 kph / 45.38 mph
2 G. Moll   Bugatti
3 P. Etancelin   Alfa Romeo

1935 Pau

1 T. Nuvolari   Alfa Romeo   83.94 kph / 52.17 mph
2 R. Dreyfus   Alfa Romeo
3 G. Soffietti   Maserati

1936 Pau

1 P. Etancelin   Maserati   82.06 kph / 51.00 mph
2 C. E. Martin   Alfa Romeo
3 M. Lehoux   Bugatti

1937 Pau

1 J-P. Wimille   Bugatti   82.41 kph / 51.22 mph
2 R. Sommer   Lago-Talbot
3 R. Dreyfus   Delahaye

1938 Pau

1 R. Dreyfus   Delahaye   87.92 kph / 54.64 mph
2 R. Caracciola/ H. Lang   Mercedes-Benz
3 G. Comotti   Delahaye

1939 Pau

1 H. Lang   Mercedes-Benz   88.66 kph / 55.10 mph
2 M. von Brauchitsch   Mercedes-Benz
3 P. Etancelin   Lago-Talbot

1947 Pau

1 N. Pagani   Maserati   83.59 kph / 51.95 mph
2 P. Levagh   Delage
3 H. Louveau   Maserati

1948 Pau

1 N. Pagani   Maserati   85.39 kph / 53.07 mph
2 Y. G. Cabantous   Lago-Talbot
3 C. Pozzi   Lago-Talbot

1949 Pau

1 J-M. Fangio   Maserati   84.71 kph / 52.65 mph
2 E. de Graffen-ried   Maserati
3 B. Campos   Maserati

SPANISH GP

1913 Guadarrama

1 C. de Sala-manca   Rolls Royce   86.89 kph / 54.00 mph
2 Marquis de Aulencia   de Dietrich
3 E. Platford   Rolls Royce

1923 Sitges-Terramar

1 A. Divo   Sunbeam   96.91 kph / 60.22 mph
2 L. Zborowski   Miller
3 Carreras   Elizalde

1926 Lasarte

1 B. Constantini   Bugatti   123.70 kph / 76.88 mph
2 J. Goux   Bugatti
3 L. Wagner/ R. Benoist   Delage

1927 Lasarte

1 R. Benoist   Delage   129.56 kph / 80.52 mph
2 C. Conelli   Bugatti
3 E. Bourlier   Delage

1928 Lasarte

1 L. Chiron   Bugatti   126.98 kph / 78.92 mph
2 E. Bouriano   Bugatti
3 Delemer   EHP

1929 Lasarte

1 L. Chiron   Bugatti   116.49 kph / 72.40 mph
2 L. Philippe/ G. Bouriat   Bugatti
3 M. Lehoux   Bugatti

1930 Lasarte

1 A. Varzi	Maserati	139.69 kph / 86.82 mph
2 A. Maggi	Maserati	
3 H. Stoffel	Peugeot	

1933 Lasarte

1 L. Chiron	Alfa Romeo	134.06 kph / 83.32 mph
2 L. Fagioli	Alfa Romeo	
3 M. Lehoux	Bugatti	

1934 Lasarte

1 L. Fagioli	Mercedes-Benz	156.33 kph / 97.16 mph
2 R. Caracciola	Mercedes-Benz	
3 T. Nuvolari	Bugatti	

1935 Lasarte

1 R. Caracciola	Mercedes-Benz	163.99 kph / 101.92 mph
2 L. Fagioli	Mercedes-Benz	
3 M. von Brauchitsch	Mercedes-Benz	

SWISS GP

1934 Bremgarten

1 H. Stuck	Auto-Union	140.32 kph / 87.21 mph
2 A. Momberger	Auto-Union	
3 R. Dreyfus	Bugatti	

1935 Bremgarten

1 R. Caracciola	Mercedes-Benz	144.73 kph / 89.95 mph
2 L. Fagioli	Mercedes-Benz	
3 B. Rosemeyer	Auto-Union	

1936 Bremgarten

1 B. Rosemeyer	Auto-Union	161.70 kph / 100.50 mph
2 A. Varzi	Auto-Union	
3 H. Stuck	Auto-Union	

1937 Bremgarten

1 R. Caracciola	Mercedes-Benz	158.57 kph / 98.55 mph
2 H. Lang	Mercedes-Benz	
3 M. von Brauchitsch	Mercedes-Benz	

1938 Bremgarten

1 R. Caracciola	Mercedes-Benz	143.91 kph / 89.44 mph
2 R. J. B. Seaman	Mercedes-Benz	
3 M. von Brauchitsch	Mercedes-Benz	

1939 Bremgarten

1 H. Lang	Mercedes-Benz	154.50 kph / 96.02 mph
2 R. Caracciola	Mercedes-Benz	
3 M. von Brauchitsch	Mercedes-Benz	

1947 Bremgarten

1 J-P. Wimille	Alfa Romeo	153.53 kph / 95.42 mph
2 A. Varzi	Alfa Romeo	
3 C. Trossi	Alfa Romeo	

1948 Bremgarten

1 C. Trossi	Alfa Romeo	146.11 kph / 90.81 mph
2 J-P. Wimille	Alfa Romeo	
3 L. Villoresi	Maserati	

1949 Bremgarten

1 A. Ascari (Jnr)	Ferrari	146.03 kph / 90.76 mph
2 L. Villoresi	Ferrari	
3 R. Sommer	Lago-Talbot	

Mille Miglia

One of the greatest of all sports car road races ever run, the Mille Miglia was first held in 1927 and, by tradition, cars set off at one-minute intervals from the centre of Brescia, raced down to Rome and returned. The course changed over the years and, in 1957, following a tragic accident, the last Mille Miglia was held although smaller versions of the race around Brescia continued to be staged, and a series of nostalgic races has been held since 1982. (See also feature on page 171)

1927

1 F. Minoia/ A. Morandi	OM	
77.22 kph / 47.99 mph		
2 T. Danieli/ R. Balestrero	OM	
3 M. Danieli/ A. Rosa	OM	

1928

1 G. Campari/ G. Ramponi	Alfa Romeo	
84.10 kph / 52.27 mph		
2 F. Mazotti/ A. Rosa	OM	
3 G. Strazza/ Varallo	Lancia	

1929

1 G. Campari/ G. Ramponi	Alfa Romeo	
89.67 kph / 55.73 mph		
2 A. Morandi/ A. Rosa	OM	
3 A. Varzi/ G. Colombo	Alfa Romeo	

1930

1 T. Nuvolari/ B. Guidotti	Alfa Romeo	
100.43 kph / 62.42 mph		
2 A. Varzi/ G. Canavesi	Alfa Romeo	
3 G. Campari/ A. Marinoni	Alfa Romeo	

1931

1 R. Caracciola/ W. Sebastian	Mercedes-Benz	
101.13 kph / 62.85 mph		
2 G. Campari/ A. Marinoni	Alfa Romeo	
3 A. Morandi/ A. Rosa	OM	

1932

1 B. Borzacchini/ A. Bignami	Alfa Romeo	
109.86 kph / 68.28 mph		
2 A. Brivio/ C. F. Trossi	Alfa Romeo	
3 Scarfiotti/ d'Ippolito	Alfa Romeo	

1933

1 T. Nuvolari/
   Compagnoni   Alfa Romeo
   108.54 kph / 67.46 mph
2 L. Castelbarco/
   F. Cortese   Alfa Romeo
3 P. Taruffi/
   Pellegrini   Alfa Romeo

1934

1 A. Varzi/
   A. Bignami   Alfa Romeo
   114.29 kph / 71.03 mph
2 T. Nuvolari/
   E. Siena   Alfa Romeo
3 L. Chiron/
   A. Rosa   Alfa Romeo

1935

1 C. Pintacuda/
   A della Stufa   Alfa Romeo
   114.72 kph / 71.30 mph
2 M. Tadini/
   L. Chiari   Alfa Romeo
3 G. Battaglia/
   B. Tuffanelli   Alfa Romeo

1936

1 A. Brivio/
   Ongaro   Alfa Romeo
   121.59 kph / 75.57 mph
2 G. Farina/
   Meazza   Alfa Romeo
3 C. Pintacuda/
   Stefani   Alfa Romeo

1937

1 C. Pintacuda/
   Mambelli   Alfa Romeo
   114.72 kph / 71.30 mph
2 G. Farina/
   Meazza   Alfa Romeo
3 L. Schell/
   R. Carriere   Delahaye

1938

1 C. Biondetti/
   Stefani   Alfa Romeo
   135.37 kph / 84.13 mph
2 C. Pintacuda/
   Mambelli   Alfa Romeo
3 P. Dusio/
   Boninsegni   Alfa Romeo

1939

1 E. Boratto/
   C. Sanesi   Alfa Romeo
   141.37 kph / 87.86 mph
2 C. Biondetti/
   Monzani   Alfa Romeo
3 C. Pintacuda/
   Mambelli   Alfa Romeo
(Held on a course between Tobruk
and Tripoli)

1940

1 H. von Hanstein/
   Baumer   BMW
   166.69 kph / 103.60 mph
2 G. Farina/
   Mambelli   Alfa Romeo
3 Brudes/
   Rosese   BMW
(Held over a short course around
Brescia)

1941–46

Not held

1947

1 C. Biondetti/
   Romano   Alfa Romeo
   110.43 kph / 68.63 mph
2 T. Nuvolari/
   Carena   Cisitalia
3 I. Bernabei/
   Pacini   Cisitalia

1948

1 C. Biondetti/
   Navone   Ferrari
   120.93 kph / 75.16 mph
2 Compirato/
   Dumas   Fiat
3 Apruzzi/
   Apruzzi   Fiat

1949

1 C. Biondetti/
   Salani   Ferrari
   131.18 kph / 81.53 mph
2 F. Bonetto/
   Carpani   Ferrari
3 F. Rol/
   Richiero   Alfa Romeo

1950

1 G. Marzotto/
   Crosara   Ferrari
   123.56 kph / 76.79 mph
2 D. Serafini/
   Salani   Ferrari
3 J-M. Fangio/
   Zanardi   Alfa Romeo

1951

1 L. Villoresi/
   Cassani   Ferrari
   121.51 kph / 75.52 mph
2 G. Bracco/
   U. Maglioli   Lancia
3 P. Scotti/
   Ruspaggiari   Ferrari

1952

1 G. Bracco/
   Rolfo   Ferrari
   128.56 kph / 79.90 mph
2 K. Kling/
   Klenk   Mercedes-Benz
3 L. Fagioli/
   Borghi   Lancia

1953

1 G. Marzotto/
   Crosara   Ferrari
   142.32 kph / 88.45 mph
2 J-M. Fangio/
   Sala   Alfa Romeo
3 F. Bonetto/
   Peruzzi   Lancia

1954

1 A. Ascari   Lancia
   139.61 kph / 86.77 mph
2 V. Marzotto   Ferrari
3 L. Musso/
   Zocca   Maserati

1955

1 S. Moss/
   D. Jenkinson   Mercedes-Benz
   157.62 kph / 97.96 mph
2 J-M. Fangio   Mercedes-Benz
3 U. Maglioli   Ferrari

1956

1 E. Castellotti   Ferrari
   137.41 kph / 85.40 mph
2 P. Collins/
   L. Klemen-
   taski   Ferrari
3 L. Musso   Ferrari

1957

1 P. Taruffi   Ferrari
   152.60 kph / 94.84 mph
2 W. von Trips   Ferrari
3 O. Gendebien/
   Wascher   Ferrari

Most Wins (Drivers)

4 C. Biondetti (1938, 1947, 1948,
   1949)
2 G. Campari (1928, 1929)
2 G. Ramponi (1928, 1929)
2 T. Nuvolari (1930, 1933)
2 A. Bignami (1932, 1934)
2 C. Pintacuda (1935, 1937)
2 G. Marzotto (1950, 1953)

Fast Winning Speed

157.62 kph / 97.96 mph S. Moss/
D. Jenkinson (Mercedes-Benz) 1955
(Von Hanstein and Baumer (BMW)
won at 166.69 kph / 103.60 mph in
1940; the race was over the shortened
course around Brescia.

Most Wins (Cars)

12 Alfa Romeo (1928–30, 1932–39,
   1947)
8 Ferrari (1948–53, 1956–57)

• The *Brooklands Gazette*, fore-runner of *Motor Sport*, was first published in August 1924. It was the first publication devoted entirely to motor sport in Britain.

• The first television coverage of a motor race was by the BBC in October 1938, when they televised heats from the Imperial Trophy at Crystal Palace.

Targa Florio

The last of the truly great road races, the Targa Florio was the brainchild of wealthy Sicilian Vincenzo Florio who had a great love of racing cars. The first Targa Florio was held on 6 May 1906 and that race, like all subsequent ones, was over a difficult and testing winding Sicilian course which varied over the years. The last real Targa Florio was staged in 1973, thereafter it became a much 'tamer' affair and ceased to be part of the Sports Car World Championship.

The narrow Sicilian streets make an unusual setting for a motor race but the Targa Florio was one of the most popular, and prestigious, of long-distance road races during its 67-year life between 1906–73. (I. Morrison)

1906
1 A. Cagno   Itala
   46.95 kph / 29.18 mph
2 E. Graziana   Itala
3 P. Bablot   Berliet

1907
1 F. Nazzaro   Fiat
   53.90 kph / 33.50 mph
2 V. Lancia   Fiat
3 M. Fabry   Itala

1908
1 V. Trucco   Isotta-Fraschini
   57.06 kph / 35.46 mph
2 V. Lancia   Fiat
3 M. Ceirano   SPA

1909
1 R. Ciuppa   SPA
   54.37 kph / 33.79 mph
2 V. Florio   Fiat
3 G. Airoldi   Lancia

1910
1 F. Cariolato   Franco
   47.27 kph / 29.38 mph
2 L. de Prosperis   Sigma
   (only two finished)

1911
1 E. Ceirano   SCAT
   46.79 kph / 29.08 mph
2 M. Cortese   Lancia
3 B. Soldatenkoff   Mercedes

1912
1 C. Snipe   SCAT
   44.44 kph / 27.62 mph
2 Garetto   Lancia
3 G. Giordano   Fiat

1913
1 F. Nazarro   Nazarro
   54.35 kph / 33.78 mph
2 G. Marsaglia   Aquila-Italiana
3 A. Mariani   De Vecchi

1914
1 E. Ceirano   SCAT
   58.05 kph / 36.08 mph
2 A. Mariani   De Vecchi
3 L. Lopez   Fiat

1915–18
Not held

1919
1 A. Boillot   Peugeot
   55.01 kph / 34.19 mph
2 A. Moriendo   Itala
3 D. Gamboni   Diatto

1920
1 G. Meregalli   Nazzaro
   51.07 kph / 31.74 mph
2 E. Ferrari   Alfa Romeo
3 L. Lopez   Darracq

1921
1 G. Masetti   Fiat
   58.23 kph / 36.19 mph
2 M. Sailer   Mercedes
3 G. Campari   Alfa Romeo

1922
1 G. Masetti   Mercedes
   63.81 kph / 39.66 mph
2 J. Goux   Ballot
3 G. Foresti   Ballot

1923
1 U. Sivocci   Alfa Romeo
   59.16 kph / 36.77 mph
2 A. Ascari   Alfa Romeo
3 F. Minoia   Steyr

1924
1 C. Werner   Mercedes
   66.00 kph / 41.02 mph
2 G. Masetti   Alfa Romeo
3 P. Bordino   Fiat

1925
1 B. Constantini   Bugatti
   71.60 kph / 44.50 mph
2 L. Wagner   Peugeot
3 A. Boillot   Peugeot

1926
1 B. Constantini   Bugatti
   73.50 kph / 45.68 mph
2 F. Minoia   Bugatti
3 J. Goux   Bugatti

1927
1 E. Materassi   Bugatti
   71.78 kph / 44.61 mph
2 B. Conelli   Bugatti
3 A. Maserati   Maserati

1928
1 A. Divo   Bugatti
   73.45 kph / 45.65 mph
2 G. Campari   Alfa Romeo
3 C. Conelli   Bugatti

1929
1 A. Divo   Bugatti
   74.35 kph / 46.21 mph
2 F. Minoia   Bugatti
3 G. Brilli-Peri   Alfa Romeo

1930
1 A. Varzi   Alfa Romeo
   78.00 kph / 48.48 mph
2 L. Chiron   Bugatti
3 C. Conelli   Bugatti

1931
1 T. Nuvolari   Alfa Romeo
   64.83 kph / 40.29 mph
2 B. Borzacchini   Alfa Romeo
3 A. Varzi   Bugatti

1932
1 T. Nuvolari   Alfa Romeo
   79.28 kph / 49.27 mph
2 B. Borzacchini   Alfa Romeo
3 L. Chiron/
   A. Varzi   Bugatti

1933

1 A. Brivio   Alfa Romeo
   76.52 kph / 47.56 mph
2 R. Balestrero   Alfa Romeo
3 G. Carraroli   Alfa Romeo

1934

1 A. Varzi   Alfa Romeo
   69.20 kph / 43.01 mph
2 N. Barbieri   Alfa Romeo
3 G. Magistri   Alfa Romeo

1935

1 A. Brivio   Alfa Romeo
   79.13 kph / 49.18 mph
2 L. Chiron   Alfa Romeo
3 N. Barbieri   Maserati

1936

1 G. Magistri   Lancia
   67.08 kph / 41.69 mph
2 S. di. Pietro   Lancia
3 'Gladio'   Lancia

1937

1 F. Severi   Maserati
   66.92 kph / 41.58 mph
2 G. Lurani   Maserati
3 E. Bianco   Maserati

1938

1 G. Rocco   Maserati
   71.02 kph / 44.13 mph
2 G. Ralph   Maserati
3 L. Villoresi   Maserati

1939

1 L. Villoresi   Maserati
   84.78 kph / 52.68 mph
2 P. Taruffi   Maserati
3 N. Barbieri   Maserati

1940

1 L. Villoresi   Maserati
   88.41 kph / 54.94 mph
2 F. Cortese   Maserati
3 G. Rocco   Maserati

1941–47

Not held

1948

1 C. Biondetti/
   I. Troubetskoy   Ferrari
   89.30 kph / 55.50 mph
2 P. Taruffi/
   Rabia   Cisitalia
3 Macchieraldo/
   Savio   Cisitalia

1949

1 C. Biondetti/
   Benedetti   Ferrari
   82.53 kph / 51.29 mph
2 F. Rol/
   Richiero   Alfa Romeo
3 G. Rocco/
   Prete   AMP

The Isotta-Fraschini team make final
preparations before setting off on the
1907 Targa Florio — sheep permitting
that is! (National Motor Museum)

1950

1 F. Bornigia/
   M. Bornigia   Alfa Romeo
   86.68 kph / 53.87 mph
2 I. Bernabei/
   Pacini   Ferrari
3 S. LaMotta/
   Alterio   Ferrari

1951

1 F. Cortese   Frazer Nash
   73.32 kph / 45.57 mph
2 F. Cornacchia/
   G. Bracco   Ferrari
3 I. Bernabei
   Pacini   Maserati

1952

1 F. Bonetto   Lancia
   79.97 kph / 49.70 mph
2 L. Valenzano   Lancia
3 E. Anselmi   Lancia

1953

1 U. Maglioli   Lancia
   80.61 kph / 50.10 mph
2 E. Giletti   Maserati
3 S. Mantovani/
   J-M. Fangio   Maserati

1954

1 P. Taruffi   Lancia
   89.86 kph / 55.85 mph
2 L. Musso   Maserati
3 R. Prioli   Lancia

1955

1 S. Moss/
  P. Collins   Mercedes-Benz
  95.90 kph / 59.60 mph
2 J-M. Fangio/
  K. Kling   Mercedes-Benz
3 E. Castellotti/
  R. Manzon   Ferrari

1956

1 U. Maglioli/
  H. von
  Hanstein   Porsche
  90.70 kph / 56.37 mph
2 P. Taruffi   Maserati
3 O. Gendebien/
  H. Herrmann   Ferrari

1957

Not held

1958

1 L. Musso/
  O. Gendebien Ferrari
  94.79 kph / 58.91 mph
2 J. Behra/
  G. Scarlatti   Porsche
3 W. von Trips/
  M. Hawthorn   Ferrari

1959

1 E. Barth/
  W. Seidel   Porsche
  91.29 kph / 56.74 mph
2 E. Mahle/
  H. Linge/
  P. Strahle   Porsche
3 A. Pucci/
  H. von
  Hanstein   Porsche

1960

1 J. Bonnier/
  H. Herrmann   Porsche
  95.32 kph / 59.24 mph
2 W. von Trips/
  P. Hill   Ferrari
3 O. Gendebien/
  H. Herrmann   Porsche

1961

1 W. von Trips/
  O. Gendebien Ferrari
  103.41 kph / 64.27 mph
2 D. Gurney/
  J. Bonnier   Porsche
3 E. Barth/
  H. Herrmann   Porsche

1962

1 W. Mairesse/
  R. Rodriguez/
  O. Gendebien Ferrari
  102.12 kph / 63.47 mph
2 G. Baghetti/
  L. Bandini   Ferrari
3 N. Vaccarella/
  J. Bonnier   Porsche

1963

1 J. Bonnier/
  C. M. Abate   Porsche
  103.89 kph / 64.57 mph
2 L. Bandini/
  L. Scarfiotti/
  W. Mairesse   Ferrari
3 H. Linge/
  E. Barth   Porsche

1964

1 C. Davis/
  A. Pucci   Porsche
  100.21 kph / 62.28 mph
2 H. Linge/
  G. Balzarini   Porsche
3 R. Bussinello/
  N. Todaro   Alfa Romeo

1965

1 N. Vaccarella/
  L. Bandini   Ferrari
  102.49 kph / 63.70 mph
2 C. Davis/
  G. Mitter   Porsche
3 U. Maglioli/
  H. Linge   Porsche

1966

1 W. Mairesse/
  H. Muller   Porsche
  98.91 kph / 61.47 mph
2 G. Baghetti/
  J. Guichet   Ferrari
3 A. Pucci/
  V. Arena   Porsche

1967

1 P. Hawkins/
  R. Stommelen   Porsche
  108.78 kph / 67.61 mph
2 L. Cella/
  G. Biscaldi   Porsche
3 J. Neerpasch/
  V. Elford   Porsche

1968

1 V. Elford/
  U. Maglioli   Porsche
  111.09 kph / 69.04 mph
2 N. Galli/
  I. Giunti   Alfa Romeo
3 M. Casoni/
  L. Bianchi   Alfa Romeo

1969

1 G. Mitter/
  U. Schutz   Porsche
  117.44 kph / 72.99 mph
2 V. Elford/
  U. Maglioli   Porsche
3 H. Herrmann/
  R. Stommelen Porsche

1970

1 J. Siffert/
  B. Redman   Porsche
  120.15 kph / 74.66 mph
2 P. Rodriguez/
  L. Kinnunen   Porsche
3 N. Vaccarella/
  I. Giunti   Ferrari

1971

1 N. Vaccarella/
  T. Hezemans   Alfa Romeo
  120.06 kph / 74.61 mph
2 A. de Adamich/
  G. van Lennep Alfa Romeo
3 J. Bonnier/
  R. Attwood   Lola

1972

1 A. Merzario/
  S. Munari   Ferrari
  122.54 kph / 76.15 mph
2 H. Marko/
  N. Galli   Alfa Romeo
3 T. Hezemans/
  A. de Adamich   Alfa Romeo

1973

1 H. Muller/
  G. van Lennep Porsche
  114.69 kph / 71.27 mph
2 S. Munari/
  J. C. Andruet   Lancia
3 L. Kinnunen/
  C. Haldi   Porsche

Most Wins (Drivers)

3 O. Gendebien (1958, 1961, 1962)
Many other drivers have won the race
twice

Fastest Winning Speed

122.54 kph / 76.15 mph A. Merzario/
  S. Munari (Ferrari) 1972

Most Wins (Cars)

11 Porsche (1956, 1959–60, 1963–64,
   1966–70, 1973)
 9 Alfa Romeo (1923, 1930–35, 1950,
   1971)

● The Can-Am series of races
were instituted in 1966 but it was
not until Peter Revson's victory in
1971 that an American won the
series. Britain's John Surtees and
New Zealanders Denny Hulme and
Bruce McLaren had domin-
ated the series until then.

● Jim Clark (GB) and Jack
Brabham (Aus) hold the distinc-
tion of winning the British Grand
Prix at three different venues.
Clark won at Aintree in 1962,
Silverstone in 1963, 1965 and
1967, and at Brands Hatch in
1964. Brabham won at Aintree in
1959, Silverstone in 1960 and
Brands in 1966.

CAN-AM Series

The Canadian-American Challenge Cup series of international road races in the United States and Canada was first introduced in 1966 in an attempt to bring the excitement of Grand Prix racing to the new North American road circuits that had sprung up. The first race was the Player's Quebec Race at Mont Tremblant, St. Jovite on 11 September 1966. Following a decline in interest in the mid-1970s the series was revived but the Sports Car Club of America discontinued their organization of the races in 1984. They are, however, hoping to revive the series in 1988 when it is hoped to restore it to its former glory.

Bruce McLaren (NZ) was one of the most respected Formula One drivers, and then constuctor of Formula One cars. He also enjoyed great success with his Can-Am cars. He won nine races as a driver on his way to two championships across the Atlantic, and his cars won a record 42 races, including 23 in succession between 1968–70. (National Motor Museum)

Individual race winners and Champions

1966

Mont Tremblant	J. Surtees	Lola	155.56 kph / 96.68 mph
Bridge-hampton	D. Gurney	Lola	169.88 kph / 105.58 mph
Mosport	M. Donohue	Lola	163.91 kph / 101.87 mph
Laguna Seca	P. Hill	Chaparral	158.33 kph / 98.40 mph
Riverside	J. Surtees	Lola	171.94 kph / 106.86 mph
Las Vegas	J. Surtees	Lola	175.78 kph / 109.25 mph

Final Championship Standing

1	J. Surtees	27 pts
2	M. Donohue	21 pts
3	B. McLaren	20 pts

1967

Elkhart Lake	D. Hulme	McLaren 168.10 kph / 104.55 mph
Bridge-hampton	D. Hulme	McLaren 175.52 kph / 109.13 mph
Mosport	D. Hulme	McLaren 170.47 kph / 105.93 mph
Laguna Seca	B. McLaren	McLaren 163.20 kph / 101.61 mph
Riverside	B. McLaren	McLaren 184.12 kph / 114.41 mph
Las Vegas	J. Surtees	Lola 180.90 kph / 112.41 mph

Final Championship Standing

1	B. McLaren	30 pts
2	D. Hulme	27 pts
3	J. Surtees	16 pts

1968

Elkhart Lake	D. Hulme	McLaren 152.15 kph / 94.54 mph
Bridge-hampton	M. Donohue	McLaren 179.15 kph / 111.32 mph
Edmonton	D. Hulme	McLaren 166.00 kph / 102.90 mph
Laguna Seca	J. Cannon	McLaren 131.76 kph / 85.60 mph
Riverside	B. McLaren	McLaren 184.03 kph / 114.46 mph
Las Vegas	D. Hulme	McLaren 182.01 kph / 113.10 mph

Final Championship Standing

1	D. Hulme	35 pts
2	B. McLaren	24 pts
3	M. Donohue	23 pts

1969

Mosport	B. McLaren	McLaren 170.39 kph / 105.90 mph
Mont Tremblant	D. Hulme	McLaren 156.96 kph / 97.55 mph
Watkins Glen	B. McLaren	McLaren 202.72 kph / 125.99 mph
Edmonton	D. Hulme	McLaren 167.90 kph / 104.35 mph
Lexington	D. Hulme	McLaren 151.58 kph / 94.21 mph
Elkhart Lake	B. McLaren	McLaren 172.94 kph / 107.48 mph
Bridge-hampton	D. Hulme	McLaren 182.98 kph / 113.72 mph
Michigan	B. McLaren	McLaren 173.93 kph / 108.10 mph
Laguna Seca	B. McLaren	McLaren 170.28 kph / 105.83 mph
Riverside	D. Hulme	McLaren 194.37 kph / 120.80 mph
Texas	B. McLaren	McLaren 176.75 kph / 109.85 mph

Final Championship Standing

1	B. McLaren	165 pts
2	D. Hulme	160 pts
3	C. Parsons	85 pts

Nigel Mansell

Britain's Nigel Mansell. After coming so close to winning the title in 1986, surely the world crown cannot be too far away?

Nigel Mansell not only carried the good wishes of all Manxmen as he went into the final round of the 1986 World Championship with a seven-point lead over Frenchman Alain Prost and Brazilian Nelson Piquet, but with all of Britain backing him. Millions stayed awake until the early hours of the morning to see if he could finish in third place, or better, so that he would be assured of Britain's first title for ten years.

He started the race at Adelaide in pole position and was looking comfortable in third position on lap 63 when, coming up the Brabham Straight at about 320 kph (200 mph), one of his rear tyres exploded. Amidst a mass of sparks, Mansell was seen by millions as he struggled courageously, and brilliantly, to keep the car under control, avoiding a major disaster. While he saved his life, and possibly that of others, his season lay in tatters as he watched Alain Prost (Fra) and Williams team-mate Nelson Piquet (Bra), the two men who could deprive him of the championship, battle it out to see who would win the crown. That honour went

to Frenchman Prost who took the title by two points.

Nigel Mansell reached the top the hard way, with sheer determination. He started Karting in 1968, aged 15. When he took up motor racing seriously in 1976, he gave up a lucrative job with Lucas, where he worked as a qualified engineer at one of their plants near to his Birmingham home. A month after turning professional, in May 1977, Mansell broke his neck in two places in a racing accident—but five weeks later he was racing again. Mansell moved from Formula Ford to Formula Three in 1978, after selling his house to help finance his new career.

The following year he secured a contract with the Unipart Formula Three team and his performances impressed Lotus enough for him to be invited for a testing session. He attended that session suffering great pain from a back injury sustained at Oulton Park a few weeks earlier, but he emerged from the test with a Formula One contract for the 1980 season.

He made his Grand Prix debut in the Lotus 81 at the Osterreich-

ring. But, having finished no higher than third place (on four occasions) in five seasons at Lotus, Mansell moved to the Frank Williams team in 1985 and that was the start of his push towards the championship.

After finishing second in the Belgian Grand Prix he won the next race, the European Grand Prix at Brands Hatch. His victory at Kyalami two weeks later ended a great debut season with Williams.

Mansell and car were ready for the 1986 World Championship but that burst tyre on lap 63 at Adelaide decided the outcome. When Nigel Mansell returned to his Isle of Man home after failing to win the championship he still returned a hero and was greeted by signs that were calling for the renaming of the island to the 'Isle of Mansell'. Mansell had survived a potentially horrific accident, determined to try even harder to win that world title for Britain in 1987.

Mansell (No. 5) with team-mate Piquet in pursuit. Despite dominating the 1986 season with nine wins between them, they still had to surrender the world title to Alain Prost (FRA)

1979

Hall County	K. Rosberg	Spyder	188.23 kph / 116.97 mph
Charlotte	J. Ickx	Lola	168.39 kph / 104.64 mph
Mosport	J. Ickx	Lola	182.94 kph / 113.67 mph
Mid-Ohio	A. Jones	Lola	161.16 kph / 100.14 mph
Watkins Glen	K. Rosberg	Spyder	184.40 kph / 114.58 mph
Road America	J. Ickx	Lola	181.78 kph / 112.96 mph
Brainerd	J. Ickx	Lola	188.43 kph / 117.09 mph
Trois Rivieres	E. Forbes-Robinson	Spyder	137.31 kph / 85.32 mph
Laguna Seca	R. Rahal	Prophet	182.19 kph / 113.21 mph
Riverside	J. Ickx	Lola	192.77 kph / 119.79 mph

Final Championship Standing

1	J. Ickx	51 pts
2	E. Forbes-Robinson	45 pts
3	G. Lees	32 pts

1980

Sears Point	P. Tambay	Lola	162.68 kph / 101.09 mph
Mid–Ohio	P. Tambay	Lola	160.86 kph / 99.96 mph
Mosport	P. Tambay	Lola	185.30 kph / 115.15 mph
Watkins Glen	P. Tambay	Lola	174.11 kph / 108.19 mph
Road America	A. Holbert	CAC	174.61 kph / 108.50 mph
Brainerd	P. Tambay*	Lola	188.61 kph / 117.20 mph
Trois Rivieres	P. Tambay	Lola	—
Hall County	G. Brabham	Lola	—
Laguna Seca	A. Unser	Frissbee	174.96 kph / 108.72 mph
Riverside	A. Holbert	CAC	191.41 kph / 118.94 mph

Final Championship Standing

1	P. Tambay	61 pts
2	A. Holbert	40 pts
3	G. Brabham	26 pts

1981

Mosport	T. Fabi	March	185.92 kph / 115.53 mph
Mid-Ohio	T. Fabi	March	161.59 kph / 100.41 mph
Watkins Glen	A. Holbert	CRC	180.29 kph / 112.05 mph
Road America	G. Brabham	Lola	185.34 kph / 115.17 mph
Edmonton	G. Brabham	VDS	170.87 kph / 106.18 mph
Trois Rivieres	A. Holbert	CRC	132.67 kph / 82.44 mph
Mosport	T. Fabi	March	188.74 kph / 117.28 mph
Riverside	A. Holbert	CRC	192.02 kph / 119.32 mph
Laguna Seca	T. Fabi	March	186.51 kph / 115.90 mph
Las Vegas	D. Sullivan	Frissbee	151.20 kph / 93.96 mph

Final Championship Standing

1	G. Brabham	487 pts
2	T. Fabi	456 pts
3	A. Holbert	420 pts

1982

Hall County	A. Unser	Frissbee	160.47 kph / 99.72 mph
Mosport	A. Unser	Frissbee	177.59 kph / 110.35 mph
Mid-Ohio	A. Holbert	VDS	164.52 kph / 102.23 mph
Elkhart Lake	A. Holbert	VDS	184.78 kph / 114.82 mph
Trois Rivieres	A. Holbert	VDS	140.57 kph / 87.35 mph
Mosport	A. Unser	Frissbee	187.71 kph / 116.64 mph
Las Vegas	D. Sullivan	March	146.82 kph / 91.23 mph
Riverside	A. Holbert	VDS	193.88 kph / 120.48 mph
Laguna Seca	A. Unser	Frissbee	183.71 kph / 114.15 mph

Final Championship Standing

1	A. Unser	540 pts
2	A. Holbert	500 pts
3	D. Sullivan	390 pts

1983

Mosport	J. Villeneuve	Frissbee	179.89 kph / 111.78 mph
Lime Rock Park	J. Crawford	Ensign	172.92 kph / 107.45 mph
Road America	J. Fitzpatrick	Porsche	174.74 kph / 108.50 mph
Trois Rivieres	J. Villeneuve	Frissbee	140.37 kph / 87.23 mph
Mosport	J. Crawford	Ensign	187.18 kph / 116.31 mph
Sears Point	J. Villeneuve	Frissbee	163.77 kph / 101.77 mph

Final Championship Standing

1	J. Villeneuve	96 pts
2	J. Crawford	93 pts
3	B. Roos	63 pts

1984

Mosport	M. Roe	VDS	154.05 kph / 95.74 mph
Dallas	M. Roe	VDS	109.39 kph / 67.98 mph
Brainerd	M. Roe	VDS	190.20 kph / 118.21 mph
Lime Rock Park	M. Roe	VDS	173.43 kph / 107.79 mph
Hall County	J. Crawford	March	175.94 kph / 109.35 mph
Trois Rivieres	J. Crawford	March	138.10 kph / 85.83 mph
Mosport	M. Roe	VDS	183.02 kph / 113.75 mph
Sears Point	M. Roe	VDS	160.16 kph / 99.54 mph
Riverside	M. Roe	VDS	192.58 kph / 119.69 mph
Green Valley	J. Crawford	March	150.78 kph / 93.71 mph

Final Championship Standing

1	M. Roe	162 pts
2	J. Crawford	156 pts
3	H. Kroll	119 pts

Most Championship Wins

2	B. McLaren (1967, 1969)
2	D. Hulme (1968, 1970)
2	P. Tambay (1977, 1980)

Most Race Wins (Drivers)

22	D. Hulme
12	P. Tambay
10	A. Holbert
9	B. McLaren
9	M. Donohue
7	G. Follmer
7	M. Roe

Most Wins (Cars)

42	McLaren
38	Lola
15	Porsche
15	Frissbee
12	VDS

Most Wins One Season (Drivers)

7 M. Roe (1984)

Formula One World Champions who have won races

D. Hulme (22)	
A. Jones (6)	
J. Surtees (4)	
K. Rosberg (2)	
J. Stewart (2)	
P. Hill (1)	

Most Consecutive Wins

6 M. Donohue (1973)

Most Wins One Season (Car)

11 McLaren (1969)

Most Consecutive Wins

23 McLaren (1968–70)

Tasman Cup Series

Racing in Australia and New Zealand became very popular with Formula One teams and drivers in the mid-fifties. As a result, an International series, known as the Tasman Cup, was introduced in 1964 for the old 2½-litre formula. As more and more Grand Prix races were added to the Formula One calendar the Cup lost its international appeal and in 1976 the Cup was abolished to make way for the Formula Pacific Series in New Zealand, and the Formula 5000 Series in Australia.

Individual race winners and champions

1964

Levin	D. Hulme	Brabham	118.05 kph / 73.37 mph
Pukekohe (New Zealand GP)	B. McLaren	Cooper	141.35 kph / 87.85 mph
Christchurch	B. McLaren	Cooper	150.26 kph / 93.39 mph
Invercargill	B. McLaren	Cooper	123.96 kph / 77.04 mph
Sandown Park (Australian GP)	J. Brabham	Brabham	155.69 kph / 96.76 mph
Warwick Farm	J. Brabham	Brabham	132.53 kph / 82.37 mph
Lakeside	J. Brabham	Brabham	143.14 kph / 88.96 mph
Longford	G. Hill	Brabham	179.73 kph / 111.70 mph

Final Championship Standing

1	B. McLaren	39 pts
2	J. Brabham	33 pts
3	D. Hulme	23 pts
	T. Meyer	23 pts

1965

Pukekohe (New Zealand GP)	G. Hill	Brabham	141.43 kph / 87.90 mph
Levin	J. Clark	Lotus	124.18 kph / 77.18 mph
Christchurch	J. Clark	Lotus	154.21 kph / 95.84 mph
Invercargill	J. Clark	Lotus	136.68 kph / 84.95 mph
Warwick Farm	J. Clark	Lotus	139.18 kph / 86.50 mph
Sandown Park	J. Brabham	Brabham	153.34 kph / 95.30 mph
Longford (Australian GP)	B. McLaren	Cooper	177.52 kph / 110.33 mph

Final Championship Standing

1	J. Clark	35 pts
2	B. McLaren	24 pts
3	J. Brabham	21 pts

1966

Pukekohe (New Zealand GP)	G. Hill	BRM	128.69 kph / 79.97 mph
Levin	R. Attwood	BRM	129.31 kph / 80.35 mph
Christchurch	J. Stewart	BRM	154.39 kph / 95.94 mph
Invercargill	J. Stewart	BRM	147.92 kph / 91.92 mph
Warwick Farm	J. Clark	Lotus	135.94 kph / 84.47 mph
Lakeside (Australian GP)	G. Hill	BRM	152.32 kph / 94.65 mph
Sandown Park	J. Stewart	BRM	162.03 kph / 100.69 mph
Longford	J. Stewart	BRM	186.89 kph / 116.13 mph
Surfers' Paradise	S. Martin	Brabham	155.52 kph / 96.64 mph

Final Championship Standing

1	J. Stewart	36 pts
2	J. Clark	25 pts
3	J. Palmer	19 pts

1967

Pukekohe (New Zealand GP)	J. Stewart	BRM	162.38 kph / 100.90 mph
Levin	J. Clark	Lotus	139.10 kph / 86.44 mph
Christchurch	J. Clark	Lotus	154.33 kph / 95.90 mph
Invercargill	J. Clark	Lotus	143.20 kph / 88.98 mph
Lakeside	J. Clark	Lotus	156.11 kph / 97.01 mph
Warwick Farm (Australian GP)	J. Stewart	BRM	141.09 kph / 87.67 mph
Sandown Park	J. Clark	Lotus	163.99 kph / 101.90 mph
Longford	J. Brabham	Brabham	191.85 kph / 119.22 mph

Final Championship Standing

1	J. Clark	45 pts
2	J. Stewart	18 pts
	F. Gardner	18 pts
	J. Brabham	18 pts

1968

Pukekohe (New Zealand GP)	C. Amon	Ferrari	164.95 kph / 102.50 mph
Levin	C. Amon	Ferrari	143.23 kph / 89.00 mph
Christchurch	J. Clark	Lotus	165.40 kph / 102.78 mph
Invercargill	B. McLaren	BRM	136.80 kph / 85.01 mph
Lakeside	J. Clark	Lotus	160.05 kph / 99.46 mph
Warwick Farm	J. Clark	Lotus	143.23 kph / 89.00 mph
Sandown Park (Australian GP)	J. Clark	Lotus	164.02 kph / 101.92 mph
Longford	P. Courage	McLaren	156.03 kph / 96.96 mph

Final Championship Standing

1	J. Clark	44 pts
2	C. Amon	36 pts
3	P. Courage	34 pts

1969

Pukekohe (New Zealand GP)	C. Amon	Ferrari	169.14 kph / 105.10 mph
Levin	C. Amon	Ferrari	142.75 kph / 88.70 mph
Christchurch	J. Rindt	Lotus	167.37 kph / 104.00 mph
Invercargill	P. Courage	Brabham	156.72 kph / 97.39 mph
Lakeside (Australian GP)	C. Amon	Ferrari	161.22 kph / 100.18 mph
Warwick Farm	J. Rindt	Lotus	125.04 kph / 77.70 mph
Sandown Park	C. Amon	Ferrari	170.59 kph / 106.00 mph

Final Championship Standing

1	C. Amon	44 pts
2	J. Rindt	30 pts
3	P. Courage	22 pts

1970

Levin	G. Lawrence	Ferrari	142.43 kph / 88.51 mph
Pukekohe (New Zealand GP)	F. Matich	McLaren	168.17 kph / 104.50 mph
Christchurch	F. Matich	McLaren	163.10 kph / 101.35 mph
Invercargill	G. McRae	McLaren	154.34 kph / 95.91 mph
Surfers' Paradise	G. McRae	McLaren	162.96 kph / 101.26 mph
Warwick Farm	K. Bartlett	Mildren	146.47 kph / 91.02 mph
Sandown Park	N. Allen	McLaren	164.23 kph / 102.05 mph
Warwick Farm (Australian GP)	F. Matich	McLaren	153.73 kph / 95.53 mph

Final Championship Standing

1	G. Lawrence	30 pts
2	F. Matich	25 pts
3	K. Bartlett	19 pts
	M. Stewart	19 pts

1971

Levin	G. McRae	McLaren	141.53 kph / 87.95 mph
Pukekohe (New Zealand GP)	N. Allen	McLaren	173.64 kph / 107.90 mph
Christchurch	G. McRae	McLaren	168.88 kph / 104.94 mph
Invercargill	N. Allen	McLaren	157.72 kph / 98.01 mph
Warwick Farm	F. Gardner	Lola	149.99 kph / 93.20 mph
Sandown Park	G. McRae	McLaren	172.37 kph / 107.11 mph
Surfers' Paradise	F. Matich	McLaren	166.71 kph / 103.61 mph

Final Championship Standing

1	G. McRae	35 pts
2	F. Matich	31 pts
3	N. Allen	27 pts

1972

Pukekohe (New Zealand GP)	F. Gardner	Lola	171.15 kph / 106.35 mph
Levin	G. McRae	Leda	148.64 kph / 92.36 mph
Christchurch	G. McRae	Leda	181.74 kph / 112.93 mph
Invercargill	K. Bartlett	McLaren	141.30 kph / 87.80 mph
Surfers' Paradise	G. McRae	Leda	165.08 kph / 102.58 mph
Warwick Farm	F. Matich	Matich	152.81 kph / 94.96 mph
Sandown Park (Australian GP)	G. McRae	Leda	176.19 kph / 109.48 mph
Adelaide	D. Hobbs	McLaren	162.06 kph / 100.70 mph

Final Championship Standing

1	G. McRae	39 pts
2	M. Hailwood	28 pts
3	F. Gardner	25 pts

1973

Pukekohe (New Zealand GP)	J. McCormack	Elfin	144.78 kph / 89.97 mph
Levin	G. McRae	McRae	151.44 kph / 94.10 mph
Christchurch	G. McRae	McRae	183.90 kph / 114.28 mph
Invercargill	A. Rollinson	McRae	132.15 kph / 82.12 mph
Surfers' Paradise	F. Matich	Matich	165.51 kph / 102.85 mph
Warwick Farm	S. Thompson	Chevron	130.88 kph / 81.33 mph
Sandown Park	G. McRae	McRae	174.26 kph / 108.29 mph
Adelaide	J. McCormack	Elfin	168.66 kph / 104.81 mph

Final Championship Standing

1	G. McRae	40 pts
2	J. McCormack	29 pts
3	F. Matich	27 pts

1974

Levin	J. Walker	Lola	—
Pukekohe	P. Gethin	Chevron	156.82 kph / 97.45 mph
Christchurch (New Zealand GP)	J. McCormack	Elfin	134.13 kph / 83.35 mph
Invercargill	M. Stewart	Lola	—
Oran Park	M. Stewart	Lola	—
Surfers' Paradise	T. Pilette	Chevron	168.93 kph / 104.97 mph
Sandown Park	P. Gethin	Chevron	178.72 kph / 111.06 mph
Adelaide	W. Brown	Lola	—

Final Championship Standing

1	P. Gethin	41 pts
2	M. Stewart	26 pts
3	T. Pilette	22 pts

1975

Levin	G. Lawrence	Lola	151.70 kph / 94.27 mph
Pukekohe (New Zealand GP)	W. Brown	Lola	148.60 kph / 92.34 mph
Christchurch	G. McRae	McRae	185.80 kph / 115.46 mph
Invercargill	C. Amon	Talon	—
Oran Park	W. Brown	Lola	157.70 kph / 97.99 mph
Surfers' Paradise	J. Walker	Lola	167.93 kph / 104.35 mph
Adelaide	G. Lawrence	Lola	172.00 kph / 106.88 mph
Sandown Park	J. Goss	Matich	163.10 kph / 101.35 mph

Final Championship Standing

1	W. Brown	31 pts
2	G. Lawrence	30 pts
	J. Walker	30 pts

1976

Pukekohe (New Zealand GP)	K. Smith	Lola	162.78 kph / 101.15 mph
Fielding	M. Stewart	Lola	120.52 kph / 74.89 mph
Christchurch	K. Smith	Lola	180.00 kph / 111.85 mph
Invercargill	G. Lawrence	Lola	163.61 kph / 101.67 mph
Oran Park	V. Schuppan	Lola	—
Adelaide	K. Smith	Lola	—
Sandown Park	J. Cannon	March	—

Final Championship Standing

1	K. Smith	39 pts
2	V. Schuppan	24 pts
3	K. Bartlett	17 pts

Most Championship Wins

3 J. Clark (1965, 1967, 1968)
3 G. McRae (1971, 1972, 1973)

Most Race Wins (Drivers)

14 J. Clark
13 G. McRae
 7 C. Amon
 6 J. Stewart
 6 F. Matich

Most Wins One Season (Drivers)

5 J. Clark (1967)

**Formula One World Champions
who have won races**

J. Clark (14)
J. Stewart (6)
G. Hill (4)
J. Brabham (4)
J. Rindt (2)
D. Hulme (1)

Most Wins (Cars)

17 Lola
15 Lotus
15 McLaren
10 Brabham
10 BRM

Most Wins One Season (Cars)

7 BRM (1966)

Race of Champions

A Formula One event, the first Race of Champions was held in 1965 and, like all subsequent races, was held at Brands Hatch. It was the traditional opening race of the Formula One season in Britain but, with an ever-increasing number of World Championship Formula One races on the calendar, the event was dropped after the 1979 race but made a temporary comeback in 1983.

1965

1 M. Spence   Lotus
   155.40 kph / 96.58 mph
2 J. Stewart   BRM
3 J. Bonnier   Brabham

1966

No Race

1967

1 D. Gurney   Eagle
   158.78 kph / 98.67 mph
2 L. Bandini   Ferrari
3 J. Siffert   Cooper

1968

1 B. McLaren   McLaren
   162.17 kph / 100.77 mph
2 P. Rodriguez   BRM
3 D. Hulme   McLaren

1969

1 J. Stewart   Matra
   174.85 kph / 108.65 mph
2 G. Hill   Lotus
3 D. Hulme   McLaren

1970

1 J. Stewart   March
   175.59 kph / 109.11 mph
2 J. Rindt   Lotus
3 D. Hulme   McLaren

1971

1 C. Regazzoni   Ferrari
   174.45 kph / 108.40 mph
2 J. Stewart   Tyrrell
3 J. Surtees   Surtees

1972

1 E. Fittipaldi   Lotus
   180.60 kph / 112.22 mph
2 M. Hailwood   Surtees
3 D. Hulme   McLaren

1973

1 P. Gethin   Chevron
   178.37 kph / 110.84 mph
2 D. Hulme   McLaren
3 J. Hunt   Surtees

1974

1 J. Ickx   Lotus
   160.87 kph / 99.96 mph
2 N. Lauda   Ferrari
3 E. Fittipaldi   McLaren

1975

1 T. Pryce   Shadow
   183.13 kph / 113.80 mph
2 J. Watson   Surtees
3 R. Peterson   Lotus

1976

1 J. Hunt   McLaren
   173.74 kph / 107.96 mph
2 A. Jones   Surtees
3 J. Ickx   Hesketh

1977

1 J. Hunt   McLaren
   187.26 kph / 116.36 mph
2 J. Scheckter   Wolf
3 J. Watson   Brabham

1978

No Race

1979

1 G. Villeneuve   Ferrari
   189.45 kph / 117.72 mph
2 N. Piquet   Brabham
3 M. Andretti   Lotus

1980

No Race

1981

No Race

1982

No Race

1983

1 K. Rosberg   Williams
   189.72 kph / 117.89 mph
2 D. Sullivan   Tyrrell
3 A. Jones   Arrows

Most Wins (Drivers)

2 J. Stewart (1969, 1970)
2 J. Hunt (1976, 1977)

Fastest Winning Speed

189.72 kph / 117.89 mph
   K. Rosberg (Williams) 1983

**Winners of Race of Champions
and World Drivers' Championship in the same year**

1969 J. Stewart
1972 E. Fittipaldi
1976 J. Hunt

Most Wins (Cars)

3 Lotus (1965, 1972, 1974)
3 McLaren (1968, 1976, 1977)

● Stirling Moss in 1961, Jackie Stewart in 1973, and Nigel Mansell in 1986 are the only motor racing drivers to win the BBC Sports Personality of the Year award. John Surtees won the trophy in 1959 but that was before he turned to four wheels.

Above Jackie Stewart (GB) steering his March 701 to victory in the 1970 Race of Champions at Brands Hatch. Stewart, having won the race the previous year, became the first man to win it twice. (National Motor Museum)

Jubilation for Canadian Gilles Villeneuve, after winning the 1979 Race of Champions from Nelson Piquet (BRA) and Mario Andretti (USA). (Michelin Tyre Co. Ltd.)

Grovewood Award

The Grovewood Motor Racing Awards were instituted in 1963 as a result of an idea conceived by John Danny, chairman of Grovewood Securities Limited, operators of Brands Hatch, Snetterton and Oulton Park. The award offers financial and other assistance to a driver who, in the opinion of an independent panel of motor racing journalists, has shown outstanding promise in the early stages of his career.

Winners:

1963	Richard Attwood	1975	Brian Henton
1964	Roger Mac	1976	Tiff Needell
1965	Piers Courage	1977	Bruce Allison
1966	Chris Lambert	1978	Kenneth Acheson
1967	Alan Rollinson	1979	Mike Thackwell
1968	Tim Schenken	1980	David Leslie
1969	Mike Walker	1981	Dave Scott
1970	Colin Vendervell	1982	Martin Brundle
1971	Roger Williamson	1983	Andrew Gilbert-Scott
1972	David Morgan	1984	Mark Blundell
1973	Tom Pryce	1985	Russell Spence
1974	Bob Evans		

The Birth of the Turbocharger

When the Renault RS01 1500 cc turbo-charged car failed on lap 17 of the 1977 British Grand Prix at Silverstone, there must have been many people who did not see a future for this power-booster, particularly as it was the turbo-charger that caused the car's withdrawal from the race.

The RS01 had a twin o.h.c. V6 1492 cc engine with four valves per cyclinder but was aided by a turbine compressor powered by the car's exhaust gases. The unit, located between the engine and gearbox, was capable of producing 510 b.h.p. at 11 000 r.p.m. Such was the improvement in turbo cars in such a short space of time that they were soon capable of producing anything up to 1300 b.h.p.

Renault showed they had a winner for the first time at the 1979 French Grand Prix when Jean-Pierre Jabouille (Fra) was first, with team-mate Rene Arnoux third. Other manufacturers soon followed suit, notably Ferrari and Alfa Romeo. Ferrari, in 1982, were

the first Constructors' champions with a turbo car and within four years all manufacturers were running turbo-charged engines. Ken Tyrrell, an opponent of them since 1979, was the last manufacturer to power his cars with turbo-chargers.

Ten seasons after the introduction of the Renault RS01 all manufacturers ran turbo-charged cars and, because of the increased power generated, the sport's governing body saw a need to curtail its use.

The sport's governing body

Zakspeed are one of the newest Formula One teams and they powered their cars with the S4 turbo engine. (West Zakspeed)

announced plans in 1986 for the phasing out of turbos, to be complete by the start of the 1989 season. The phasing out will be gradual with two World Championships in 1987 and 1988, one for turbo cars, and one for normally aspirated cars, with a complete return to 3.5 litre normally aspirated cars thereafter and thus bringing an end to the turbocharger... born 1977, died 1988.

The car that started the Turbo revolution in 1977, the Renault RS01. (National Motor Museum)

INDEX

Page numbers in *italics* refer to illustrations and their captions. Colour plates are indicated by *col*.

Tables are indexed by title; their contents – drivers, manufacturers, etc – are not indexed separately when found in the tables only.